TRICOLORE Total

Teacher's Book

1

Nelson Thornes

Sylvia Honnor
Heather Mascie-Taylor
Michael Spencer

CW01572758

Text © Sylvia Honnor, Heather Mascie-Taylor and Michael Spencer 2008
Original illustrations © Nelson Thornes Ltd 2008

The rights of Sylvia Honnor, Heather Mascie-Taylor and Michael Spencer to be identified as authors of this work has been asserted by them in accordance with the Copyright, Designs and Patents Act 1988.

All rights reserved. No part of this publication may be reproduced or transmitted in any form or by any means, electronic or mechanical, including photocopy, recording or any information storage and retrieval system, without permission in writing from the publisher or under licence from the Copyright Licensing Agency Limited, of Saffron House, 6-10 Kirby Street, London EC1N 8TS.

Any person who commits any unauthorised act in relation to this publication may be liable to criminal prosecution and civil claims for damages.

Tricolore first published in 1980 by E. J. Arnold and Sons Limited
Encore Tricolore first published in 1992 by Thomas Nelson and Sons Limited
Encore Tricolore nouvelle édition first published in 2000 by Thomas Nelson and Sons Limited

Tricolore Total first published in 2008 by:
Nelson Thornes Ltd
Delta Place
27 Bath Road
CHELTENHAM
GL53 7TH
United Kingdom

09 10 11 12 / 10 9 8 7 6 5 4 3 2

A catalogue record for this book is available from the British Library

978-0-7487-9989-3

Cover photo courtesy of Photolibrary
Page make-up by Pantek Arts Ltd, Maidstone, Kent
Printed in China

Acknowledgements

The authors and publisher would like to thank the following people for their help in producing this book:

Hilary Bates for editing the materials.
Alan Wesson, Jackie Coe, Teresa Huntley, Heather Rendall, Sheila Blackband, Andrew Colley, Keith Faulkner, Arnold Klein, Jane Bayliss, Victoria Dutchman-Smith, Frédérique Jouhandin, Seonaid Loader, Collège Missy, Parc Asterix.

Special thanks to all schools who took part in the formal and informal market research on Tricolore Total and provided valuable feedback; Mrs S Hotham of Wakefield Girls' High School; Ms Bethany Honnor, Florence Picard and the French staff at Latymer School; Hilary Munday and the French staff and students at Royal Grammar school, High Wycombe; Collège Chante Cigale

Recordings produced by Footstep Productions Ltd

Tricolore Total 1

Contents

Section 1
General information

Section 2
Activities and resources

Section 3
Teacher's notes

Introduction

Tricolore Total builds on the proven strengths and approach of *Tricolore* and *Encore Tricolore* and incorporates new features to bring it into line with current teaching requirements.

The course features:

- lively, interesting and motivating materials for learning the French language
- a systematic and comprehensive approach to grammar progression, with clear explanations and extensive practice
- material to develop cultural awareness through authentic contexts and activities from France and other French-speaking countries
- systematic training in language learning, study and thinking skills
- user-friendly reference sections to encourage independent learning
- opportunities for differentiation through flexible use of activities, but a common core of material for all students

Key features of the new edition are:

- increased emphasis on language-learning skills, drawing out similarities between French and English, patterns in French, etc.
- ideas and activities for starters and plenaries in line with the MFL framework
- increased guidance on Assessment for Learning covering individual, peer and teacher assessment
- a new Student's Book design with each spread covering specific learning objectives
- an integrated, contemporary ICT resource, providing presentations, video sequences, interactive tasks, electronic worksheets, and record and playback facilities for pronunciation and speaking.

Components

Tricolore Total 1 covers one complete year's work.

The components are:

Student's Book

Teacher's Book

Audio CDs

Copymasters and Assessment Book

Grammar in Action 1

Tricolore Total 1 online resource
(includes Flashcard Bank)

Student's Book

The Student's Book is the main teaching tool of the course and contains the essential core material and reference sections. It comprises:

- **10 units**

Each unit is organised in spreads and each spread is a self-contained entity with explicit learning objectives and a full range of activities to practise language and thinking skills. Every unit finishes with a unit summary (*Sommaire*). (The *Sommaires* are also provided on copymasters.) In *Tricolore Total*, grammar explanations are

given in *Dossier-langue* boxes and skills are covered in *Stratégies* boxes.

- **Au choix**

This section contains further practice and extension tasks for each unit. Most of these require reading and writing skills only, but a few involve listening.

- **Presse-Jeunesse**

Starting after *Unité 4* and at regular intervals throughout the book, these four magazine-style sections provide material for reading for pleasure and to enhance cultural awareness. They can be used flexibly and are intended for students to work on alone. Although they use mainly the vocabulary and structures previously taught, they also contain a small amount of additional language. Comprehension and practice tasks are provided on copymaster.

- **Rappel**

These double-page, revision sections are placed after *Unités 3, 5, 7* and *9*, alternating with the *Presse-Jeunesse* sections. Each *Rappel* section provides reading and writing activities, suitable for students working independently, for homework or during cover lessons. They contain a variety of tasks including practice of vocabulary, grammar and topic revision.

- **Grammaire**

The reference section covers the main grammar points and irregular verbs taught in *Tricolore Total 1*.

- **Glossaires**

French–English and English–French glossaries at the end of the Student's Book encourage students to use reference sources.

- **Vocabulaire de classe**

This gives a list of useful classroom phrases and rubrics with their meaning.

Teacher's Book

The Teacher's Book has three sections:

- **Section 1:**

This provides general information, such as details of components, reference and planning documents, etc.

- **Section 2:**

This includes details of games and songs which can be used at various points in the course.

- **Section 3:**

This provides detailed teaching notes and solutions for all items in the Student's Book and in the Copymasters. It also includes a full transcript of all recorded items, ideas for starters and plenaries, Assessment for Learning and notes on formative assessment (*Épreuves*) and summative assessment (*Contrôles*).

Each unit begins with an overview grid to help with planning. This summarises the objectives, key language, grammar and skills and is correlated to National Curriculum levels, KS3 Framework Objectives, etc. The teaching suggestions follow the sequence of spreads in the Student's Book and include ideas for starters, plenaries, Assessment for Learning and differentiation. The Section 3 notes indicate linked ICT activities (available in the *Tricolore Total* online resource) in their suggested teaching sequence, but detailed teaching notes for all online activities and materials are provided in full in the online resource.

The following symbols are used in the Teacher's Book:

 39 Student's Book page number

3 Task number

 2/4 Copymaster number (unit/number)

 1 p12 Grammar in Action 1 page number

 1 tr 12 Recorded item (CD number and track)

 Présentation ICT PowerPoint presentation

 Fiche de travail/Activité Online worksheet activity/Online interactive activity

Audio CDs

The CDs provide a wide variety of lively material, recorded by French native speakers and at a speed and level which the students can understand.

List of CDs	Student CD (CD 6)
CD 1: Unités 1–3	Tu comprends? Unités 4–10
CD 2: Unités 4–5	Chantez! Unités 2, 3, 6, 8, 9, 10
CD 3: Unités 6–7	
CD 4: Unités 8–9	
CD 5: Unité 10 and *Contrôles*	

Copymasters and assessment

The 128 copymasters provide a wide variety of material for practice in all four skills. Pdf files of the copymasters are also available with the teacher's materials in the online resource.

Some worksheets are intended to be expendable, e.g. those containing crosswords, word searches or listening grids. Others can be cut up and used for pair or group activities. The *Sommaire* and grammar practice sheets can be stuck into the student's exercise book or file for future reference.

Mini-flashcards

These worksheets are initially used for a writing activity, but can then be cut up and used for group or pairwork activities and games.

Presse-Jeunesse

These are linked to each *Presse-Jeunesse* section in the Student's Book and give practice in reading and writing.

Assessment

There are student sheets for the assessment tests, *Épreuves* (informal) and *Contrôles* (formal) and a record sheet.

Tu comprends?

These self-instructional listening tasks are used with the accompanying Student CD for homework or for independent work in class.

List of copymasters

Unité 1
1/1 La France
1/2 Écoutez bien!
1/3 Sommaire

Unité 2
2/1 J'habite en France
2/2 Trois conversations
2/3 Les jours de la semaine
2/4 Sommaire

Unité 3
3/1 La famille Techno
3/2 Masculin, féminin
3/3 À la maison
3/4 C'est où?
3/5 Sommaire
3/6 Épreuve: Écouter
3/7 Épreuve: Lire
3/8 Épreuve: Écrire et grammaire

Unité 4
4/1 Les animaux [mini-flashcards]
4/2 Les animaux de mes amis
4/3 C'est moi!
4/4 Questions et réponses
4/5 Des conversations au choix
4/6 Tu comprends?
4/7 Sommaire
4/8 Épreuve: Écouter
4/9 Épreuve: Lire
4/10 Épreuve: Écrire et grammaire

Unité 5
5/1 Des dates A, B
5/2 être
5/3 Les numéros
5/4 Des vêtements [mini-flashcards]
5/5 Jeux de vocabulaire
5/6 Des cadeaux et des vêtements
5/7 avoir
5/8 Des descriptions
5/9 Tu comprends?
5/10 Sommaire
5/11 Épreuve: Écouter
5/12 Épreuve: Lire
5/13 Épreuve: Écrire et grammaire

Unité 6
6/1 Le temps [mini-flashcards]
6/2 Vocabulaire: la météo et les saisons
6/3 La météo A, B
6/4 Tom et Jojo
6/5 Les verbes
6/6 Des activités
6/7 Des cartes postales
6/8 Tu comprends?
6/9 Sommaire
6/10 Épreuve: Écouter
6/11 Épreuve: Lire
6/12 Épreuve: Écrire et grammaire

Unité 7
7/1 En ville (1) [mini-flashcards]
7/2 Vocabulaire – les endroits
7/3 C'est quelle direction?
7/4 Où va-t-on?
7/5 C'est où?
7/6 En ville (2) [mini-flashcards]
7/7 Ma ville/mon village
7/8 Un plan à compléter A, B
7/9 aller
7/10 Tu comprends?

7/11   Sommaire
7/12   Épreuve: Écouter
7/13   Épreuve: Lire
7/14   Épreuve: Écrire et grammaire

Unité 8
8/1   Quelle heure est-il? [mini-flashcards]
8/2   Qui est-ce? A, B
8/3   Jeux de vocabulaire: les matières
8/4   La vie scolaire
8/5   On fait beaucoup de choses
8/6   Mon, ton, son
8/7   Des questions et des réponses (notre/nos, votre/vos)
8/8   Tu comprends?
8/9   Sommaire
8/10   Épreuve: Écouter
8/11   Épreuve: Lire
8/12   Épreuve: Écrire et grammaire

Unité 9
9/1   On mange et on boit [mini-flashcards]
9/2   C'est quel mot?
9/3   Des jeux de vocabulaire
9/4   La forme négative
9/5   À table
9/6   Qu'est-ce qu'on va faire?
9/7   Tu comprends?
9/8   Sommaire
9/9   Épreuve: Écouter
9/10   Épreuve: Lire
9/11   Épreuve: Écrire et grammaire

Unité 10
10/1   faire
10/2   Grands mots croisés: la musique
10/3   Les loisirs
10/4   Manon et Clément A, B
10/5   La semaine dernière
10/6   24 heures
10/7   Qu'est-ce que tu as fait?
10/8   Tu comprends?
10/9   Sommaire
10/10   Épreuve: Écouter
10/11   Épreuve: Lire
10/12   Épreuve: Écrire et grammaire

CM 103   Presse-Jeunesse 1 (for SB 40–41)
CM 104   Presse-Jeunesse 2 (for SB 74–75)
CM 105   Presse-Jeunesse 3 (for SB 108–109)
CM 106   Presse-Jeunesse 4 (for SB 138–139)
CM 107   Presse-Jeunesse 4: La page des sports
CM 108–109   Premier contrôle: Écouter
CM 110   Premier contrôle: Parler
CM 111–112   Premier contrôle: Lire
CM 113   Premier contrôle: Écrire
CM 114–115   Deuxième contrôle: Écouter
CM 116   Deuxième contrôle: Parler
CM 117–118   Deuxième contrôle: Lire
CM 119   Deuxième contrôle: Écrire
CM 120–121   Troisième contrôle: Écouter
CM 122   Troisième contrôle: Parler
CM 123–124   Troisième contrôle: Lire
CM 125   Troisième contrôle: Écrire
CM 126   Contrôles: record sheets
CM 127   À l'ordinateur
CM 128   Voici la France

Flashcards
There are 100 visuals for colour flashcards available on the *Tricolore Total* online resource. This allows the teacher to view and print images individually and in groups, as needed. They are used to present vocabulary and for oral work and games. (See TB 22).

List of flashcards
1 happy face
2 sad face

Places
3 town
4 village
5 house and garden
6 flat
7 farm
8 street
9 grocer's shop
10 supermarket
11 café
12 cinema

Rooms
13 bedroom
14 kitchen
15 bathroom
16 lounge
17 dining room

Animals
18 hamster
19 dog
20 cat
21 rabbit
22 fish
23 horse
24 mouse
25 budgerigar
26 guinea pig

Weather
27 hot weather
28 cold weather
29 raining
30 fine sunny weather
31 windy weather
32 snow
33 fog

Activities
34 watching TV
35 listening to radio/CDs/iPod
36 doing homework
37 using computer
38 playing table tennis
39 playing basketball
40 playing volleyball
41 playing with games console
42 playing cards

Places in town
43 market
44 restaurant
45 swimming pool
46 campsite

47 museum
48 town hall
49 school
50 tourist office
51 youth hostel
52 hospital
53 post office
54 station
55 church
56 castle
57 mosque
58 ice rink
59 library
60 football pitch

Food and drink
61 ham
62 roast chicken
63 roast red meat
64 fish
65 omelette
66 potatoes
67 chips
68 carrots
69 peas
70 cauliflower
71 cabbage
72 French/green beans
73 lettuce
74 apple
75 orange
76 pear
77 peach
78 banana
79 grapes
80 strawberries
81 baguette
82 croissants
83 cheese
84 yoghurts
85 cake
86 wine
87 mineral water
88 lemonade
89 coke
90 fruit juice
91 coffee
92 tea
93 hot chocolate
94 milk

Leisure activities
95 playing chess
96 skate-boarding
97 roller skates/blades
98 mountain bike
99 drumkit
100 drawing

Grammar in Action 1

This expendable workbook provides additional practice of the grammar introduced in Stage 1. The workbook is designed for independent use by students and includes clear explanations, exercises at a range of levels and reference material. It provides a useful reference and revision resource for students to retain for personal use.

Tricolore Total 1 online resource

This resource plays an integral role in *Tricolore Total*. There are ICT activities to support the teaching sequence in each unit. Students can access interactive tasks, electronic worksheets, readers and quizzes. Teachers can use a range of resources including presentations, flashcards (with flashcard viewer function), a copymaster bank, audio transcripts, and text files from the core material, grammar and glossary.

Using Information and Communication Technology (ICT)

The Dearing Review (2007) highlighted the importance of ICT in language learning,

'We have made earlier references to the value of ICT in teaching and learning languages.

Young people's familiarity with ICT offers a great opportunity to language teachers. It seems to us that a determined commitment to use this world, which is so familiar to young people, is a key to increasing the engagement of young people of all ages with languages. New technologies can facilitate real contacts with schools and young people in other countries. They can also provide stimulus for creative and interactive work.'

ICT has been fully integrated into *Tricolore Total 1* and is seen as a routine part of learning French and of life in French-speaking countries.

The *Tricolore Total 1* Online Resource provides a full range of integrated ICT activities. Appropriate ICT activities are indicated at regular points in the Section 3 unit teaching notes and detailed notes for each ICT activity are provided in the online resource itself.

This integrated approach to ICT is fully in line with the National Curriculum for Modern Foreign Languages in England and Wales and with similar requirements elsewhere. Students will benefit to the full from frequent opportunities to use technology through this blended learning approach.

Some key ICT uses include:

- reading and replying to e-mail
- word processing, e.g. writing frames, re-drafting text, framework poems (poems made out of a list of words supplied by the teacher), simple narratives, comic strips, postcards, letters, shopping lists, menus
- using tables or spreadsheets, e.g. for verb paradigms and vocabulary lists
- on-screen marking
- text manipulation, e.g. to help develop grammatical awareness, comprehension and spelling
- presentation, e.g. new vocabulary, grammar points, dialogues and simple picture stories
- internet, e.g. to support learning about aspects of French life and culture
- use of online dictionaries and reference sources.

This website from CILT and ALL provides a gateway to information and guidance for teachers of languages on using Information and Communications Technology in the classroom: **http://www.languages-ict.org.uk**

Planning the course

Stage 1 Overview

Unité 1 Bonjour! SB Page 6

• greet and say goodbye to a French-speaking person • tell someone your name and age and ask their name and age • ask someone how they are and tell them how you are • talk about school items and things in the classroom • understand simple classroom instructions	• numbers up to 20 • the gender of nouns (masculine and feminine) • make nouns plural	• using a dictionary • comparing French and English pronunciation • pronunciation – plural words, the letter *i*

Unité 2 J'habite ici SB Page 12

• understand people saying where they live • say where you live and ask someone where they live • days of the week • use the French alphabet	• numbers up to 30 • use *dans*, *à*, *en* to say 'in' for homes, towns or countries • ask how to say things in French	• shortening words before a vowel • spotting similarities between English and French

Unité 3 Chez moi SB Page 18

• talk about your family and your home • talk about other people's homes and families • say who things belong to • say where things are	• the definite article, *le* and *la* (the) • the indefinite article, *un* and *une* (a) • possessive adjectives, *mon*, *ma*, *mes* (my) and *ton*, *ta*, *tes* (your with *tu*) • the singular of the verb *être* (to be) and *avoir* (to have) • numbers up to 70 • use prepositions *sous* (under) and *sur* (on) • more about masculine and feminine words	• pronunciation – *è*, *ou*, *u*, *et*, *est* • number patterns

Rappel 1 – revision activities SB Page 28

Unité 4 Les animaux SB Page 30

• talk about animals, especially pets • describe animals and other things • talk about your preferences and give opinions	• make adjectives agree • understand the negative, *ne ... pas* (not) • ask questions • the singular of the verb *avoir* (to have) • more about plurals • how to say 'you' in two different ways	• improving creative work • using adjectives of size correctly • using qualifiers • expressing opinions • more about shortening words before a vowel • pronunciation – words spelt the same in French and English

Presse-Jeunesse 1 – magazine section SB Page 40

Unité 5 Des fêtes et des festivals SB Page 42

• ask for and give the date • festivals and other important annual events • greetings for special days • birthdays and presents • discuss prices • talk about clothes • describe yourself and other people	• the full present tense of the verb *être* (to be) • the plural form of nouns and adjectives • the full present tense of the verb *avoir* (to have) • numbers 0–100	• coping with new vocabulary • spelling and pronouncing the months • learning irregular adjectives with a noun • 3 kinds of words – nouns, verbs and adjectives • developing and practising your listening skills • accents: *é*, *è*, *ê* • the letters *qu*

Rappel 2 – revision activities + tips for learning vocabulary SB Page 58

Unité 6 Qu'est-ce que tu fais? SB Page 60

• talk about the weather • say what the temperature is • understand simple weather information • talk about months and seasons • talk about sport • talk about family activities • say what you do at weekends • talk about different activities according to the weather	• some regular –er verbs • the pronoun on • more about accents and ç	• using some 'high frequency' words (souvent, quelquefois, normalement) • pronunciation: syllables ending in –n and –m • reading French handwriting • practising and improving speaking skills • writing a postcard

Presse-Jeunesse 2 – magazine section SB Page 74

Unité 7 En ville SB Page 76

• talk about places in a town • ask for and understand directions and information • understand and say how far away places are • talk about your own town and area • understand tourist information	• the preposition à, au, à la, à l', aux (to, at) • other prepositions devant (in front of), derrière (behind), entre (between) etc • use the verb aller	• pronunciation: h, final –t • using connectives, like et and mais • listening to longer texts

Rappel 3 – revision activities SB Page 90

Unité 8 Une journée scolaire SB Page 92

• ask about and tell the time • arrange a time to meet • talk about daily routine and a typical day • talk about school subjects • say what you think of school subjects • find out about Senegal, a French-speaking country in Africa	• the verb faire (to do, make) • possessive adjectives son, sa, ses (his, her, its); notre, nos (our); votre, vos (your, plural or formal); leur, leurs (their) • some examples of reflexive verbs • ask questions using quel	• pronconciation: oi, ui, r • English and French spelling patterns: –y and –ie • using qualifiers • translating phrases (le prof d'histoire) • working out the meanings of new words • preparing a presentation

Presse-Jeunesse 3 – magazine section SB Page 108

Unité 9 C'est bon, ça! SB Page 110

• meals in France • talk about food and drink • fruit and vegetables • healthy eating • discuss what you like to eat and drink • having a meal with a French family • plan some meals and picnics • festival foods in other countries	• the partitive article du, de la, de l', des (some) • the verb prendre (to take) • the verb manger (to eat) • the negative ne … pas (not) • pas de – (not any) • use aller + infinitive to talk about the future	• saying 'please' and 'thank you' • improving your reading • pronunciation: g

Rappel 4 – revision activities SB Page 122

Unité 10 Amuse-toi bien! SB Page 124

• talk about sport • talk about music and the Fête de la Musique • discuss other leisure activities • give opinions • understand and talk about what you did last weekend/last week • find out about Astérix and the Parc Astérix • use the 24 hour clock	• faire + de + activity • jouer à + sport/de + instrument • recognise and use some phrases in the past tense	• writing a letter to a friend • clues to phrases about the past • adding more detail • linking nouns and verbs of similar meaning • understanding and using some sequencing words

Presse-Jeunesse 4 – magazine section SB Page 138

Au choix SB Page 140
Extra activities to practise and extend the language learnt in Unités 1–10.

Grammaire SB Page 158

Glossaire Français–anglais SB Page 165

Glossaire Anglais–français SB Page 171

Vocabulaire de Classe SB Page 174

Covering the curriculum in England and Wales

The MFL Framework

The 'Framework for teaching modern foreign languages: Years 7, 8 and 9' (DfES, 2003) is part of a wider initiative, the Key Stage 3 National Strategy, to improve standards in schools in England and Wales. It sets out a set of objectives for each year, based on the National Curriculum Programme of Study, which aims to ensure that the MFL curriculum is accessible to both teachers and students alike. It emphasises the provision of a 'firm foundation' for Year 7 students, allowing them to build confidence and strategies in using the target language.

The framework is organised under five headings:

- Words
- Sentences
- Texts: reading and writing
- Listening and speaking
- Cultural knowledge and contact

Each of these 'strands' has between five and nine objectives, which guide teachers towards well-planned lessons, allowing clear criteria against which to monitor students' progress. Within this structure, there should be a degree of flexibility and scope for variation.

Thinking skills

Some of the framework objectives are aimed at 'developing pupils' ability to bring independent and personal thinking to their use of the language'. In *Tricolore Total*, students are encouraged to apply a deductive approach to understanding grammar, to use former knowledge to work out meanings and to consider how they can use new language in different contexts. The *Dossier-langue* and *Stratégies* sections particularly focus on the development of thinking skills and language learning skills.

Assessment for learning

Assessment for learning is formative assessment, which provides feedback to the student on what has been achieved and what requires further work. The first step is to share learning objectives with students as they begin work on each spread, so that they are aware of the purpose of what they are doing. Refer back to these spread objectives as appropriate and in the final plenary session. In the unit teaching notes, certain tasks are identified as being suitable for assessment. Individual, peer and teacher assessment are all effective ways to track progress. Students also need to be aware of 'how' they are learning, and the steps they need to adopt to meet the assessment criteria.

A key aspect is to give students opportunities to discuss what they have learnt, what they find easy or difficult and how they feel they can improve. Constructive feedback could include modelling successful work, identifying next steps in learning and highlighting ways to evaluate what has been achieved so far.

In addition to the Assessment for learning tasks, there are *Épreuves* at the end of each unit. (See p20)

The *Rappel* sections in the Student's Book enable students to revisit vocabulary and topics taught earlier to consolidate their learning.

Lesson planning

Framework lessons have three parts: starter, teaching sequence and plenary.

Starters

Starters should focus on receptive activities that will help students to settle and switch into a 'learning French' mindset. Receptive activities are best, where students are given the target language and have to manipulate, order and categorise vocabulary, etc.

Starters should make all students equally active. When checking an activity, make sure that everyone takes part. The same type of activity can be used in different lessons so students don't waste time working out how to do the activity.

Suitable activities include:

- a game of *Effacez!* – for numbers, words, etc. (See p21)
- matching tasks (French/English, subject/verb, etc.)
- identifying the odd word out or putting words in groups

A grid on the following lines could be pre-printed for 5-4-3-2-1 activities where similar words are grouped together.

5	4	3	2	1

Ideas for starters are given in the unit notes and suitable material and grids are provided in the *Tricolore* online resource.

Plenaries

The purpose of a plenary is for students to review their work and take stock of what they have learnt and for the teacher to monitor progress and plan subsequent lessons accordingly. The final plenary of each spread should review actual learning against the spread learning objectives. Some suggestions:

- Reflect on the importance of correct pronunciation. Give students some cognates to practise saying in French. See if they are beginning to grasp spelling and pronunciation patterns.

- Students think about how they read and listen for gist. Discuss useful strategies e.g. similarity to English, context, type of word, need to know, etc.

- Students should discuss tips for remembering regular verb endings, e.g. writing out a verb in a table and using colour to distinguish the stem and the ending, using a spider diagram.

- Review the spread objectives: how well do students think they have done? Can they explain the main points to a partner? What did they find easy or difficult?

- **Think, pair and share** In pairs, students tell each other the two most useful, interesting or strange things they have learnt in the unit so far. They then compare with other pairs and a spokesperson relays their findings to the rest of the class.

- Discuss what students find most difficult about learning nouns (gender, spellings, etc.). Share useful tips, such as (Look, say, copy, spell, hide and repeat, or similar). With gender, ask how students are learning this and whether their strategies are successful. Has anyone worked out any patterns?

Framework Strand Coverage

The following grids show examples from *Tricolore Total 1* of the Framework Objectives for each of the five strands.

Words		Unité 1	Unité 2	Unité 3	Unité 4	Unité 5
7W1	Everyday words	Well-covered throughout the Student Book.				
7W2	High-frequency words		p. 13 *Dossier-langue*, ex. 1–2	p. 18 ex. 1, p. 20 *Dossier-langue*, p. 21 ex. 3, p. 21 *Dossier-langue*, p. 21 ex. 4, p. 23 ex. 4b, p. 24 ex. 1–2, p. 25 *Dossier-langue*, p. 25 ex. 3, p. 26 ex. 1–4	p. 30 ex. 1, p. 31 ex. 4, p. 32 *Stratégies*, p. 33 ex. 2–3, p. 33 *Stratégies*, p. 37 ex. 3, p. 37 *Dossier-langue*, p. 38 ex. 1, p. 38 ex. 2	p. 42 ex. 1, p. 42 ex. 2, p. 50 ex. 1, p. 51 *Dossier-langue*, p. 52 ex. 1, p. 53 ex. 2, p. 53 ex. 4, p. 55 ex. 6
7W3	Classroom words	p. 9 ex. 3, p. 9 ex. 4, p. 10 ex. 1, p. 10 ex. 2, p. 11 *Sommaire*	p. 16 *Stratégies*			
7W4	Gender and plural	p. 8 ex. 1, p. 8 *Dossier-langue*, p. 8 *Stratégies*, p. 9 *Dossier-langue*, p. 11 *Sommaire*	p. 12 ex. 2	p. 18 *Prononciation*, p. 19 *Dossier-langue*, p. 20 *Dossier-langue*, p. 20 ex. 1–2, p. 25 *Dossier-langue*, p. 25 ex. 3–4	p. 31 ex. 3, p. 32 ex. 1, p. 33 *Dossier-langue*, p. 33 ex. 2–3, p. 36 *Dossier-langue*	p. 48 ex. 2, p. 49 *Dossier-langue*, p. 49 ex. 4–6, p. 53 *Dossier-langue*, p. 53 ex. 3
7W5	Verbs present (+ past)			p. 19 *Dossier-langue*, p. 22 *Dossier-langue*, p. 22 ex. 1–3, p. 24 ex. 2	p. 35 ex. 4, p. 35 *Dossier-langue*	p. 46 ex. 1, p. 46 ex. 2, p. 47 *Dossier-langue*, p. 47 ex. 3–4, p. 55 *Dossier-langue* and ex. 4, p. 55 ex. 5
7W6	Letters and sounds	p. 9 *Prononciation*, p. 10 *Prononciation*	p. 15 *Stratégies*, p. 16 ex. 2, p. 17 *Prononciation*	p. 18 *Prononciation*, p. 19 *Prononciation*, p. 22 *Prononciation*, p. 24 *Prononciation*	p. 35 *Prononciation*, p. 38 *Prononciation*	p. 42 *Prononciation*, p. 47 *Prononciation*, p. 51 *Prononciation*, p. 53 *Prononciation*, p. 56 *Prononciation*, p. 56 ex. 1–3
7W7	Learning about words	pp. 8–9	p. 16 *Stratégies*	p. 26 *Stratégies (1)*, p. 26 *Stratégies (2)*	p. 31 *Dossier-langue*	p. 42 *Stratégies*, p. 45 *Stratégies*, p. 49 *Stratégies*, p. 51 *Dossier-langue*
7W8	Finding meanings	p. 8 *Stratégies*	p. 16 *Stratégies*		p. 38 *Stratégies*	p. 44 ex. 2, p. 49 ex. 5
Sentences						
7S1	Typical word order			p. 23 ex. 5	p. 34 *Dossier-langue*	
7S2	Sentence gist	p. 9 ex. 3	p. 13 *Stratégies*	p. 19 ex. 5, p. 22 ex. 1–3		p. 48 ex. 3, p. 55 ex. 4
7S3	Adapting sentences	p. 6 ex. 2, p. 8 ex. 2		p. 25 ex. 5		p. 48 ex. 2
7S4	Basic questions	p. 6 ex. 2, p. 7 ex. 3, p. 10 ex. 3	p. 12 ex. 2, p. 14 ex. 2, p. 15 ex. 5, p. 16 ex. 2	p. 19 ex. 4, p. 20 ex.2	p. 34 *Stratégies*, p. 34 ex. 2, p. 37 ex. 4	p. 48 ex. 2, p. 56 ex. 4
7S5	Basic negatives	p. 7 ex. 3		p. 19 ex. 4	p. 32 *Dossier-langue*, p. 36 *Stratégies*	
7S6	Compound sentences				p. 36 ex. 1	p. 48 ex. 3

Code	Topic					
7S7	Time and tenses					p. 47 Prononciation
7S8	Punctuation					p. 54 ex. 3
7S9	Using simple sentences	p. 7 Stratégies			p. 35 ex. 4, p. 38 ex. 2	
Text: reading and writing						
7T1	Reading using cues		p. 14 ex. 1, p. 15 ex. 4	p. 18 ex. 2, p. 19 ex. 4, p. 22 ex. 1–2, p. 23 ex. 4, p. 24 ex. 1	p. 30 ex. 1, p. 36 ex. 1	p. 44 ex. 1, p. 46 ex. 2, p. 50 ex. 2, p. 51 ex. 3, p. 52 ex. 1
7T2	Reading aloud		p. 15 ex. 3			p. 48 ex. 2
7T3	Checking before reading	p. 9 ex. 3				p. 54 ex. 4
7T4	Using resources	p. 8 ex. 1				
7T5	Assembling text	p. 10 ex. 3		p. 18 ex. 3, p. 23 ex. 5	p. 37 ex. 2	p. 47 ex. 4, p. 55 ex. 6
7T6	Texts as prompts for writing	p. 8 ex. 2		p. 18 ex. 3, p. 26 ex. 2–3, p. 26 ex. 4		
7T7	Improving written work	p. 13 Dossier-langue		p. 26 Stratégies	p. 33 Stratégies	
Listening and speaking						
7L1	Sound patterns	p. 6 ex. 1, p. 7 ex. 3, p. 9 Prononciation, p. 10 Prononciation	p. 17 Prononciation	p. 18 Prononciation, p. 19 Prononciation, p. 22 Prononciation, p. 26 ex. 1, p. 24 Prononciation	p. 35 Prononciation, p. 38 Prononciation	p. 42 Prononciation, p. 47 Prononciation, p. 51 Prononciation, p. 53 Prononciation, p. 56 ex. 1–3
7L2	Following speech	p. 6 ex. 1, p. 7 ex. 3	p. 14 ex. 2	p. 18 ex. 1, p. 19 ex. 5, p. 21 ex. 3, p. 23 ex. 4, p. 24 ex. 1	p. 36 ex. 1a	p. 52 ex. 1
7L3	Gist and detail	p. 7 ex. 4	p. 12 ex. 1, p. 13 Stratégies, p. 15 ex. 3, p. 16 ex. 1, p. 16 ex. 3	p. 19 ex. 5	p. 30 ex. 2, p. 31 ex. 3, p. 34 ex. 1	p. 42 ex. 1, p. 44 ex. 1, p. 46 ex. 1, p. 48 ex. 1, p. 49 ex. 6, p. 50 ex. 1, p. 51 ex. 4, p. 51 ex. 5, p. 54 ex. 1, p. 56 ex. 4–5
7L4	Classroom talk	p. 9 ex. 3b, p. 10 ex. 1	p. 16 Stratégies			
7L5	Spontaneous talk		p. 15 ex. 5		p. 31 ex. 5, p. 34 ex. 2, p. 37 ex. 4, p. 38 ex. 3	p. 53 ex. 4, p. 54 ex. 2, p. 55 ex. 7
7L6	Improving speech	p. 6 ex. 2, p. 7 Stratégies	p. 12 ex. 2	p. 19 ex. 4		p. 43 ex. 3, p. 48 ex. 2
Cultural knowledge and contact						
7C1	Geographical facts	p. 3 map				
7C2	Everyday culture					p. 43 ex. 4, p. 44 ex. 1, p. 45 ex. 3–4, p. 51 ex. 5
7C3	Contact with native speakers	p. 9 ex. 3b				
7C4	Stories and songs	Online Resource (ppt 03) Présentation				
7C5	Social conventions	p. 6 ex. 1, p. 7 ex. 3			p. 37 Dossier-langue	

Words		Unité 6	Unité 7	Unité 8	Unité 9	Unité 10
7W1	Everyday words	Well-covered throughout the Student Book.				
7W2	High-frequency words	p. 61 ex. 2, p. 62 ex. 1 and Dossier-langue, p. 62 Stratégies and ex. 2, p. 64 ex. 1, p. 70 Dossier-langue, p. 72 ex. 3	p. 78 ex. 1–4, p. 82 ex. 1, p. 82 Dossier-langue and ex. 2, p. 83 ex. 5–7, p. 84 ex. 1–2, p. 84 Dossier-langue, p. 85 Stratégies	p. 96 ex. 1–3, p. 99 ex. 5 and Stratégies, p. 101 Dossier-langue, p. 102 Dossier-langue and ex. 5, p. 103 Dossier-langue and ex. 6, p. 105 ex. 2	p. 110 ex. 1–2, p. 111 Dossier-langue and ex. 3, p. 111 ex. 4, p. 112 ex. 1, p. 113 ex. 5, p. 117 Stratégies	p. 124 ex. 1, p. 126 ex. 1, p. 126 ex. 4, p. 128 ex. 1, p. 128 Dossier-langue and ex. 2, p. 129 Stratégies, p. 130 Stratégies, p. 135 Stratégies
7W3	Classroom words			p. 96 ex. 1–3		
7W4	Gender and plural	p. 64 Dossier-langue	p. 79 Dossier-langue, p. 82 Dossier-langue, p. 82 ex. 2, p. 82 ex. 3, p. 84 ex. 3, p. 86 ex. 1	p. 96 ex. 1, p. 100 Dossier-langue and ex. 2, p. 100 ex. 3, p. 100 ex. 5, p. 101 Dossier-langue and ex. 7, p. 102 ex. 5, p. 103 Dossier-langue and ex. 5, ex. 6	p. 111 Dossier-langue, p. 112 ex. 1, p. 112 ex. 3 and Dossier-langue	p. 130 Stratégies
7W5	Verbs present (+ past)	p. 65 Dossier-langue and ex. 4–5, p. 67 ex. 3 and Dossier-langue, p. 67 ex. 4, p. 68 ex. 1–2, p. 69 ex. 3–4, p. 71 ex. 6	p. 86 ex. 1 and Dossier-langue, p. 86 ex. 2, p. 87 ex. 3–4	p. 95 Dossier-langue and ex. 2, p. 95 ex. 5, p. 97 Stratégies, p. 98 ex. 1, p. 98 Dossier-langue and ex. 2–3	p. 112 Dossier-langue, p. 113 Dossier-langue and ex. 6, p. 115 ex. 3, p. 115 Dossier-langue, p. 118 ex. 1, p. 118 Dossier-langue, p. 119 ex. 3	p. 125 ex. 3, p. 125 Dossier-langue, p. 125 ex. 4–5, p. 128 ex. 1, p. 128 ex. 3, p. 130 Dossier-langue and ex. 2–3, p. 134 ex. 1, p. 134 Dossier-langue and ex. 2, p. 136 ex. 1
7W6	Letters and sounds	p. 62 Dossier-langue, p. 63 ex. 6, p. 63 ex. 6, p. 64 Dossier-langue, p. 67 Dossier-langue, p. 70 Prononciation	p. 76 Prononciation, p. 78 Prononciation, p. 82 Dossier-langue	p. 96 Prononciation, p. 105 Prononciation	p. 112 Prononciation, p.114 ex. 1	
7W7	Learning about words		p. 76 ex. 2	p. 97 Stratégies, p. 99 ex. 5 and Stratégies, p. 103 Stratégies, p. 105 ex. 2	p. 112 Dossier-langue, p. 113 Dossier-langue, p. 120 Stratégies 1	p. 126 ex. 1, p. 126 Dossier-langue, p. 128 Dossier-langue, p. 129 Stratégies, p. 130 Stratégies, p. 134 Stratégies
7W8	Finding meanings	p. 61 Stratégies		p. 105 ex. 2	p. 114 ex. 2, p. 120 Stratégies 1	p. 125 Dossier-langue, p. 133 Stratégies
Sentences						
7S1	Typical word order		p. 84 Dossier-langue	p. 103 Stratégies		p. 131 ex. 3
7S2	Sentence gist	p. 60 ex. 1, p. 62 ex. 1, p. 63 Dossier-langue	p. 83 ex. 6	p. 98 ex. 1, p. 103 Stratégies		p. 125 ex. 3, p. 129 ex. 4
7S3	Adapting sentences	p. 64. ex. 2, p. 71 ex. 5, p. 72 ex. 1–2		p. 100 ex. 5	p. 117 ex. 4	p. 128 ex. 3, p. 131 ex. 6, p. 132 ex. 1, p. 135 ex. 5
7S4	Basic questions	p. 63 ex. 6, p. 64 ex. 1 and 3, p. 69 ex. 5, p. 70 ex. 3, p. 71 ex. 5, p. 72 ex. 1	p. 78 ex. 3, p. 80 ex. 1–2, p. 81 ex. 6, p. 81 ex. 7, p. 82 ex. 2, p. 83 ex. 4	p. 97 ex. 6, p. 98 ex. 1, p. 100 ex. 1, p. 100 Dossier-langue and ex. 2, p. 100 ex. 3–4, p. 105 ex. 3	p. 113 ex. 6, p. 115 ex. 4	p. 124 ex. 1, p. 126 ex. 3, p. 128 ex. 3, p. 131 ex. 4, p. 135 ex. 4, p. 136 ex. 2
7S5	Basic negatives		p. 84 ex. 4		p. 116 ex. 1, p. 116 Dossier-langue, p. 116 ex. 2, p. 117 ex. 3	
7S6	Compound sentences					

7S7	Time and tenses		p. 87 ex. 5	p. 92 ex. 1–3, p. 93 ex. 4–5, p. 96 ex. 2	p. 115 ex. 3	p. 130 *Stratégies* and ex. 1, p. 130 ex. 2, p. 131 ex. 3–5, p. 131 ex. 7, p. 133 ex. 3, p. 134 ex. 1, p. 135 ex. 4, p. 135 ex. 6
7S8	Punctuation	p. 62 *Dossier-langue*, p. 63 ex. 6				
7S9	Using simple sentences	p. 70 ex. 2	p. 78 ex. 4			
Text: reading and writing						
7T1	Reading using cues	p. 61 ex. 5, p. 63 ex. 4, p. 66 ex. 1–2	p. 78 ex. 2, p. 79 ex. 5, p. 80 ex. 3, p. 81 ex. 6, p. 88 *Stratégies* and ex. 1	p. 93 ex. 4, p. 94 ex. 1, p. 96 ex. 2, p. 104 ex. 1, p. 105 ex. 3, p. 106 ex. 1	p. 115 ex. 3, p. 116 ex. 1, p. 118 ex. 2, p. 119 ex. 3, p. 120 *Stratégies*, p. 120 ex. 1	p. 125 ex. 3, p. 127 ex. 4–5, p. 132 ex. 1–2, p. 133 ex. 4, p. 135 ex. 5, p. 136 ex.1
7T2	Reading aloud	p. 71 ex. 5	p. 76 ex. 1, p. 82 ex. 2	p. 101 ex. 6		p. 124 ex. 1, p. 127 ex. 5
7T3	Checking before reading	p. 71 ex. 6				
7T4	Using resources					
7T5	Assembling text	p. 67 ex. 4, p. 69 ex. 4, p. 71 ex. 4a	p. 79 ex. 6, p. 85 ex. 7, p. 87 ex. 5	p. 95 ex. 3, p. 97 ex. 7, p. 101 ex. 6, p. 102 ex. 4, p. 105 ex. 4	p. 113 ex. 4, p. 119 ex. 4	p. 129 ex. 5, p. 131 ex. 7, p. 135 ex. 6, p. 136 ex. 2
7T6	Texts as prompts for writing	p. 63 *Dossier personnel*, p. 65 ex. 6, p. 68 ex. 1, p. 71 ex. 6				
7T7	Improving written work	p. 62 *Stratégies*, p. 62 *Dossier-langue*	p. 85 *Stratégies*	p. 99 *Stratégies*		p. 129 *Stratégies*, p. 129 ex. 5, p. 135 *Stratégies*
Listening and speaking						
7L1	Sound patterns	p. 63 ex. 6	p. 76 *Prononciation*, p. 78 *Prononciation*	p. 96 *Prononciation*, p. 105 *Prononciation*	p. 112 *Prononciation*	
7L2	Following speech	p. 66 ex. 1	p. 76 ex. 1, p. 80 ex. 3	p. 94 ex. 1, p. 102 ex. 1, p. 104 ex. 1	p. 115 ex. 3, p. 117 ex. 4	p. 134 ex. 3
7L3	Gist and detail	p. 61 ex. 3, p. 64 ex. 1, p. 69 ex. 4, p. 71 ex. 4, p. 72 ex. 3	p. 78 ex. 3, p. 80 ex. 1, p. 81 ex. 4–5, p. 83 ex. 4, p. 84 ex. 2, p. 86 ex. 2, p. 88 ex. 2	p. 92 ex. 1, p. 92 ex. 3, p. 96 ex. 1 and 3, p. 97 ex. 5, p. 98 ex. 1, p. 99 ex. 4, p. 98 ex. 5, p. 100 ex. 1, p. 102 ex. 1	p. 110 ex. 3, p. 112 ex. 2, p. 115 ex. 5, p. 118 ex. 2, p. 119 ex. 3	p. 124 ex. 2, p. 126 ex. 2, p. 128 ex. 1, p. 130 ex. 1, p. 131 ex. 5, p. 133 ex. 3, p. 134 ex. 1
7L4	Classroom talk	p. 71 ex. 5, p. 72 ex. 4	p. 80 ex. 2, p. 85 ex. 6	p. 93 ex. 5, p. 99 ex. 6, p. 100 ex. 3–4	p. 115 ex. 4	p. 126 ex. 3, p. 131 ex. 4, p. 135 ex. 4
7L5	Spontaneous talk	p. 61 ex. 4, p. 69 ex. 5, p. 70 ex. 3, p. 72 ex. 4	p. 85 ex. 5	p. 93 ex. 5, p. 106 ex. 2	p. 115 ex. 6	p. 136 ex. 2
7L6	Improving speech	p. 63 ex. 6, p. 64 ex. 3, p. 69 ex. 6, *Stratégies*, p. 71 ex. 5	p. 81 ex. 7, p. 82 ex. 2, p. 85 *Stratégies*	p. 97 ex. 6, p. 99 ex. 6		p. 128 ex. 3, p. 133 *Stratégies*
Cultural knowledge and contact						
7C1	Geographical facts	Spreads A & B	All spreads	Spread G		
7C2	Everyday culture	Spread C		Spreads B and F and H	All spreads	p. 126 ex. 5, p. 129 *Stratégies*, Spread E
7C3	Contact with native speakers					
7C4	Stories and songs	p. 62				
7C5	Social conventions				p. 117 *Stratégies*	

National Curriculum Programme of Study: Knowledge, Skills and Understanding

Tricolore Total 1 covers attainment levels 1–4 (and some aspects of levels 5 and 6) of the National Curriculum.

Developing knowledge, skills and understanding	
1 Acquiring knowledge and understanding of the target language	*Tricolore Total 1*
Pupils should be taught:	
a the principles and interrelationship of sounds and writing in the target language	*Prononciation* sections, listening and speaking tasks.
b the grammar of the target language and how to apply it	A major feature of the course. Grammar is explained in *Dossier-langue* sections of the Student's Book and presented and practised extensively.
c how to express themselves using a range of vocabulary and structures.	A major feature of the course.
2 Developing language skills	
Pupils should be taught:	
a how to listen carefully for gist and detail	A major feature of the course with regular practice tasks for class and individual work. Strategies for listening set out in teacher's notes in *Unité 2*.
b correct pronunciation and intonation	*Prononciation*
c how to ask and answer questions	Taught and practised throughout the course, with numerous pairwork activities. Questions with *Est-ce que* introduced in *Unité 4*; other question words and forms used throughout. *Questions et réponses* is a series of tasks which practises matching correct answers to questions.
d how to initiate and develop conversations	Many activities practise this, e.g. *Inventez des conversations* and information gap tasks on copymaster.
e how to vary the target language to suit context, audience and purpose	Practised through substitution tables, but mainly covered in later stages of *Tricolore Total*.
f how to adapt language they already know for different contexts	Discussed in plenaries. Core structures and vocabulary re-applied in new contexts.
g strategies for dealing with the unpredictable (for example, unfamiliar language, unexpected responses)	Reading strategies set out in several units.
h techniques for skimming and for scanning written texts for information, including those from ICT-based sources	*Presse-Jeunesse* sections in the Student's Book and related copymasters, *Tricolore Total* online resource.
i how to summarise and report the main points of spoken or written texts, using notes where appropriate	Reading comprehension tasks in Student's Book. Tasks on copymaster, linked with *Presse-Jeunesse* pages.
j how to redraft their writing to improve its accuracy and presentation, including the use of ICT.	Suggestions in the Teacher's Book for using a range of ICT tools efficiently to draft, bring together and refine information and create documents and presentations. Writing frames and electronic worksheets in *Tricolore Total* online resource.
3 Developing language-learning skills	
Pupils should be taught:	
a techniques for memorising words, phrases and short extracts	Grouping words into topics (*Sommaires*), colour-coding genders, identifying word endings of nouns to indicate gender, memory games, routine practice of useful phrases and expressions. Tips listed in *Rappel 1*. Discussed in plenaries.
b how to use context and other clues to interpret meaning (for example, by identifying the grammatical function of unfamiliar words or similarities with words they know)	*Stratégies* and reading comprehension tasks in the Student's Book, (especially U8G, U9F) *Presse-Jeunesse* and related copymasters.
c to use their knowledge of English or another language when learning the target language	*Stratégies* and *Dossier-langue* sections in the Student's Book include comparisons with English.
d how to use dictionaries and other reference materials appropriately and effectively	Students encouraged to use the glossary, reference grammar provided in the Student's Book and dictionaries.
e how to develop their independence in learning and using the target language.	Many tasks are self-instructional, e.g. in *Rappel* and *Presse-Jeunesse* sections. *Tu comprends?* is a series of listening for independent use. *Vocabulaire de classe* reference section provides support for using target language in class.

Developing knowledge, skills and understanding

4 Developing cultural awareness	*Tricolore Total 1*
Pupils should be taught about different countries and cultures by:	
a working with authentic materials in the target language, including some from ICT-based sources (for example, handwritten texts, newspapers, magazines, books, video, satellite television, texts from the internet)	Authentic printed materials used in the Student's Book, where appropriate. Suggestions for internet sites given in the Teacher's Book. *Presse-Jeunesse* sections include slightly adapted articles from French magazines for young people.
b communicating with native speakers (for example, in person, by correspondence)	Suggestions for forming class links and sending e-mails.
c considering their own culture and comparing it with the cultures of the countries and communities where the target language is spoken	Festivals (*Unité 5*), mealtimes (*Unités 8, 9*), school life and everyday routine (*Unité 8*).
d considering the experiences and perspectives of people in these countries and communities.	Recordings, letters, articles, etc. from people from different French-speaking countries and communities.

5 Breadth of study	
During Key Stages 3 and 4, pupils should be taught the knowledge, skills and understanding through:	
a communicating in the target language in pairs and groups, and with their teacher	A major feature of the course, with detailed suggestions in the Teacher's Book and Student's Book.
b using everyday classroom events as an opportunity for spontaneous speech	Suggestions in the Teacher's Book for using target language for class communication. *Vocabulaire de classe* sections in the Student's Book provide support for this.
c expressing and discussing personal feelings and opinions	Likes, dislikes (*Unités 4, 6, 8, 10*), opinions (*Unités 8, 10*).
d producing and responding to different types of spoken and written language, including texts produced using ICT	A major feature of the course, with detailed suggestions in the Teacher's Book and Student's Book.
e using a range of resources, including ICT, for accessing and communicating information	Suggestions in the Teacher's Book and Student's Book for useful resources, including internet sites.
f using the target language creatively and imaginatively	*Dossier personnel* sections in the Student's Book encourage students to personalise and vary language learnt.
g listening, reading or viewing for personal interest and enjoyment, as well as for information	Recorded stories, songs, *Presse-Jeunesse* sections, readers and presentations in *Tricolore* online resource, etc.
h using the target language for real purposes (for example, by sending and receiving messages by telephone, letter, fax or e-mail)	Tasks in the Student's Book for writing letters, messages and e-mails (e.g. *Unité 8*).
i working in a variety of contexts, including everyday activities, personal and social life, the world around us, the world of work and the international world.	*Tricolore Total* covers the full range of contexts

Covering the QCA Programme of Study: Modern Foreign Languages

Tricolore Total has taken into account the QCA Programme of Study, with its emphasis on key concepts (linguistic competence, knowledge about language, creativity and intercultural understanding); and key processes (developing language learning strategies and language skills).

Throughout the course, students have opportunities to:

- hear, speak, read and write in French within the classroom and beyond through accessing material on the internet
- communicate in pairs, groups and as a class for a variety of purposes
- use a range of language, including some complex structures
- make links with English
- use a range of resources, including ICT
- listen to, read or view materials (including some from authentic sources) for personal interest and enjoyment
- develop language skills in a variety of contexts
- use the target language in connection with other areas of the curriculum (health education, geography, ICT)

Source: Programme of Study: Modern Foreign Languages (Key Stage 3) (QCA, 2007)

DCSF Languages Ladder and Asset Languages

The Languages Ladder has been developed by the DCSF to define grades of competence in each linguistic skill: listening, speaking, reading, writing. The grades are further grouped into six stages: Breakthrough, Preliminary, Intermediate, Advanced, Proficiency, Mastery.

The Asset Languages qualifications provide a flexible system of assessment of these stages by assessing each skill separately.

See: **http://www.assetlanguages.org.uk/**

Tricolore Total 1 covers grades 1–4 and some aspects of grades 5–6.

Covering the Scottish Modern Languages Guidelines (5–14)

The structure, content and teaching approach of *Tricolore Total* is closely aligned to the principles of breadth, balance, coherence, continuity and progression of the Scottish Guidelines.

The course emphasises learning how to use grammar and structures in a flexible way and how to recognise the spelling patterns and unique features of the language. Grammar is first presented in use, then explained in a *Dossier-langue* section, then practised through a variety of different activities. Students are encouraged to identify similarities and differences between English and French.

It provides extensive practice in all four linguistic skills as outlined by the Guidelines.

Listening

'Pupils will listen and react verbally and non-verbally to a wide range of texts in varying forms. They will listen for a variety of purposes: to extract information and instructions, to react to others and for enjoyment. Listening may also involve watching.'

Speaking

'Pupils will develop the fluency and, where the task and the degree of support allow, accuracy to speak in the foreign language for a variety of purposes, including transactions, social interaction and the expression of opinions and feelings.'

Reading

'Pupils will read a growing range of printed and screen material for a variety of purposes, including the gathering of information, the deduction of meaning and the enjoyment of the texts themselves. Reading is also closely connected to writing and speaking, encouraging young people to see the relationship between the written and spoken forms of the language.'

Writing

'Pupils will write or word-process texts for a variety of purposes, including the transfer of information, the consolidation of understanding, the establishment of contact and the creation of imaginative pieces.'

Source: Modern Languages: 5–14 National Guidelines, Scottish Executive and Learning and Teaching Scotland

Covering the Curriculum in Northern Ireland

Tricolore Total is fully in line with the learning outcomes and objectives of the MFL curriculum in Northern Ireland. Students are encouraged to become effective and creative communicators, with opportunities to develop awareness of language, to make inter-cultural comparisons, to use previously learnt language in new contexts, etc. The varied activities enable students to research and manage information, think critically, develop creativity and work effectively with others, etc.

1 Developing pupils as Individuals

There are many opportunities for students to communicate an understanding of self and others (personal conversation in several units); to explore issues relating to lifestyle and choice (hobbies *Unités 6, 10*, healthy eating *Unité 9*); to contribute actively to a positive learning environment (class interaction, *vocabulaire de classe*); to develop an awareness of cultural similarities and differences (*Unités 5, 8*, etc.).

2 Developing pupils as Contributors to Society

Students have opportunities to explore social issues which relate to everyday lives (giving opinions *Unités 4, 8*, expressing future plans *Unité 9*, reporting recent events *Unité 10*); to make inter-cultural comparisons (festivals *Unité 5*, food *Unité 9*); to develop an awareness of media and media resources (use of websites and authentic resources throughout the course); to discuss ethical issues (environment *Unité 7*).

3 Developing pupils as Contributors to the Economy and Environment

This objective is developed more fully in Stages 2 and 3.

Building on earlier learning

The Primary National Strategy for Literacy

Tricolore Total builds on the knowledge about language that students will bring with them from their primary school. They are encouraged to:

- read, write, speak and listen for a range of purposes and contexts
- read and write using both paper and screen
- interact with peers through group discussion
- comprehend and interpret texts
- create and modify texts

Language learning at KS2

'The learning of a foreign language in primary school provides a valuable educational, social and cultural experience for all pupils. Pupils develop communication and literacy skills that lay the foundation for future language learning.' (The National Curriculum Online, 2007)

Tricolore Total 1 should be ideal for building on this foundation, and has very similar aims to those listed in the non-statutory guidelines and the QCA scheme of work for Key Stage 2.

Besides the actual teaching of a new language, *Tricolore Total* emphasises the development of language-learning skills, incorporating comparison of the new language with English, encouraging cultural awareness, and building up confidence and positive attitudes towards language learning.

The actual topics covered in the QCA primary languages programme are very similar to those which appear in *Tricolore Total 1*, so it should be relatively easy for teachers to ensure continuity of learning. Levels of competence and prior knowledge will vary. By using the diversity of material offered by the course, such as the Copymasters, the *Au Choix*, *Rappel* and *Presse-Jeunesse* sections and especially the integrated online resource, teachers will be able to tailor their teaching to different learning needs. Assessment and progress is checked regularly through AfL tasks, *Épreuves* and *Contrôles*.

Pairwork can also play a useful part in integration and continuity, maybe pairing a more experienced language learner to help a newer learner. 'Carousel' sessions can also be organised with some groups of students working on harder items than others, but all linked with a common theme.

Another way to build on diversity is for groups of students with prior knowledge to prepare presentations to help other groups. Some of these could involve internet research using websites about e.g. La Rochelle, schools in France, the French-speaking world, food and shopping.

Some more able students might also communicate directly with a linked French school or town, writing simple e-mails and reporting back to the class on their findings.

For detailed guidelines on the new Key Stage 2 scheme of work for French, see **http://www.qca.org.uk/**

Teaching approach

Developing listening skills

Training in careful listening for detail and for gist is a key feature of the course and should be developed from the outset. Two key strategies are:

- Building confidence by introducing language gradually with clues for what is to be listened for. This will help convince students that they can understand spoken French.
- Encouraging guesswork, especially of cognates, and emphasising that you don't need to understand every word.

There are no 'paused' recordings so the teacher can judge when there should be pauses, and the speed of building up from simple to more demanding tasks. The only exception to this is in the *Contrôles*, which simulate examination-type conditions.

Recorded listening material can be broadly grouped as follows:

Intensive listening

Students know what to listen for and have to select specific information from the recorded text and listen in sufficient detail to respond, e.g. by matching a description to a picture or answering simple *Vrai ou faux?* questions.

In many cases, students are also encouraged to listen for an opinion or for additional details.

Most of the listening practice in *Tricolore Total 1* is intensive.

Listening for gist

Students listen to find out what happened at the end of a story or to discover the type of information. Students should not worry if they can't understand every word but should just listen for the main points, as they probably will do when they hear real French people talking.

Interrelationship between sounds and writing

There are regular items on pronunciation.

Independent listening

From *Unité 4* onwards, there are recorded listening items, with linked tasks on the copymaster. These *Tu comprends?* sections are based on the language content of the unit and are graded in difficulty.

Developing speaking skills

The National Curriculum states that students should learn how to express themselves using a range of vocabulary and structures.

Particular emphasis is placed on the following:

- correct pronunciation and intonation
- how to ask and answer questions
- how to initiate and develop conversations
- how to vary the target language to suit context, audience and purpose.

These are addressed fully in the course, for example:

- individual pronunciation
- using the target language for class activities, supported by the *Vocabulaire de classe* section. Students are expected to use French for class activities, and to use English only when necessary (for example, when discussing a grammar point or when comparing English and the target language).
- questions – using *Est-ce que* (*Unité 4*), asking for personal details (*Unités 1–4*), more general questions (*Unités 5–10*)
- pairwork and role-play practice and 'information gap' activities, using copymasters
- 'colour-coded conversations', called *Inventez des conversations*. Students practise a basic conversation, then vary and adapt it by substituting other words and expressions from the colour-coded sections.

The *Tricolore Total* online resource provides a record and playback facility, particularly useful for practice in pronunciation and speaking.

Developing reading skills

There is a wide range of reading material, including practice in intensive reading and reading for gist.

Reading strategies, e.g. techniques for skimming and for scanning written texts, using context and other clues to interpret meaning, appear at regular points in the *Stratégies* sections of the Student's Book.

Presse-Jeunesse

These magazine sections can just be used alone or with the accompanying copymasters.

ICT and reading skills

The *Tricolore* online resource includes a reader for each unit for class or individual use and several interactive reading tasks allowing students to work on reading texts at their own pace.

Using dictionaries and other reference material

There is regular practice in using dictionaries and the French–English and English–French glossaries

Developing writing skills

There is systematic training in writing e.g.

Copywriting

In the early units, the main emphasis is on copywriting of words and phrases to help familiarise students with spelling patterns. Some simple creative work can be introduced quite quickly, through word games, sorting words and making labels or posters for the classroom.

Learning new words

The *Sommaire* sections, at the end of each unit and on copymasters, encourage students to learn and practise lists of vocabulary on a regular basis.

Adapting a model by substituting text/adapting known language to new contexts

These begin with simple sentence work, using substitution tables. More creative and open-ended writing is gradually introduced, especially through the *Dossier personnel* items in which students adapt the language they have learnt to their personal situation, state likes and dislikes and express opinions.

Developing independence in learning and using the target language

Students are encouraged to use dictionaries and other reference materials appropriately.

Re-drafting writing to improve its accuracy

Although this is quite advanced work for students using *Tricolore Total 1*, early training is given by the following types of task:

- *Vrai ou faux?* tasks, followed by correcting false statements
- *Chasse à l'intrus* activities in which students add explanations for their answers
- sentence completion tasks, based on information from short articles or letters
- working on the computer with text re-sequencing activities
- unjumbling and completing sentences
- using substitution tables.

Developing understanding and application of grammar

Grammar is a central feature of *Tricolore Total*. New grammatical structures are introduced in context and students are encouraged to work out rules for themselves. Key points are explained in the *Dossier-langue* sections, which is immediately followed by practice activities so students absorb the grammatical patterns and use them.

There is a grammar reference section, including verb tables, and students are encouraged to make up their own electronic verb tables.

- **Grammar in Action**

  Grammar in Action is a series of self-instructional workbooks to accompany each stage of *Tricolore Total*. The books provide extensive practice in French grammar to reinforce and extend the correct use of grammar.

Developing language-learning skills

The National Curriculum emphasises training in language-learning skills stating that pupils should be taught:

- **techniques for memorising words, phrases and short extracts**

In *Tricolore Total 1*, students are given regular hints for memorising, e.g. learning nouns with their gender, using spider diagrams, using visual imagery, making associations, etc.

The *Masculin, féminin* tasks in the *Rappel* sections are supported by a *Pour t'aider* note which indicates common word endings linked to masculine or feminine words. These are also given in the *Grammaire*.

The *Sommaire* sections at the end of each unit bring vocabulary together for easy reference. This gives a sense of progress and emphasises the importance of regular learning as an essential language-learning skill.

- **to use their knowledge of English or another language when learning the target language**

Grammar is explained in English, and the *Dossier-langue*, *Stratégies* and Plenary sections draw out comparisons with English and other languages.

- **to look out for clues**

Students are taught to use clues to discover meaning, such as similarities to English (cognates), as well as context and grammatical function.

Developing cultural awareness

Tricolore Total features many aspects of everyday life in France (meals, daily routine, school life, leisure) and also other French-speaking countries, such as Sénégal (*Unité 8*). The French town of La Rochelle provides the background for *Unité 7*. There is coverage of popular festivals in France (*Unité 5*) and around the world (*Unité 9*), the *Fête de la science* (*Unité 6*) and the *Fête de la musique* (*Unité 10*). Authentic materials and websites are used to extend knowledge about the French-speaking world.

Cross-curricular links

Tricolore Total provides cross-curricular links with other subjects such as English (comparisons between grammar and vocabulary); ICT (standard terminology, use of internet sites, software applications, the *Tricolore* online resource, etc); maths (using numbers, simple statistics, prices); PHSE (healthy eating) and geography (towns, areas and climate of France, French-speaking countries in Africa, etc).

Differentiation

Tricolore Total 1 contains material for most of the ability range. In the first few units it is assumed that the class will work at much the same pace, although suggestions for adapting the level of difficulty are included in the teacher's notes.

For classes in which some or all of the students have already learnt French in the Primary School, differentiation can be organised by using the *Au choix* section of the Student's Book, the Copymasters and also the Grammar in Action books. See also p18, Language learning at KS2.

The *Au choix* section of the Student's Book provides material for extension (harder items) and consolidation (more practice at the same level). In most cases, students can work on these tasks independently.

The Copymasters provide flexibility and include some support and some extension work. Many have an incline of difficulty, to allow even the less able students to try harder items if they wish.

Differentiation by outcome

Some tasks, especially the open-ended ones such as the *Dossier personnel*, can be used at various levels according to ability. For example, to offer more support for the less able, the task could be treated as a class activity and a description built up on the board to be copied down. In other cases, gap-filling tasks can be made easier by giving students options to choose from, which can be written on the board and copied.

Selective use of items

The teaching of each new area of language follows a sequence of steps: presentation, discovery and explanation of new language, practice of new vocabulary and structures, leading to full communicative use.

The initial presentation, through oral/aural work, the explanation of new structures and some practice is appropriate for all.

After this, there is room for selection, for example, by choosing appropriate tasks, games and ICT activities.

Assessment

In addition to the Assessment for Learning strategy, described on p10, there are two types of assessment tests.

Épreuves (formative assessment)

These appear after *Unité 3* and all subsequent units. Full details (solutions, mark allocations) are given with the relevant unit notes. The skills tested are listening, reading and writing combined with grammar.

The *Épreuves* relate specifically to the unit just completed and could be used during two lessons: one for listening and another for reading and writing.

There is an incline of difficulty, starting with easy tasks at Level 1. Students will find the *Épreuves* useful to check their own progress and pinpoint areas for further revision. They can be used for continuous assessment or more informally in class, for homework or as extra practice and consolidation.

Contrôles (summative assessment)

Tricolore Total 1 includes three blocks of formal assessment in all four skills. The student's sheets are at the end of the Copymasters, and the teaching notes are given at the end of Section 3. These should be used as follows:

> *Premier contrôle* – after *Unité 4*
>
> *Deuxième contrôle* – after *Unité 7*
>
> *Troisième contrôle* – after *Unité 10*

The *Contrôles* have been designed to provide:

- a means of checking how much of the language and structures in preceding units has been assimilated
- evidence to help determine the National Curriculum Levels attained by students in each of the four language skills (Attainment Targets)
- a way of recording progress made by students – a Record sheet for students (CM 126) is provided for this purpose
- a pointer towards lack of progress (enabling the teacher to take the necessary steps for support)
- an introduction, at a basic level, to the type of target-language testing used in formal examinations, giving students a head start in developing the examination techniques they are going to need at a later date.

The three *Contrôles* each provide a series of tasks at various levels, with an incline of difficulty within each paper, so that all students can start together at the beginning and work through the tasks as far as they are able.

> *Premier contrôle*: Levels 1–2
>
> *Deuxième contrôle*: Levels 1–3
>
> *Troisième contrôle*: Levels 2–4 (+some elements of Levels 5 and 6)

Full details are given on pp207–213.

The mark scheme, and the tasks themselves, are closely linked to the approach set out by the QCA Exemplification Materials and Optional Tests and Tasks for Key Stage 3.

The following points should be borne in mind in relation to the various sets of papers:

Listening

- These papers are designed to be expendable.
- Each item is recorded twice, without any sound effects or interruptions and is clearly spoken by a native French speaker. It must be remembered that playing the material a third time, except where specified, could affect a student's performance and cause an artificially high score to be obtained.

Speaking

- These sheets are designed to be re-used and there is no need for students to write on them.
- The teacher is best placed to decide when to give out the tasks prior to the assessment and whether to allow students to record their own work.

Reading

- These papers are designed to be expendable.
- The use of dictionaries should not be permitted.

Writing

- These sheets are designed to be re-used.
- The use of dictionaries should not be permitted.
- Because these tasks are open-ended, the marking is quite complicated, but full details are provided in the individual mark schemes.

Finally, it is important to remember that the assessment tasks of the three *Contrôles* should not be used in isolation to determine the National Curriculum levels attained by students. They are designed to supplement rather than replace knowledge accumulated by the teacher from everyday assessment of student performance as they work through the various activities.

Games for language learning

Many of the games described here can be used for a wide range of language practice. A game which is particularly appropriate for a specific area is mentioned in the relevant unit notes.

In many games the teacher is the caller at the beginning, but students can soon be encouraged to take over this role.

1 Number games

Continue!

The caller counts aloud, stopping at intervals and pointing at someone, who must say the next number or s/he is out.

Chef d'orchestre

This is a more complicated version of *Continue!* The class is divided into two teams (*en avant* and *en arrière*). The 'conductor' says any number and points to one of the teams who must call out the next or the previous number depending on which team is indicated.

Dice games

Ordinary dice can be used for number games or special ones made using higher numbers or with words on, such as the six persons of the verb paradigm, etc.

The simplest form of dice games is for a player to throw the dice and say aloud the number or word that they throw. One group can throw for another and students unable to say the right words are out.

Loto! (Bingo)

Students can make a class set of Bingo cards, and play with buttons as counters. Similarly, they can play a simpler version by just writing any four numbers on a scrap of paper and crossing them off as they are said by the caller. This game is useful when the numbers are learnt as words, as the winner must show her/his paper to the teacher and will be eliminated if the words are incorrectly spelt.

This type of Bingo is also an excellent standby for practice of almost any set of vocabulary, days of the week, colours, etc. For example, when learning the date, students write four days in words on a piece of paper and cross them off as the caller says them, saying *Loto!* when all four have been said. (For a sample set of cards, see TB 23.)

Le dix magique

This is a pontoon-type game. The French for pontoon is *vingt et un*, but this version uses a total of ten so is called *Le dix magique*.

Students make a simple set of cards with numbers 1–10. They place the cards upside down and turn them over one at a time, saying the number, until they get exactly 10. If they get 11 or more they are 'bust' (*fichu!*) and they must start again. The best of five turns is the winner.

Onze!

Students stand up and take turns to call out numbers in sequence i.e. *un, deux, trois, quatre, cinq, six, sept, huit, neuf, dix, onze*. Students may choose to call out one number, two numbers or three numbers. Whoever calls out *Onze* has to sit down. It can get very tactical with the boys trying to get rid of all the girls and vice versa. When it gets down to the last two then the one going first should win if they think carefully. Whoever says *sept* will lose.

Countdown

This is a familiar game show format based on the long-running French show called *Le jeu des Chiffres et des Lettres*. It is played as a whole class activity and practises numbers as well as simple arithmetical operations such as *plus, moins, multiplié par, divisé par* and *égale*. Someone nominates and gives six numbers – four single-figure digits and two numbers which must be 25, 50, 75 or 100. Write them on the board. (Alternatively you can download a Countdown random number generator if you look around on the web.) You then 'randomly' put a three figure number on the board and the class have two minutes to arrive at that figure using some or all of their chosen numbers. They must not use a number more than once. When a student thinks they have solved the calculation you get them to explain it whilst you write it up on the board. To help them write up the terms they will need to explain the calculation.

This game works well with near beginners up to intermediate. Classes could use calculators, but it is probably better for them to use pencil and paper solutions.

Zut-alors (Fizz-buzz)

Another mental arithmetic game for the whole class. Explain that you are going to count up to 100, but whenever you get to a number with a 5 in, or a multiple of 5, they must say ZUT. When they arrive at a number with 7 in, or a multiple thereof, they must say ALORS. When 5 and 7 are involved they must say ZUT-ALORS.

It takes about 15 minutes to get to 100.

Quelle heure est-il?

This is a 'signalling' game in which the caller holds her/his arms upright to symbolise the hour, to the right to symbolise quarter past, to the left to symbolise quarter to and downwards to symbolise half past and the class or individuals say the time.

The game could be played in the manner of *Jacques a dit* (see TB 24), with the teacher saying the time and the students doing the hand signals. Alternatively, students could write down a sequence of times signalled and check them back orally.

2 General vocabulary games

These can be used for practising numbers and areas of vocabulary, e.g. food, pets, etc.

Attention!

Everyone in the class is given a word or number at the beginning of a week and a list of these is written on a notice or at the side of the board. At any odd time during the French lessons for that week, the teacher will call out one of the words or numbers listed and the correct student should stand up. If not, s/he is out and crossed off the list. The winners are those still in at the end of the week.

This game can be used to practise any vocabulary, each member of the class being allocated a colour, fruit, part of a verb, etc.

Effacez!

Numbers, pictures or words are displayed in random order. When the caller names an item on the board, a student must rush out and delete the item.

This can be played by the teacher just pointing at the next student, who has five seconds only to locate and delete the right item. It can also be played in groups or in teams. In the latter case it is advisable to write two sets of

items, each in a different colour. If the teacher wants the items left on for further practice they could be highlighted instead of being deleted. This is an excellent game for matching the written word to vocabulary previously met only aurally.

Les deux échelles (a dice game)

Two or more six-rung ladders can be drawn on the board with a number (or word, part of verb, etc.) on each rung. Each team or group throws the dice and reads out the number or word and, if it is the next on the ladder, it is crossed off and the team moves up to the next rung. No number or word must be crossed off until that rung is reached and the first team to reach the top of the ladder wins.

See also Dice games and *Loto!* (TB 23).

Qu'est-ce qu'il y a dans la boîte?

This game can be played with any selection of objects linked with a recent vocabulary topic, e.g. classroom objects, pictures of animals, clothes, etc.

First show the class the things to be used and practise the vocabulary. The objects are then taken out of sight and placed one at a time in a box for the class to guess which one is there each time.

Vrai ou faux? (True and false chairs)

This is a useful game for mixed or lower ability classes as it does not involve all the class in speaking or writing. Each team has two chairs labelled *vrai* and *faux*. The teacher (or a student) makes any statement and a member of each team comes out and sits on the true chair if s/he thinks the statement is true and on the false one if not. Sitting on the right chair wins a point for that team. (If the teams are too level, points can be given for the first child to sit on the right chair each time.)

Je touche

This is a cumulative game (chain game), in which the first person gets up and touches something, saying what he/she is doing, e.g. *Je touche le livre de Jean*, and then chooses someone to continue. The next person repeats what has been said and adds on something else, and so on.

For writing practice the class could try to write the whole list down from memory at the end.

Another alternative is to make, from memory, a numbered list of drawings. This list can be used again for pairwork, e.g. *Numéro 4, qu'est-ce que c'est?*

Touché-coulé (Battleships)

This well-known game (best played in pairs) can be adapted to practise various bits of language. In its simplest form students are given the area of vocabulary to be practised, e.g. a verb paradigm, numbers, days of the week, etc. or a set of flashcards is put up as a reminder. Each person writes down on paper any three of the alternatives. Each player in turn guesses one item that the other person has written and if guessed correctly, the player must cross it out. The first one to eliminate their partner's items has won.

More complicated versions, nearer to the original, involve writing the items in a particular place on squared paper or a plan so that one player says to their opponent, e.g. *A3, tu as …!*)

Using Battleships to practise the verb 'être'

(as for *Unités 3* or *5*)

Each partner marks where s/he is on a simple plan of a house or flat. Then each asks the other, in turn, e.g. *Es-tu dans la cuisine?* answering, e.g. *Oui, je suis dans la cuisine* or *Non* if incorrect. The first one to discover where the other is has won.

When the whole paradigm has been learnt, the game can be extended to include the third person and the plural persons of the verb, e.g. *Les enfants sont dans le salon*, etc.

Je pense à quelque chose

The basic guessing game, in which someone thinks of a word (within a given range) and the others have to guess it by asking *C'est un/une …?* (See *Unité 1* – SB 9.)

Le jeu des Scarabées (Beetle)

Again, various areas of vocabulary which can have visual interpretation can be adapted to this, e.g. Beetle house. Students draw a square divided into six for a house. They throw the dice and fill in the correct parts as follows:

1 *la cuisine*
2 *la salle à manger*
3 *la salle de bains*
4 *la chambre*
5 *la porte*
6 *le jardin*

The first to complete her/his house has won. Other possible subjects are pets (*Unité 4*), clothes (*Unité 5*), lessons on a timetable (*Unité 8*) and courses of a meal (*Unité 9*).

Jeu de mémoire (Kim's game)

Everyone looks at a set of objects, words or information for a set time (say, two minutes). Then one or more of these is removed or the whole lot are covered up, and the class has to remember as many objects, facts or words as possible.

3 Flashcard games

For guessing games involving flashcards the class should always be shown all the cards to be used first and the French for these should be practised or checked before the game begins.

Qu'est-ce que c'est? (Guess the back of the flashcard)

It is better to limit the cards to a single topic, so that there are not too many to choose from.

The pile of flashcards is shuffled and the caller holds up a card with the picture facing her/him and says *Qu'est-ce que c'est?* Other students ask *C'est un/une* (+ noun)? and the person who guesses correctly comes out and acts as caller.

Qu'est-ce qu'il/elle fait?

This game is similar to the one above but is played with flashcards depicting actions (e.g. flashcards 34–42 and 95–100).

Quel temps fait-il?

This is played in the same way as above, but with cards 27–33.

Ce n'est pas … (Guess what the card isn't)

This is played with the whole class, as a group game or in pairs. One player holds up a card, face away, and the other person(s) guess what it is not, e.g.

– *Ce n'est pas un chien.*
– *Vrai.*
– *Ce n'est pas une souris.*
– *Vrai.*
– *Ce n'est pas un lapin.*
– *Faux – c'est un lapin.*

This is a good morale booster as the answer is more often right than wrong!

Des questions

The teacher picks up one of a group of flashcards and asks a question about it. S/he gives the card to the student who answers correctly. When all the cards are given out, the students with them come to the front and ask a question about their card to someone else in the class who then receives the card if s/he answers correctly. This goes on until all the class have had a turn.

Où vas-tu?

To practise the verb *aller*, all the flashcards referring to places should be put up around the room. The teacher or a student tells someone, e.g. *Va à la gare!* The student gets up and goes to the relevant place and on the way is asked *Où vas-tu?* If s/he answers correctly s/he continues and the teacher asks someone else *Où va-t-il/elle?* If s/he replies incorrectly s/he sits down and someone else is told to go somewhere. If s/he replies correctly and arrives at the destination s/he has a point.

Trois questions (Mind reading)

This is good for practising verbs + nouns.

Tell students that you are going to read their minds. Put up a number of flashcards and tell a student to think hard about one of them (get the thinker to tell her/his neighbour or write down which s/he has chosen, as a safeguard). Then ask three questions and if you have read her/his mind by then you get a point, if not the class gets a point.

Examples:

1 *être* (+ room)

   Teacher: *Tu es dans la salle à manger?*

   Student: *Non, je ne suis pas dans la salle à manger.*

   Teacher: *Tu es dans le salon?*

   Student: *Non, je ne suis pas dans le salon.*

   Teacher: *Tu es dans la cuisine?*

   Student: *Oui, je suis dans la cuisine.*

   or *Non, je ne suis pas dans la cuisine.*

   or *Non, je suis* (+ correct place)

2 *avoir* (+ pets)

   Teacher: *Tu as un lapin.*

   Student: *Oui, j'ai un lapin.*

   or *Non, je n'ai pas de lapin,* etc.

3 *aller* (+ place)

   Teacher: *Tu vas à l'église.*

   Student: *Oui, je vais à l'église.*

   or *Non, je ne vais pas à l'église,* etc.

This game can be adapted for use with a wide range of structures and can be played teacher v class, group v group, team v team, girls v boys, etc.

4 Mini-flashcard games

The flashcard games which follow can be played in pairs or small groups, with the sets of mini-flashcards made from the worksheets.

Pelmanism (group or pair game)

Use double sets of word cards, mini-flashcards or picture cards + matching word cards. In turn, students turn over a pair of cards to see if they match. They say the word on or represented by the cards, then turn them face

downwards again in the same place – unless they form a pair, in which case they pick them up and keep them.

Le jeu des sept familles (Happy Families or Fish!)

Using four sets of mini flashcards for each group, or a set of home-made cards, this game can be played as normal, using *As-tu…?/Oui, j'ai/Non, je n'ai pas …*

Loto de vocabulaire (Flashcard Bingo)

Students could make their own sets of Loto cards with pictures of four items. Each group of students could make sets of cards dealing with a different vocabulary area. The example below uses vegetables and fruit.

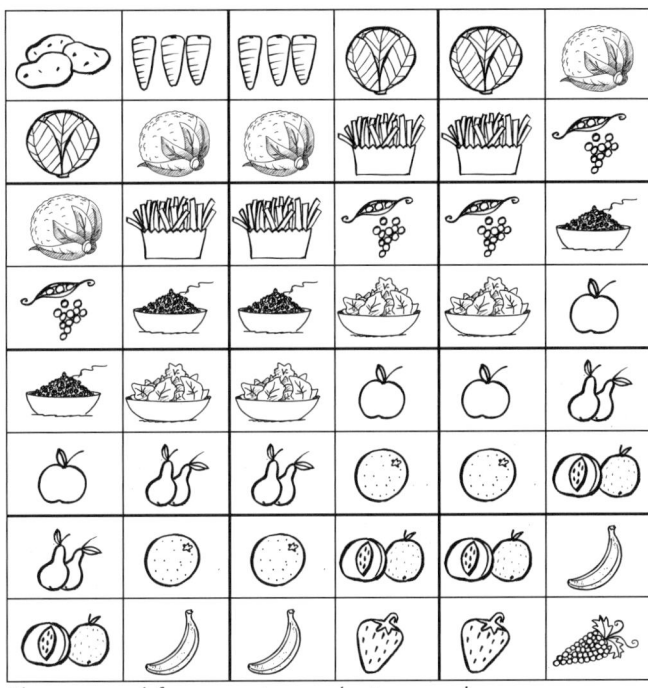

Players need four counters or buttons each.

The caller should shuffle the relevant flashcards and turn them up one at a time saying *Voilà des pommes de terre,* etc.

The winner (who must shout *Loto!*) is the player whose card is first full and who can also say the four things shown on it in French. If the first to finish cannot say the words in French s/he is out and the caller continues until the next card is full.

Suitable vocabulary areas for this are *En ville, À la maison, Les animaux* and weather.

The statements to be made by the caller can be extended to practise relevant structures, e.g. *J'aime les pommes de terre. Il y a des carottes.*

For a text-based item, teachers could use the grid in the *Tricolore Totale* online resource, Starters and Plenaries section. This is a grid for 34 different cards (enough for one each in a fairly large class) using text for various items (e.g. *Unité 3* covers 15 items of vocabulary on rooms and contents). Teachers could adapt the grid for other vocabulary topics and just replace a word or a picture.

'Carousel' version

Each group could have sets of flashcards, each on a different subject. Then groups could rotate after five minutes or so to practise different sets of vocabulary.

Games with 2 sets of cards

- **Bataille! (Snap)**

  Flashcard snap in which they say the name of each card as they put it down. The first player to call *Bataille* wins the pile of cards.

- **Contre la montre**

  This is a race against time in which each student sorts their cards into fruit and vegetables, masculine and feminine, good and bad weather, inside or outside, as appropriate.

- **Mots et images**

  One player says the name of an object from their hand. The other player selects the appropriate card from their own hand and puts it on the table. Then this player says a name and the first player puts the appropriate card on the table, and so on.

5 Games for practising verbs

These are in addition to those already mentioned.

Verb dice

Make a big cardboard dice, but instead of numbers write on it *je*, *tu*, *il/elle/on*, *nous*, *vous*, *ils/elles*. Students throw the dice in turn and must say or write the correct part of the verb. The verbs could also be used in sentences, e.g. *Je suis à l'épicerie*.

Loto des verbes

Students write down three or four persons of a verb on their paper and play as before. Alternatively, about ten infinitives (of regular verbs) should be put on the board and everyone writes down the same person of four of them (this enables one person + relevant ending to be practised at a time).

Le jeu des mimes (Miming)

Students take turns to mime an action. The teacher or group leader says *Qu'est-ce qu'il/elle fait?* Students guess the action by asking *Tu regardes la télévision? Tu écoutes la radio?* etc. The actor answers *Oui, je regarde la télévision* or *Non, je ne regarde pas la télévision*, as appropriate.

Le jeu des mimes (Group version)

Students could work in groups of four or five, a representative of each group doing a mime in turn, and the members of the other groups writing down a guess for each mime. When enough mimes have been done (say, two or three per group), the groups can then be asked to guess in turn and to score a point for each correct guess. The points are totalled to find the winning group.

Chef d'orchestre

(See Number games, TB 21.) The teams must give the next person before or after the one quoted, in the standard paradigm or any agreed order. (Some classes will need the pronouns in order on the board as a visible prompt.)

Les verbes en cercle (Circle paradigm practice)

A number of subjects (nouns and pronouns) are written on the board, in random order, in the form of a circle, e.g.

Christophe
Je   *Magali et Olivier*
Nous   *Tu*
On   *Ils*
Vous

The teacher calls out a sentence, e.g. *Je joue au tennis*, and then points to any of the subjects in the circle and asks someone to modify the sentence accordingly. The person chosen then continues clockwise round the circle until stopped by the teacher. This practice drill should move quickly, with frequent changes of speaker, sentence and points on the circle. Different nouns and pronouns should be used whenever this is played.

Jacques a dit (or Simon dit)

An old favourite in which students carry out actions preceded by *Jacques a dit* (or *Simon dit*) but not otherwise, e.g. *Jacques a dit* (*Simon dit*): *jouez au football! Asseyez-vous!* etc.

Les verbes en désordre (Scrambled verbs)

Write the pronouns and the six (or nine) parts of the verb in random order on each side of the board. One from each team comes out and rings *je* and the part which goes with it. Then, when this is done correctly, the next marker comes out and rings *tu* and the verb in a different colour, and so on until one team has correctly unscrambled the verb.

6 Spelling games

Dix secondes

Words linked with a particular topic are written on the board. A member of each team in turn has to see how many of the words s/he can spell correctly in, say, ten seconds. (The speller stands facing away from the board.) The words are crossed out or ticked when spelt so the choice gets smaller.

Je vois (I spy)

Play as in English: *Je vois quelque chose qui commence par …*

This game is particularly useful from *Unité 2* onwards, when the French alphabet has been introduced.

Spelling consequences

Students in groups spell words one letter at a time, in turn. Each group has to say a new letter and must be 'on the way' to making a French word that makes sense, preferably from a given vocabulary area, e.g. *En ville* or *Les fruits et les légumes*.

If anyone thinks they know the word, they put their hand up, the spelling stops and they guess. If correct, their group gets a point and takes over, starting a new word. If wrong, the speller says which word they were spelling and the speller's group start a new word, gaining one point. If anyone suspects that a group has added a letter when they had not got a word in mind, they can challenge. If they were right, they gain a point and take over with a new word. If wrong, the speller's group gets a point and starts a new word.

Songs

1 Using the songs

There are six songs on CD and the online resource, especially written and performed for *Tricolore Total*. The words of the songs and musical scores, comprising melodies, guitar chords and words, are on photocopiable pages of this Teacher's Book, TB 26–31. There is no music for *Attention, c'est l'heure!* which is a rap.

Un, deux, trois (Unité 2)

L'alphabet (Unité 4)

Le premier mois (Unité 6)

Attention, c'est l'heure! (Unité 8)

Pique-nique à la plage (Unité 9)

Samedi, on part en vacances (Unité 10)

There are two recorded versions of each song, one version including the words and the other an instrument-only version.

The version of each song which includes the words can be:

- listened to by the students simply for enjoyment
- used as the stimulus material for various types of listening comprehension tasks or games
- used as a device to teach the song to students – they may be able to sing along with this version, or sing along with the teacher (who may choose to play the accompaniment or not) independently of the recording.

The instrument-only version of each song may be used in class as a means of encouraging students to perform the song without vocal support from the recording, and thus this version lends itself to independent preparation and performance by small groups. (The publishers recommend that students preparing the song independently of the teacher use a security copy in order to prevent the risk of damage to the master CD; Nelson Thornes copyright conditions allow one such security copy to be made per purchasing establishment.)

Students preparing the songs in this way may be encouraged to perform them in extra- or cross-curricular contexts, for example departmental parents' evenings, school assemblies or as projects in conjunction with performing arts departments within the school.

The instrumental backing of the songs has been designed to be accessible and relatively simple in terms of musical structure and progression; thus, students with some musical training (in conjunction with music teachers or musically-able language teachers) might be expected to be able to produce full instrumental and vocal interpretations of these songs, by studying the recording and melody/guitar chords score.

Attention, c'est l'heure!

This rap 'song' practising times can be used at any appropriate point in *Unité 8* or later.

> Déjà sept heures moins dix, dix, dix,
> Vite, vite, je vais être en retard.
> Sept heures et quart je me prépare,
> Je quitte la maison, enfin je pars.
> Attention, c'est l'heure!
> Ça y est, huit heures du mat, matin,
> On entre en gare, j'arrive en train.
> La cloche sonne à huit heures vingt,
> Je suis au collège, tout va bien.
> Attention, c'est l'heure!
> Enfin midi, j'ai faim, faim, faim,
> On va manger à la cantine.
> Il est cinq heures, viens Géraldine,
> La fin des cours, vive les copines.
> Attention, c'est l'heure!
> Il est six heures du soir, soir, soir,
> Je fais mes devoirs, ouf, ça y est!
> Huit heures, on prend tous le dîner,
> Et puis, on regarde la télé.
> Attention, c'est l'heure!
> Besoin d'un bon dodo, dodo,
> Très fatigué, je vais au lit.
> Eh oui, il est dix heures et demie,
> Alors à bientôt, bonne nuit.
> Attention, c'est l'heure!

Games and songs

2 Words and music for the songs

L'alphabet

Tricolore Total 1 © Nelson Thornes 2008

Un, deux, trois

Un, deux, trois, Sa - lut! C'est moi! Qua-tre, cinq, six, J'ha - bite à Nice,

Sept, huit, neuf, Dans la rue El - beuf. Dix, onze, douze, Et toi? — Tou-louse.

Treize, qua-torze, quinze, Dans l'a-ven-ue de Reims. Seize, dix-sept, Je m'ap-pelle Col-ette.

Dix - huit, dix - neuf, vingt, C'est la fin! Re - comm-ence au num - é - ro un...

– 1, 2, 3,
Salut! C'est moi!

4, 5, 6,
J'habite à Nice.

7, 8, 9,
Dans la rue Elbeuf.

10, 11, 12,
Et toi?

– Toulouse.
13, 14, 15,
Dans l'avenue de Reims.

16, 17,
Je m'appelle Colette.

18, 19, 20,
C'est la fin!

Recommence au numéro un …

Tricolore Total 1 © Nelson Thornes 2008

Le premier mois

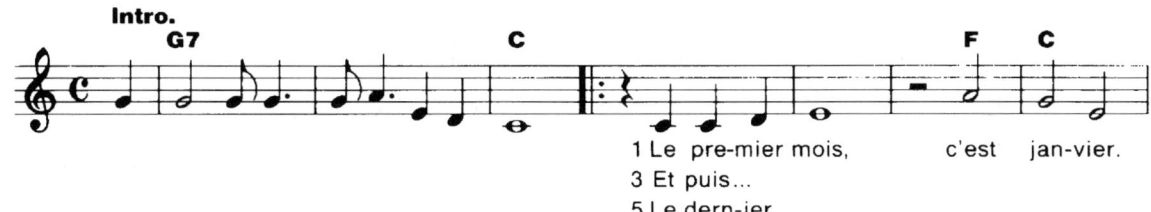

1 Le pre-mier mois, c'est jan-vier.
3 Et puis...
5 Le dern-ier...

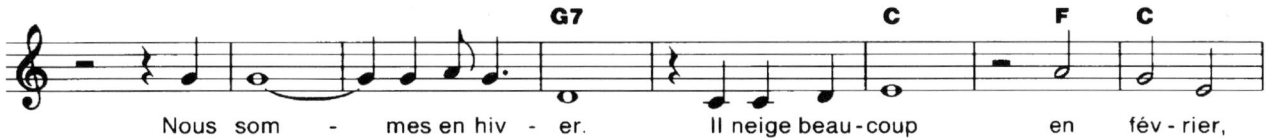

Nous som - mes en hiv - er. Il neige beau-coup en fév - rier,

3rd time end here

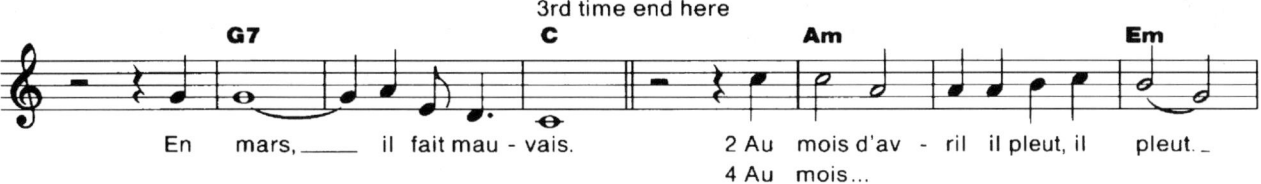

En mars,____ il fait mau - vais. 2 Au mois d'av - ril il pleut, il pleut. _
4 Au mois...

Nous som - mes au prin - temps. Il fait très

beau au mois de mai,____ La____ mét - éo dit: beau temps!

1 Le premier mois, c'est janvier.
   Nous sommes en hiver.
   Il neige beaucoup en février,
   En mars, il fait mauvais.

2 Au mois d'avril, il pleut, il pleut.
   Nous sommes au printemps.
   Il fait très beau au mois de mai,
   La météo dit: beau temps!

3 Et puis c'est juin, et juillet, août.
   Nous sommes en été.
   Il fait très chaud pour les vacances,
   Ma saison préférée.

4 Au mois de septembre la rentrée.
   Octobre, c'est l'automne.
   Du brouillard pendant novembre.
   Oh! qu'est-ce qu'il fait du vent!

5 Le dernier mois, on fête Noël.
   Nous sommes en décembre.
   Il fait très froid, mais moi, j'ai chaud –
   Je reste dans ma chambre!

Tricolore Total 1 © Nelson Thornes 2008

Pique-nique à la plage

Bonne jour - née! Bonne jour -

- née! Tout le monde va pique-niqu - er. Va cher - cher le pan-i - er! Pique-nique,

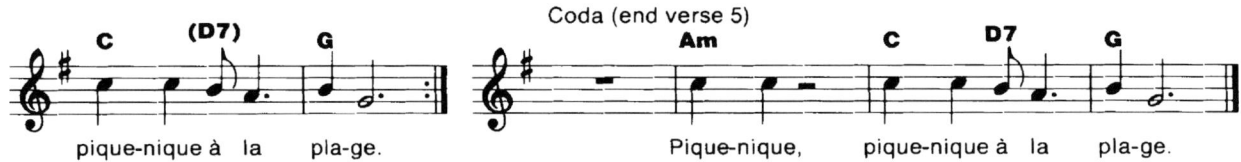

pique-nique à la pla-ge.   Pique-nique,   pique-nique à la pla-ge.

1 Bonne journée! Bonne journée!
   Tout le monde va pique-niquer.
   Va chercher le panier!
   Pique-nique, pique-nique à la plage.

2 Bonne journée! Bonne journée!
   Qu'est-ce que nous allons manger?
   Des sandwichs, une grande quiche.
   Pique-nique, pique-nique à la plage.

3 Bonne journée! Bonne journée!
   Regarde dans le panier.
   Oh, chouette, une galette!
   Pique-nique, pique-nique à la plage.

4 Bonne journée! Bonne journée!
   Il ne faut pas oublier
   Les chips, le vin, les petits pains.
   Pique-nique, pique-nique à la plage.

5 Quelle journée! Quelle journée!
   Tout le monde va pique-niquer.
   Allons trouver le soleil!
   Pique-nique, pique-nique à la plage.

Tricolore Total 1 © Nelson Thornes 2008

Samedi, on part en vacances

Samedi, on part en vacances.
Samedi, on part en vacances.

1 Nice et Cannes, Toulouse et Sète,
Ma valise est presque faite.
Samedi, on part en vacances.
Samedi, on part en vacances.

2 Oui, c'est vrai, on part demain.
Où est mon maillot de bain?
Nice et Cannes, Toulouse et Sète,
Ma valise est presque faite.
Samedi, on part en vacances.
Samedi, on part en vacances.

3 Pour le soleil, mes lunettes,
Pour le volley, mes baskets.
Oui, c'est vrai, on part demain.
Où est mon maillot de bain?
Nice et Cannes, Toulouse et Sète,
Ma valise est presque faite.
Samedi, on part en vacances.
Samedi, on part en vacances.

4 Faire du vélo, faire du ski,
Faire du camping, allons-y!
Pour le soleil, mes lunettes,
Pour le volley, mes baskets.
Oui, c'est vrai, on part demain.
Où est mon maillot de bain?
Nice et Cannes, Toulouse et Sète,
Ma valise est presque faite.
Samedi, on part en vacances.
Samedi, on part en vacances.

5 Sète, Toulouse et Nice et Cannes,
Nous allons en caravane.
Faire du vélo, faire du ski,
Faire du camping, allons-y!
Pour le soleil, mes lunettes,
Pour le volley, mes baskets.
Oui, c'est vrai, on part demain.
Où est mon maillot de bain?
Nice et Cannes, Toulouse et Sète,
Ma valise est presque faite.
Samedi, on part en vacances.
Samedi, on part en vacances.

6 Que nous avons de la chance,
C'est bientôt les vacances!
Sète, Toulouse et Nice et Cannes,
Nous allons en caravane.
Faire du vélo, faire du ski,
Faire du camping, allons-y!
Pour le soleil, mes lunettes,
Pour le volley, mes baskets.
Oui, c'est vrai, on part demain.
Où est mon maillot de bain?
Nice et Cannes, Toulouse et Sète,
Ma valise est presque faite.
Samedi, on part en vacances.
Samedi, on part en vacances.

Tricolore Total 1 © Nelson Thornes 2008

Aims and objectives	Key language/Culture	Grammar and skills	National criteria
Introduction p3 • introduce France • learn where some places are in France	*Voici …* *Ça, c'est …* **Culture**: Finding out about the geography of France	**Skills** Learning some geographical facts about France **Cross-curricular** Geography	**Attainment** AT1 Level 1, AT3 Level 1, AT4 Level 1 **Framework** 7C1 **Languages ladder/Asset languages** Grade 1
1A Toi et moi pp6–7 • greet someone and say goodbye • tell someone your name and age in French and ask what their name and age is • ask someone how they are and tell them how you are	Greetings: *Bonjour monsieur/madame/mademoiselle …* *Salut (+ name) … Au revoir.* *Comment t'appelles-tu? … Je m'appelle …* *Ça va? … Oui, ça va bien. Et toi?* *… Non, pas très bien. … Comme ci, comme ça.* Numbers 1–20 *Quel âge as-tu? … J'ai (+ number) ans.* **Culture**: social conventions	**Skills** Asking and answering questions	**Attainment** AT1 Level 1–2, AT2 Level 1–2, AT3 Level 1–2, AT4 Level 1 **Framework** 7S3/4/5/9, 7T1/2, 7L1/2/3/6, 7C5 **Languages ladder/Asset languages** Grades 1–3 **Assessment for learning*** ex 3, Stratégies
1B Qu'est-ce que c'est? pp8–9 • learn about numbers and things in the classroom • learn about the gender of nouns • learn how to make nouns plural	*Qu'est-ce que c'est?* *C'est un bic/cahier/cartable/crayon/livre/ordinateur/stylo/taille-crayon …* *C'est une boîte/calculatrice/chaise/gomme/règle/table/trousse …* *baladeur (iPod, lecteur mp3)/classeur/fenêtre/feuille de papier/feutre/lecteur CD/portable/porte/poubelle/sac à dos/tableau interactif/trombone* *Combien? Il y a combien de (+ noun)?* *Il y a (number) (+ noun).* *Ce n'est pas un/une (+ noun)* *Ce sont des (+ plural noun)*	**Grammar** Masculine and feminine nouns with indefinite article (*un/une*) Forming plurals **Skills** Learning gender as you learn new nouns **Pronunciation** Different pronunciation of words which look the same in French and English	**Attainment** AT1 Level 1–2, AT2 Level 1–2, AT3 Level 1–2, AT4 Level 1–2 **Framework** 7W3/4/6/8, 7S2/3, 7T3/4/6, 7L1/4, 7C3 **Languages ladder/Asset languages** Grades 1–2 **Assessment for learning** ex 3
1C En classe pp10–11 • practise classroom commands and vocabulary • practise some questions and answers	Classroom commands: *Asseyez-vous/Complète/Comptez/Copie/Écoute(z)/Écris/Écrivez/Ferme(z)/Jouez à deux/Levez-vous/Ouvre(z)/Regarde(z)/Répétez/Réponds/Travaillez à deux/Trouve*	**Pronunciation** The letter *i*	**Attainment** AT1 Level 1–2, AT2 Level 1–2, AT3 Level 1–2, AT4 Level 1–2 **Framework** 7W3/4/6, 7S4, 7T1/5, 7L1/4, **Languages ladder/Asset languages** Grades 1–2

Other resources: Online resource *Unité 1*, Copymasters CM 1/1–1/3, 128 CD 1 tracks 2–16, Flashcards 1–2

* AfL: Throughout the course, the plenaries provide a good opportunity for students to assess their progress against the spread objectives and share thoughts on effective learning strategies.

Introduction   page 3

Aims and objectives	Grammar and skills	Resources
• introduce France • learn where some places are in France	**Skills** Learning some geographical facts about France **Cross-curricular** Geography	**Key language:** see p32 **Online resource:** *Unité 1* int01 **Copymasters:** 1/1, 128

 3   **AT1**

La France

Many teachers like to begin with an introduction to France itself. The ICT presentation, the maps in the Student's Book and on CM128 and the quiz on CM1/1 are ideal for this.

Speak about the map (SB 3) very simply in French, e.g.

Voici la France. Ça, c'est Paris – voici la Tour Eiffel et Disneyland Paris. Voici les montagnes, les Alpes, les Pyrénées etc.

Ask a few questions to find out how many of the class have visited France, how to get there, if they know any French people or can speak any French. etc.

Maybe talk about France from your own point of view, perhaps showing some photos, and tell the class about other countries where French is spoken and how useful it is as an international language.

The map also presents a good opportunity to tie in geographical facts to the towns (such as famous buildings, certain foods, etc.). It can be used later to assess students' knowledge of France. Point out the different spelling and pronunciation of some towns/cities and stress the importance of correct pronunciation at this early stage.

 **Activité (int01)**   **AT1, AT3**

Voici la France

This online activity presents and practises the information on the map of France.

1/1   **AT3, AT4; 7C1**

La France

1   Voici la France

This accompanies the map on page 3 and *Presse-Jeunesse* item *Le sais-tu? La France*, SB 40.

It could be done at the beginning of learning French or later for interest or consolidation. The multi-choice quiz could be used for class discussion or as a written task, or as a group quiz 'against the clock'.

> **Solution:**
>
> **1 Voici la France**
>
> **1** a, **2** b, **3** a, **4** b, **5** b, **6** a, **7** c, **8** c
>
> **2 Chasse à l'intrus**
>
> **1** *la Seine*, **2** *le Rhône*, **3** *la mobylette*, **4** *Dieppe (others are capital cities)*, **5** *la Manche*, **6** *Le Mont Blanc*, **7** *la Suisse*, **8** *Londres*
>
> **3 Mots mêlés**
>
> Note that words are horizontal, vertical and diagonal.

I	L	I	F	K	A	L	P	E	S	S
Q	I	B	O	R	D	E	A	U	X	I
X	L	T	O	L	O	I	R	E	T	A
H	L	U	F	Q	S	E	I	N	E	L
R	E	I	L	Y	O	N	S	I	Q	A
N	A	V	I	G	N	O	N	C	O	C
G	F	X	Z	R	H	Ô	N	E	U	O
I	D	I	S	N	E	Y	L	A	N	D

Students could be encouraged to find out more about France themselves, such as obtaining leaflets from a travel agent for a classroom display round a centrally placed map.

1A Toi et moi   pages 6–7

Aims and objectives	Grammar and skills	Resources
• greet someone and say goodbye • tell someone your name and age in French and ask what their name and age is • ask someone how they are and tell them how you are	**Skills** Asking and answering questions	**Key language:** see p32 **Online resource:** *Unité 1* int02/03, ppt01, ws02 **CD** 1 tracks 2–4 **Flashcards:** 1–2

Starters (pages 6–7)

 Fiche de travail (ws02)

The material required for starters and plenaries can be found on one online worksheet for each unit. This can be used to display on the interactive whiteboard or to print out.

1 **5-4-3-2-1** This is the first of a regular type of starter. Display the words in random order and ask students to find 5 towns/cities, 4 rivers, 3 mountains, 2 seas and 1 country.

Solution:

des villes	des rivières	des montagnes	des mers	un pays
La Rochelle	Garonne	Alpes	Atlantique	France
Lyon	Loire	Pyrénées	Méditerranée	
Marseille	Rhône	Vosges		
Paris	Seine			
Strasbourg				

If the online map activity has not yet been used, students could use that and talk briefly about France, before beginning to learn greetings, etc.

2 (Use after task 2 and the follow-up activities.) For a quick revision of introducing people, walk around the class, suddenly pointing to someone and asking the class *Qui est-ce?* When they reply, ask the person concerned *Comment t'appelles-tu?*

As this is simple revision, it needs to be done quickly, pointing to students behind you, on the other side of the class, etc. After a short while, able students could have a turn at this random pointing and questioning.

Introduction	AT2

Greetings

Introduce the class to French greetings and appropriate replies, both when addressed as a class and individually, e.g.

1 – *Bonjour, les enfants/les élèves/la classe!*
– *Bonjour, Monsieur/Madame/Mademoiselle.*

2 – *Bonjour, Ellie/Olivia/Jack/Noah* etc.
– *Bonjour, M./Mme/Mlle.*

Greet individuals by name, perhaps shaking hands with them.

Explain the use of *Salut* as a more informal greeting (Hi!) and bring this into the conversation as well.

Salut, Lauren. Salut, Harry, etc.

Introduce the other titles one at a time by using cards with names on, e.g. *M. Duval, Mme Cresson, Mlle Leclerc*.

Give out one or two cards and introduce those holding them to the class.

– *Voici Monsieur Duval. Répétez.*
– *Bonjour, Monsieur* etc.

To make things more amusing, you could attach the name labels to hats which can then be put on a variety of children, who, in turn, exchange greetings with the class or individuals.

When the class is confident with this, introduce *Au revoir* and practise in a similar way.

sb 6   1 tr 2   AT1, AT2; 7T1, 7L1, 7L2, 7C5

1 Bonjour!

The class listens to the greetings while looking at the photos.

Ask pupils what they think they'll be learning, before eliciting the lesson objective, e.g. by the end of the lesson you will be able to meet and greet someone in well pronounced French.

Then play the recordings again, this time with the students repeating after the speakers and then try out the conversations without the support of the recording.

As you do this, begin to introduce some classroom commands, e.g.

Écoute! Écoutez! Ouvrez le livre à la page …
Regardez le livre.

Comment, if you wish, on the fact that shaking hands and sometimes kissing each other on the cheek, as shown in the photos, is quite usual in France for both boys, girls and adults.

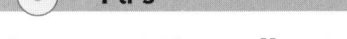

Bonjour!

1 – Bonjour, Coralie.
 – Bonjour, Sébastien.
2 – Salut, Olivier!
 – Salut, Magali!
3 – Au revoir, Isabelle.
 – Au revoir, Loïc.
4 – Bonjour, Monsieur Garnier.
 – Bonjour, Madame Lucas.

As a follow-up, after a short demonstration, ask students to get up and each say hello, then goodbye to four other people in French.

Integrate with greetings the teaching and practice of the commands:

Lève-toi/Levez-vous, Assieds-toi/Asseyez-vous, Viens/Venez ici and *Retourne à ta place*. The game *Jacques a dit* (TB 24) could be used here as a class activity to consolidate understanding of the new classroom commands.

| ● 1 tr 3 | AT1 |

Comment t'appelles-tu?

Explain that the class will now hear some of the people shown in the photographs being asked what their names are. Ask the class to listen carefully to see how they reply.

Comment t'appelles-tu?

– Comment t'appelles-tu?
– Je m'appelle Coralie.
– Comment t'appelles-tu?
– Je m'appelle Sébastien.
– Comment t'appelles-tu?
– Je m'appelle Olivier.
– Comment t'appelles-tu?
– Je m'appelle Magali.
– Comment t'appelles-tu?
– Je m'appelle Loïc.
– Comment t'appelles-tu?
– Je m'appelle Isabelle.

After playing the recording, introduce yourself: *Je m'appelle* (+ name) and then point to several students and get them to say *Je m'appelle* (+ name).

Gradually start to ask the question *Comment t'appelles-tu?* and practise this question and answer work until most students can answer correctly.

| sb 6 | AT2; 7S3, 7S4, 7T2, 7L6 |

2 Une conversation

This illustrated dialogue shows the printed form and should prove a useful prompt for practice in pairs. Make sure that everyone understands the rubric *Travaillez à deux*.

As a follow-up, get students to go round the class asking four different people their names before they sit down.

| Introduction | AT2, AT4 |

C'est …?

The aim of the next activities is to be able to introduce people. Point to a student and ask *Comment t'appelles-tu?* The student replies. Then point to the student and say to the class. *C'est …*

Gradually expand this as follows:

1 **Teacher:** *C'est …? Oui/Oui, c'est …*
2 **Teacher:** *Qui est-ce? C'est …? Oui? Oui, c'est …*
3 **Teacher:** *Qui est-ce?*
 Student: *C'est …*
 Teacher: *Oui, c'est …*
4 **Teacher:** *Qui est-ce? C'est* (+ wrong name)? *Non, c'est* (+ correct name).
5 **Teacher:** *Qui est-ce? C'est* (+ wrong name)?
 Student: *Non, c'est* (+ correct name).

| sb 140 Au choix | AT2, AT4 |

1 Qui est-ce?

These are close-ups from the photos of the same people featured in *Bonjour!* (task 1 above). Students jot down the numbers and match them up with the people.

This short item could be corrected orally.

> **Solution: 1** *C'est Loïc,* **2** *C'est Coralie,* **3** *C'est Monsieur Garnier,* **4** *C'est Olivier,* **5** *C'est Isabelle,* **6** *C'est Madame Lucas,* **7** *C'est Sébastien,* **8** *C'est Magali*

| Jeu | AT2, AT3 |

Devinez le prénom

(Use at any point after task 2)

Write a selection of about ten common French *prénoms* on cards and spread them out, face down.

Students take turns to pick up and look at one of the cards, which then becomes his/her name. Other students are asked to guess the card-holder's name (*Qui est-ce?*) finally asking *Comment t'appelles-tu?* The student who guessed correctly picks a card next.

Continue until all the names have been used.

Several students could pick up cards and ask each other's names as a chain game.

As an alternative version, one student picks up a card and the others have three chances to guess her/his correct name.

Each pupil could keep a card and it could become his/her 'French name'.

| sb 7 ● 1 tr 4 FC1–2 | AT1; 7L1, 7L2, 7S4, 7S5, 7C5; AfL |

3 Ça va?

Tell the class they are going to learn how to ask people how they are or if they're OK. The class repeat *Ça va?* several times. Then get some students to ask you the question and, showing flashcard 1 (happy face), say *Oui,*

ça va bien, merci. After a while, add to this *Et toi?* Hand the card to the questioner and get her/him to reply.

When everyone has practised this, introduce the possibility of not feeling too good, miming pain or sadness and using flashcard 2 (sad face) to teach *Non, pas très bien*.

Students copy down the names of the six people illustrated in silhouette or just write the numbers, then listen to the conversations between Julie and her friends and put a tick or a cross to show if each person is OK or not.

Pause the recording after the first conversation, refer to the example to make sure everyone knows what to do before playing the rest of the recording. Eventually correct the item orally with the class, perhaps playing the recording again and stopping after each conversation to say *Ça va? Oui ou non?*

> **Solution: 1** *Lauryne* ✓, **2** *Julien* ✓,
> **3** *Sanjay* ~, **4** *Chloé* ✗, **5** *Léa* ✓, **6** *Alexandre* ~

transcript

Ça va?

1 – Bonjour, Lauryne.
  – Ah, bonjour, Julie. Ça va?
  – Oui, ça va bien, merci, et toi?
  – Oui, oui. Ça va très bien.

2 – Bonjour, Julien, c'est Julie.
  – Ah, bonjour, Julie. Ça va?
  – Oui, ça va bien, merci, et toi?
  – Oui. Ça va très bien, merci.

3 – Bonjour, Sanjay.
  – Ah, salut Julie.
  – Ça va, Sanjay?
  – Oh, comme ci comme ça.

4 – Bonjour, Chloé.
  – Qui est-ce?
  – C'est Julie. Ça va, Chloé?
  – Non, Julie. Ça ne va pas très bien.

5 – Bonjour, Léa.
  – Qui est-ce? C'est Julie?
  – Oui, oui, c'est moi. Ça va, Léa?
  – Ah, salut, Julie! Oui, oui, ça va bien, merci.

6 – Bonjour, Alexandre, c'est Julie.
  – Ah, bonjour, Julie. Ça va?
  – Oui, ça va bien, merci, et toi?
  – Bof, comme ci comme ça.

For further practice, choose pairs of students to come out and ask each other *Ça va?* and cue their replies with the flashcards. This practice could continue as pair or group work and is an opportunity for peer assessment, with mini-flashcards made quickly by the students. Refer students to the spread objectives and agree the criteria for success. This allows students to demonstrate the skills acquired so far. If appropriate, display a model of a perfect answer.

| Activité (int02) | AT1, AT3 |

Bonjour! Ça va?

Use this animated interaction to practise recognition of answers to the question 'How are you?'

Numbers 1–20

Many students will have at least some idea of the French numbers, but it is important to get pronunciation right at this point.

It is a good idea to teach the numbers three at a time with students repeating them after you, and only move on to the next three when the previous group is properly learnt. Tell pupils that our brains recall information best when it's remembered in chunks.

Number games

There is a wide selection of these (see TB 21) e.g. *Loto!, Continue!, Onze* and *Le dix magique*. For games which have a winner, teach *J'ai gagné* and *(Name) a gagné*.

The numbers need plenty of practice, so one or two number games could be played in each lesson during the first few weeks of French, with higher numbers being added unit by unit as they are introduced. *Zéro* could also be taught, perhaps as part of a 'countdown'.

| Activité (int03) | AT1 |

Qui parle?

Once students are familiar with numbers up to 20, they could do this simple matching activity.

| sb 7 | AT2; 7L3 |

4 Quel âge as-tu?

Students look at the question and answer printed at the top of the task and can be helped to work out how to slot different ages into the same answer structure. They can then go on to practise this with the puzzle.

1 Students follow the lines and work out each person's age, perhaps noting them down, e.g. *Laura 11*.

2 They work in pairs, in turns asking the age of their partner who replies for the person named, as in the example.

> **Solution:** *Théo 5, Hugo 10, Laura 11, Manon 7,
> Noah 3, Camille 18, Julien 8, Marine 17*

| Dialogue | AT2 |

Students could now add age to the dialogue previously used to ask each other's name (see SB 6, task 2).

First revise greetings and asking names, demonstrating with a student.

Teacher: (shaking hands) *Bonjour.*

Student: *Bonjour M./Mme/Mlle.*

Teacher: *Comment t'appelles-tu?*

Student: *Je m'appelle …*

Teacher: (shaking hands) *Au revoir* (name).

Student: *Au revoir M./Mme/Mlle.*

Get students to practise this in pairs, choosing a few to demonstrate this to the class.

Then add in the new question and answer and get pairs of students to practise the complete dialogue, perhaps recording some of them.

 7 **Stratégies** **AT2; 7S9, 7L6; AfL**

This item provides consolidation of the three types of question and answer learnt so far and is a good opportunity for peer assessment. Remind students of the spread objectives and agree the criteria for success.

Students work in pairs to see how long a conversation

they can make up. This could then be developed into a class competition to see which pair's conversation is the longest (as well as being correct).

 **Présentation (ppt01)** **AT2**

Quel âge?

In this PowerPoint activity, students have to guess people's ages from photos.

Plenaries (pages 6–7)

 Fiche de travail (ws02)

1 Students write down two sentences summarising the lesson, then share these with the class. Discuss the key points to remember and what aspects might cause difficulties.

2 Discuss strategies for remembering words and phrases and urge students to practise at home – maybe with brothers and sisters.

1B Qu'est-ce que c'est?   pages 8–9

Aims and objectives	Grammar and skills	Resources
• learn about numbers and things in the classroom • learn about the gender of nouns • learn how to make nouns plural	**Grammar** Masculine and feminine nouns with indefinite article (*un/une*) Forming plurals **Skills** Learning gender as you learn new nouns **Pronunciation** Different pronunciation of words which look the same in French and English	**Key language:** see p32 **Online resource:** *Unité 1* int04/05, ppt02, ws02/03/04 **Copymasters:** 1/2 **CD** 1 tracks 5–9

Starters (pages 8–9)

Fiche de travail (ws02)

1 Everyone stands up. Go quickly round the class asking people questions, alternating between their name, age and if they are well.

   If they answer correctly they sit down, until all are seated.

2 (Use before task 2) The lesson could start with a game to see if students remember the classroom vocabulary, e.g. *Jeu de mémoire* (Kim's game – see TB 22) or *Je touche* (TB 22). Use actual objects in the classroom, or the PowerPoint game below (ppt02).

Introduction **AT2**

Gender

Grammatical gender is still a difficult concept, to be introduced gradually, stressing its importance but not making it sound too difficult.

The words *garçon* and *fille* have occurred in the number games, but in any case they are good ones to start with.

Revise the questions and answers learnt already and move on from *Qui est-ce? C'est Jean* to *Qui est-ce? C'est un garçon. C'est un garçon? Oui, c'est un garçon.*

The best way to teach classroom objects, initially, is to handle them, introducing the words orally. A good standard teaching sequence is as follows:

Écoutez!/Répétez! C'est un(e) …

Oui ou non?/Choix – c'est un stylo ou un crayon?

Corrige-moi. C'est un crayon.

Non, c'est un stylo.

Qu'est-ce que c'est? etc.

Introduce the French for five masculine classroom objects (*un livre, un stylo, un cahier, un crayon, un cartable*) and practise them with the question *Qu'est-ce que c'est?*

Then help students to deduce that the word for 'a' used with the other words is *un* (like *un* before *garçon*).

Next point to a girl and say *C'est un garçon?* (In single-sex classes, use alternatives such as flashcards or a PowerPoint presentation.) When you get the answer *Non*, say *Non, c'est une fille. Répétez. C'est une fille.* Elicit the difference in sound from pupils.

Now teach five feminine objects (*une chaise, une règle, une table, une gomme, une boîte*) with *Qu'est-ce que c'est?*

Draw attention to the word *une* and link it with *une fille.*

Explain briefly that, in French, all objects are either *un* or *une* words, and mention the terms masculine and feminine. Tell the students to make sure that they always learn whether a word is masculine or feminine. You could introduce an ongoing presentation technique with PowerPoint: use one colour background for masculine words, one for feminine and one for plurals and get pupils to always do the same. Tell the students this is helpful as we learn in three ways – through seeing, hearing and doing, and this particular technique helps visual memory.

Or give each student two pieces of card, one in blue for masculine nouns, one in red for feminine nouns. When practising new vocabulary, students hold up the blue or red card as appropriate. This makes them think about the gender, and the colour helps cement the gender for some students. (See the Starters & Plenaries file (ws02) in the online resource for a printable version of these cards.)

Next, teach a few more classroom objects (*un ordinateur, un classeur, un sac à dos, un trombone, un taille-crayon, une calculatrice, une trousse*) and practise these as before.

As further practice, play some fast-paced vocabulary games at the end.

Stress that masculine/feminine is not to do with the essence of the thing – stereotypically manly things are not necessarily masculine or girly things feminine.

| Activité (int04) | AT1, AT2, AT3 |

Les affaires scolaires

Use this online activity to present and practise the classroom objects.

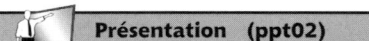

| Présentation (ppt02) | AT2 |

Jeu de mémoire: Mes affaires scolaires

This is a teacher-led Kim's Game where there are several classroom objects on the page.

| 8 | 1 tr 5 | AT1, AT4; 7W4, 7T4 |

1 Des affaires scolaires

Ask the class to look at the pictures of classroom objects, noticing that they are divided into masculine (*un*) and feminine (*une*) words (surrounded with red or blue frames as an added reminder).

Explain *affaires* if they have not already met the phrase *Rangez vos affaires!*

Students write down the numbers from 1–15, listen to the recording and write down the letter for each object as it is mentioned in the recording.

This task could be corrected by playing the recording again and stopping to check each answer in turn.

Reinforce gender here by asking students, as they listen, to say whether they heard *un* or *une* and what that, therefore, tells them about the noun, i.e. that it is masculine or feminine (*c'est masculin/féminin*).

The written form of the names for classroom objects can be introduced as soon as students are confident enough in their pronunciation. They should refer to the list in the *Sommaire* on page 11.

This is a suitable time for students to start their own vocabulary books, perhaps adopting the idea of writing or underlining masculine words in blue and feminine ones in red.

Solution: 1 C, **2** I, **3** J, **4** A, **5** E, **6** N, **7** B, **8** D, **9** F, **10** H, **11** M, **12** L, **13** K, **14** O, **15** G

transcript

Des affaires scolaires

1. – Qu'est-ce que c'est?
   – C'est un cahier.
2. – Et ça? C'est une règle?
   – Ah oui, c'est une règle.
3. – Qu'est-ce que c'est?
   – C'est une gomme.
4. – C'est un livre?
   – Oui, c'est un livre.
5. – Qu'est-ce que c'est?
   – C'est un cartable.
6. – Et voici une chaise.
   – Oui, oui, c'est une chaise.
7. – Et ça, qu'est-ce que c'est?
   – C'est un stylo.
8. – Voici un crayon.
   – C'est vrai. C'est un crayon.
9. – Et ça, qu'est-ce que c'est?
   – C'est un taille-crayon, c'est mon taille-crayon.
10. – Et voici un bic.
    – Oui, un bic. C'est important, ça!
11. – Et une calculatrice, regarde!
    – Ah bon, c'est ma calculatrice, ça!
12. – Oui? Dans la trousse? C'est ça?
    – Oui, oui. Dans la trousse.
13. – Et ça, c'est une boîte?
    – Oui, c'est une boîte.
14. – Et ça, c'est une table.
    – Oui, c'est vrai, c'est une table.
15. – Et voici un ordinateur.
    – Oui, un ordinateur. Ça, c'est très important!

| 8 | Dossier-langue | 7W4 |

Masculine and feminine (gender)

Draw students' attention to this brief *Dossier-langue*, which sums up the gender of nouns.

8   Stratégies   AT3; 7W4, 7W8, 7T4

This explains the use of gender and provides some added practice involving using a dictionary. Make sure that students are clear about the significance of *m* and *f*, and remind them of this from time to time, getting them to look up new words as they occur.

140   Au choix   1 tr 6   AT1, AT2

2 Télé-jeu: 30 secondes

This is a fun listening item for practice of classroom vocabulary.

Ask students to look at the picture, then explain it briefly:

Voilà, c'est un jeu à la télévision. Regardez les prix.

Chloé gagne quatre choses et Max gagne six choses.

Explain *gagne*, if not guessed.

Some teachers may wish to give their class the written words (on the board in random order).

As follow-up, students can play the game themselves. One student sees how many prizes s/he can win in thirty seconds, without looking at the book and with suitable applause from the class. Soon, a student can play the quizmaster, or the game can be played in groups. More prizes could be added.

Solution: Chloé 1, 2, 4, 6 **Max** 1, 3, 5, 7, 8, 9

transcript

Télé-jeu: 30 secondes

– Voilà, Chloé et Max, regardez les prix – ce sont des prix fantastiques, non?
– Oui, oui, fantastiques!
– Bon, tu as trente secondes: 3 … 2 … 1 … zéro!
– Eh bien, numéro un, c'est un lecteur CD et deux, euh, c'est un portable.
– Très bien, super! Continue!
– Alors trois, numéro trois, c'est … c'est une télévision?
– Ah, non. Mais …
– Ah non, euh, la télé, c'est numéro quatre. Et numéro six, euh, c'est un baladeur …
– Trente secondes! Très bien, Chloé. Tu as gagné un lecteur CD, un portable, une télé et un baladeur.
– Oh, merci, merci, monsieur.
– Et maintenant, Max. Ça va?
– Euh … oui, oui, ça va.
– Tu as trente secondes: 3 … 2 … 1 … zéro! Commence!
– Numéro un est un lecteur CD, euh … oui, numéro trois, c'est une calculatrice; numéro cinq, des crayons; numéro sept, un lasseur; numéro huit, une poubelle, numéro neuf, un cartable et …
– Trente secondes! Fantastique, Max! Tu as gagné six prix, six! Voilà: un lecteur CD, une calculatrice, des crayons, un classeur, une poubelle et un cartable. Félicitations et au revoir!

Introduction   AT2

Combien?

Teach *Combien?* and *C'est combien?* orally using groups of classroom objects, holding up fingers, writing figures on the board, etc., first asking and answering the questions yourself then getting students to do so.

Gradually use numbers plus nouns, saying: *Il y a combien de* (+ noun)? *Il y a* (+ number and noun).

8   AT2; 7S3, 7T6

2 Combien?

First ask a few questions based on the picture to check that students remember the words involved. Then show the class how to work in pairs asking each other *Il y a combien de* (+ noun)?

They answer using the structure suggested.

Solution: 1 *Il y a 3 crayons,* **2** *Il y a 5 livres,* **3** *Il y a 8 règles,* **4** *Il y a 2 stylos,* **5** *Il y a une trousse,* **6** *Il y a 6 gommes,* **7** *Il y a 7 taille-crayons,* **8** *Il y a 4 calculatrices.*

(Note: The written form of the numbers is not given in the Student's Book until *Unité 2*. If the spelling of numbers is required at this point, refer to the *Sommaire* on page 17 of the Student's Book.)

Fiche de travail (ws03)   AT3

Un ou une?

This online activity revises the classroom objects learnt so far, together with their gender.

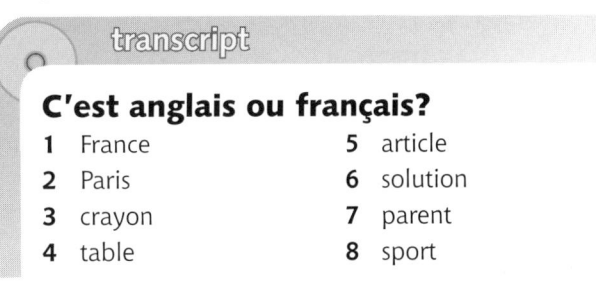

9   1 tr 7   AT2; 7W6, 7L1

Prononciation: c'est anglais ou français?

This is the first in a series of items featuring different sounds.

This short item focuses on the difference in pronunciation between English and French words, even though they might look the same.

transcript

C'est anglais ou français?

1	France	**5**	article
2	Paris	**6**	solution
3	crayon	**7**	parent
4	table	**8**	sport

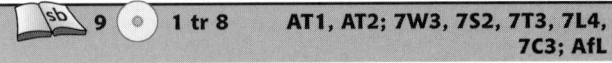

9   1 tr 8   AT1, AT2; 7W3, 7S2, 7T3, 7L4, 7C3; AfL

3 Qu'est-ce que c'est?

a Revise the classroom objects already taught using the structure *Qu'est-ce que c'est?*

C'est un [bic/cahier/cartable/crayon/livre/ordinateur/stylo/taille-crayon.]

C'est une [boîte/calculatrice/chaise/gomme/règle/table/trousse.]

Voici/Voilà un … Oui/Non.

1B Qu'est-ce que c'est?

Then teach *un tableau interactif, un baladeur, un CD, un lecteur CD, un portable, un classeur, un sac à dos, un trombone, un feutre,* **une** *calculatrice,* **une** *feuille de papier,* **une** *poubelle,* **une** *fenêtre,* **une** *porte.* Use flashcards, objects or the online presentation (*Activité (int04)* above).

The word *baladeur* is taught here as it is the generic term, but you may also wish to teach *un iPod* and *un lecteur mp3.*

When students are familiar with the new vocabulary, they can do the listening activity. For this they listen to French children playing the game *Je pense à quelque chose,* using a mixture of masculine and feminine nouns. Before they do this, explain simply how the game works, e.g.

– *Je pense à quelque chose. Qu'est-ce que c'est?*

– *C'est un livre?*

– *Non, ce n'est pas ça.*

– *C'est un feutre?*

– *Oui, c'est ça. Très bien!*

Play the game with them a few times, using first the objects in the masculine box (*un*), then in the feminine box (*une*). Play a few more rounds with students taking the teacher's role.

Students can then listen to the recording and write down the numbers of any objects mentioned.

Solution: 4, 8, 10, 1, 7, 5, 3

Qu'est-ce que c'est?

– Je pense à quelque chose. Qu'est-ce que c'est?
– C'est un classeur.
– Non, ce n'est pas ça.
– C'est un feutre?
– Non, ce n'est pas ça.
– C'est une fenêtre?
– Non, ce n'est pas ça.
– C'est un tableau interactif?
– Oui, c'est un tableau interactif. Très bien!

– Je pense à quelque chose. Qu'est-ce que c'est?
– C'est un trombone?
– Non, ce n'est pas ça.
– C'est un sac à dos?
– Non, ce n'est pas ça.
– C'est un portable?
– Oui, c'est ça. C'est un portable.

b Students can now play the game in pairs or groups, using both masculine and feminine singular nouns. This is an opportunity for peer assessment. Remind students of the spread objectives and agree the criteria for success. Show how their work can be improved by praising good examples and letting them demonstrate to other groups or the whole class.

For further practice, students could play a version of *Je pense à quelque chose* using mini whiteboards. Working in pairs, they each draw (in secret) three items they might find in a pencil case/classroom. They have to guess their partner's items by asking, e.g. *Un stylo, s'il te plaît.* If their partner has drawn this item, they get another go; if not, they swap over. The winner is the person who identifies all three with the fewest guesses.

sb 9 **Dossier-langue** 1 tr 9 AT1; 7W4

Plural

This explains plurals.

The listening activity focuses on the sound of singular and plural forms. Students should then look at the difference between French and English plurals. If necessary, compare with the *Prononciation* activity above.

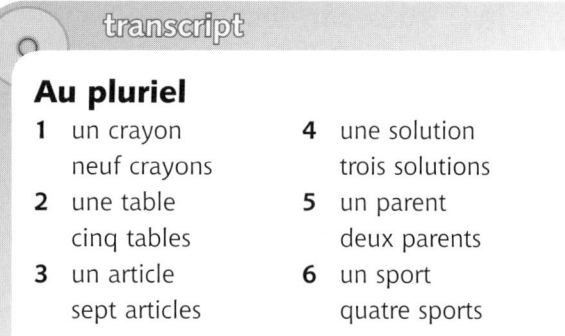

transcript

Au pluriel

1	un crayon	**4**	une solution
	neuf crayons		trois solutions
2	une table	**5**	un parent
	cinq tables		deux parents
3	un article	**6**	un sport
	sept articles		quatre sports

sb 9 AT3, AT4; 7W3

4 Au collège

a Students read through the statements about Mathilde's possessions, and copy down only those which match the picture.

Solution: 1 *Il y a quatre crayons,* **3** *Il y a une trousse,* **4** *Il y a trois livres,* **5** *Il y a un portable*

b This time, students refer to the picture and write complete sentences to describe it.

Solution: *Dans le sac de Thomas, il y a* **un** *taille-crayon. Il y a* **deux** *classeurs.*

Il y a cinq **règles**, *une* **calculatrice**, *quatre* **gommes** *et* **un** *baladeur.*

Activité (int05) AT2

Combien?

Use this online recording activity to practise talking about classroom objects in the singular and plural.

Fiche de travail (ws04) AT3, AT4

Singulier ou pluriel?

This online worksheet provides written practice of classroom items in the singular and plural.

sb 140 **Au choix** AT3

3 C'est quelle image?

Students match the conversations to the pictures.

Solution: 1 B, **2** A, **3** G, **4** C, **5** D, **6** E, **7** F, **8** H

cm 1/2 1 tr 10–12 AT1

Écoutez bien!

A listening quiz on language taught in this unit. Students write down 'Section 1' and numbers from 1–5. They look at the pictures and write the letter of the correct one as they hear it.

Solution: 1 d, **2** b, **3** e, **4** a, **5** c

In Section 2, the class number again from 1–5, then listen for the age of each speaker.

Solution: 1 e, **2** a, **3** b, **4** d, **5** c

In Section 3, students number from 1–10, then listen for classroom objects.

Solution: 1 j, **2** c, **3** b, **4** d, **5** g, **6** a, **7** i, **8** f, **9** h, **10** e

transcript

Écoutez bien!

Section 1

1 Bonjour! Je m'appelle Pierre.
2 Bonjour! Je m'appelle Françoise.
3 Bonjour! Je m'appelle Catherine.
4 Bonjour! Je m'appelle Jean-Pierre.
5 Bonjour! Je m'appelle Michèle.

Écoutez bien!

Section 2

1 – Quel âge as-tu?
  – J'ai six ans.
2 – Quel âge as-tu?
  – J'ai quatre ans.
3 – Quel âge as-tu?
  – J'ai douze ans.
4 – Quel âge as-tu?
  – J'ai cinq ans.
5 – Quel âge as-tu?
  – J'ai dix ans.

Écoutez bien!

Section 3

1 C'est une gomme.
2 C'est un livre.
3 C'est un cartable.
4 C'est une règle.
5 C'est une boîte.

6 – Qu'est-ce que c'est?
  – C'est un crayon.
7 – Qu'est-ce que c'est?
  – C'est un cahier.
8 – Qu'est-ce que c'est?
  – C'est une table.
9 – Qu'est-ce que c'est?
  – C'est un stylo.
10 – Qu'est-ce que c'est?
  – C'est une chaise.

Plenaries (pages 8–9)

Fiche de travail (ws02)

1 Use the game *Qu'est-ce qu'il y a dans la boîte?* (see TB 22). Make sure that there are sometimes several of the same object in the box.

When students have identified an object, encourage them to think about whether they should use *un/une* or a number and how they remembered which to use. If there is only one object, ask how to make this plural. Similarly, for plural objects, elicit whether one of them would be *un* or *une*.

A number of images are provided on the online worksheet for a version of this activity if required.

2 Follow up the *Prononciation* item on this spread by leading a discussion of the correlation between sound and spelling, based on place names on the map (SB 3), e.g.

• *France* – looks like English: sounds totally different
• *Paris, Calais* – final consonant not sounded
• *Lyon*/Lyons – languages often spell towns differently
• *Honfleur* – silent 'h'

This could lead into a further discussion about learning strategies and identifying patterns in language (including comparisons with patterns in English).

Some words are provided on the online worksheet for a version of this activity if required.

1C En classe   pages 10–11

Aims and objectives	Grammar and skills	Resources
• practise classroom commands and vocabulary • practise some questions and answers	**Pronunciation** The letter *i*	**Key language:** see p32 **Online resource:** *Unité 1* int06/07, ws02/05 **Copymasters:** 1/3 **CD** 1 tracks 13–16

Starters (pages 10–11)

 Fiche de travail (ws02)

1 As all the items on this double page spread are intended to consolidate the language covered in the first weeks of learning French, another look at the online map of France would be appropriate.

Students could see how quickly they can identify the places on the map and then work in groups to see how many of the words on the map and how many snippets of information about France they can remember.

2 **5-4-3-2-1** game. Display the list of words in random order, then ask students to name 5 electrical/electronic items, 4 things to write with, 3 containers, 2 pieces of furniture, 1 book.

Solution:

un baladeur, un lecteur CD, un ordinateur, un portable, un tableau interactif
un bic, un crayon, un feutre, un stylo
une boîte, un sac, une trousse
une chaise, une table
un cahier

Introduction

Classroom instructions

Gradually introduce *s'il te plaît* and *merci bien* and, if wished, *Je ne sais pas/Je voudrais un …*

Begin to use as often as possible such commands as *regardez, ouvrez, fermez, écrivez*, so that the class gets used to the lesson being conducted in French.

10 1 tr 13 AT1, AT3; 7W3, 7T1, 7L4

1 Vocabulaire de classe

a   In part **a**, students read the classroom commands and match them to the illustrated activities.

Solution: 1 C, **2** A, **3** H, **4** B, **5** G, **6** D, **7** F, **8** E

b   Students listen to the recording and write down the letter for the correct picture.

Solution: 1 H, **2** D, **3** G, **4** C, **5** E, **6** B, **7** F, **8** A

transcript

Vocabulaire de classe

1 Travaillez à deux.	5 Asseyez-vous.
2 Répétez.	6 Levez-vous.
3 Écris.	7 Comptez.
4 Écoute.	8 Regardez.

Activité (int06) AT1, AT3

Vocabulaire de classe (1)

This online activity supports the classroom vocabulary by matching the French commands to the spoken version and to the English translations. It can be used at any stage to revise or assess the main classroom commands used so far.

10 AT3, AT4; 7W3

2 Complète les phrases

This activity provides written practice of the classroom commands in context. Students could read out their answers and direct student(s) or the teacher to follow the appropriate instruction.

Solution: 1 *tableau interactif,* **2** *crayons,* **3** *porte,* **4** *fenêtre,* **5** *lecteur CD,* **6** *bic,* **7** *livre,* **8** *cahier*

 Fiche de travail (ws05) AT3

Dans la salle de classe

This online worksheet provides further practice of the classroom vocabulary and its meaning.

10 1 tr 14–16 AT1, AT2; 7W6, 7L1

Prononciation: la lettre 'i'

a   Students listen to the words and match them with the printed version.

Solution: 1 a, **2** e, **3** c, **4** d, **5** f, **6** b

b   Students pronounce the words and check their pronunciation.

This is a good task for students to work on individually so they can concentrate fully on getting the pronunciation correct. However, it could also be used for whole-class oral work.

c   The silly sentence helps fix the sound for students.

transcript

Prononciation: la lettre 'i'

a	1 dix	4	un bic
	2 il y a	5	un stylo
	3 merci	6	unité

b   six   écris   livre   dis   oui   fille
c   Minnie la souris lit dix livres à Paris.

10 AT3; 7S4, 7T5

3 Trouve la question

Students find the appropriate question to match the answers supplied.

Solution: 1 c, **2** e, **3** f, **4** a, **5** d, **6** b

11 1/3 7W3, 7W4

Sommaire

This is a summary of the main language and structures taught in this unit. It is also on copymaster for ease of reference.

On each *Sommaire* page is a useful strategy for learning vocabulary.

Activité (int07) AT3

Vocabulaire (1)

This online game provides practice of all the vocabulary of the unit.

Plenaries (pages 10–11)

 Fiche de travail (ws02)

1 Get students to construct a mind map. Provide a blank sheet with headings for the topics covered (greetings, name and age, health, numbers, classroom objects, classroom commands). Students write notes or vocabulary for each of the headings, based on their learning so far, then discuss these with the teacher.

2 Referring to the *Sommaire* for help, students work in pairs to see how long a conversation they can make up, using greetings, questions and answers about name, age and health and also about what things are and how many of them there are.

Encourage discussion about what students have learnt, what parts are easier and what proved more difficult.

Aims and objectives	Key language/Culture	Grammar and skills	National criteria
2A Venez en France pp12–13			
• understand people saying where they live • learn how to say 'in' a place	*J'habite à* (+ town) *en/au* (+ country) *dans + un appartement/une ferme/une maison* *près de…* *une île/un port/un village/une ville/à la montagne*	**Grammar** Prepositions for locations: *à/a/en/dans* **Skills** Using clues to work out meaning	**Attainment** AT1 Level 1–2, AT2 Level 1–2, AT3 Level 1–2, AT4 Level 1–2 **Framework** 7W2/4, 7S2/4, 7T7, 7L3/6 **Languages ladder/Asset languages** Grades 1–2 **Assessment for learning** ex 2
2B Où habites-tu? pp14–15			
• say where you live • ask someone where they live • use numbers up to 30	*Où habites-tu ? Tu habites où?* *en France/en Angleterre/en Écosse/en Irlande (du Nord)/au Pays de Galles* Numbers 1–30	**Skills** Elision: *je* or *j'* Inversion to form questions	**Attainment** AT1 Level 1–3, AT2 Level 1–3, AT3 Level 1–2, AT4 Level 1–3 **Framework** 7W6, 7S4, 7T1/2, **7L2/3/5, 7C4** **Languages ladder/Asset languages** Grades 1–3 **Assessment for learning** ex 2, ex 5
2C Comment ça s'écrit? pp16–17			
• learn the days of the week • spell words using the French alphabet	*Quel jour sommes-nous?/C'est quel jour?* *lundi/mardi/mercredi/jeudi/vendredi/samedi/dimanche* *à la maison* *Comment ça s'écrit?* *Comment ça se dit?* *Comment dit-on […] en français/anglais?*	**Skills** Identifying patterns in language for days of the week Learning useful phrases for the classroom **Pronunciation** The French alphabet The letter é	**Attainment** AT1 Level 1–3, AT2 Level 1–3, AT3 Level 1–3, AT4 Level 1–3 **Framework** 7W2/3/6/7, 7S4, 7L1/3/4, 7C4 **Languages ladder/Asset languages** Grades 1–3 **Assessment for learning** ex 2

Other resources: Online resource *Unité 2*. Copymasters CM2/1–2/4. CD 1 tracks 17–31, Flashcards 3–7

2A Venez en France   pages 12–13

Aims and objectives	Grammar and skills	Resources
• understand people saying where they live • learn how to say 'in' a place	**Grammar** Prepositions for locations: *à/a/en/dans* **Skills** Using clues to work out meaning	**Key language:** see p44 **Online resource:** *Unité 2* int01, ppt01, ws02 **Copymasters:** 2/1 **CD** 1 track 17 **Flashcards:** 3–7

Starters (pages 12–13)

 Fiche de travail (ws02)

1 Display words and phrases from the previous unit randomly on the screen (see below or the online worksheet for a suggested list). In pairs, students create as many different phrases as they can.

11 ans	*as-tu*	*Au revoir*	*Bonjour*
calculatrice	*Ça va*	*Comment*	*elle*
il	*j'ai*	*je*	*m'appelle*
Non	*ordinateur*	*Oui*	*pas très bien*
portable	*Quel âge*	*sac*	*s'appelle*
Salut	*t'appelles*	*très bien*	*tu*
un	*une*		

2 (For use after *habite à* is taught.) Make up a *Vrai ou faux?* item about where famous people live. Start them off, then students make up their own statements, e.g.

David Beckham habite à Los Angeles.
Michael Jackson habite à Manchester.
Le Prince Harry habite en Angleterre.
Homer Simpson habite à Springfield.
Nessie habite en Écosse.
Sherlock Holmes habite à Londres en Angleterre.

Introduction

Share the spread objectives with students at the start of each lesson. Give them every opportunity to demonstrate their knowledge and skills and to evaluate their progress.

Draw attention to these basic phrases.

Qui est-ce?	*Il y a …*
Qu'est-ce que c'est?	*Oui, c'est ça.*
C'est …	*Non, ce n'est pas ça.*
Ce n'est pas …	*Voici …*

13   Stratégies   **7S2, 7L3**

Using clues

Some simple training in strategies for listening can be built into the materials from the outset. (See also TB 18, **Developing listening skills**.)

1 Build up confidence by introducing language gradually with clues for what is to be listened for. This will help convince students that they can understand spoken French.

2 Encourage guesswork and emphasise that you don't need to understand every word. For example, this item includes some new, but easily guessable, words: *super, fantastique, moderne, important(e)*.

 **Activité (int01)**   **AT1, AT3**

J'habite en France

An audio and graphic presentation of the places mentioned on the map and the new vocabulary.

Introduction   **AT2**

J'habite …

Teach how to say where you live using the online presentation (see above) and repetition of *J'habite à* (+ place). Then students say the phrase in answer to the question *Où habites-tu?* Finally, students could question others.

Using the presentation, gradually teach *C'est une ville/un village/un port* and ask:

(Name of place), *c'est une ville? C'est un village?*

Write the names of some well-known towns or villages in Britain and France on the board and use them for oral practice, e.g.

Teacher: – (Student A), *Paris, c'est une ville?*

Student A: – *Oui, c'est une ville.*

Alternatively, students could work on this in pairs, e.g.

Student A: *Paris.*

Student B: *C'est une ville.*

This provides an opportunity for the teacher to monitor who is able to say the words and who understands the work.

In a similar way, teach *une maison* and *un appartement*. Then ask *Tu habites dans une maison ou dans un appartement?* Teach *une ferme* and practise these nouns using a flashcard game (FC 3–7, see TB 22).

 **sb 12** ● **1 tr 17** **AT1, AT2, 7L3**

1 J'habite en France

Use the photos to teach or revise *garçon*, *fille*, *homme*, *femme*, e.g.

Voici une femme.

Elle s'appelle Mme Dumas. Elle habite ici.

Et voici une fille. Elle habite dans une maison.

Next look at all the pictures in turn, speaking briefly about them, e.g.

Voici Paris. C'est une ville? Oui, c'est une ville.

Et voici Strasbourg. C'est une ville aussi.

Répétez – Strasbourg.

Mme Dumas habite à Strasbourg.

Et voici une ferme. C'est un appartement? Non, c'est une ferme, près de Trouville.

Et voici une fille. La fille habite ici, dans la maison.

Et voici un homme. Répétez. Il s'appelle M. Lebrun etc.

Now play the whole recording once while students follow in their books. Play it a second time, using the pause button to give them time to identify each speaker.

 transcript

J'habite en France

1 J'habite à Paris. C'est fantastique!

2 Moi, j'habite à Lille. J'habite dans un appartement en ville.

3 Moi, j'habite ici, en Normandie. J'habite dans une ferme, près de Trouville.

4 J'habite ici, à Strasbourg, avec ma famille. J'habite dans une maison en ville.

5 Moi, j'habite à La Rochelle. C'est un port en France.

6 Moi, j'habite dans un village, à la montagne. C'est dans les Alpes, près de Grenoble.

7 Moi, j'habite ici, à l'Île de Ré. C'est une île près de La Rochelle.

8 Moi, j'habite à Nice. C'est super!

Présentation (ppt01) **AT2**

Jeu de mémoire: Où habites-tu?

Use this PowerPoint version of Kim's Game to practise the vocabulary introduced in task 1.

 **cm 2/1** ● **1 tr 17** **AT1, AT3**

1 J'habite en France

As a support activity to the above item, students listen again to the recording, first identifying the speakers and noting down the names, then filling in the grid on the sheet. This activity is ideal for use with individual listening facilities.

Solution:

	ville/port	village	île	maison	appt.	ferme
Lucas	✓					
Camille	✓				✓	
M. Lebrun						✓
Mme. Dumas	✓			✓		
Nicolas	✓					
Mathilde		✓				
Julie			✓			
Jean-Pierre	✓					

2 Où sont les voyelles?

This could be done for further consolidation in class or for homework.

 Solution: 1 *ferme*, 2 *Paris*, 3 *maison*, *famille*, 4 *appartement*, 5 *Grenoble*, 6 *habite*, 7 *ville*, 8 *habite*, *La Rochelle*

 **sb 12** **AT3; 7W4, 7S4, 7L6; (AfL)**

2 Vrai ou faux?

Teach *Vrai ou faux?* by making statements about members of the class or classroom objects, e.g. (holding up a book) *Voici une règle – c'est vrai ou faux? – C'est faux!*

Use the example to check that everyone knows how to do the task.

The task could be done as a class activity or individually with the answers checked orally. Some students might be ready to read out some of the statements being checked or they could just be repeated by the class.

Solution: 1 *vrai*, 2 *vrai*, 3 *vrai*, 4 *faux*, 5 *faux*, 6 *faux*, 7 *vrai*, 8 *vrai*, 9 *vrai*, 10 *faux*

Students could then to try to make up further *vrai ou faux* statements about the photos. As follow-up, they could make up similar statements about their own town and set them as a class activity, e.g. *St Albans est en France. Huddersfield est en Angleterre. Liverpool est près de Paris*, etc.

As follow-up and a simple but effective opportunity for AfL, ask students: How do you say (for example) 'in a house'? Students tell their partner, who checks and corrects if necessary. Take feedback from the class. This links to both objectives for this spread and allows students to demonstrate their ability to recall and generate the language they have learnt.

sb 13 Dossier-langue **7W2, 7T7**

Work briefly through the explanation and ask students to complete rules 1, 2 and 3. Encourage them to refer back to them as they do the next few tasks.

Solution: 1 *à*, 2 *en*, 3 *dans*

Students could build up their own list of strategies for learning and remembering new language, e.g. in a personal file/exercise book. These rules could be added to their list.

Plenaries (pages 12–13)

Fiche de travail (ws02)

1 In pairs, students tell their partner three things about where they live. They then pair up with another two students – how many different phrases can they say? Take feedback from the class.

2 Sticky notes: students write one phrase (or more, depending on the class) about where they live

(*j'habite à …, j'habite dans …, j'habite en …, c'est une ville …, c'est super/fantastique*, etc.). They stick the notes on an agreed place in the classroom (e.g. a display board headed *J'habite ici*). Teacher monitors the sticky notes for accuracy and uses this as an AfL opportunity, asking students to give feedback and suggestions for improvement. These can also be used to start the next lesson.

2B Où habites-tu? pages 14–15

Aims and objectives	Grammar and skills	Resources
• say where you live • ask someone where they live • use numbers up to 30	**Skills** Elision: *je* or *j'* Inversion to form questions	**Key language:** see p44 **Online resource:** *Unité 2* int02/03/04, ppt02 ws02/03/04/05/06 **Copymasters:** 2/2 **CD** 1 tracks 18–22

Starters (pages 14–15)

Fiche de travail (ws02)

1 **Chain questioning** (Use this to revise personal information before SB page 15, task 4)

Display the questions *Comment t'appelles-tu? Quel âge as-tu?* and *Ça va?* and choose a student to ask someone one of the questions. If they answer correctly, that student asks another person one of the other two questions, and so on.

This could be done as a competition in rows or groups,

2 Use a number game (see TB 21) to revise the numbers taught so far.

 **14** | **AT4; 7T1**

1 Écris des phrases complètes

Students find the correct words from the box to complete these core sentences.

They could just note down the numbers and matching letters and the answers could be checked orally, with students supplying the full sentence. Any students ready to start writing could copy down the complete sentences. This could be used as a homework task.

Solution: 1 b, 2 f, 3 c, 4 a, 5 e, 6 d, 7 h, 8 g

 **14 Dossier-langue**

This short item introduces the concept of inversion to form questions. Go over the example to ensure students recognise the change of word order. Some students may be able to make up other questions such as *Habites-tu en France/dans une maison/à Londres?* Avoid other parts of the verb at this stage.

 **14** ⦿ **1 tr 18** | **AT1, AT2; 7S4, 7L2; AfL**

2 Et toi? Où habites-tu?

Students listen to the model dialogue, then make up their own answers and use them in conversation, based on the illustrated examples.

Students could learn the conversations for homework. This can be the basis of an early speaking assessment. It is also an ideal opportunity for peer assessment, allowing students to demonstrate their skills and to give or receive feedback.

transcript

Et toi? Où habites-tu?
– Où habites-tu?
– J'habite à Wakefield. Et toi, où habites-tu?
– Moi, j'habite dans un village, près de Leeds.

 Fiche de travail (ws03) | **AT3, (AT4)**

Où?

A word snake matching activity practising *dans, en, au, à*.

 **2/2** ⦿ **1 tr 19** | **AT1**

Trois conversations

Students should first look through the illustrations for the conversations and the multiple choice items, before working on the recorded version and ticking the correct options. This item would be useful with individual listening equipment or in a multi-media facility.

Solution: 1 Ab, Bc, Cb, Dc
2 Aa, Bc, Ca, Da
3 Aa, Bb, Ca, Db

transcript

Trois conversations

1 Première Conversation

– Bonjour. Je m'appelle Monique. Comment t'appelles-tu?
– Je m'appelle Marcel.
– Quel âge as-tu, Monique?
– J'ai quatorze ans. Et toi?
– J'ai dix ans.

2 Deuxième Conversation

– Bonjour. Je m'appelle Marc. Comment t'appelles-tu?
– Je m'appelle Françoise. Tu habites où?
– J'habite dans un village, près de La Rochelle. Et toi?
– J'habite dans un village, près de Marseille.

3 Troisième Conversation

– Bonjour. Je m'appelle Philippe. Et toi? Tu t'appelles comment?
– Je m'appelle Martine. Tu habites où?
– J'habite à Sainte-Marie. C'est un village. Et toi?
– J'habite à Bordeaux. C'est une ville en France.

| | 141 Au choix | AT2, AT4 |

1 C'est où?

Students make up sentences, using the appropriate prepositions with the names of towns or countries. This could be an oral or written activity.

Solution:

1 *Glasgow, c'est une ville en Écosse.*
2 *Manchester, c'est une ville en Angleterre.*
3 *Paris, c'est une ville en France.*
4 *La Rochelle, c'est une ville en France.*
5 *Bordeaux, c'est une ville en France.*
6 *Dublin, c'est une ville en Irlande.*
7 *Leeds, c'est une ville en Angleterre.*
8 *Belfast, c'est une ville en Irlande du Nord.*
9 *Swansea, c'est une ville au pays de Galles.*
10 *Aberdeen, c'est une ville en Écosse.*

| | 141 Au choix | AT3, AT4 |

2 Complète les phrases

This gap-fill activity practises the prepositions with places, towns and countries. Students could write out the full sentences or do the activity orally.

Solution: 1 *dans, à,* 2 *dans, dans,* 3 *en, dans,* 4 *à, près, au,* 5 *en, dans, près*

| | Fiche de travail (ws04) | AT4 |

Écris des phrases

This activity gives further written consolidation of prepositions with places, towns and countries.

| | Présentation (ppt02) | AT1, AT2, AT3; 7C4 |

Chantez! Un, deux, trois

A song revising numbers 1–20 which could be used now as preparation for the next group of numbers. For the words and music, see TB 28.

Teaching numbers up to 30

Teach the numbers orally, using the ICT activity (below), repetition and number games (see TB 21).

| | Activité (int02) | AT1, AT2, AT4 |

Les nombres 1–30

This online activity includes listening, speaking and writing tasks to practise the numbers 1–30. It can be used at any point from now on for consolidation or revision.

| | Fiche de travail (ws05) | AT3 |

Comptez

This online reading activity practises matching numbers to words and can be used in conjunction with the previous activity.

| | 15 ⊙ 1 tr 22 | AT1; 7T2, 7L3 |

3 Qui habite où?

Revise the pronunciation of the names and ask the class to read aloud the numbers of the houses. Then play the recording, pausing after each speaker to look at the example, and for students to write down the correct answers.

Check the results orally, perhaps with further questions, e.g. *Qui habite au numéro sept? Où habite Magali?* etc.

Solution: 1 *Olivier 7,* 2 *Coralie 21,* 3 *Magali 25,* 4 *Loïc 30,* 5 *Sébastien 14,* 6 *M. Garnier 28,* 7 *Jean-Marc 5,* 8 *Isabelle 15*

This activity could also be used more competitively: say one of the people's names and students race to say the correct number. If considered appropriate, the 3rd person could also be introduced, e.g.

Teacher: *Magali.*
Student: *Elle habite au numéro 25.*

transcript

Qui habite où?

1 – Où habites-tu, Olivier?
– J'habite à Paris, dans la Villa Violette.
– C'est quel numéro?
– Numéro sept.

2 – Et toi, Coralie? Où habites-tu?
  – J'habite à La Rochelle, dans la rue Gambetta.
  – Quel numéro?
  – Vingt et un.

3 – Salut, Magali. Est-ce que tu habites au numéro vingt-cinq?
  – Oui, c'est ça. Au vingt-cinq.

4 – Et toi, Loïc, tu habites dans cette rue, non?
  – Oui, j'habite au numéro trente.

5 – Salut, Sébastien.
  – Salut!
  – Où habites-tu, Sébastien?
  – À La Rochelle, au numéro quatorze, rue du Pont.

6 – Et vous habitez aussi dans la rue du Pont, M. Garnier. C'est vrai?
  – Oui, mais moi, j'habite au numéro vingt-huit.

7 – Et Jean-Marc, aussi. Il habite au numéro cinq.
  – Oui, c'est ça. Moi, j'habite au cinq.

8 – Et toi, Isabelle, où habites-tu?
  – Moi, j'habite à Rennes, dans la rue de Paris.
  – Quel numéro?
  – Quinze, j'habite au numéro quinze.

 **15** AT3, AT4; 7T1

4 C'est moi!

a This task is suitable for students ready for independent reading. In part **a**, students match up the two halves of sentences. In part **b**, they write out the sentences in full.

Solution:

a **1** b, **2** a, **3** e, **4** f, **5** d, **6** c

b **1** *Je m'appelle Sonia Charbonnier.*
  2 *J'ai douze ans.*
  3 *J'habite dans une maison.*
  4 *Ma maison est dans un petit village.*
  5 *Le village est près de La Rochelle.*
  6 *La Rochelle est une ville en France.*

 Activité (int03) AT1, AT2

Où habites-tu?

In this online role-play activity, students listen to two people greeting each other and asking their name, age and where they live.

 **15** AT2; 7S4; 7L5; AfL

5 Inventez des conversations

This pairwork activity offers a good AfL opportunity. First agree the criteria for success with students; they can then check their conversation with partners and know exactly what they must do to be successful.

As follow-up, students could be encouraged to prepare and perform presentations of themselves (or a famous person or friend, in the first person), saying name, age, where they live and anything else they have learnt. They could do this in pairs, asking and answering as many questions as possible, using props and role play. The activity is fun and gives them a real sense of how much they have already learnt.

 15 Stratégies 7W6

Students might have worked out the answer to this question, while using *j'habite*.

Explain that *h* is often not sounded in French. With *habite*, this has the effect of making it seem as if the word begins with a vowel. Stress to students that this also has the effect of making *j'habite* sound like one word.

Solution: 1 *Je,* **2** *J',* **3** *J',* **4** *Je*

 Fiche de travail (ws06) AT2, AT4

Carte d'identité

Students complete an identity card for themselves and a friend.

 Activité (int04) AT1, AT3

Rue Danton: Une nouvelle famille dans la rue

This is a suitable point at which to use the first episode (covering *Unités 1* and *2*) of the video soap opera. The language is closely linked to the unit, but the video also provides some extension and valuable cultural background. The online activities help focus students on the key language.

Plenaries (pages 14–15)

Fiche de travail (ws02)

1 Brainstorming session in which students work out how much they could now tell a French person about themselves, e.g. name, age, state of health, where they live, how many CD players, MP3 players etc. they have. This also could take the form of a mind map if preferred.

2 Students reflect on the objectives of the unit and how much they have achieved. They could find two things they've found easy, one thing they've found hard; say what is the most important fact they have learnt this unit and what is the oddest fact. They should comment on any aspects of French culture they have been exposed to (especially if they have watched the Rue Danton video) and compare these with their own.

2C Comment ça s'écrit? pages 16–17

Aims and objectives	Grammar and skills	Resources
• learn the days of the week • spell words using the French alphabet	**Skills** Identifying patterns in language for days of the week Learning useful phrases for the classroom **Pronunciation** The French alphabet The letter é	**Key language:** see p44 **Online resource:** *Unité 2* int05/06/07/08, ppt03/04, ws02/07 **Copymasters:** 2/3, 2/4 **CD** 1 tracks 23–31

Starters (pages 16–17)

Fiche de travail (ws02)

1 **Trouve les paires** Display a selection of sentences and phrases in French. Students match them to the English translations. (See online worksheet.)

1	*Ça va?*	a	In a flat.
2	*Il habite à la montagne.*	b	Not very well.
3	*Asseyez-vous.*	c	She's called Françoise.
4	*Dans un appartement.*	d	How are you?
5	*Pas très bien.*	e	Sit down.
6	*Où habites-tu?*	f	It's a town in France.
7	*C'est une ville en France.*	g	Where do you live?
8	*Elle s'appelle Françoise.*	h	He lives in the mountains.

■ **Solution:** **1** d, **2** h, **3** e, **4** a, **5** b, **6** g, **7** f, **8** c

2 **Chasse à l'intrus** Display groups of words from *Unités 1* and *2*. Students identify the odd word out of each group and justify their choice. (See online worksheet.)

A	B	C	D	E	F
crayon	**Ça va.**	une boîte	seize	je	maison
stylo	Copie.	**un cartable**	sept	**jeudi**	ferme
classeur	Écoute.	une poubelle	six	il	**montagne**
feutre	Écris.	une trousse	**samedi**	elle	appartement

Activité (int05)   AT1, AT3

Un calendrier

Use this activity to present and practise the days of the week.

📖 16 ⏺ 1 tr 23   AT1, AT2, AT3; 7W2, 7L3

1 La semaine de Lou

Make sure students know the days of the week before presenting this item. See if they have spotted the link between *di* and day.

Once students have read and understood the text, they find the five true sentences in activity **b** below. Follow this up with some oral work – teacher-led at first, then handed over to students, e.g.

C'est lundi. Où est Lou?

Il est en Angleterre – c'est quel jour?

As an extension activity, students could be encouraged to do their own cartoon strip. Discuss places Lou Leroux might report from and suggest sources for illustrating their work (presentation pictures or clip art of town, village, house, flat, farm, etc.). These could provide an interesting wall display and be a stimulus for further oral work.

■ **Solution:** Sentences 1, 3, 5, 6 and 8 are true.

transcript

La semaine de Lou

Voici Lou Leroux. Il est reporter à Télé-France.

Il voyage beaucoup.

Lundi, il est dans un village en Écosse.

Mardi, il est à Londres, en Angleterre.

Mercredi, il est au pays de Galles.

Jeudi, Lou est à Belfast, en Irlande du Nord.

Vendredi, il est dans une ferme à la montagne, en France.

Samedi, Lou est à Paris,

Lou est à la maison. Ouf!! Lou adore le dimanche!

Activité (int06)   AT1, AT2

L'alphabet

This is an animated presentation of the alphabet.

Introduction   AT1, AT2

L'alphabet

Before doing the remaining SB activities, the French alphabet should be taught. Use the online presentation (above) or the song (below) or follow this suggested sequence:

- The class repeats a few letters at a time – ask them to spot the 'catches' as they arise (*e/i*, *g/j*, etc.).

- Gradually work up to the whole alphabet using such strategies as stopping and seeing if the class or one group can go on alone, dividing the class into two or more groups and 'conducting' them, moving swiftly from one group to another, one group carrying on as the other leaves off.

- Teach students to spell their names and introduce *Comment ça s'écrit?*

- Help the class to get used to asking the teacher to spell any word they are not sure of.
- Practise spelling a few words regularly and perhaps play a spelling game, e.g.

Ton nom s'écrit comme ça?

The teacher, and later one of the class, spells out someone's name in French. Anyone who thinks their name is being spelt should stand up. If the wrong person stands up or the person named fails to stand up, they lose a point. If the person named stands up, they have the next turn at spelling a name.

When students have learnt the alphabet, suggest that every time they learn a new French word, they should try to spell it in French.

The introduction of the French alphabet could be linked with ICT, providing a good opportunity to explore the keyboard, which would be useful for those students with poor keyboard skills.

The most basic activity is *Trouve la touche*. Dictate spellings or phrases by saying, for example, *Tapez 'd', tapez 'e', tapez 'u', tapez 'x' – C'est quel mot?*

 Présentation (ppt03)   **AT1, AT2, AT3; 7C4**

Chantez! L'alphabet

The alphabet song provides an alternative and popular way of presenting and practising the alphabet. For words and music, see TB 26.

AT1

C'est quel jour?

Now students are familiar with the alphabet, provide further practice of days of the week with a simple listening task. Spell out days of the week (in random order) and students either spot which one is being spelt from a calendar-type list or write it down.

 **2/3**

Les jours de la semaine

This provides extra practice of the days of the week, numbers and spelling.

Solution:

1 Mots mêlés

T	O	L	U	N	D	I	T
P	Q	N	I	C	I	I	G
E	I	D	R	A	M	D	N
S	E	Z	N	O	A	U	I
I	D	E	R	D	N	E	V
X	T	I	U	H	C	J	B
I	D	E	U	X	H	Q	F
D	Y	S	A	M	E	D	I

(The missing day is *mercredi*.)

 **16**   **AT2; 7W6, 7S4; AfL**

2 La semaine de Camille

1 *Lundi, elle est à la ferme.*
2 *Vendredi, elle est à la plage* (or *Nice*).
3 *Samedi, elle est au match de foot.*
4 *Mardi, elle est à La Rochelle.*
5 *Mercredi, elle est à Paris.*
6 *Jeudi, elle est à la montagne.*
7 *Dimanche, elle est à la maison.*

2 Comment ça s'écrit?

This pairwork activity consolidates the work on spelling. Students should act out the conversation in pairs then adapt it by changing the names to whatever they want.

This activity provides another opportunity for peer assessment. Remind them of the objectives of the spread and agree the criteria for success before they proceed to demonstrate their skill.

 **16**   **Stratégies**   **7W3, 7W7, 7L4**

This provides some useful phrases for finding out new words, helping students to respond to face-to-face instructions, questions and explanations. Practise the questions and some answers with a quick quiz around the class.

Student A: *Comment dit-on 'jeudi' en anglais?*
Student B: *Comment dit-on 'book' en français?*
Student C: *Comment ça s'écrit?*

16   **1 tr 26**   **AT1; 7L3**

3 Comment ça se dit?

Look at the pictures with students and talk through them first before playing the recording.

Students then match the recording to the correct picture.

Solution: **1** D, **2** C, **3** A, **4** B

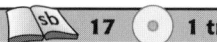 **transcript**

Comment ça se dit?

1 J'ai 30 chansons sur mon lecteur MP3.
2 Je réponds à l'invitation de Kévin, tu vois? RSVP.
3 Ah, regarde les lettres: IRL. C'est une voiture irlandaise.
4 Samedi, je regarde un DVD avec Chloé.

17   **1 tr 27**   **AT1, AT2; 7W6, 7L1**

Prononciation

L'alphabet

Some useful tips to help students remember the more difficult letters of the French alphabet. Encourage students to think up their own ideas as this helps cement the pronunciation in their minds.

The key letters and words are recorded as a model for students, with sound effects which can reinforce the learning for some students.

transcript

Prononciation: L'alphabet

i – j ... comme l'île de Fiji.

g comme génie

h comme hache

C'est un VW, comme Volkswagen.

17 1 tr 28–29 **AT1, AT2**

Pronounciation

la lettre é (e with an acute accent)

This listen-and-match activity practises the pronunciation é (e, accent aigu).

For extra practice, get more able students to spell words containing é.

Other words that have appeared so far include *numéro, écris/écrit, télé, vérifie, zéro, idée, stratégie* and *unité* as well as some people's names.

Solution: a 1 c, **2** e, **3** a, **4** f, **5** b, **6** d

transcript

Prononciation: La lettre é

a	1	*détail*	b	*Écosse*
	2	*école*		*écris*
	3	*écoute*		*télévision*
	4	*éléphant*		*réponds*
	5	*cinéma*		*téléphone*
	6	*énorme*		

141 Au choix 1 tr 30 **AT1, AT4**

3 Qu'est-ce que c'est?

This activity gives further practice of singular and plural nouns with *c'est* and *voici*. (*Voici* has been used at this stage as *ce sont* is not explicitly taught in this unit.) In part **a**, students listen and match the captions with the pictures.

Solution: a 1 C, **2** A, **3** D, **4** E, **5** B, **6** G, **7** F, **8** H

In part **b**, students write sentences about the eight pictures, using the substitution table to help them.

transcript

Qu'est-ce que c'est?

1	C'est une boîte.	5	C'est un baladeur.
2	Voici des baladeurs.	6	C'est une calculatrice.
3	Voici des boîtes.	7	C'est un enfant.
4	Voici des enfants.	8	Voici des calculatrices.

141 Au choix 1 tr 31

4 Jean-Pierre a des problèmes

Students first listen straight through to get the gist of the story. They then look at the things which the teacher asks for and listen to the recording, writing down the order in which the objects are asked for.

Finally see if the class can explain why Jean-Pierre has apparently come without a lot of his equipment.

Solution: C, D, F, E, A, B

transcript

Jean-Pierre a des problèmes

– Jean-Pierre, donne-moi ton cahier, s'il te plaît.

– Oui, monsieur ... euh ... mon cahier ... mais monsieur, mon cahier est dans mon cartable.

– Bien. Voici ton cartable. Donne-moi ton cahier de mathématiques.

– Mais monsieur, mon cahier n'est pas ici.

– Ah ... ton cahier n'est pas là. Montre-moi ta calculatrice alors.

– Ma calculatrice ... mais monsieur, ma calculatrice n'est pas dans le cartable.

– Jean-Pierre, c'est la leçon de mathématiques et ton cahier n'est pas dans ton cartable, et ta calculatrice n'est pas dans ton cartable! Alors, regarde bien dans le cartable. Il y a des crayons?

– Oui, monsieur, il y en a deux. Mais monsieur ...

– Et il y a une gomme?

– Oui, monsieur, il y a une gomme, mais monsieur ...

– Tais-toi, Jean-Pierre! Il y a une règle?

– Oui, monsieur, il y en a une, mais monsieur ...

– Et un livre? Il y a un livre de mathématiques?

– Oui, monsieur ...

– Bon, c'est bien, alors!

– Mais non, monsieur, ce n'est pas bien!

– Jean-Pierre, qu'est-ce qu'il y a, alors?

– Ça, c'est le cartable de Sébastien. Voilà mon cartable et voici mon cahier et ma calculatrice!

Activité (int07) **AT1, AT3**

Vocabulaire de classe (2)

This online matching activity provides examples of classroom vocabulary, building on those from the previous unit.

Fiche de travail (ws07)/Présentation (ppt04) AT3

Le baladeur d'Anne-Sophie

This online worksheet provides extended reading practice of the language of the first two units. It should be printed out and folded to make a simple reader. There are short comprehension activities on the final page.

Use the PowerPoint presentation for whole-class presentation of the text.

Each unit from now on has a similar reader, providing a mixture of fact and fiction.

 sb 17 cm 2/4

Sommaire

A summary of the main language and structures of the unit, also on copymaster for ease of reference.

There is a vocabulary-learning tip included on the page.

 **Activité (int08)**   **AT3**

Vocabulaire (2)

This online game provides practice of all the vocabulary of the unit.

Plenaries (pages 16–17)

 Fiche de travail (ws02)   **AT3**

1 Students agree on (for instance) 10 words that they are going to find more difficult to remember from this unit. They then suggest and discuss things they are going to do to remember them.

2 Students produce a spider diagram of everything learnt in the unit. This could be in groups or as a whole-class activity with students contributing to the mind map on the board.

Aims and objectives	Key language/Culture	Grammar and skills	National criteria
3A Ma famille pp18–19			
• talk about your family • practise saying 'the' and 'a' • use parts of the verb avoir (to have)	J'ai … un père/une mère/une sœur/deux sœurs/un frère/trois frères/un demi-frère/une demi-sœur/un cousin/une cousine/un beau-père/une belle-mère/un grand-père/une grand-mère/des parents/des grands-parents Je suis … fils unique/fille unique/enfant unique/le frère/la sœur de Tu as/As-tu des frères et sœurs? Qui est-ce? C'est … Voici/Voilà mon/ma/mes … Il/Elle s'appelle comment? Il/Elle s'appelle … Il/Elle a quel âge? Il/Elle a … ans Il/Elle habite où? Il/Elle habite à …	**Grammar** Masculine and feminine definite and indefinite articles (revision) Avoir (1st, 2nd and 3rd person singular) **Pronunciation** Identifying rhyming words Final consonants	**Attainment** AT1 Level 1–3, AT2 Level 1–3, AT3 Level 1–3, AT4 Level 1–3 **Framework** 7W2/4/5/6. 7S2/4/5, 7T1/5/6, 7L1/2/3/6 **Languages ladder/Asset languages** Grades 1–3 **Assessment for learning** ex 2, ex 3, Pronunciation. ex 5, Au choix ex 6
3B C'est à qui? pp20–21			
• use the words for 'my' and 'your' • say who things belong to	mon, ma, mes ton, ta, tes C'est le/la (+ noun) de (+ name)	**Grammar** Possessives (mon/ma/mes, ton/ta/tes) de to indicate possession	**Attainment** AT1 Level 1–3, AT2 Level 1–3, AT3 Level 1–3, AT4 Level 1–3 **Framework** 7W2/4, 7S4, 7L2 **Languages ladder/Asset languages** Grades 1–3 **Assessment for learning** ex 2
3C Ma maison pp22–23			
• use parts of the verb être (to be) • talk about your home	Qu'est-ce qu'il y a? il y a … le salon/la salle à manger/la cuisine/les toilettes/la chambre/la salle de bains/le jardin/le garage/la pièce/le lit/la console/la radio/le téléphone/le chat	**Grammar** Être (1st, 2nd and 3rd person singular) **Pronunciation** et, st Discriminating between similar sounds in French	**Attainment** AT1 Level 1–3, AT2 Level 1–3, AT3 Level 1–3, AT4 Level 1–3 **Framework** 7W2/5/6, 7S1/2, 7T1/5. 7L1/2 **Languages ladder/Asset languages** Grades 1–3 **Assessment for learning** ex 4, ex 5
3D C'est où? pp24–25			
• use prepositions to say where things are • learn more about masculine and feminine • practise the sounds ou and u	Où est …? sur sous dans	**Grammar** Masculine and feminine – definite, indefinite and possessive articles (revision) Use prepositions **Pronunciation** sur and sous	**Attainment** AT1 Level 1–3, AT2 Level 1–3, AT3 Level 1–3, AT4 Level 1–3 **Framework** 7W2/4/5/6, 7S3. 7T1, 7L1/2 **Languages ladder/Asset languages** Grades 1–3
3E Les nombres pp26–27			
• learn and practise the numbers up to 70 • practise language you have learnt in this Unit	numbers up to 70 Classroom language and rubrics: Pour vos devoirs … Copiez vos devoirs. Faites l'exercice à la page … C'est pour lundi. Apprenez le vocabulaire à la page.. C'est pour un contrôle. vendredi. Lisez «X» à la page …	**Skills** Identifying patterns when counting Building vocabulary **Cross-curricular** Numeracy	**Attainment** AT1 Level 1–2, AT2 Level 1–3, AT3 Level 1–2, AT4 Level 1–3 **Framework** 7W2/7. 7T6/7. 7L1 **Languages ladder/Asset languages** Grades 1–3 **Assessment for learning** ex 4

Other resources: Online resource Unité 3. Copymasters 3/1–3/8. CD 1 tracks 32–47, Flashcards 13–17, GIA pp5–7

3A Ma famille pages 18–19

Aims and objectives	Grammar and skills	Resources
• talk about your family • practise saying 'the' and 'a' • use parts of the verb *avoir* (to have)	**Grammar** Masculine and feminine definite and indefinite articles (revision) *Avoir* (1ˢᵗ, 2ⁿᵈ and 3ʳᵈ person singular) **Pronunciation** Identifying rhyming words Final consonants The letter è	**Key language:** see p54 **Online resource:** *Unité 3* int01/02, ppt01, ws02/03/04 **Copymasters:** 3/1 **CD** 1 tracks 32–34 **GiA:** p5

Starters (pages 18–19)

Fiche de travail (ws02)

1 Revise and practise days of the week and numbers up to 30. Each lesson, ask which day it is (*Quel jour sommes-nous? Aujourd'hui, c'est …*) and what the date is. Show a month page from a calendar (see online worksheet) and point to a date, asking, for example, *Le 15, c'est quel jour?* Follow this with questions such as *Deux jours après/avant le 15, c'est quel jour?*, reinforcing the use of *avant* and *après* by pointing at the appropriate date.

2 (use after task 3) Display a family tree on the board (see online worksheet) – two grandparents, two parents, three children. Use stick figure symbols to represent males and females and label the middle child *moi*. Write these family nouns on the board in random order: *le père, la mère, la sœur, le frère, le grand-père, la grand-mère*. Ask students to match them to the different members of the tree in relation to *moi*.

Introducing reading

A number of activities and ideas are suggested for the introduction of reading in the course of the book (see TB 19) and some of these could be used with this unit.

Présentation (ppt01)   **AT3**

La famille

Use the PowerPoint presentation to introduce the family members.

 18 1 tr 32   **AT1, AT2; 7W2, 7L2**

1 Ma famille

Speak about the Laurent family using the photos to introduce the recording.

Students can go on to listen to the recorded text several times, with or without the printed version.

For extra practice, the teacher could say a number from 1 to 5 and the name of a student who could then the corresponding sentence aloud.

Ma famille

1 – Je m'appelle Thomas Laurent et j'ai douze ans. Dans ma famille, il y a cinq personnes: mes parents et trois enfants.

2 – Voici mon frère. Il s'appelle Daniel et il a dix ans.

3 – Voici ma sœur. Elle a quatorze ans.
– Je m'appelle Louise et je suis la sœur de Thomas et Daniel.

4 – Voici ma mère, Madame Claire Laurent.

5 – Voici mon père, Monsieur Jean-Pierre Laurent.

 18   **AT3, AT4; 7T1; AfL**

2 Qui est-ce?

Students read through the statements and, referring back to the text if necessary, decide who is speaking or described each time.

The activity could be corrected orally. This provides an opportunity for peer assessment if students read out the answers. They should review the objectives and agree the criteria first.

> **Solution:** **1** *C'est Thomas,* **2** *C'est Louise,* **3** *C'est Daniel,* **4** *C'est M. Laurent,* **5** *C'est Louise,* **6** *C'est Mme Laurent,* **7** *C'est M. Laurent,* **8** *C'est Louise*

 18   **AT3, AT4; 7T5, 7T6; AfL**

3 La famille Laurent

Students complete the description, orally or in writing, using the words in the box.

They should read out the full sentence when correcting this task, which provides another opportunity for peer assessment. Review objectives and agree criteria first.

> **Solution:** **1** *père,* **2** *mère,* **3** *famille,* **4** *fille,* **5** *fils,* **6** *frères,* **7** *sœur*

Activité (int01) AT1, AT3

La famille de Kévin

Practise family members, relationship and age with this online drag-and-drop listening activity.

 Fiche de travail (ws03) AT3, AT4

La famille Roland

This online worksheet provides consolidation of family vocabulary. Students complete a gapped version of the same family tree as in the previous activity.

 **18** AT2, AT3; 7W4, 7W6, 7L1; AfL

Prononciation

This activity could be done in pairs first, with students checking on each other's answers and practising pronunciation. Agree the criteria and use this for peer assessment. It could then be checked as a class activity.

> **Solution: 1** *frères, père, mère,* **2** *frères,* **3** no, **4** no – s usually sounded in English, **5** a, e

 19 Dossier-langue

Masculine and feminine

This short explanation should help to familiarise students with *le* and *la*. It is covered again later in the fuller item on gender, (SB 25).

 **19** AT3; 7S4, 7S5, 7T1, 7L6

4 Une grande famille

As preparation, tell the class you are going to ask them whether they have any brothers and sisters and ask *Tu as (As-tu) des frères et sœurs?* with just *Oui* or *Non* for the answers to begin with.

The short cartoon then introduces the printed version of the question *Tu as des frères et sœurs?* and supplies examples of how to answer it.

Talk the class through the cartoon to check it has been understood, e.g.

Voici une fille. Elle dit, 'Tu as des frères et sœurs?'
Et voici un garçon. Il répond …
Regarde les photos. Le garçon dit, 'J'ai quatre sœurs' etc.

Write on the board:

Oui, j'ai … sœur(s).

Oui, j'ai … frère(s).

Then ask some students to answer more fully the question *Tu as des frères et sœurs?*, choosing first those you know to have siblings. Eventually teach orally *Non, je suis fille/fils/enfant unique.* Add this to the list on the board, and go on to the next item.

 **19** ⊙ **1 tr 33** AT1, AT3; 7S2, 7L2, 7L3; AfL

5 Trois familles

First give the class a few minutes to look at the photos and text.

Add to the list on the board *demi-frère, demi-sœur, grand-père, grand-mère, grands-parents, cousin(e).*

Ask the class to repeat these words and work out the meaning.

Go through each of the statements with the class, pointing at the relevant words on the board as you say them, e.g.

Voici Talia. Elle est fille unique. Voici Simon. Il est fils unique. Il habite avec sa grand-mère et son grand-père/avec ses grands-parents.

Voici Alice. Elle a un demi-frère et une demi-sœur.

Some students may want to know more about step-parents and siblings. They may be able to spot that *demi* is invariable whereas *beau* and *belle* agree. They could even look up the plurals in the glossary and find the 'mother/father-in-law' meaning, too.

Now use the recording, and incorporate a range of listening and reading strategies with varying amounts of support.

The reading task in part **b** is based on the photos and text above, but with the verbs in the third person. It could be done orally as a class activity or by students working in pairs, providing an opportunity for peer assessment. More able students, working alone, could write corrected versions of the false sentences.

> **Solution:** (suggested corrections): **1** *faux (Talia est fille unique./Talia a deux cousins.),* **2** *faux (Simon a un père et des grands-parents/un grand-père et une grand-mère.),* **3** *vrai,* **4** *vrai,* **5** *faux (Simon est fils/enfant unique.),* **6** *faux (Alice a un demi-frère et une demi-sœur.),* **7** *vrai,* **8** *vrai,* **9** *vrai,* **10** *vrai*

 **transcript**

Trois familles

1 – Talia, tu as des frères et sœurs?

– Non, je suis fille unique.

– Tu as des cousins?

– Oui, j'ai une cousine, Delphine et un cousin, Nicolas.

2 – Et toi, Simon, as-tu des frères et sœurs?

– Non, je suis fils unique.

– Et tu habites avec ta grand-mère et ton grand-père, c'est ça?

– Oui, j'habite avec mon père et mes grands-parents.

3 – Et toi, Alice. Tu es fille unique aussi?

– Non, non. Dans ma famille, il y a ma mère, mon beau-père et aussi mon demi-frère, David, et ma demi-sœur, Erika. Ils sont fantastiques!

 Activité (int02) AT1, AT2

Des frères et sœurs

This online matching activity provides consolidation of family vocabulary. The second part can be used as a noughts-and-crosses team game – to win a square students must say the phrase that matches it. This could also provide a starter for future lessons.

19 Dossier-langue   **7W4, 7W5**

This item summarises the singular paradigm of *avoir* and the use of *avoir* in talking about age.

 **Fiche de travail (ws04)**   **AT2**

Des cartes d'identité

An online speaking activity based on the language presented in exercises 4 and 5.

This leads in to SB 143 *Au choix*, task 6 (*Ma famille*) where students use the same formulae about themselves.

For further speaking practice, see CM 3/1 below.

Yellow card

There should be no use of English in oral pairwork tasks like this one. A 'yellow card' system can be introduced with appropriate sanctions for offenders.

 **143 Au choix**   **AT4; AfL**

6 Ma famille

The brief item can be exploited with varying degrees of support, depending on ability, as an AfL task. Use the spread objectives as a focus for discussion and remember that it is important to model how to do tasks of this kind.

At the simplest level, students could design a poster for classroom display, including sketches or photos with labels. However, some students will be able to write a fuller description of their family, and this can form part of their *Dossier personnel*. This text could then be used as a basis for pair work.

As a variation, students could swap over and pretend to be someone else answering questions for them. Discuss how students' work has met the assessment criteria, and provide encouragement for improving skills where necessary.

Some posters could be put up in the classroom and used later for oral practice of *son/sa/ses*, e.g. *Son frère, comment s'appelle-t-il? Quel âge a-t-il?* etc.

The posters are also good for a guessing game. Cover the name at the top of the poster and say, for example: *Son frère s'appelle Thomas, sa sœur a 6 ans. Qui est-ce?*

                  AT2

Une famille imaginaire

For this follow-up speaking activity, students each invent a family for themselves and note down the details. They then work in pairs or small groups, finding out about these 'new families', by using the questions and answers learnt on this spread.

 **19**   **1 tr 34**   **AT2; 7W6, 7L1**

Prononciation

La lettre 'è'

This brief item practises pronunciation of the è sound and mentions use of the grave accent on other vowels.

 transcript

La lettre 'è'

père, très, après, chère

 142 Au choix   **AT2**

1 Combien?

This activity gives further practice of question and answer work about families and could be done orally in class or used as a written extension activity. This is suitable as a written homework activity.

Students could go on to design various different families for each other, using pencil and paper and stick men (or clip art on the computer or whiteboard). They then change over, answering questions about each other's families.

> **Solution:**
> **1** *J'ai deux frères et une sœur.*
> **2** *J'ai une sœur.*
> **3** *Je suis enfant unique.*
> **4** *J'ai quatre frères.*
> **5** *J'ai un frère et une sœur.*
> **6** *J'ai trois sœurs.*
> **7** *J'ai un frère.*
> **8** *J'ai un frère et deux sœurs.*

 3/1   **AT2, AT4**

La famille Techno

This is an information-gap activity, based on a family tree. Students work in pairs, asking questions in turn to complete the ages of the people on their allocated family tree.

Hot seat

For further speaking practice, use the subject of one's family as a 'Hot seat' topic – one student answers questions asked by various members of the class for about a minute, e.g. *Ton frère/Ta sœur, comment s'appelle-t-il/elle?/Quel âge a-t-il/elle?* etc.

Plenaries (pages 18–19)

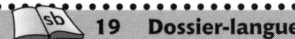 **Fiche de travail (ws02)**

1 In pairs, students tell their partner three things about their family. They then pair up with another two students – how many different phrases can they say? Take feedback from the class.

2 In pairs or groups, students discuss strategies for remembering family vocabulary – *frère*, *mère*, *père* all rhyme; how to remember *sœur? enfant* is like which English word? (infant)

or How many cognates or near cognates can students remember? (e.g. *unique*)

3B C'est à qui? pages 20–21

Aims and objectives	Grammar and skills	Resources
• use the words for 'my' and 'your' • say who things belong to	**Grammar** Possessives (*mon/ma/mes, ton/ta/tes*) *de* to indicate possession	**Key language:** see p54 **Online resource:** *Unité 3* int03, ppt02, ws02/05/06 **CD** 1 track 35 **GiA:** pp6–7

Starters (pages 20–21)

 Fiche de travail (ws02)

1 Display a number of words randomly on the board/ screen (see below and online worksheet for suggestions). Students try pronouncing them silently to themselves putting the correct word for 'the' in front of each. After one minute, point to a word and then point to or name a student; the student says the word with *le/la/l'* in front.

appartement, baladeur, boîte, chaise, crayon, fenêtre, gomme, livre, maison, ordinateur, taille-crayon, porte, poubelle, règle, stylo, trousse, village, ville

The rest of the class agree (*Oui, c'est ça/correct*) by calling out the correct article.

In this activity, students …

• are building up internal sound checking skills
• are encouraged always to sound out silently before trying words out loud
• are reminded that there is more than one form of the definite article.

2 (use before task 3) Revise days of the week and classroom objects, using one of the following:

• Give the days of the week with missing letters and ask students to fill in the gaps.
• Display jumbled spellings of the days of the week and ask students to write them correctly.
• Write the days of the week on the board in one location and a list of classroom items in another, then play a chain game in groups or as a class, e.g. *Lundi, j'ai un cartable. Mardi, j'ai un cartable et un baladeur. Mercredi, j'ai un cartable, un baladeur et …*

baladeur, boîte, crayon, cahier, calculatrice, cartable, classeur, feutre, gomme, livre, portable, règle, stylo, taille-crayon, trousse

Introduction	AT2

My and your

Teach *mon* and *ma, ton* and *ta* orally, by picking up classroom objects and saying *Voici mon crayon. Où est ton crayon?/C'est ta gomme, ça? Oui, c'est ma gomme,* etc.

Go round the class 'stealing' possessions from students. When you have assembled a pile of these, ask students *C'est ton crayon/ta gomme?* etc. They can only claim their possessions back by correctly saying *C'est mon crayon* etc.

Gradually extend this type of activity to include some plurals, *tes cahiers, mes livres,* etc.

When most students are getting the idea, move on to the explanation on SB 20.

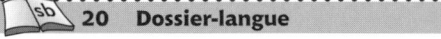 **20 Dossier-langue** 7W2, 7W4

How to say 'my' and 'your'

Get the class to read through the explanation and see if they have worked out the rule and understood it, first by getting one or two of them to explain it to the class, then asking the whole class to work in pairs and explain the rule to each other.

For practice, divide the class in half, one team being 'my' and one 'your'. When you say a French word, perhaps also holding up an object, the members of each team take it in turns to say, e.g. *mon stylo/ta règle/mes affaires* etc. The teams take it in turns to answer first and the winner is the first to get, say, 20 points for correct answers.

If students produced posters for SB 143 *Au choix* task 6 (see TB 57), these could be used for pairwork, e.g. *C'est ta sœur? Non, c'est ma mère,* etc.

 1 pp6–7

Further practice of the possessive adjectives *mon, ma, mes* and *ton, ta, tes.*

 **Activité (int03)** AT3

À moi, à toi

This online activity reinforces the *Dossier-langue* and prepares students for task 1.

20 AT2, AT3, AT4; 7W4

1 La famille Corpuscule

Talk about this unusual family, using the illustrations and getting students to repeat the names of the family, preferably in short sentences, e.g.

Voici la famille Corpuscule. C'est une famille de Vampires.

Voici le père. Il s'appelle Tombô. Voici la mère. Elle s'appelle Draculine, etc.

Then move on to the task which involves supplying the correct possessive adjective either orally or in writing.

Voici Désastre. Il présente sa famille. Complète la description pour Désastre.

Solution: 1 *Ma, mon,* **2** *mes,* **3** *Mon, mon,* **4** *Ma, ma,* **5** *mes, ma*

AT2

Les Corpuscule

As a follow-up speaking activity, put the names of the Corpuscule family on pieces of paper. Students pick one and have to say two things (or as much as they can) as if they are that person, e.g. *Je m'appelle Draculine. Mon fils s'appelle Désastre et ma fille s'appelle Enferina.*

Alternatively, students sit in the Hot seat and others ask them questions, e.g. *Ton fils, comment s'appelle-t-il?*

 142 Au choix

2 Des questions utiles

Students supply the correct adjective: *ton, ta* or *tes*.

This could be an oral exercise or the answers could be written and checked orally.

Solution: 1 *Ton,* **2** *Ta,* **3** *Tes,* **4** *Ton,* **5** *ton,* **6** *Ton,* **7** *ta,* **8** *tes*

 Fiche de travail (ws05)   AT2, AT3, AT4

Interview d'une vampire

As support for the above task, the questions form the basis of an online worksheet. This could form part of the students' *Dossier personnel.*

 20   AT2, AT4; 7W4, 7S4; AfL

2 Tu as tes affaires?

Further practice of the two possessive adjectives. Draw students' attention to the colour-coding suggested in the *Stratégies* box (masculine nouns in blue and feminine ones in red), indicating the thought process necessary to carry out the task. Remind students of the learning objectives and how this task will allow them to demonstrate their skills. Students could do this task orally in pairs, changing over roles half way through. More able students could then write the answers as consolidation (just possessives + noun).

Encourage students to check and correct each other's work, displaying correct answers as appropriate.

Solution: 1 *ta; ma,* **2** *ta; ma,* **3** *tes; mes,* **4** *tes; mes,* **5** *ton; mon,* **6** *ton; mon,* **7** *ta; ma,* **8** *ton; mon*

 20 **Stratégies**

This item suggests ways of remembering the gender of nouns.

AT2

Dans mon cartable …

Working in pairs or small groups, each student puts two or three of their possessions in their school bag and they each have to ask questions in turn to find out what they are, e.g. *Tu as ton livre? Oui, voici mon livre* (puts it on the table) (or *Non!*). The first one to guess all the other one's possessions has won.

Introduction   AT2

C'est le/la … de …

Introduce this structure by going round the classroom and picking up objects, saying, e.g.

Voici la règle de Martin, et ça, qu'est-ce que c'est?
C'est le stylo de Linda.
C'est le crayon de David. Vrai ou faux?

Use some games for practice, e.g.

1 Put a few objects in a box. Take one out and hold it behind your back. Students guess what it is and who it belongs to, e.g. *C'est la règle de Chantal?*

2 *Je touche …* (See Games TB 21.)

3 *Je pense à quelque chose,* played as usual, but with each person guessing using the construction *C'est le livre de Caroline* etc. (See Games TB 21.)

The choice of objects could be limited in order to stop one person's turn from going on interminably.

 21   1 tr 35   AT1, AT3; 7W2, 7L2

3 Dani

Play the recording as students follow the cartoon strip. Then ask them some questions, on similar lines to those in the exercise which follows, e.g. *Regardez le baladeur. C'est le baladeur de Dani? Non? C'est le baladeur de son frère? Oui, c'est ça.*

transcript

Dani

Presenter – **Lundi**, Dani est à la maison.

Dani – Voici une carte postale de mon frère, Louis. Il est à Nice.

Presenter – Aujourd'hui, c'est **mardi**. Dani est content.

Dani – Voici le baladeur de mon frère. C'est super, hein?

Presenter – **Mercredi**, il est à la campagne.

Dani – C'est le vélo de mon frère. J'aime le vélo!

Presenter – **Jeudi**, Dani a un livre.

Dani – Très intéressant! C'est le livre de mon frère.

Presenter – **Vendredi**, il cherche son cartable.

Dani – Où est mon cartable? Ah, je prends le sac à dos de mon frère.

Presenter – **Samedi**, il est avec une amie.

Dani – Je vais à la discothèque. Voici la copine de mon frère.

Presenter – Mais **dimanche** ... qui est-ce?!

Dani – Aïe! Voici mon frère!

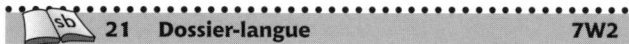

21   Dossier-langue   7W2

Go through the presentation of *de* + noun and ask students to give further examples to reinforce the new structure.

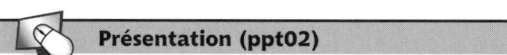

Présentation (ppt02)   AT3

Les articles

Use this PowerPoint presentation to introduce and practise the use of definite and indefinite articles and possessive adjectives.

21   7W2

4 Dani et son frère

Students write down the true statement in each pair. This can be corrected orally, with students reading out the full sentence each time, e.g.

Regardez 'a'. C'est le baladeur de Dani? Oui? Non?

Et regardez 'b'. C'est le baladeur de son frère. C'est vrai? Oui, c'est vrai.

Solution: 1 b, **2** b, **3** b, **4** a, **5** a, **6** b

AT2

Qu'est-ce qui manque?

As follow-up, this group speaking task provides practice of classroom objects + *de* + name. Everyone in the group puts something in the middle, e.g. pencil. ruler, rubber. They shut their eyes while the teacher mixes the objects up and removes one thing. Then in turn students pick up something and identify it saying, *C'est le crayon de Paul* etc. At the end they are asked *Qu'est-ce qui manque?* and have to say what is missing.

Fiche de travail (ws06)   AT4

C'est le crayon de ...?

This online worksheet provides more writing practice of *de*.

Plenaries (pages 20–21)

Fiche de travail (ws02)

1 Students write down two sentences summarising the lesson, then share these with the class. Discuss the key points to remember and what aspects might cause difficulties.

2 Students shut their books and take stock of what they have learnt so far in this unit: vocabulary for members of the family, differences between masculine and feminine, using possessive adjectives, using the different word order of *le/la* (+ noun) *de* (+ name).

3C Ma maison   pages 22–23

Aims and objectives	Grammar and skills	Resources
• use parts of the verb *être* (to be) • talk about your home	**Grammar** *Être* (1ˢᵗ, 2ⁿᵈ and 3ʳᵈ person singular) **Pronunciation** *et, est* Discriminating between similar sounds in French	**Key language:** see p54 **Online resource:** *Unité 3* int04/05, ppt03, ws02/07 **CD** 1 tracks 36–38 **Flashcards:** 13–17

Starters (pages 22–23)

Fiche de travail (ws02)

1 Reinforce the focus on masculine and feminine. Present an assortment of 12–15 nouns learnt so far, without the articles (see below and online worksheet). Give each student two pieces of card, one in blue for masculine nouns, one in red for feminine nouns. Now read out the list of words. Students hold up the blue card if the word is masculine, red for feminine.

cahier, calculatrice, cartable,
chaise, classeur, fenêtre,
lecteur CD, maison, porte,
poubelle, sac, stylo,
table, tableau interactif, village

2 (use after task 3) Play *Loto!* using visuals or text. Prepare a card for each student with any four rooms or items in the Laurent family's house in French (see online worksheet). Students pick them up as they enter the classroom. The first student to get all four places calls *Loto!* and has to say the four places in French.

An alternative version of this is 'strip bingo' – items are listed vertically on a strip of paper and students can only tear items from the top or the bottom when they are called out.

Ma maison

22   Dossier-langue   7W5

être (to be)

As the singular parts of *être* have occurred in context, this is now explained and practised. The full paradigm is covered in *Unité 5*. If teachers wish to cover the full paradigm in this unit, an online task is provided below.

For oral practice, use flashcards (13–17) for the rooms, giving them to students and asking questions, e.g.

– *Où es-tu?*
– *Je suis dans la chambre.*
– *Où est Richard? Il est dans la cuisine?*
– *Non, il est dans la salle à manger,* etc.

 **22**   **1 tr 36**   **AT1; 7W6, 7L1**

Prononciation
est (is), *et* (and)

This item focuses on the sound of *est* (is) and *et* (and). It is accompanied by a short listening differentiation task. Emphasise to students that understanding the context helps them work out which word is being used. Also mention that the final *t* of *est* is sounded before a vowel or silent *h*, but the *t* on *et* is never sounded.

Solution: **1** *et,* **2** *est,* **3** *et,* **4** *est,* **5** *est,* **6** *est,* **7** *et,* **8** *est*

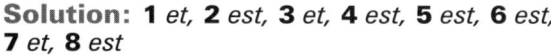

Prononciation: *est* (is), *et* (and)

1 J'ai une sœur et un frère.
2 Mon frère est très amusant.
3 Il a une souris et un rat.
4 La souris est amusante.
5 Mais le rat est horrible.
6 Ma sœur est très petite.
7 Elle déteste le rat et la souris.
8 Mais elle adore son petit chat. Il est fantastique!

   Fiche de travail (ws07)   **AT3, AT4**

Le verbe être

This online task practises the verb *être*. It contains both singular and plural forms, but these are split to allow the plural to be optional.

 **22**   **AT3, AT4; 7W5, 7S2, 7T1**

The next three items are a set of e-mails to practise the singular of *être* and other vocabulary.

1 Un message d'Yvan

Students read the first e-mail which could be followed by a brief discussion about the verbs used. They then do the short *Vrai ou faux?* task. Point out the word *sportif* in preparation for the feminine form which appears in the next e-mail.

Solution: **1** *faux,* **2** *vrai,* **3** *vrai,* **4** *faux,* **5** *faux,* **6** *vrai,* **7** *vrai,* **8** *faux*

2 Un message de Karine

As the e-mail is sent by a girl, comment on the use of *sportive.*

Solution: *Je suis ta correspondante; Il est amusant; Elle est fantastique!; Es-tu sportive comme moi?*

3 Salut!

Students now write their own e-mail, filling in the gaps. More able students could add a few more sentences here.

 **22**   **Stratégies**

This item focuses on the use of emphatic pronouns *moi* and *toi.*

   Présentation (ppt03)   **AT3**

Des maisons françaises

This PowerPoint presentation introduces the rooms of a house, and includes a picture of a house and a flat. It then presents some of the contents of various rooms.

Using the PowerPoint presentation, revise:

– *Tu habites où? – J'habite …*

Qu'est-ce que c'est? – C'est une maison/un appartement.

Then present and practise the names of the rooms in the house and finally move on to include the word *pièce* and objects or items of furniture which appear in the rooms. Before presenting the contents, revise *table, chaise, télévision, radio, ordinateur, lecteur CD* and add *lit, téléphone, console.*

 **23**   **1 tr 37 AT1, AT2, AT3; 7W2, 7T1, 7L2; AfL**

4 La maison de la famille Laurent

a   First get the class to look at the plan of the house and talk briefly about the rooms, e.g.

La salle à manger, c'est la lettre …?

La lettre A, c'est quelle pièce? C'est la chambre.

Et voici la cuisine. Regardez. Dans la cuisine il y a une radio etc.

1   Use a range of reading strategies with varying amounts of support.

2   Ask questions about the plan, introducing *Qu'est-ce qu'il y a?* and *Il y a …* and gradually train the class to answer and then ask each other these, e.g.

a – *C'est le salon?*
  – *Oui, c'est le salon./Non, c'est la salle à manger.*

b – *Il y a une table/une radio/un lit dans la salle à manger/la cuisine/la chambre de Louise? Oui ou non?*

c – *Où est le lecteur CD/l'ordinateur?*
  – *Dans la chambre de Louise/de Thomas et Daniel* etc.

d – *Qu'est-ce qu'il y a dans la chambre de Louise?*
  – *Dans la chambre de Louise, il y a un lit, un chat et un lecteur CD.*

3   Finally play the recording again, this time with students not following the printed text.

Tricolore Total 1 Teacher's Notes   **61**

transcript

La maison de la famille Laurent

Je suis Louise Laurent. Voici notre maison et notre jardin.

Et voici le garage. Dans la maison, il y a huit pièces: le salon, la salle à manger, la cuisine, les toilettes, la salle de bains et trois chambres.

Dans la chambre de mes parents, il y a un lit et un lecteur CD. Dans la chambre de Thomas et Daniel, il y a deux lits, une console de jeux et toutes les affaires de mes frères.

Il y a une télévision dans le salon et aussi dans la chambre de mes parents et de mes frères. Il y a aussi un téléphone dans la chambre de Maman et Papa.

Dans la salle à manger, il y a une table et cinq chaises.

Dans la cuisine, il y a une radio et un téléphone.

Dans ma chambre, il y a mon lecteur CD, mon ordinateur et, regardez, sur mon lit, il y a mon chat Mimi!

b This matching task consolidates the vocabulary for rooms. Ask questions such as *Le salon, c'est où? La cuisine, c'est la lettre 'B', oui ou non?* Answers can be checked orally. Students could check each other's work in pairs as an opportunity for peer assessment. Remind them to refer to the spread objectives and agree criteria for success before assessing their work.

Solution: 1 J, **2** G, **3** H, **4** I, **5** A, **6** C, **7** B, **8** D, **9** E, **10** F

Once all the areas of the house have been identified, do further oral practice of the new vocabulary, e.g. *La lettre 'D', c'est quelle pièce?*

For further practice, print the pictures from the PowerPoint presentation (above) as flashcards and play any of the flashcard games (see TB 22) or adapt the games for the whiteboard. A useful one here is 'Guess which room it is' or 'Guess which room it isn't'. Hold a flashcard face down, or hide the whiteboard picture, and ask, for example,

– *Ce n'est pas la cuisine?*

– *Vrai.*

– *Ce n'est pas la salle à manger?*

– *Faux, c'est la salle à manger. Regarde!*

 **Activité (int04)** | **AT1, AT3, AT4**

Les pièces

These online tasks present and practise the new vocabulary.

 **23** | **AT3; 7S1, 7T5; AfL**

5 Les pièces

This entails matching two halves of a sentence. Answers could be checked through in pairs first as an opportunity for peer assessment. Then correct the task orally, to give practice in reading out the complete sentences.

Solution: 1 b, **2** i, **3** g, **4** h, **5** e, **6** a, **7** d, **8** c, **9** f, **10** j

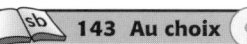 **143 Au choix** | **1 tr 38** | **AT1**

5 Samedi

This item is to practise the verb *être* and also includes some possessive adjectives and rooms of the house. Go through the text and pictures with the class, commenting on where everyone is and asking questions such as *Où est Louise? Ah, voilà, elle est dans sa chambre* etc.

Students could then do part **b** in which they complete the sentences. They should then listen to the recording and follow the text, checking their answers as they go.

Solution: 1 *est*, **2** *est*, **3** *es*, **4** *suis*, **5** *es*, **6** *suis*, **7** *est*, **8** *es*, **9** *suis*, **10** *est*

Finally, students could read the conversation aloud in groups of four, perhaps recording some of them. Some groups of students might like to act this now or later.

If more oral work is required, use flashcards of rooms to give to a ro.w of students. asking them questions, e.g. *Tu es dans le salon? Es-tu dans la cuisine?* etc.

Then get students to make up *vrai ou faux* statements to ask others, e.g.

Corrie est dans la salle à manger. Tyler est dans la salle de bains, etc.

transcript

Samedi

– C'est samedi chez la famille Laurent. Où sont les enfants?

– Où est Louise? Je pense qu'elle est dans sa chambre … Louise, tu es dans ta chambre?

– Oui, Maman. Je suis ici. J'écoute des CD.

– Et Thomas? Il est dans sa chambre aussi? Thomas, tu es dans ta chambre?

– Non, Maman. Je suis dans le salon. Je regarde la télé.

– Très bien. Mais où est Daniel? Daniel, tu es dans ta chambre?

– Oui, Maman, je suis dans ma chambre. Je range mes affaires.

– Tu ranges tes affaires?!

– Mais oui, Maman! Dimanche, c'est le concert rock en ville, non? Et moi, j'adore la musique!

 **Activité (int05)** | **AT1, AT2**

Ma famille et ma maison

This online guided role play practises much of the language covered so far. Students could use this as the basis for further extended dialogues.

Plenaries (pages 22–23)

Fiche de travail (ws02)

1 Find out from students how they remember the spelling and pronunciation of the rooms and the objects in them. They work in pairs, then report back to the whole class. If necessary, provide some ideas to start them off, e.g. *salon* – like 'saloon'; *cuisine* – spell it rhythmically C-U … I-S … I-N-E.

2 Ask students to look at the objectives for SB pages 22–23: how well do they think they have done? Can they explain the main points to a partner? What did they find easy or difficult?

3D C'est où? pages 24–25

Aims and objectives	Grammar and skills	Resources
• use prepositions to say where things are • learn more about masculine and feminine • practise the sounds *ou* and *u*	**Grammar** Masculine and feminine – definite, indefinite and possessive articles (revision) Use prepositions **Pronunciation** *sur* and *sous*	**Key language:** see p54 **Online resource:** *Unité 3* int06, ppt04, ws02/08 **Copymasters:** 3/2 **CD** 1 tracks 39–41 **GiA:** p5

Starters (pages 24–25)

Fiche de travail (ws02)

1 Write a random list of vocabulary items on one area of the board (see online worksheet – rooms, furniture, objects). Begin to draw any one of the items. Students tell you as soon as they know what it is. Bad drawing 'adds to the interest'. Students then continue in pairs. (This provides good preparation for the vocabulary used in work on prepositions.)

2 Show the picture of Thomas and Daniel's room (SB 24 and ws02) and play *Sur ou sous?* Explain that holding your arms up means that an object is *sur*; holding them down means it is *sous*. Say sentences containing *sur* or *sous* (e.g. *la trousse de Thomas est sur la chaise*). Students listen and when they hear *sur* their arms go up, when they hear *sous* their arms go down under the desks. Alternatively, they could only do the action if the information is correct (as a version of *Jacques a dit* …).

Introduction	AT2

Où est …?

There are a variety of ways to teach and practise *sur*, *sous* and *dans*, e.g. with classroom objects, piling them up, putting them in, on or under things and asking questions beginning with *Où est* …? At first supply the answers too, then get the class to answer. Eventually students can ask and answer similar questions. The small diagram on SB 24 gives the meaning of the three words.

Several oral games provide useful practice, e.g. *Qu'est-ce qu'il y a dans la boîte?* (see TB 22).

Présentation (ppt04)	AT1, AT2, AT3

C'est où?

This PowerPoint presentation introduces and practises the prepositions *dans*, *sur* and *sous*.

sb 24	1 tr 39	AT1, AT3; 7W2, 7T1, 7L2

1 Notre chambre

Use the picture for oral discussion. Students then listen to Thomas describing the room and guess which is his side.

After this first hearing, go through the whole item more thoroughly using the printed text. Use listening and reading strategies as appropriate.

Ask questions about the picture, e.g. *Où sont les livres de Thomas?/Où est le lit de Daniel? – Voici/Voilà …*

Où est le sac à dos?/Qu'est-ce qu'il y a dans la trousse? etc.

Notre chambre

Je suis Thomas Laurent, et Daniel est mon petit frère.

Voici notre chambre et voici notre console, avec les jeux vidéo et les manettes.

Voici mes affaires. Mes livres sont sur la table, et mes crayons sont dans la boîte. Mon stylo est sur le cahier et mes classeurs sont sous la table. Et voilà mon baladeur.

Et voici les affaires de mon frère Daniel.

Où est le sac à dos? Ah oui, il est sur le lit! Dans le sac, il y a une règle et des livres. Et qu'est-ce qu'il y a sous le lit? Voilà! Le baladeur de Daniel est sous le lit. Et voici la trousse de Daniel: elle est sur la chaise. Et qu'est-ce qu'il y a dans la trousse? Regardez! Il y a une gomme dans la trousse, mais les crayons et le stylo sont sous la chaise!

3D C'est où?

2 Dans la chambre

Students supply the word *sur, sous* or *dans* to complete these sentences. Most are given in the text, but one or two have to be discovered through the picture of the bedroom. The answers should be checked orally afterwards, with students reading aloud each completed sentence.

 Solution: 1 *dans,* **2** *sur,* **3** *dans,* **4** *sur,*
5 *dans, sur,* **6** *dans,* **7** *sous,* **8** *sur*

Use similar questions and answers to consolidate the new vocabulary and to introduce the pronouns *il* and *elle*.

Consolidation

The following worksheet and *Au choix* activities present a selection of differentiated activities which could be used here to consolidate work on rooms in the house, prepositions and expressing possession.

 Fiche de travail (ws08)   AT4

Invente des phrases

This online worksheet provides writing practice of the prepositions *dans, sur* and *sous*.

 142 Au choix   **1 tr 40**   AT1, AT4

3 La maison de la famille Lambert

This task is suitable for most students. Students listen to the recording and complete the text. This could be done as an oral exercise with students requiring extra support.

Solution: 1 *maison,* **2** *chaises,* **3** *table,*
4 *salle à manger,* **5** *salon,* **6** *la télévision,* **7** *un,*
8 *affaires,* **9** *la,* **10** *de*

 **transcript**

La maison de la famille Lambert

Voici la maison et le jardin de la famille Lambert.

Dans la cuisine, il y a trois chaises et une table.

Mme Lambert est dans la salle à manger.

Anne-Marie Lambert est dans le salon. Elle regarde la télévision.

Voici la chambre de Christophe Lambert. Dans sa chambre, il y a un lit et aussi ses affaires.

Voici la salle de bains.

 **142 Au choix**   AT4

4 Jeu de mémoire

This brings together work on the rooms of the house and also revises possession. Students study the pictures on SB 23 and 24 before trying to identify the objects, using the substitution table to help them. The task could be done in writing and checked orally.

Solution:
1 *C'est la radio de la famille Laurent.*
2 *C'est le lit de Thomas.*
3 *C'est le stylo de Daniel.*
4 *C'est le baladeur de Thomas.*
5 *C'est la télévision de la famille Laurent.*
6 *C'est le chat de Louise.*
7 *C'est le sac à dos de Daniel.*
8 *C'est le lecteur CD de Louise.*

Optionally, this task could be followed by more oral questions about the objects shown, practising *C'est le (+ noun) de (+ name).*

Some students may be able to cope with the alternative structure *C'est à qui? C'est à (+ name)* – see *Grammaire* 4.3 (SB 160). This could be done first with the teacher asking questions, then with some students making up similar questions about the objects shown or about things in the classroom, e.g.

– *Le baladeur, c'est à Louise?*   – *Non.*

– *C'est à qui?* – *C'est à Simon.*

– *Et ce cahier, c'est à James?*   – *Oui.*

– *Ah oui, c'est le cahier de James,* etc.

Prononciation: Suzanne et Suzette Souris

This item focuses on the pronunciation of the sound *ou* and *u*, already met in the words *sur* and *sous*. Students could try saying the sentences as a tongue twister.

transcript

Prononciation: Suzanne et Suzette Souris

Suzanne Souris est sur la boîte. La boîte est sur la table.

Voici sa sœur, Suzette Souris. Suzette est amusante.

La boîte est sous la table. Suzanne et Suzette Souris sont aussi sous la table.

Masculine and feminine

By now students have met all the articles and several possessive adjectives and pronouns, so this item really serves as a reference table for revision, bringing the main examples together. Go through the table with students and check that they can complete it accurately.

The completed table …

- sets out more fully the link between *un* and *le/une* and *la* (already mentioned on SB 19)

- includes *l'* + vowel

- mentions the use of the pronouns *il* and *elle* to mean 'it'
- explains that gender applies to things as well as people in French.

If some students are not too clear about any of these points, give them more examples, e.g.

Voici un stylo. (Write *un stylo* on the board.)

C'est le stylo de Vivienne, oui? (Write *le stylo* under *un stylo*.)

Put the pen in a box, or any other suitable place.

Bon, le stylo de Vivienne est dans la boîte. Il est dans la boîte. (Write *il* under *le*.)

Coloured pens could be used to highlight masculine and feminine words.

Continue in the same way using feminine objects and with words beginning with a vowel, so that students can see the pattern.

 **25**   **7W2, 7W4**

3 Masculin ou féminin?

Draw the attention of the class to the words in the box and emphasise that words other than the definite and indefinite article show if a noun is masculine or feminine.

Students then work on writing the two lists of nouns, showing their gender and their meaning.

> **Solution:**
>
> ### masculin
>
> | français | anglais |
> |---|---|
> | un livre | a book |
> | un crayon | a pencil |
> | ton ami | your friend |
> | un ordinateur | a computer |
> | le cartable | the satchel |
> | le baladeur | the personal stereo |
> | mon grand-père | my grandfather |
>
> ### féminin
>
> | français | anglais |
> |---|---|
> | ta gomme | your rubber |
> | ma calculatrice | my calculator |
> | ta chaise | your chair |
> | l'amie | the (girl)friend |
> | une table | a table |

 **25**   **AT3; 7W4**

4 Où est ...?

This task practises the prepositions *sur*, *sous* and *dans* and also involves matching the correct pronoun (*il* or *elle*) with a masculine or feminine noun.

Mention two things to look for when doing the task:

1 get the right preposition
2 match the genders (*il* for masculine noun, *elle* for feminine noun)

Solution: 1 c, 2 a, 3 d, 4 b, 5 g, 6 e, 7 h, 8 f

           AT2

C'est où?

For further practice of prepositions and pronouns, play a game. Someone places/hides objects around the classroom and asks where they are. Others reply using

pronouns. This could be a team game – one mark for the correct place, one for the correct preposition, one for using the correct pronoun.

 **25**   **AT2, AT4; 7S3**

5 Ma chambre

Students could discuss this activity in pairs first, noting the phrases and vocabulary they will need. The task could then be done orally as a class activity, asking students questions such as: *Qu'est-ce qu'il y a dans ta chambre? Où est ton ordinateur? Tu as une télévision dans ta chambre?*

Students can then write out a short description of their room (or their ideal room, if they prefer). The final version of this can form part of students' *Dossier personnel*.

 3/2

Masculin, féminin

This gives practice of gender. There is a built-in incline of difficulty, so less able students may need help with tasks 3 and 4.

> **Solution:**
>
> **1 Les mots féminins**
>
> The following should be underlined: *la famille, la maison, une demi-sœur, la trousse, la mère, la télévision, une carte postale, la radio, une calculatrice, la grand-mère*
>
> **2 5-4-3-2-1**
>
> 5 *un frère, une demi-sœur, le père, la mère, la grand-mère*
> 4 (any 4) *la télévision, un ordinateur, un lecteur CD, la radio, une calculatrice*
> 3 *samedi, vendredi, dimanche*
> 2 *un stylo, un crayon*
> 1 (any one) *une maison, un cinéma*
>
> **3 Fais deux listes**
>
> | | |
> |---|---|
> | *l'animal* | *la ferme* |
> | *le baladeur* | *la maison* |
> | *le grand-père* | *la rue* |
> | *le jardin* | *la sœur* |
> | *l'ordinateur* | |
> | *le sac* | |
>
> **4 Les blancs**
>
> This is an open-ended task.

 **1 p5**

Masculine and feminine

This grammar explanation and practice covers material in *Unités 1–3* and can be used here for consolidation.

 Activité (int06)   **AT1, AT3**

Rue Danton: L'appartement de Manon et Hugo

This is a suitable point to use the ongoing video 'soap'. This episode provides extension material on rooms and contents.

3E Les nombres

Plenaries (pages 24–25)

Fiche de travail (ws02)

1 In pairs, students tell their partner three things about where things are in their house or room. They then pair up with another two students – how many different phrases can they say? Take feedback from the class.

2 Show visuals of some of the items of vocabulary that students have met in this unit (and also from the first two units). Which, if any, do students find hard to remember? Is it easy to remember the gender? Discuss, as a class, ways of memorising the more difficult words.

3E Les nombres   pages 26–27

Aims and objectives	Grammar and skills	Resources
• learn and practise the numbers up to 70 • practise language you have learnt in this Unit	**Skills** Identifying patterns when counting Building vocabulary **Cross-curricular** Numeracy	**Key language:** see p54 **Online resource:** *Unité 3* int07/08/09, ppt05, ws02/09 **Copymasters:** 3/3, 3/4, 3/5 **CD** 1 tracks 42–43

Starters (pages 26–27)

Fiche de travail (ws02)

1 Display the numbers up to 30 in words in French on the board, out of sequence. Invite students to work out the right order silently to themselves and then to call them out in sequence. Point to the first student who starts – *un, deux*. Then point to another student (not the next one) who continues – *trois, quatre, cinq*. Point to a third student – *six* – etc.

2 Display words with the vowels é and è missing. Students hold up a piece of paper with é or è on it. It is helpful if these are on different coloured paper, perhaps orange for é and green for è. Suggestions: *écoute, réponse, numéro, stratégie, zéro, idée, vérifie, télévision, téléphone, intéressant, vélo, père, mère, frère, pièce, complète, règle* and one to really test them: *répète*.

26 Stratégies   **7W7, 7T7**

If students have not already done so, this is a good point to encourage them to write their own vocabulary book, building it up with every unit. Discuss the different ways they could organise it. In pairs or small groups, students could say which method they think will work best for them.

26   1 tr 42   **AT1; 7W2, 7L1**

1 C'est quel nombre?

This listening activity practises aural discrimination of numbers up to 70.

Solution: 1a 30, **2a** 60, **3b** 31, **4b** 70, **5a** 59, **6b** 13.

transcript

C'est quel nombre?

1	trente	4	soixante-dix
2	soixante	5	cinquante-neuf
3	trente et un	6	treize

26   **AT2, AT4; 7W2, 7T6**

2 Les nombres

Students have to supply the missing number in each straightforward sequence. This could be done orally first, then ask students to write out the missing numbers.

Solution: 1 *vingt-huit,* **2** *soixante-deux,* **3** *quarante-quatre,* **4** *quatorze,* **5** *cinquante,* **6** *trente-cinq*

26   1 tr 43   **AT1, AT3, AT2; 7W2, 7T6**

3 Complète les listes

This is a more demanding task as the numbers are not sequential, but follow varying patterns and directions. Students work out the missing numbers, then listen to the recording to check.

Solution: 1 *quatre,* **2** *seize,* **3** *quinze,* **4** *trente,* **5** *cinquante-cinq,* **6** *soixante,* **7** *trente et un,* **8** *cinquante*

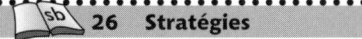

Complète les listes

1 dix, huit, six, quatre
2 quatre, huit, douze, seize
3 cinq, dix, quinze, vingt
4 dix, vingt, trente, quarante
5 vingt-deux, trente-trois, quarante-quatre, cinquante-cinq
6 soixante-dix, soixante, cinquante, quarante
7 vingt et un, trente et un, quarante et un, cinquante et un
8 soixante-cinq, soixante, cinquante-cinq, cinquante

Follow this up with more oral work, such as a chain game where you start off a sequence of numbers and students continue as far as they can up to 70. The sequence can be varied at any point, the direction can be reversed, etc.

 **26 Stratégies**   7W7

Students could look at the questions in groups, then go through the answers in class, with students saying the appropriate numbers.

> **Solution:**
> How many contain the word *dix*? (five: 10, 17, 18, 19, 70)
> How many contain *un*? (six: 1, 21, 31, 41, 51, 61)
> How many contain *et*? (five: 21, 31, 41, 51, 61)

Try to elicit a rule for these numbers. This will help students remember the pattern and make the next group of numbers (71–100) less daunting.

 **26**   AT2, AT4; 7W2, 7T6; AfL

4 Ma maison

Students write a description of their house based on the model. This item can be exploited with varying degrees of support, depending on ability, as an AfL task. Use the spread objectives as a focus for discussion and use the model to show students how to do tasks of this kind. The final version of this can be included in the students' *Dossier personnel*.

As an option for more able groups, this could be in the form of an oral presentation, made from prepared notes or even recorded.

This might be a good opportunity to suggest that students could build up a recorded equivalent of the *Dossier personnel* if suitable facilities are available.

At the simplest level, students complete the gap-fill text and eventually learn the corrected version.

 3/3   AT4

À la maison

This support sheet consolidates household vocabulary and prepositions and practises writing them.

Activité (int07)   AT1, AT3

Vocabulaire de classe (3)

An online activity in which students match up some French and English classroom language.

 Fiche de travail (ws09)/Présentation (ppt05) AT3

La famille Souris

This worksheet can be printed and folded to form a reader on the subject of families. It is in the form of a poem and provides extension material for the unit. The PowerPoint presentation can be used for whole-class presentation of the text.

 3/4   AT3, AT4

C'est où?

This copymaster provides further reading and writing support for rooms, contents and prepositions.

> **Solution:**
> **1 Vrai ou faux?**
>   **a** V, **b** F, **c** V, **d** F, **e** F, **f** V, **g** V, **h** F, **i** V, **j** F
> **2 Attention! Il y a des erreurs!**
>   **a** *Il y a <u>une télévision</u> dans la salle de bains.*
>   **b** *Le cartable est <u>sur</u> le lit.*
>   **c** *Le baladeur est <u>sous</u> la table <u>dans</u> le salon.*
>   **d** *La table est dans <u>la chambre</u>.*
>   **e** *L'ordinateur est <u>dans la cuisine</u>.*
>   **f** *La chaise est <u>sous le lit</u>.*
>   **g** *Dans la cuisine, <u>il y a une télévision</u>.*
>   (any order for **h, i, j**; accept any correct answer)
>   **h** *Il y a <u>un chat sur la table dans la chambre</u>.*
>   **i** *<u>Il y a une radio dans la chambre.</u>/<u>La radio est dans la chambre</u>.*
>   **j** *<u>Le lit est dans le salon.</u>/<u>Il y a un lit dans le salon</u>.*

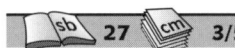 **27** **3/5**

Sommaire

A summary of the main language and structures of the unit, also on copymaster for ease of reference.

The page also includes a vocabulary-learning tip.

 Activité (int08)   AT3

Vocabulaire (3)

An online game which tests the vocabulary of the unit.

 Activité (int09)   AT1, AT3, AT4

Quiz Unités 1–3

This online activity provides assessment of the first three units. There are ten questions covering a range of grammar, vocabulary and skills.

Plenaries (pages 26–27)

 Fiche de travail (ws02)

1 With their books closed, students reconstruct the different language they have learnt in this unit. Write up the information as a mind-map with *Chez moi* at the centre (see online worksheet).

Surround *Chez moi* with some sentences/sentence starters, e.g.

Dans ma famille, j'ai un frère, …

Dans mon appartement, il y a …

Dans ma chambre, j'ai …

Mon ordinateur est sur la table, …

2 Discuss what students have been able to include in their *Dossier personnel* at the end of this unit. Students could assess how far they have come in the first three units (before moving on to the first *Rappel* section) and summarise what they now know.

Unité 3 Consolidation and assessment

Épreuves Unités 1–3

These worksheets can be used for an informal test of listening, reading and writing or for extra practice, as required.

For general notes on the *Épreuves*, see TB 20.

 3/6 Écouter ● **1 tr 44–47**

As the first item of each task is given as an example, each task is effectively out of 5, giving a total of 20 marks for the listening test.

A Des affaires scolaires

Solution: 1 b, **2** f, **3** e, **4** d, **5** a, **6** c (mark /5)

> **transcript**
>
> **Des affaires scolaires**
>
> Voici des affaires scolaires:
> 1 Regarde la trousse, c'est ma trousse.
> 2 Et voici un cartable. C'est le cartable de Suzanne.
> 3 Et où sont les cahiers? Ah oui, voici les cahiers.
> 4 Voici une console. C'est ma console.
> 5 Et voilà mes crayons. Il y a douze crayons.
> 6 Et où est ma règle? Ah oui, voici ma règle!

B C'est moi!

Solution: 1 a, **2** a, **3** a, **4** a, **5** b, **6** a *(mark /5)*

> **transcript**
>
> **C'est moi!**
>
> 1 Salut! Je m'appelle Sophie.
> 2 J'ai douze ans.
> 3 Je suis fille unique.
> 4 J'habite dans une maison.
> 5 Voici ma chambre et voici mon baladeur.
> 6 Et voici ma mère dans la salle à manger.

C C'est quelle phrase?

Solution: 1 a, **2** a, **3** b, **4** b, **5** b, **6** b (mark /5)

> **transcript**
>
> **C'est quelle phrase?**
>
> Exemple: **1**a
> **1** a Voici Michel avec ses deux sœurs.
>   b Voici Michel avec ses deux frères.
> **2** a Voici Marie avec son demi-frère.
>   b Voici Marie avec sa demi-sœur.
> **3** a Il y a un cahier sur la table.
>   b Il y a un cahier sous la table.
> **4** a Voici une photo de mes grands-parents avec ma sœur et moi.
>   b Voici une photo de mon grand-père avec ma sœur et moi.
> **5** a Voici une ville. Elle est près de Paris.
>   b Voici un village. Il est près de Calais.
> **6** a Dans la cuisine, il y a une table et trois chaises. Il y a aussi une radio.
>   b Dans la cuisine, il y a une petite table et deux chaises. Il y a aussi un téléphone.

D Je pense à quelque chose

Solution: 1 b, **2** e, **3** a, **4** c, **5** f, **6** d (mark /5)

> **transcript**
>
> **Je pense à quelque chose**
>
> – Je pense à quelque chose. Qu'est-ce que c'est?
> – C'est un crayon?
> – Non, ce n'est pas ça.
> – Ce sont des gommes?
> – Non, non. Ce n'est pas ça.
> – Je sais, je sais, c'est une calculatrice.
> – Non, ce n'est pas une calculatrice.
> – Ce sont des livres?
> – Des livres? Non, ce n'est pas ça.
> – Zut … qu'est-ce que c'est, alors? C'est une règle, c'est juste?
> – Non, non. Ce n'est pas juste.
> – Alors, c'est un baladeur?
> – Oui, fantastique! C'est un baladeur.

 **3/7 Lire**

There are three reading tests, effectively out of 6, 7 and 7, giving a total of 20 marks.

A Notre maison

Solution: 1 g, **2** e, **3** d, **4** f, **5** b, **6** a, **7** c
(mark /6)

B C'est quelle image?

Solution: 1 f, **2** d, **3** a, **4** g, **5** e, **6** c, **7** b, **8** h
(mark /7)

C Le télé-quiz

Solution: 1 vrai, **2** vrai, **3** faux, **4** vrai, **5** faux,
6 vrai, **7** vrai, **8** vrai (mark /7)

 3/8   Écrire et grammaire

There are three writing and grammar tests, effectively
out of 6, 6 and 8, giving a total of 20 marks.

A Les mots corrects

Solution: 1 une maison, **2** une ville, **3** un
village, **4** la France, **5** une porte, **6** des cahiers,
7 des livres (mark /6)

B Les images et les descriptions

Solution:
1e   Voici une fille.
2b   Voici un garçon.
3f   Les crayons sont dans la trousse.
4g   Le livre est sur la table.
5a   Voici un ordinateur.
6c   La famille Lebrun.
7d   La calculatrice est sous la boîte. (mark /6)

C Un e-mail de Martin

Solution: 1 suis, **2** j'ai, **3** J'ai, **4** Mon, **5** ma,
6 as, **7** es, **8** Mes, **9** ta   (mark /8)

Rappel 1

 **28–29**   **AT3, AT4**

This section can be used at any point after Unité 3 for
revision and consolidation. It provides reading and
writing activities which are self-instructional and can be
used by students working individually for homework or
during cover lessons.

1 Deux conversations

Solution:

1 – Bonjour, Marc.
  – Bonjour, Suzanne, ça va?
  – Oui, ça va bien, merci, et toi?
  – Ça va, merci.

2 – Bonjour, Lucie.
  – Bonjour, David, ça va?
  – Oui, ça va bien, merci, et toi?
  – Non, pas très bien. Au revoir, David.
  – Au revoir, Lucie.

2 Masculin, féminin

Solution:

masculin		féminin	
frère	mon	elle	mère
garçon	père	fille	sœur
il	ton	la	ta
le	un	ma	une

3 Un multi-quiz

Solution:

En France: **1** c, **2** b, **3** a
Au collège: **4** a, **5** b, **6** c
En famille: **7** c, **8** c

4 Le jeu des images

Solution: 1 B, **2** A, **3** D, **4** I, **5** E, **6** C, **7** F, **8** G,
9 H, **10** J

5 Des descriptions

This task requires production of vocabulary involving
some knowledge of gender and number.

Solution:
1 une table, une chaise et un livre
2 des maisons et un cinéma
3 famille, fille, garçons, parents (adultes). La,
ans

6 Les petits mots

This task requires production of articles and possessive
adjectives.

Solution: a 1 une, **2** une, **3** ton, **4** ta, **5** le,
6 ton

b 7 ma, **8** mon, **9** ma, **10** mon, **11** le

7 Questions et réponses

This is a predominantly open-ended task testing key
language from Unités 1–3.

Solution: 1–5 open-ended, **6** sur la table,
7 sous la table, **8** Il est sur le livre, **9** une
maison, **10** Non, c'est le chat de Louise.

Aims and objectives	Key language/Culture	Grammar and skills	National criteria
4A Tu as un animal? pp30–31			
• talk about pets • learn adjectives to describe colour and size	*Tu as un animal? J'ai … un animal (des animaux)* *un chat/une chatte/un chien/un cochon d'Inde/un hamster/un lapin/un oiseau/un perroquet/une perruche/un poisson (rouge)/un rat/une souris/une tarentule* *De quelle couleur est-il/elle?* *blanc (blanche)/bleu(e)/brun(e)/gris/jaune/marron/noir/orange/ rouge/vert(e)* *grand(e)/gros(se)/petit(e)* *je préfère*	**Grammar** Adjectives (receptive)	**Attainment** AT1 Level 1–3, AT2 Level 1–3, AT3 Level 1–3. AT4 Level 1 **Framework** 7W2/4/7. 7T1. 7L3/5 **Languages ladder/Asset languages** Grades 1–3 **Assessment for learning** ex 5
4B Les adjectifs pp32–33			
• use adjectives to describe things • learn how to make adjectives 'agree'	*Il/Elle est comment? Il/Elle est… Il/Elle n'est pas…* *grand(e)/gros(se)/petit(e)/énorme/méchant(e)/mignon(ne)* *blanc (blanche)/bleu(e)/brun(e)/gris(e)/jaune/marron/noir/orange/ rouge/vert(e)* Qualifiers: *très, assez, pas très*	**Grammar** Adjective agreement Understanding the negative *ne … pas* (not) **Skills** Describing things Using qualifiers	**Attainment** AT1 Level 1–3, AT2 Level 1–2, AT3 Level 1–3. AT4 Level 1–3 **Framework** 7W2/4, 7S5. 7T7 **Languages ladder/Asset languages** Grades 1–3 **Assessment for learning** *Dossier-langue. Au choix* ex 3
4C Tu as des questions? pp34–35			
• learn how to ask questions • revise the singular of the verb *avoir* (to have)	*Est-ce que … ?* *avoir – j'ai/tu as/il/elle a* *Comment?/quel?* *Comment ça s'écrit?*	**Grammar** Avoir (1st, 2nd and 3rd person singular) Asking questions using *Est-ce que…?* Shortening words before a vowel **Pronunciation** *à, as, a*	**Attainment** AT1 Level 1–3, AT2 Level 1–3, AT3 Level 1–3. AT4 Level 1–3 **Framework** 7W5/6, 7S1/4/9. 7L1/3/5 **Languages ladder/Asset languages** Grades 1–3
4D Tu aimes ça? Et vous aussi? pp36–37			
• learn how to give opinions • learn two ways to say 'you'	*J'aime …J'aime beaucoup …J'adore …Je préfère …* *Je n'aime pas… Je n'aime pas beaucoup …Je déteste …* *… parce que …* *animaux* *chevaux* *oiseaux* *jeux* *extraordinaire/naturellement* **Culture** *Tu* and *vous*	**Grammar** *tu* and *vous* Making plurals using *–x* **Skills** Expressing opinions	**Attainment** AT1 Level 1–3, AT2 Level 1–3, AT3 Level 1–3. AT4 Level 1–3 **Framework** 7W2/4, 7S4/5/6, 7T1/5/7. 7L2/5, 7C5 **Languages ladder/Asset languages** Grades 1–3 **Assessment for learning** ex 4
4E Un zoo extraordinaire p38			
• practise language you have learnt	*Écoutez bien.* *Copiez ces mots.* *Viens ici.* *Répétez après moi.* *Écris ton nom.* *Vérifiez vos réponses.* *Lis à haute voix.* *Chantez!*	**Pronunciation** The letter *i* Words spelt the same in French and English	**Attainment** AT1 Level 1–2, AT2 Level 1–3, AT3 Level 1–2, AT4 Level 1–3 **Framework** 7W2/6/7, 7S9, 7L1/5 **Languages ladder/Asset languages** Grades 1–3 **Assessment for learning** ex 2, ex 3

Other resources: Online resource *Unité 4*. Copymasters 4/1–4/10. 103 (Presse-Jeunesse). 128 (map). CD 2 tracks 2–16, Flashcards 18–26, GiA pp. 8–12

4A Tu as un animal? pages 30–31

Aims and objectives	Grammar and skills	Resources
• talk about pets • learn adjectives to describe colour and size	**Grammar** Adjectives (receptive)	**Key language:** see p70 **Online resource:** *Unité 4* int01/02, ppt01, ws02/03 **Copymasters:** 4/1 **CD** 2 tracks 2–3 **Flashcards:** 18–26

Starters (pages 30–31)

 Fiche de travail (ws02)

1 Chasse à l'intrus Play an odd-one-out game, based on language encountered in *Unités 1–3*. Display sets of words, e.g.

seize, trois, quinze, crayon, vingt
chambre, télévision, cuisine, toilettes, salon
mère, cousine, frère, grand-mère, demi-sœur
habite, ai, est, suis, sur
une chaise, un cahier, un crayon, un ordinateur, un livre
une ferme, un village, un appartement, une maison, une famille

Students write down the odd one out. Collate answers as a whole-class activity with students giving a reason for their choice (some of the above groupings are deliberately ambiguous).

2 5-4-3-2-1 Play in small groups or as a class. Display the words below (or others) in random order. Suggestion: 5 rooms, (*chambre, cuisine, salle à manger, salle de bains, salon*), 4 classroom objects (*cahier, gomme, stylo, régle*), 3 words for 'in' (*à, dans, en*), 2 names of animals (*chat, lapin*), 1 verb (*habite*).

To revise the alphabet as well, this could be played as a team game, one team giving the word, the other spelling it out correctly.

 Présentation (ppt01)   **AT1, AT3**

Les animaux

This PowerPoint presentation introduces the animal vocabulary (with sound effects).

Introduction FC 18–26   **AT2**

Est-ce que tu as un animal à la maison?

Using the PowerPoint presentation (above) or flashcards 18–26, teach the names of the pets. Introduce them a few at a time, use repetition and ask: *Qu'est-ce que c'est?*

Eventually write the words on the board for a game of *Effacez!* or *Je pense à un animal*.

Start some simple copy-writing with a game of *Loto!*, in which students write down the names of four animals and the teacher or another pupil acts as caller.

When introducing the animals, use the vocabulary reinforcement techniques (see TB 25).

 Activité (int01)   **AT1**

Sondage

In this online activity, students listen for how many animals people have.

 Activité (int02)   **AT1, AT3**

Les couleurs

This online activity presents and practises colours.

Draw students' attention to the labelled colours on SB 30 after completing the interactive presentation.

When introducing the colours, use the vocabulary reinforcement techniques (see TB 25).

Teach colours with known vocabulary, e.g. *Voilà un stylo: il est noir*, and with the animal pictures, e.g. *Voilà un lapin: il est blanc et gris*. Introduce *De quelle couleur est-il/elle?* and appropriate answers. Gradually encourage students to ask each other about colours, masculine nouns only.

 **30**   **AT2, AT3; 7W2, 7T1**

1 Grand Concours National

Ask students if they can guess the meaning of the words *concours national* and *finalistes*.

Talk about the animals in the photos: *La photo A, c'est quel animal? Le chien, c'est quelle photo?*

Introduce the words *grand/gros* and *petit* and refer to classroom objects etc. to emphasise the meaning.

Refer to the note on SB 31 about the use of *grand* and *gros*.

The feminine version of *chat* has been introduced as this is commonly used when referring to pets. It avoids students making sentences like *J'ai un chat. Elle s'appelle Mimi*. If appropriate for your students, you could also teach *une chienne*.

Tell the class to read through the eight descriptions of the animals and do the simple task, matching the descriptions with the photos.

■ **Solution: 1** C, **2** A, **3** E, **4** F, **5** B, **6** D, **7** H, **8** G

This could be checked orally, e.g. *Numéro 2, c'est Minnie. C'est quelle photo?*

Further oral work could be based on the photos and descriptions, e.g.

Est-ce que Minnie est blanche/grise/noire?
Le hamster, comment s'appelle-t-il?
Est-ce que Samba est gros ou petit?
Est-ce que le lapin s'appelle Minou?
Il est noir et blanc. C'est Samba?

 **4/1** **AT3, AT4**

Les animaux

This is a support worksheet for practising animal vocabulary. Students copy the names of the animals onto the correct square and colour according to the instructions. These could be stuck onto card, cut up and used as mini-flashcards for pair or group practice (see TB 23–24).

 Fiche de travail (ws03) **AT3**

Trouve les animaux

This online worksheet practises recognition of animals and sorting them according to gender.

 **30** **2 tr 2** **AT1, AT2, AT3; 7L3**

2 Vote, vote, vote!

a Draw students' attention to the *Stratégies* box which suggests different ways of answering. Ask students, *Tu préfères quel animal?* After a few oral answers, ask everyone to write their vote on a slip of paper as indicated. Add up the votes to find the class results – extra number practice can be given by getting the class to count out each animal's score aloud. Sort the votes into separate piles for each animal and give out the piles to individual students.

Alors qui a les votes pour Minou? Ellie? Bon, comptez les votes avec Ellie! … Très bien – sept votes pour Minou, etc.

b A recording of the results is provided. The class can listen to the first part of the recording (up to *Et finalement, voici les résultats.*) and jot down the correct letters or the names in the order in which the nine finalists are mentioned.

> **Solution:** **1**C (*Samba*), **2**A (*Minnie*), **3**D (*Tally et Lily*), **4**E (*Flic*), **5**F (*Carotte*), **6**B (*Dodu*), **7**G (*Tricolore*), **8**H (*Fifi*)

Then play the rest of the recording so that the class can compare their results with those of the national competition.

transcript

Vote, vote, vote!

Bonsoir, bonsoir! Voici des résultats importants, les résultats du Grand Concours National. Il y a huit finalistes: Samba, un gros chien adorable; Minnie, la petite souris blanche; les deux chats, Tally et Lily; puis un petit hamster qui s'appelle Flic; Carotte, un lapin noir et blanc; un cochon d'Inde qui s'appelle Dodu; Tricolore, le petit poisson; et Fifi, la petite perruche bleue, verte et jaune.

Et finalement, voici les résultats.

En troisième place – le numéro trois … c'est Flic. Oui, Flic, le petit hamster, a gagné le troisième prix.

Le deuxième prix … c'est pour Samba, le chien. Alors, Samba est numéro deux.

Et finalement, le premier prix, le numéro un … c'est pour Dodu, le cochon d'Inde. Alors, Dodu a gagné le concours, le grand concours national!

Félicitations à tous les animaux et bonsoir!

> **Solution:** **1** *Dodu, le cochon d'Inde,* **2** *Samba, le chien,* **3** *Flic, le petit hamster*

 **31** **2 tr 3** **AT1, AT3, AT4; 7W4, 7L3**

3 Tu as un animal?

Students should first listen and follow the conversation, then listen again without looking at the text. Play the recording again, but pause at key places, asking students to supply the next word from memory, e.g.

C'est une ……… Elle s'appelle ………

Oui, j'ai un ……… Il s'appelle ………

C'est un ………

Finally, students can write out the gapped text as completed sentences.

> **Solution:** **1** *une perruche,* **2** *Coco,* **3** *jaune,* (the next three sentences will vary)

transcript

Tu as un animal?

Girl J'ai un oiseau. C'est une perruche jaune. Elle s'appelle Coco. Et toi, Noah? As-tu un animal?

Boy Oui, Sophie, j'ai un animal. Il s'appelle Roland.

Girl Qu'est-ce que c'est?

Boy C'est un rat, un gros rat noir!

Girl Aïe!

31 **Dossier-langue** **7W7**

Make sure students understand the difference between *gros, grand* and *petit*. Students could find examples of *gros* on these pages (e.g. *Le gros chien s'appelle Samba./C'est un rat, un gros rat noir.*)

31 **AT3, AT4; 7W2**

4 C'est à qui?

This task practises recognition of colours. The maze puzzle is not quite as straightforward as might at first appear. Although students should have no trouble in tracing the owners of each animal by using the lines, they will have to look carefully to distinguish between the actual pets, since the puzzle includes three birds, two fish and two horses, all of different colours.

Note that both *brun* and *marron* are used in the colours as they are both in common usage for describing animals. Point out, when appropriate, that *marron* is invariable (see *Dossier-langue* SB 33).

Make sure everyone is clear what has to be done, e.g.

Regardez l'oiseau bleu et vert – il est mignon, non? Mais il est à qui? Suivez la ligne … voilà – il est à Hugo.

Maintenant, regardez les descriptions des animaux … Numéro 1, l'oiseau bleu et vert … c'est ça.

Students can just write the number and the name (or initial) of the owner or they can write out the whole sentence for practice. When checking answers, ask for the full sentence. See TB 64 for explaining the construction *c'est à* (+ name) if not already done.

Adjectival agreement is covered in the next spread, but can be briefly explained if students enquire about it.

Solution: **1** *Hugo,* **2** *Magali,* **3** *Coraline,* **4** *Eléna,* **5** *M. Lebrun,* **6** *Coraline,* **7** *Thomas,* **8** *Thomas*

For further practice, make up some true or false statements or questions, *Est-ce que M. Lebrun a un poisson? Thomas a un poisson rouge, orange et vert. C'est vrai?*

 **31** AT2; 7L5; AfL

5 Et toi, as-tu un animal?

Students make up conversations in pairs, using the dialogue in task 3 as a model. Suggest that if they do not have their own pet they can talk about a pet belonging to a friend or relation. Check that they understand the phrase *je n'ai pas d'animal.*

This conversation is for basic pair practice at this stage but will be expanded as the unit progresses, since agreement and position of adjectives are taught in the next spread. Teachers who wish to explain this straight away, can refer back to task 4 and get pupils to deduce rules from this.

Some of the dialogues could be recorded or presented to the class.

Note: if students want to use the plural of *animal, cheval* or *oiseau,* direct them to the note on SB 36 (*Dossier-langue*).

This activity offers an excellent opportunity for AfL. Agree the criteria for success with students. They prepare their work, check it against the agreed criteria, check with a partner, and then they could even record their dialogue. It can be a classic WALT and WILF exercise: We Are Learning Today ... and What I'm Looking For ...

 **144 Au choix** AT2

1 Combien d'animaux?

Students identify the number of different pets in the picture writing the answers as figures or in full.

Solution: **1** *trois hamsters,* **2** *quatre chiens,* **3** *un oiseau,* **4** *deux chats,* **5** *une souris,* **6** *deux poissons,* **7** *un lapin*

Plenaries (pages 30–31)

 Fiche de travail (ws02)

1 Ask how many students can name at least one animal in French. All hands should go up. Two? Three? Keep going until only a few hands are left up, then challenge these students to name them. Follow this with a discussion on which animals students are most likely to remember? Why? Which memorisation techniques did they use?

2 Students find something in the classroom for each colour they have learnt. They touch it and say *C'est jaune* etc. They then discuss different techniques they can use to help remember the colours and how to spell them, e.g. visualising the words spelt out in coloured letters, identifying a colour with a particular coloured item, etc.

4B Les adjectifs pages 32–33

Aims and objectives	Grammar and skills	Resources
• use adjectives to describe things • learn how to make adjectives 'agree'	**Grammar** Adjective agreement Understanding the negative *ne … pas* (not) **Skills** Describing things Using qualifiers	**Key language:** see p70 **Online resource:** *Unité 4* int03, ppt01,ws02/04 **Copymasters:** 4/2 **CD** 2 track 4 **GiA:** p8

Starters (pages 32–33)

 Fiche de travail (ws02)

1 Display the first part of the transcript of *Vote, vote, vote!* with key words blanked out. Display the missing words in a random list (see online worksheet). Students work in pairs to decide which words go where. Finally, students try to read the gapped text, supplying the missing words from memory, but prompted by the list.

Solution: (gapped words underlined)

Bonsoir, bonsoir! Voici des résultats importants – les résultats du Grand Concours National. Il y a neuf finalistes: Samba, un gros chien adorable; Minnie, la petite souris blanche; les deux chats, Tally et Lily; puis un petit hamster qui s'appelle Flic; Carotte, un lapin noir et blanc; un cochon d'Inde qui s'appelle Dodu; Tricolore, le petit poisson; et Fifi, la petite perruche bleue, verte et jaune.

2 En groupes (use at some point after task 2)

Display a mixture of masculine and feminine adjectives in random order (see online worksheet and Solution below).

Display a 3-column grid with the first word in each column already filled in. Students have to place the words in the correct box. As an extension they could give an example (*blanc – masculin – mon chat est blanc*).

Solution:

masc	fém	masc <u>et</u> fém
blanc	bleue	moderne
gros	brune	rouge
méchant	grise	énorme
noir	petite	jaune
petit	blanche	orange
vert	mignonne	fantastique

Alternatively, students could hold up cards for *masculin*, *féminin* or *masculin <u>et</u> féminin*.

 Présentation (ppt01) AT2

Les animaux

Use the PowerPoint presentation again and play a game with several pictures of animals for oral practice. Show the pictures and say, e.g. *il est gros? petit? noir? blanc? méchant? mignon?* etc.

 **32** AT3; 7W4

1 Une histoire de chats

This task gives practice with adjectives and feminine agreements.

First introduce the words *mignon/mignonne* and *méchant/méchante*, e.g. using some of the animals from page 30 or using the PowerPoint images above:

Regardez Minnie/la souris. Elle est mignonne, non?

Et voilà Lily/une chatte. Elle est mignonne aussi, elle n'est pas méchante.

Write the words on the board.

Refer to the *Dossier-langue* section (below) which gives a brief introduction to the negative.

The class then reads through the story, first silently, then aloud. Ask them some questions, e.g.

Est-ce que César est jaune?
Est-ce que Mimi est grosse?
Est-ce que Minette est mignonne?
Est-ce que César est le chat de Monsieur Lenoir?
Est-ce que tu préfères Mimi ou César?

Eventually students can complete the sentences.

More able students could act the story or make up a similar sketch.

Solution: 1 *César*, **2** *Mimi*, **3** *Géant*, **4** *Minette*, **5** *César/Géant*, **6** *Mimi*

 **32 Dossier-langue** 7S5

The negative

A brief introduction to the negative.

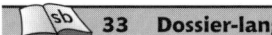 **33 Dossier-langue** 7W4; AfL

Adjectives – how to describe things in French

This covers adjectival agreement (singular only) and the difference in position of some adjectives. Plurals are introduced receptively in *Unités 1–5*, but not fully explained until *Unité 5*.

Tell the class to spot the differences in the spelling of *blanc*, *petit* and *mignon* (in the description of the dog and the mouse) and work out and explain the reason for these.

Students could read aloud the masculine and feminine forms of the adjectives, perhaps with half the class saying the feminine form and the other the masculine, changing over from time to time.

Explain the two words for 'brown': *marron* is invariable, i.e. does not change for feminine or plural; *brun* is a regular adjective.

Working in pairs or groups, students spot as many adjectives as they can. Students read their list aloud in turns. Everyone with the same adjective gains 1 point. Any that no-one else has is worth 5 points. Suitable for peer assessment. Remind students of the spread objectives and agree the criteria for success.

 33 AT3; 7W2, 7W4

2 Des adjectifs

This task gives routine practice of masculine and feminine forms of common adjectives and produces a useful reference table.

Solution:

masculin		féminin		anglais
brun	1	brune		brown
noir	2	noire	6	black
gris	3	grise		grey
blanc	4	blanche	7	white
jaune		jaune	8	yellow
rouge	5	rouge	9	red
gros	10	grosse		big/fat
grand		grande	15	large
petit	11	petite	16	small
énorme	12	énorme	17	enormous
méchant	13	méchante		nasty
mignon	14	mignonne		nice

 Activité (int03) AT3

Masculin ou féminin?

This online activity provides further practice in recognising the gender of adjectives.

Fiche de travail (ws04) AT3

Albert

This online worksheet provides extension for task 2.

 **33**   **AT2, AT4; 7W2, 7W4**

3 Les animaux de Jean-Pierre

Practice in writing adjectives with the correct agreement. Go through the activity orally first, asking questions about each animal and drawing out the difference in gender. Remind students not just to look for the word with the right meaning, but also to pick the correct masculine or feminine agreement.

Students then write out the full sentences. The answers can be collated on the board.

This could be a good homework activity.

> **Solution:** **1** *petit, noir,* **2** *grosse, blanche,* **3** *gros, bleu, orange, blanc,* **4** *grosse, noire, mignonne*

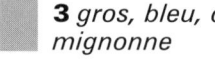 **32 Stratégies**   **7W2, 7T7**

Improve your creative work!

This covers qualifiers and their use in improving descriptions. As a follow-up, students could write their own description of an animal. This could be either their own pet or an animal belonging to a friend. Alternatively, they could draw an imaginary animal and describe it. They should be encouraged to use qualifiers in their descriptions. Students could work in pairs, each checking the other's descriptions to see if adjectives agree and seeing how many qualifiers and different adjectives are used.

Follow this with a growing-sentences chain game. Remind students to use *et* and *mais* to lengthen sentences. Start them off with a sentence such as *J'ai un chat.* This could eventually grow into something like *J'ai un très petit chat noir et blanc et assez mignon mais pas très méchant et il s'appelle Frodo, mais …* This could be played as a team game to see which team can build the longest sentence.

Jeu   **AT2, AT4**

Le message secret

This is an optional follow-up activity on adjectives and animals. Each student writes a 'secret message' on a piece of paper and signs it. The message is an instruction to draw and colour an animal (the message can be sensible or 'silly'), e.g. *Dessine un gros chien blanc et noir./Dessine trois chats, un bleu, un vert et un orange.*

Some messages might contain more detail, e.g.

Dessine Georges. C'est un cochon d'Inde. Il est noir.

Dessine Lulu. C'est une souris. Elle est blanche et très mignonne.

Dessine Noiraud. C'est un chien. Il est gros – et il est très méchant.

The messages are folded, pooled and given out at random.

The person receiving each message must carry out the instruction correctly and show it to the teacher (or group leader) to prove that it has been understood.

To make further use of these drawings and descriptions, after students have written their names on the back, the papers could be pinned up or laid on tables around and numbered. They could then be used as a matching game in which students have to match up the descriptions with the resulting picture.

 4/2   **AT3, AT4**

Les animaux de mes amis

This copymaster gives further practice of descriptive vocabulary and some dictionary practice with the names of animals. Some students might need help with the final task.

> **Solution:**
>
> **1 Où sont les voyelles?**
> **1** *chien,* **2** *poisson,* **3** *souris,* **4** *perroquet,* **5** *tarentule,* **6** *oiseau,* **7** *cheval,* **8** *lapin*
>
> **2 C'est utile, un dictionnaire**
>
> | | |
> |---|---|
> | *canard (m)* | duck |
> | *canari (m)* | canary |
> | *chameau (m)* | camel |
> | *chat (m)* | cat |
> | *chauve-souris (f)* | bat |
> | *cheval (m)* | horse |
> | *chien (m)* | dog |
> | *chimpanzé (m)* | chimp |
> | *cochon d'Inde (m)* | guinea pig |
>
> **3 Les animaux de mes amis**
> **1** *petite,* **2** *grand,* **3** *blanc,* **4** *noir,* **5** *mignonne,* **6** *gris,* **7** *méchant,* **8** *vert*

144 Au choix   2 tr 4   **AT1, AT3**

2 Chat perdu

Teach *perdu* and *trouvé,* demonstrating perhaps by putting a pencil under a book:

J'ai perdu mon crayon, où est mon crayon?
Ah, voilà mon crayon. J'ai trouvé mon crayon.

It is not necessary to explain the perfect tense other than to give the set phrases *j'ai perdu/trouvé …* = I have lost/found ….

Next talk about the advert and photograph, introducing the expression *Il est comment?*, e.g.

Regardez le chat. Il est comment?
Il est gros ou petit?
De quelle couleur est-il?
Mais le chat dans la photo est perdu, non?
Mais Mme Robert a trouvé le chat? Alors il est à qui?

Écoutez les conversations au téléphone. Est-ce que le chat est à Mme Duval, à Claire Martin ou à François Léon?

Play the three telephone conversations, stopping after each one to let the class compare the details with the photo, perhaps asking some questions, e.g.

Il est comment, le chat de Mme Duval? Il est petit ou gros? Il est blanc?

At the end of the recording, take a vote by show of hands to see who the class thinks owns the cat (*François*).

transcript

Chat perdu

– Allô. C'est Mme Robert?
– Oui.
– Je m'appelle Mme Marie Duval. J'ai perdu mon chat et …

– Ah bon. Il est comment, votre chat?
– Eh bien, il est noir, tout noir, et il est très gros.

– Allô.
– Allô. Je m'appelle Claire Martin et j'ai perdu mon petit chat, Tigre.
– Bonjour, Claire. Il est comment, ton Tigre?
– Oh, il est adorable! Il est fantastique!
– Oui, oui, mais il est comment? Il est gros ou petit? Il est de quelle couleur?
– Ben, blanc, il est blanc, mais brun aussi, et noir, et jaune aussi. Enfin, il est de toutes les couleurs, mais surtout blanc.
– Et il est gros?
– Oh oui. Il est très, très gros. Il mange beaucoup. Il est énorme!

– Allô. C'est Mme Robert?
– Oui, oui, c'est moi. Je suis Mme Robert.
– Alors, madame, je pense que vous avez trouvé notre chat. Le chat sur la photo, c'est notre chat, Magique!
– Ah bon. Il est comment, Magique?
– Il n'est pas très gros, mais il n'est pas très petit. Il est gris, blanc et noir, avec les pattes blanches.
– Et toi, comment t'appelles-tu?
– Moi, je m'appelle François Léon.

Possibilities for further exploitation of this task:

1   Students could listen again to the recording and try to complete the descriptions of the three cats:

Le chat de Mme Duval est …
Le chat de Claire est …
Le chat de François est …

2   Groups of (able) students could make up similar telephone calls. One student could draw or write a description of a cat and the others could 'phone in' and try to claim it.

3   Students could write descriptions on the computer and import pictures of pets.

 **144 Au choix** AT4; AfL

3   Des animaux

Students write simple descriptions of the animals illustrated.

As follow-up, students can draw or use clip-art to produce posters with pictures and descriptions of the animals. They can then add text labels to their pictures.

Perhaps give the students a time limit and ask them to draw and label an animal in that time – sometimes this produces amusing results!

With the most able, this could lead to a game in which one describes the other's animal from memory. Alternatively, someone describes an animal and the other person draws it on the board following instructions. Agree criteria for success, e.g. whether the description matches the picture, and use for AfL. Remind students of the spread objectives.

 1 p8

Using adjectives – singular

These self-explanatory tasks give further practice in describing animals etc. and would be useful for homework, or later for consolidation.

Plenaries (pages 32–33)

 Fiche de travail (ws02)

1   Students summarise in pairs the rules for making adjectives agree. They then make up an exercise to test other students' understanding of the rules. Discuss what sort of exercise they might make up, e.g. match question and answer, gap-fill (with missing words in a box), translation.

2   Ask students to look at the objectives for SB pages 32–33: How well do they think they have done? Can they explain the main points to a partner? What did they find easy or difficult?

4C Tu as des questions?   pages 34–35

Aims and objectives	Grammar and skills	Resources
• learn how to ask questions • revise the singular of the verb *avoir* (to have)	**Grammar** *Avoir* (1st, 2nd and 3rd person singular) Asking questions using *Est-ce que…?* Shortening words before a vowel **Pronunciation** *à, as, a*	**Key language:** see p70 **Online resource:** *Unité 4* int04, ws02/05/06 **CD** 2 tracks 5–6 **GiA:** pp10–11

Starters (pages 34–35)

 Fiche de travail (ws02)

1 **Loto!** Have cards with names of animals ready to hand out to students as they come into the classroom (see online worksheet). Vocabulary used: *un animal, un chat, une chatte, un cheval, un chien, un cochon d'Inde, un hamster, un lapin, un oiseau, un perroquet, une perruche, un poisson, un rat, une souris, une tarentule.* Hold up flashcards, saying the word for what is portrayed on each. When checking back, students must say the words correctly. Students need to listen carefully because you can say *un animal, un oiseau,* and *une chatte.*

2 **Chaque mot à sa place** Display the grid and the words below at random (see online worksheet). Give students a few minutes to read and work out the answers, then ask *Quelle est la bonne case pour chaque mot?* Students should give the number of the box before confirming the correct answer. The first row is done as an example.

Some students might be able to explain what each category is.

words: *petite, une sœur, jaune, un livre, un chat, un cahier, un cheval, un chien, une cousine, un dictionnaire, grosse, marron, une mère, mignonne, rouge*

Solution:

1	2	3	4	5
un chat	**jaune**	**petite**	**un livre**	**une sœur**
un chien	rouge	grosse	un cahier	une mère
un cheval	marron	mignonne	un dictionnaire	une cousine

 34 **Dossier-langue** 7S1, 7S4

Asking questions

Ask students to look at all the questions in *Deux interviews* (below) to see how they all begin with *Est-ce que …* Make sure that they fully understand that a sentence can be turned into a question just by putting *Est-ce que …* at the beginning.

They could then practise turning more sentences into questions, e.g.

Charlotte habite en France.
Maman est dans la maison.
La radio est dans la cuisine.
Martin/Sandra est le frère/la sœur de Nicole.

This can be developed into a pair or team activity with one person making a statement and another turning it into a question. Students should be told to confine their statements to information about other people and things so they avoid such nonsensical questions as *Est-ce que je suis un garçon?* etc.

Some of the questions could be written down on slips of paper and then re-used, one student picking out a question at random and another answering it.

 34 ⊙ 2 tr 5 AT1, AT3; 7L3

1 Deux interviews

Students look at the questions about the two interviews and listen to the recording. Pause the recording so that students can write *Oui* or *Non* after each question.

Solution:

1 *Jean-Paul*	**a** *Oui*	**b** *Oui*	**c** *Non*
2 *Charlotte*	**a** *Non*	**b** *Oui*	**c** *Non*

 **transcript**

Deux interviews

Conversation 1

– Salut, Jean-Paul! Est-ce que tu as un animal à la maison?

– Oui, j'ai un chien. Il s'appelle Pirate.

– Est-ce qu'il est gros ou petit?

– Il est très gros et tout noir – très, très noir.

Conversation 2

– Bonjour, Charlotte.

– Bonjour.

– Est-ce que tu as un animal à la maison, Charlotte?

– Non, monsieur, mais mon frère a un animal. C'est un hamster.

– Tu n'aimes pas les animaux, toi?

– Ce n'est pas ça, monsieur. J'aime les animaux, mais notre famille habite dans un appartement à Paris.

– Ah bon, je comprends.

As a follow-up to these interviews, students could be asked to make up two more similar questions, using *Est-ce que,* and put them to other students.
e.g. **1** *Est-ce que tu as un animal …………?*
2 *Est-ce qu'il (elle) est …………?*

AT2

Asking questions

First, revise the questions already learnt by playing a chain question game. One student asks someone a question and if it is answered correctly, the second student asks a question of a third person etc.

Students could refer back to *Unité 3* for ideas.

 34 AT2; 7S4, 7L5

2 Inventez des conversations

This brings together the work on questions and answers about animals and should be practised orally in pairs.

The *Dossier-langue* reminds students of other question forms and question words that have been covered.

Activité (int04) AT1, AT2, AT3

Interview

This online activity provides further role-play practice of asking questions about pets.

144 Au choix AT2, AT3, AT4

4 Des questions

Students use the substitution table to help them make up six more questions. This can be a speaking or writing activity.

 1 pp10–11 AT4

Asking questions (1) and (2)

This full-page practice on the use of *Est-ce que …* (p10) and on asking questions with question words (p11) would be useful here for homework or for revision.

 **35** (AT2), AT4

3 Une description

Students should now be able to write (and perhaps record) a short description of one of their own or a friend's pets, using the models supplied here or on the writing frame (details below).

 Fiche de travail (ws05) AT4

Tu as un animal?

This online writing frame for describing pets can be adapted by giving different levels of support to suit students of varied abilities.

 **35 Dossier-langue** 7W5

Avoir (to have)

Students find the parts of the singular paradigm of *avoir* in the conversations in *Inventez des conversations* (above).

They can also discuss the points made about shortening *je*. Ask students if they can think of any other examples of this. If you wish, tell them this is called elision.

 **Fiche de travail (ws06)** AT3, AT4

Avoir

The first activity on this online worksheet practises recognition of the correct verb form. This is followed by an extended gap-fill text.

 **35** ● **2 tr 6** AT1, AT2; 7W6, 7L1

Prononciation

Practice in working out from the context whether a word is spelt *as*, *a* or *à*.

■ **Solution:** **1** *as*, **2** *a*, **3** *a*, **4** *a*, **5** *as*, *à*, **6** *à*, *a*

transcript

Prononciation

1 Tu **as** un chat, Daniel?
2 Non, mais ma sœur **a** un petit chien.
3 Quel âge **a**-t-il?
4 Il **a** deux ans.
5 Et toi? Tu **as** un animal **à** la maison?
6 Non. Mais mon cousin habite **à** la campagne et il **a** beaucoup d'animaux.

 **35** AT3, AT4; 7W5, 7S9

4 Questions et réponses

In this three-part activity, students complete the questions with a part of *avoir*, then they complete the answers and finally they match up the correct question and answer.

■ **Solution:**

a **1** *as*, **2** *as*, **3** *as*, **4** *a*, **5** *as*, **6** *ai*
b **a** *a*, **b** *ai*, **c** *a*, **d** *ai, a*, **e** *ai*, **f** *a*
c **1** f, **2** e, **3** d, **4** a, **5** b, **6** c

 **145 Au choix** AT3

5 La chasse à l'intrus

Use this activity at any point in the unit after teaching *avoir*. In addition to spotting the odd one out, more able students could explain their choice, e.g. 10 – *brun* is masculine, the others are feminine. Encourage them to use phrases like *c'est masculin, c'est féminin, c'est un animal, c'est une couleur*, etc.

This activity could also be used as a starter.

■ **Solution:** **1** *vingt*, **2** *oui*, **3** *une maison*, **4** *un garçon*, **5** *gros*, **6** *la cuisine*, **7** *un cheval*, **8** *Paris*, **9** *treize*, **10** *brun*, **11** *à**, **12** *très*

* The correct answer is intended to be **à** because it is not part of **avoir**. However, if anyone suggests that **ai** sounds different, this could also be counted as correct as long as the explanation is given.

Plenaries (pages 34–35)

 Fiche de travail (ws02) AfL

1 Students work in pairs and explain the ways they know of making a question. This should include adding *Est-ce que …* and using intonation, but they may be able to talk about inversion and using some question words from *Unités 1–4*. They report back and share any tips on asking questions. This activity is suitable for AfL. Remind students of the spread objectives and agree the criteria for success (perhaps related to how useful the tips are).

2 Students make up a wordsearch (using the 10 x 10 square grid provided on the online worksheet) to include approximately 12 items of vocabulary from the unit so far. They then exchange these and find the words and write them down with their English meaning.

Follow this with reflection and discussion, e.g. did students all choose similar words and if so, why? Which sort of words were chosen (adjectives, nouns) and is this because they are easier to learn? Did certain groups of letters 'pop out' at them from the wordsearch?

4D Tu aimes ça? Et vous aussi? pages 36–37

Aims and objectives	Grammar and skills	Resources
• learn how to give opinions • learn two ways to say 'you'	**Grammar** *tu* and *vous* Making plurals using –x **Skills** Expressing opinions	**Key language:** see p70 **Online resource:** *Unité 4* int 05/06, ppt02/03, ws02/07 **Copymasters:** 4/3, 4/4, 4/5 **CD** 2 track 7 **GiA:** p9

Starters (pages 36–37)

 Fiche de travail (ws02)

1 Chasse à l'intrus (see online worksheet) Display or print out five sets of words from the unit, e.g.

1	2	3	4	5
un cheval un oiseau une souris un jeu	rouge jaune orange bleu	mignon petit gros grande	aime déteste beaucoup adore	as aimes es préfère

Students work in pairs to say which is the odd one out in each set, and why. There could be several reasons for being the odd one out (e.g. **1** – *jeu* is not an animal; *souris* is feminine; *souris* doesn't have a plural in -x). They then try to add one more word to each set which will not alter the odd one out.

2 Quelle est la question? On the board, display a number of answers to questions (see online worksheet) – students have to say what the question could be. There will be several possibilities for some of them. Some question beginnings are provided as a stimulus. e.g.

J'habite dans un appartement.
Oui, il s'appelle Ben.
Non, il est bleu.
Elle est noire.
Non, je déteste les chats.
J'ai douze ans.
Je préfère les jeux vidéo.

(list of question beginnings)

Comment …? Qu'est-ce que …?
De quelle couleur …? Quel …?
Est-ce que …? Tu aimes …?
Où …? Tu préfères …?

The online worksheets can be displayed on the whiteboard or printed out later and set as homework.

 **36** ● **2 tr 7** **AT1, AT3; 7S6, 7T1, 7L2**

1 Des animaux extraordinaires

This recorded passage contains a few new words, of which the most important is *parce que*. Others, probably guessable, are *extraordinaires, par exemple* and *naturellement*.

Introducing language which is unfamiliar or more challenging can help students in a number of ways. It is useful for them to understand the gist of a written or spoken sentence without necessarily knowing every word. They should also learn to understand compound sentences, using whatever cues and details are available.

Draw attention to the *Stratégies* on opinions (see below) either before part **a** of the item or before doing part **b**.

Adopt some of the suggested strategies for using recorded text to teach reading. The text is also provided as an online activity (see ICT activity (int05) below), which allows it to be presented in smaller chunks and used for different skills.

Once students are familiar with the text, they can do the *vrai/faux* task in **b**, which focuses on likes and dislikes.

Solution: 1 *vrai*, **2** *vrai*, **3** *faux*, **4** *faux*, **5** *vrai*, **6** *faux*, **7** *vrai*, **8** *faux*, **9** *faux*, **10** *faux*

Further questions could also be asked on this passage, e.g.

Est-ce qu'Éric habite dans un appartement?
Est-ce qu'il aime les chiens et les chats?
Comment s'appelle le chien de Marc?
Qu'est-ce qu'il aime? etc.

transcript

Des animaux extraordinaires

Je m'appelle Éric Garnier. J'habite dans une ferme, près de Toulouse. J'aime beaucoup les animaux, mais à la maison, il y a des animaux extraordinaires … Par exemple, il y a Télé. C'est le petit chien noir de mon frère, Marc. Il s'appelle Télé parce qu'il adore la télévision.

Et il y a aussi Blanco, le petit chat de Maman. Naturellement, il s'appelle Blanco parce qu'il est blanc. Il déteste la télévision, mais il aime beaucoup la radio et il adore la musique.

Eh bien, Télé aime la télévision, mais Blanco préfère la radio … voilà, c'est très bien … mais non! Ce n'est pas très bien parce qu'il y a aussi Jules et quelquefois, il y a Néron. Jules est le perroquet de ma sœur, Claire. Il est petit et très mignon, mais il n'aime pas la télévision, il n'aime pas la radio et il déteste la musique.

Et Néron, qui est-il? Eh bien … Néron est un gros chien noir et blanc. C'est le chien de mon grand-père et il est très méchant. Il déteste les chats, il déteste les perroquets, il déteste la radio, il déteste la musique et il n'aime pas beaucoup le chien de Marc. Alors, qu'est-ce qu'il aime, Néron? Il aime deux choses: mon grand-père et le football … à la télévision, naturellement! Il adore ça!

Activité (int05) AT3, AT4

Extraordinaire!

This set of online activities provides support and extension for *Des animaux extraordinaires* (above).

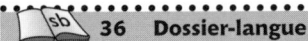 **36 Dossier-langue** 7W4

Plurals – the x factor!

This covers nouns forming their plural with *-x*. By this stage, students may want to say they have more than one particular animal or possession. For most nouns this is not a problem, but the few that form their plural with *-x* are presented here.

 Présentation (ppt02) AT2

Jeu de mémoire: Les animaux

Kim's game – this includes animals of different colours and practice of plurals with *-x*.

 **36 Stratégies** 7S5, 7T7

Useful ways of expressing your opinion

This item presents the verb phrases for expressing likes and dislikes. Make sure students understand the symbols.

 **37** AT3, AT4; 7T5

2 Et toi? Tu aimes ça?

Using the words in the box to help them, students write their own statements of likes, dislikes and preferences, completing each of the sentences 1 to 7. The completed sentences can form part of students' *Dossier personnel*.

As a follow-up, students can make a symbol chart of their own similar to the one on SB 36, using hearts and crosses to be found in a number of symbol fonts.

They could then make up their own sheet of likes and dislikes, e.g.

J'adore les chats.
J'aime beaucoup les ordinateurs.
J'aime le français.
Je n'aime pas beaucoup ma chambre.
Je n'aime pas les souris.
Je déteste les tarentules.

 **4/3** AT4

C'est moi!

This could be done now, or at the end of the unit as consolidation. Students complete their self-portrait, filling in the blanks to give name, age, address and an account of their possessions and preferences.

The corrected version of this sheet could become part of their *Dossier personnel*.

 **145 Au choix** AT3

6 Un échange

Students read through the cartoon strip and decide whether the statements are true or false.

Solution: **1** *vrai*, **2** *faux*, **3** *faux*, **4** *faux*, **5** *vrai*, **6** *faux*, **7** *faux*, **8** *faux*

 **37** AT3; 7W2

3 Qui dit ça?

Students match the correct captions to the cartoons, choosing mainly on the basis of whether *tu* or *vous* is used.

To check answers, ask students to read out the complete captions. Discuss why *tu* or *vous* has been used in each case and refer to the *Dossier-langue* which follows.

Solution: **1** D, **2** H, **3** B, **4** C, **5** E, **6** F, **7** A, **8** G

 **37 Dossier-langue** 7W2, 7C5

'You'

Go through the brief explanation with the students and, to check if they have understood it, ask them to explain the rule to each other in English. The PowerPoint presentation (below) can also be used.

 Présentation (ppt03) AT3

Tu ou vous?

This PowerPoint presentation introduces graphically the situations where *tu* and *vous* are used.

 **37** AT2; 7S4, 7L5; AfL

4 Invente des questions

This activity should be used with the *Dossier-langue* to practise the use of *tu* and *vous*. Make sure students understand the rule and work through a few examples as a whole-class activity before students make up questions in pairs. This is an opportunity for AfL. Agree the criteria for success, reminding students of the spread objectives.

Finally, collate answers as a class.

 Fiche de travail (ws07) AT3

S'il vous plaît ...?

This online worksheet practises recognition of the correct usage of *tu* and *vous*.

 **4/4** AT2, AT3, AT4

Questions et réponses

Students compile the complete conversation script, using questions from the box. When they have completed the two conversations, students can read them aloud in pairs, and some could be recorded.

The next copymaster provides follow-up speaking practice.

Solution: **A** **a** 2, **b** 3, **c** 9, **d** 5, **e** 4
B **f** 7, **g** 6, **h** 8, **i** 1, **j** 10

 **4/5** AT2

Des conversations au choix

This is a follow-up to CM 4/4. The first activity involves throwing a die or choosing questions in turns and answering from a choice of suggestions or with invented answers. Demonstrate this process first.

This is followed by a survey about pets.

 **1 p9**

Using *tu* or *vous*

This page of the Grammar in Action book provides further practice and could be used for homework or later for revision.

 Activité (int06)   **AT1, AT3**

Rue Danton: Alpha adore le foot

This is a suitable point to use the fourth episode in the ongoing soap story. Give the vocabulary item *une tortue*, or ask students if they can deduce it.

Plenaries (pages 36–37)

 Fiche de travail (ws02)

1   In pairs, students discuss the *tu/vous* rule. What do they think of the rule? Is it better in English, where there's just one word for you?

    They could then go on to make a list of five people/ groups of people/pets, etc. that would be addressed as *tu* or *vous*, writing the appropriate word next to each. They could then change pairs and see whether they agree with each other's answers.

2   In pairs, students tell each other the two most useful, interesting or strange things they have learnt in this unit so far. They then compare with other pairs. This could lead to whole-class comparison/ranking of aspects of the unit so far.

4E   Un zoo extraordinaire   pages 38–39

Aims and objectives	Grammar and skills	Resources
• practise language you have learnt	**Pronunciation** The letter *i* Words spelt the same in French and English	**Key language:** see p70 **Online resource:** *Unité* 4 int07/08, ppt04, ws02/08 **Copymasters:** 4/6, 4/7 **CD** 2 tracks 8–12 **GiA:** p12

Starters (pages 38–39)

 Fiche de travail (ws02)

1   Reinforce the focus on masculine and feminine. Present an assortment of 12–15 nouns students have learnt so far, without articles (see below and online worksheet). Read out the list of words. Students hold up a blue card if the word is masculine, red if feminine.

    Suggested vocabulary: *livre, maison, souris, chaise, poisson, fenêtre, tarentule, jardin, ordinateur, grand-père, chambre, lapin, cousine, appartement, perruche, fils.*

2   **Loto!** Use items of vocabulary from this unit (see online worksheet).

    Suggested vocabulary: *blanc, un chat, marron, jaune, un chien, vert, gros, un lapin, j'aime, rouge, énorme, un poisson, je déteste, une souris, mignon.*

    As an alternative, play 'strip bingo' (see TB 21). Students choose any four (or more) items from the list of vocabulary to be used and write the lists quickly themselves.

 **38**   **AT3; 7W2**

1 C'est extraordinaire

A matching task with some strange animals in odd colours. This practises the colours in a slightly different context.

   Solution: 1 e, **2** a, **3** f, **4** c, **5** d, **6** b, **7** h, **8** g

As follow-up, give the class three minutes to see how many words other than colours they can find in the picture (animals, singulars and plurals, etc.).

 **38   Stratégies**   **7W7**

Students should be able to guess the meaning of the names of animals as most are cognates or near cognates. The exception is *ours*, although students keen on astronomy (or Latin) may be able to work it out. In preparation for the *Prononciation* activities, students should think about the differences in spelling and pronunciation between French and English. It is also worth noting that all these animals are masculine except *une girafe*.

 **38**   **2 tr 8–9**   **AT1, AT2; 7W6, 7L1**

Prononciation

a Écoute et répète

Pronunciation practice of the zoo animals. Pay particular attention to the sound of the letter *i* (see the note with part **b** in the SB) and to the final *s* on *ours*.

b C'est quel mot?

A listening discrimination activity to point out the differences between the French and English pronunciation of similar words. Students note the language (F or A) of the animal last mentioned.

   Solution: 1 F, **2** F, **3** A, **4** A, **5** F, **6** F

transcript

Prononciation

a   Écoute et répète

1 un lion   5 un éléphant
2 un tigre   6 un chameau
3 une girafe   7 un ours
4 un zèbre   8 un gorille

b   C'est quel mot?

1 lion (F), lion (A) – lion (F)
2 tigre, tiger – tigre
3 gorille, gorilla – gorilla
4 girafe, giraffe – giraffe
5 éléphant, elephant – éléphant
6 hippopotame, hippotamus – hippopotame

 **38**   **AT2, AT4; 7W2, 7S9; AfL**

2   Trouve les couleurs

These two short activities focus on using the colours. Collate answers to the first part on the board. Students could read out their answers to the second part in pairs or small groups – this is an opportunity for them to demonstrate their skills and be assessed by others on accuracy and pronunciation. Remind students of the unit objectives and agree the criteria for success.

 **38**   **AT2, AT4; 7L5; AfL**

3   Invente des descriptions

In this two-part open-ended activity, students practise forming their own sentences about the zoo animals. The final part gives them the opportunity to make up and describe their own weird animal. The results could form a classroom display.

As a follow-up, students could make up four questions about animals They should ask another student two of these and ask the teacher the other two. (This gives extra practice of *tu* and *vous*.)

This activity consolidates the work of the rest of the page and brings in the added dimension of forming questions. This could be done orally or in writing. Once again, the questions and their answers could be used for peer assessment. Refer students to the unit objectives and agree the criteria for success. Students use this as an opportunity to demonstrate their skills.

 **1 p 12**

Asking questions (3) – using question words

These self-explanatory tasks give further practice in asking questions and would be useful for homework, or could be used later for consolidation.

 Activité (int07)   **AT1, AT3**

Vocabulaire de classe (4)

This online activity practises some more key classroom language.

 **Présentation (ppt04)/Fiche de travail (ws08) AT3**

Le sais-tu? Les animaux

This reader provides extension material with interesting facts about animals, including the sounds some common French animals make.

Use the PowerPoint for whole-class presentation of the reader.

4/6   2 tr 10–12   AT1

Tu comprends?

1   Ma chambre

Students listen to the recording and colour the picture.

transcript

Ma chambre

1 Mon lit est bleu.
2 Sur mon lit, il y a un classeur jaune et un livre brun.
3 Près de mon lit, il y a une chaise rouge.
4 Près de la table, il y a une chaise blanche.
5 La table est brune.
6 Mon ordinateur est sur la table. L'ordinateur est noir.
7 Puis il y a la porte. La porte est verte.
8 Mon chat est sur le lit, il est gris et blanc.
9 Sur la table, il y a deux crayons rouges et un taille-crayon orange.

2   Où sont les animaux?

Students draw a line to show where each animal is in the flat.

transcript

Où sont les animaux?

Aujourd'hui, il y a beaucoup d'animaux dans l'appartement. Le chat est dans la chambre de mes parents. Le poisson rouge est dans la salle de bains. La souris est dans la salle de séjour. Le chien est dans ma chambre. Le perroquet est dans la cuisine et le lapin est dans la salle à manger.

3   Qu'est-ce que c'est?

Students listen and write down the words dictated. They then spot the odd one out.

Solution: 4 *calculatrice*

Qu'est-ce que c'est?

1	dimanche (spelt out)	4	calculatrice
2	mercredi	5	lundi
3	vendredi	6	jeudi

 **39** **4/7**

Sommaire

A summary of the main language of the unit. This is also provided on copymaster.

 Activité (int08) **AT3**

Vocabulaire (4)

An online game which tests the vocabulary of the unit.

Plenaries (pages 38–39)

Fiche de travail (ws02)

1 **Think, pair and share**. In pairs, students choose one of the objectives for the unit (these could be allocated so that they are all covered), they discuss it for five minutes in pairs, then they share their findings with the class.

2 Discuss what students have been able to include in their *Dossier personnel* at the end of this unit. Students could assess how far they have come in the first four units and summarise what they now know.

Unité 4 Consolidation and assessment

Épreuves Unité 4

These worksheets can be used for an informal test of listening, reading and writing or for extra practice, as required.

For general notes on the *Épreuves*, see TB 20.

 4/8 Écouter **2 tr 13–16**

A Les animaux

Solution: **1** b, **2** c, **3** e, **4** d, **5** f, **6** a *mark* **/5**

Les animaux

1 Voici mon chien. C'est mon chien.
2 Et voici mon chat. C'est mon chat.
3 Et voilà ma souris, ma souris blanche.
4 J'ai aussi un cochon d'Inde. Mon cochon d'Inde s'appelle Dodu.
5 Puis voici ma perruche. C'est ma perruche bleue.
6 Et voilà mon lapin. Le lapin s'appelle Pierrot.

B Comment ça s'écrit?

Solution: as transcript

Comment ça s'écrit?

1 V–A–N–I–L–L–E
2 C A R O T T E
3 M I N O U
4 L A R O C H E L L E
5 P A R I S
6 B L A N C O

mark /5

C C'est quelle image?

Solution: **1** a, **2** b, **3** a, **4** a, **5** b, **6** b mark /5

C'est quelle image?

1 – Est-ce que tu as un animal à la maison?
  – Oui, j'ai un oiseau. C'est une perruche. Regarde, elle est dans sa cage.
2 – Est-ce que tu as un animal, David?
  – Oui, j'ai des poissons. J'ai trois poissons rouges.
3 – Voici mon cheval. Il est super, non?
  – Oui, oui. Il est tout blanc. Il est fantastique, ton cheval!
4 – Regarde! Dans la boîte, il y a deux petits hamsters.
  – Ah oui, ils sont mignons, tes petits hamsters! Tu as des lapins aussi?
  – Non, je n'ai pas de lapins.
5 – Attention! Ton chat est sur la table!
  – Ah non! Maman, Minou est sur la table!
6 – Voici ton prix. C'est un livre sur les animaux.
  – Oh, merci beaucoup. J'aime beaucoup les animaux.

D Un sondage: Aimez-vous les chiens?

Solution: **1** a, **2** b, **3** c, **4** a, **5** d, **6** a mark /5

Un sondage: Aimez-vous les chiens?

1 – Tu aimes les chiens?
  – Oui, j'aime les chiens.

2 – Qu'est-ce que vous préférez, mademoiselle, les chiens ou les chats?
  – J'adore tous les animaux. J'adore les chiens.

3 – Est-ce que vous aimez les chiens, monsieur?
  – Non, pas beaucoup. Enfin, non, je n'aime pas les animaux.

4 – Est-ce que tu aimes les chiens, Linda?
  – Bien sûr. J'ai deux chiens et je les aime.

5 – Tu aimes les chiens, Richard?
  – Ah non. J'aime les chats, mais je déteste les chiens. Ils sont souvent méchants!

6 – Monsieur, on pose des questions sur les chiens. Est-ce que vous aimez les chiens?
  – Euh, les chiens, oui, ça va. Oui, oui, j'aime les chiens, mais je préfère les chats. Les chats sont plus indépendants.

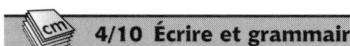 **4/9 Lire**

A Les animaux et les couleurs

Pictures to be checked for correct colouring.
mark /7

B C'est quelle description?

Solution: **1** b, **2** a, **3** a, **4** a, **5** a, **6** b   mark /5

C Chez la famille Marchadier

Solution: **1** V, **2** V, **3** V, **4** F, **5** V, **6** F, **7** F, **8** V, **9** F   mark /8

 **4/10 Écrire et grammaire**

A Un serpent

Solution: **1** un chien, **2** une perruche, **3** un chat, **4** un cheval, **5** un poisson, **6** une souris, **7** un perroquet   mark /6

B Masculin ou féminin?

Solution: **1** petit, **2** mignonne, **3** grande, **4** jolie, **5** blanche, **6** grand, **7** gros   mark /6

C Des questions

To be marked by the teacher.
mark /8

sb 40–41 cm 103–108

Presse-Jeunesse 1

These pages provide reading for pleasure. They can be used alone or with the accompanying copymasters.

See also the notes on TB page 4.

 **sb 40–41 cm 103, 128   AT2, AT3, AT4**

Bonjour, Mangetout!

Solution:

A Complète les phrases

1 chat, **2** habite, **3** sœurs, **4** aime, **5** poisson, viande, **6** Calinette

B Dans l'ordre alphabétique

aimer – to like, aussi – also, beaucoup – a lot/ very much, dans – in, dormir – to sleep, et – and, manger – to eat, pourquoi? – why?, tout – all/ everything

Le sais-tu?
La France

This is part of a series, some of which appears in other Presse-Jeunesse sections and also in online Readers. This item is also linked with the copymaster which is based on the map of France at the beginning of the Student's Book.

Students read the article and do the short tasks on copymaster. Teachers could, if wished, do a short explanation about the superlative to go with this item.

Solution:

A Trouve les mots français

1 la capitale   **2** une montagne
3 une tour   **4** du parfum
5 célèbre   **6** une cathédrale
7 un village   **8** tout le monde
9 une ville   **10** un pays

B Complète les phrases

1 Paris
2 la France
3 le Mont Blanc
4 la tour Eiffel
5 Notre-Dame

Chimène!

This can just be read for enjoyment of the story, and perhaps discussed in pairs, or followed by the copymaster activity.

Solution:

Trouve les paires

1 h, **2** d, **3** g, **4** e, **5** f, **6** b, **7** a, **8** c

Tricolore Total 1

Unité 5 Des fêtes et des festivals   pages 42–57

Aims and objectives	Key language/Culture	Grammar and skills	National criteria
5A L'année en France pp42–43 • ask for and give the date • learn about saints' days and other festivals	Months of the year Quelle est la date aujourd'hui? C'est le trente août. C'est quand, le concert/le match/ta fête? C'est le mardi premier juin. Festivals: Pâques/mardi gras/fête des Mères/la fête de la musique **Culture** Saints' days and fêtes	**Skills** Analysing spellings in French and English **Pronunciation** Comparing pronunciation of months in French and English	**Attainment** AT1 Level 1–3, AT2 Level 1–2, AT3 Level 1–3, AT4 Level 1–2 **Framework** 7W2/6/7, 7L1/3/6, 7C2 **Languages ladder/Asset languages** Grades 1–3 **Assessment for learning** ex 3
5B En France, c'est la fête pp44–45 • find out about festivals and events in France • learn greetings for special days • learn how to work out new vocabulary	le jour de l'An/la fête nationale/Noël/la Saint-Sylvestre/la fête de l'Eid/la fête des lumières Greetings: Bonne année/Joyeuses Pâques/Joyeux Noël/Bon anniversaire/Bonne fête **Culture** Festivals in France	**Skills** Working out meanings of new words	**Attainment** AT1 Level 1–3, AT2 Level 1–2, AT3 Level 1–3, AT4 Level 1 **Framework** 7W7/8, 7T1, 7L3, 7C2 **Languages ladder/Asset languages** Grades 1–3 **Assessment for learning** ex 3, ex 4
5C Mardi gras pp46–47 • talk about a Shrove Tuesday fancy dress party • practise using the verb être (to be)	être (present tense)	**Grammar** Present tense of être **Pronunciation** The letters é, è, ê	**Attainment** AT1 Level 1–3, AT2 Level 1–2, AT3 Level 1–3, AT4 Level 1–2 **Framework** 7W5/6, 7S8, 7T1/5, 7L1/3 **Languages ladder/Asset languages** Grades 1–3 **Assessment for learning** ex 4
5D Ton anniversaire, c'est quand? pp48–49 • talk about birthday dates and presents • practise using adjectives	C'est quand, ton anniversaire? Mon anniversaire est le quinze mars. C'est le dix-neuf juillet.	**Grammar** Adjective agreement **Skills** Learning irregular adjectives	**Attainment** AT1 Level 1–5, AT2 Level 1–5, AT3 Level 1–3, AT4 Level 1 **Framework** 7W4/7/8, 7S2/3/4/6, 7T2, 7L3/6 **Languages ladder/Asset languages** Grades 1–5 **Assessment for learning** ex 4
5E Des cadeaux pour tout le monde pp50–51 • learn the words for some more presents • learn some higher numbers and prices	un baladeur audio et vidéo/un ballon de foot/un billet (pour le cinéma)/des bracelets en métal argenté/une casquette/une ceinture/des chaussettes/une collection papeterie/un DVD/un jean à 5 poches/un livre de poche/des lunettes de soleil/une montre/le parfum chic fantaisie Voici un petit cadeau pour toi/vous. C'est très gentil. Merci beaucoup. De rien. Qu'est-ce que tu as reçu? J'ai reçu des vêtements. numbers 70–100, 100–999 **Culture** Saying and writing prices in euros	**Skills** Working out meanings **Grammar** Number patterns from 69 to 100s. **Pronunciation** The letters qu **Cross-curricular** Numeracy	**Attainment** AT1 Level 1–3, AT2 Level 1–2, AT3 Level 1–2, AT4 Level 1 **Framework** 7W2/6/7, 7T1, 7L1/2/3 **Languages ladder/Asset languages** Grades 1–3 **Assessment for learning** ex 2
5F Des vêtements pp52–53 • learn the French for some clothes • practise plurals	baskets (f pl)/casquette (f)/chaussette (f)/chaussure (f)/chemise (f)/cravate (f)/jogging (m)/lupe (f)/maillot (de foot) (m)/pantalon (m)/pull (m)/robe (f)/sandales (f pl)/short (m)/sweat (m)/t-shirt (m)/tennis (f pl) favori	**Grammar** Plurals **Skills** Identifying nouns, verbs and adjectives **Pronunciation** Pronunciation of clothes vocabulary (cognates and plurals)	**Attainment** AT1 Level 1–3, AT2 Level 1–2, AT3 Level 1–3, AT4 Level 1–3 **Framework** 7W2/4, 7T1, 7L1/2/5 **Languages ladder/Asset languages** Grades 1–3 **Assessment for learning** ex 4
5G Les descriptions personnelles pp54–55 • describe yourself and other people • practise using the verb avoir	avoir (present tense) J'ai/Il a/Elle a les cheveux ... longs/courts/frisés/raides/noirs/blonds/roux/bruns/châtains J'ai/Il a/Elle a les yeux ... marron/verts/bleus/gris Je/Il/Elle porte des lunettes Je suis/Il est/Elle est grand(e)/petit(e)	**Grammar** Present tense of avoir	**Attainment** AT1 Level 1–3, AT2 Level 1–4, AT3 Level 1–3, AT4 Level 1–3 **Framework** 7W2/5, 7S2/9, 7T3/5, 7L3/5 **Languages ladder/Asset languages** Grades 1–3 **Assessment for learning** ex 6, ex 7, CM 5/8
5H Écoutez bien! pp56–57 • develop and practise your listening skills	Consolidation	**Skills** Improving listening skills	**Attainment** AT1 Level 1–3, AT3 Level 1, AT4 Level 1 **Framework** 7W6, 7S4, 7L1/3 **Languages ladder/Asset languages** Grades 1–3 **Assessment for learning** ex 5

Other resources: Online resource Unité 5. Copymasters 5/1–5/13. CD 2 tracks 17–42. GIA pp13–16

5A L'année en France pages 42–43

Aims and objectives	Grammar and skills	Resources
• ask for and give the date • learn about saints' days and other festivals	**Skills** Analysing spellings in French and English **Pronunciation** Comparing pronunciation of months in French and English	**Key language:** see p85 **Online resource:** *Unité 5* int01, ws02/03 **Copymasters:** 5/1 **CD** 2 tracks 17–18

Starters (pages 42–43)

 Fiche de travail (ws02)

1 Display a selection of numbers from 1–31 for a game of *Effacez!*

2 **En groupes** Display a list of words in random order or hand this out on paper (see online worksheet). Ask students to put these into four groups, which are:

mardi, jeudi, samedi
je, tu, il
le frère, le père, l'ami
un lapin, un oiseau, une souris

Introduction

Go through the objectives for this spread.

The date

Before using the Student's Book pages, teach the date in oral and written form.

Suggested order:

Numbers

Revise the numbers 1–31 orally, perhaps using some of the number games (see TB 21).

Days of the week

a Write some days on the board, missing some out – students read them out and fill in the blanks.

b Play *Loto* with four days (or four days and four numbers) written on a piece of paper.

Months

Next, teach the months orally, in batches of three months at a time, then write these on the board.

For practice, play games such as *Chef d'orchestre, Effacez!, Loto!*, Pelmanism (see TB 21–24).

Use a French calendar, if available, for practice, e.g. *C'est* (+ month), *Oui, c'est* (+ month) if correct, or *Non, c'est* (+ correct month).

Teach *premier* and *dernier*, e.g. *Le premier mois, c'est …? Le dernier mois, c'est novembre? Non, le dernier mois, c'est décembre.*

The full date

Teach and practise the full date orally and eventually in written form, starting from today's date. Then teach and practise *le premier* before going on to other full dates. Give plenty of practice, e.g. by dictating some to be written down in figures, asking students to supply the date of the days before and after. Play *Effacez!* with the dates written in figures.

 42–43 ● 2 tr 17 AT1; 7W2, 7L3

1 Quelle est la date?

Students should look at the fourteen dates before listening to the recording. They then note down which date is linked with each conversation.

Solution: **1** L, **2** A, **3** I, **4** C, **5** E, **6** G, **7** F, **8** B, **9** H, **10** J

 transcript

Quelle est la date?

1 – C'est quand, l'anniversaire de Christophe?
– C'est le premier novembre.

2 – Salut.
– Salut. Ça va?
– Oui, ça va.
– Tu vas au grand match de foot, Marseille contre Saint-Étienne?
– C'est quand, le match?
– C'est le dimanche 20 janvier.
– Oui, je veux bien.

3 – Hé, Françoise, tu vas au concert?
– C'est quand, le concert?
– C'est le dimanche 10 août.
– Le dix août, hmm … je ne sais pas.

4 – Salut, Pascale. Tu vas à la soirée chez Noah?
– Non … c'est quand?
– C'est le jeudi 14 février.

5 – La fête au club des jeunes, c'est quand?
– C'est le mercredi deux avril.

6 – La fête de la musique, c'est quand, cette année?
  – C'est le 21 juin. C'est un samedi.
  – Excellent! J'adore ça!

7 – C'est quand, la fête des Mères?
  – C'est dimanche, le 25 mai.

8 – Mardi gras, c'est quand, cette année?
  – C'est le 5 février.

9 – Thomas, c'est quand, ta fête?
  – C'est le 3 juillet.

10 – Ingrid, c'est quand, ta fête?
  – Ma fête, c'est le deux septembre.

 42 2 tr 18 AT1; 7W6, 7L1

Prononciation

Les mois

This listening discrimination activity focuses on the similarities and differences between the pronunciation of the French and English names of the months.

Solution: **1** F, **2** F, **3** E, **4** F, **5** E, **6** F, **7** E, **8** E, **9** F, **10** F

Prononciation: Les mois

1 janvier, January – janvier
2 juillet, July – juillet
3 octobre, October – October
4 April, avril – avril
5 décembre, December – December
6 mars, March – mars
7 juin, June – June
8 February, février – February
9 septembre, September – septembre
10 November, novembre – novembre

 42 Stratégies 7W7

The months

This item focuses on the similarities and differences between the written forms of the French and English names of the months.

Solution: **1** all begin with same letter, **2** end in *-re* and *décembre* has accent **3** *février, août, décembre,* **4** begin with small letter in French

Activité (int01) AT1, AT3

C'est quelle date?

This online activity provides multiple-choice and matching tasks on dates.

 42 AT4; 7W2

2 Des dates

Students complete the dates with the correct day and month.

Solution: **1** *cinq février,* **2** *quatorze février,* **3** *deux avril,* **4** *deux septembre,* **5** *vingt janvier,* **6** *vingt-trois mars*

 Fiche de travail (ws03) AT3, AT4

C'est ma fête

This online worksheet gives practice in writing the date.

 43 AT2, AT4; 7L6; AfL

3 C'est quand?

One student asks for the date of an event and the other replies by referring to the calendar slips. If preferred, this could be done as a written task.

Solution:
1 *C'est le vingt janvier.*
2 *C'est le cinq février.*
3 *C'est le vingt et un juin.*
4 *C'est le six décembre.*
5 *C'est le premier novembre.*
6 *C'est le quatorze février.*
7 *C'est le trente et un décembre.*
8 *C'est le dix août.*

As follow-up, students could ask each other in turn the date for other events, e.g.
– *La fête des Mères, c'est quand?*
– *C'est le vingt-cinq mai.*

This is an opportunity for peer assessment. Remind students of the spread objectives and agree the criteria for success.

 43 AT3; 7C2

4 Bonne fête

This short reading passage gives some background information about the traditional practice of naming French children after saints and celebrating the saint's day as their *fête*. France is a catholic country and, in the past, everyone had to be given the name of a saint as a Christian name. Whereas laws still govern what you can call a child, names now often reflect celebrities, popular TV soaps, etc., as elsewhere in the world.

When students have read the text, they should find the *fêtes* for the names listed and answer the questions orally and/or in writing.

If students enquire why *la* is used with the names of masculine saints, point out that *la Saint-Olivier* is short for *la fête de Saint Olivier.*

Solution: **1** *C'est le 31 décembre,* **2** *C'est le 6 décembre,* **3** *C'est le 25 mai,* **4** *C'est le 5 février,* **5** *C'est le 25 octobre,* **6** *C'est le 2 septembre,* **7** *C'est le 23 mars,* **8** *C'est le 3 juillet*

5B En France, c'est la fête

 43   AT3

Students might use the internet to research saints' days. Information can be downloaded for use off-line.

For further research on names, students might like to look on the internet for lists of the most popular names for different years (search for '*prénoms populaires France*' to find a number of useful sites).

 5/1   AT2

Des dates

In this information-gap task, students have to find out details about dates and events.

 146 Au choix   AT4

1 Les mois de l'année

In this short task, students write out several different months.

> **Solution: 1** *mars,* **2** *avril,* **3** *août,* **4** *novembre,*
> **5** *janvier,* **6** *décembre,* **7** *mai,* **8** *septembre*

       AT2

Avant/après

This game provides good practice of days and dates. Start by saying, e.g. *C'est le jeudi 15 mars.* Then say, e.g. *Deux jours après* and point to a student (as they don't know who is going to be picked, everyone has to think about the answer). The chosen student should reply *C'est le samedi 17 mars.* Using this date or a new one, point to another student and say, e.g. *Un jour avant.* Keep up a brisk pace. This could also be played in groups.

 146 Au choix   AT4

2 L'année prochaine

This task is best done before or near the beginning of a new year. Students consult a calendar and note down the days and dates of significant events, birthdays, Easter, etc.

Additional activities/Consolidation

Jeu: Rendez-vous?

Students note down two free days in a diary for next week. They then work in pairs to see if they have a free day in common and to see who is first to discover the other person's two free days. They can then play the game again with other partners and continue until they find another person with the same free days as theirs.

Tu es libre le lundi 27 janvier?
Non. Et toi, tu es libre le jeudi 31 janvier?
Oui. Voilà. Alors rendez-vous le jeudi 31 janvier.

Plenaries (pages 42–43)

     Fiche de travail (ws02)

1 Students should discuss tips for remembering the sound and spelling of the days, months and numbers up to 31. These tips could be collated and assessed by others for their usefulness, perhaps by a show of hands for those who found it helpful.

2 Ask students to look at the objectives for pages 42–43: how well do they think they have done? Can they explain the main points to a partner? What did they find easy or difficult?

5B En France, c'est la fête   pages 44–45

Aims and objectives	Grammar and skills	Resources
• find out about festivals and events in France • learn greetings for special days • learn how to work out new vocabulary	**Skills** Working out meanings of new words	**Key language:** see p85 **Online resource:** *Unité 5* ppt01, ws02 **CD** 2 track 19

Starters (pages 44–45)

 Fiche de travail (ws02)

1 **En ordre** Display the names of the months in random order on the board. Ask students to write these in order using abbreviated spellings (*jan., fév.,* etc.) Ask students randomly for each month in the correct order, e.g. *Le premier mois, c'est quoi? Après janvier, c'est quel mois?* etc.

2 **Chasse à l'intrus** Display or print out the following lists and ask students to write down the odd word out in each list (shown in bold). Students exchange answers for checking. Ask several students for the correct answer before confirming this.

1	2	3	4	5
la chatte	mercredi	**dans**	le salon	noir
la chambre	vendredi	deux	la salle de bains	bleu
le cheval	dimanche	dix	**le classeur**	**sous**
le chien	**difficile**	douze	la cuisine	gris

Présentation (ppt01)   **AT1, AT3**

L'année en France

This PowerPoint presentation introduces special days and greetings.

 **44** ● **2 tr 19**   **AT1, AT3; 7T1, 7L3, 7C2**

1   Les fêtes en France

Play the complete passage with the class following the text in their books.

Use the illustrations to help students understand the information about each event and explain aspects they might not know about, in English if necessary, e.g. *La fête des Rois*.

Here are some notes for guidance.

La fête des Rois:

This is a very popular festival. A cardboard crown is supplied with the cake in the shops. The person who gets the lucky charm (*la fève*) is the king or queen and 'rules' for the rest of the day. *Fève* originally means a bean – a white bean was used for the charm, but nowadays this is a Baby Jesus or other plastic or porcelain animal, etc.

Pâques:

At Easter in France, the bells fly back to Rome (in celebration of the Resurrection) and leave chocolate eggs, rabbits, fish, chicks, etc. for the children.

Poisson d'avril:

There are various accounts of this custom. In 1565 Charles IX changed the New Year from 1 April (start of spring) to 1 January (when the days start getting longer). On 1 April, some pranksters gave 'false' New Year presents and played all sorts of tricks. This was also mixed with other customs, e.g. the *Poisson* sign of the zodiac; prolonging Lent when you were only allowed to eat fish instead of meat; confusing simple people by offering them fish at a time of year when fishing was not allowed.

For further information about saints' days, there are a number of websites on the subject.

●●●●●●●●●●●●●●●●●●●●●●●●●●●●●●●●●●●●●●

 **45   Stratégies**   **7W7**

Coping with new words

This item focuses on strategies for finding the meaning of new vocabulary.

 transcript

Les fêtes en France

1   Le premier janvier, c'est le jour de l'An. On dit «Bonne Année» à ses amis.

2   Le six janvier, c'est la fête des Rois. On mange un gâteau spécial: la galette des Rois. Dans la galette, il y a une fève. La personne qui trouve la fève est le roi et porte une couronne.

3   Au mois de février ou de mars, il y a mardi gras. On mange des crêpes.

4   En mars ou en avril, il y a Pâques. On mange des œufs en chocolat … et aussi des lapins et des oiseaux en chocolat. On dit «Joyeuses Pâques!».

5   Le premier avril, on fait des poissons d'avril. Ça, c'est amusant!

6   Au mois de mai, il y a la fête des *Mères*. Les enfants donnent une carte ou des fleurs à leur mère.

7   Le 21 juin, c'est le premier jour de l'été. En France, c'est la fête de la musique.

8   Le 14 juillet, c'est la fête nationale. Il y a un défilé dans les rues. Le soir, il y a un feu d'artifice.

9   Le 25 décembre, c'est la fête de Noël. On chante des chants de Noël. Le Père Noël apporte des cadeaux aux petits enfants. On mange un repas délicieux, souvent pendant la nuit du 24 au 25 décembre. On dit «Joyeux Noël» à tout le monde.

10 Le 31 décembre, c'est la Saint-Sylvestre. Le soir, on mange un bon repas. À minuit, on téléphone à ses amis et on dit «Bonne Année» à tout le monde.

11 Il y a aussi d'autres fêtes en France, par exemple la fête de l'Eid, pour la religion musulmane, et la fête des lumières à Diwali, pour la religion hindoue.

 **45**   **AT3; 7W8**

2   Ça veut dire quoi?

This task provides a focus to implement the strategies for finding the meaning of new vocabulary.

Solution:

a 1 *premier*   premier, first
   2 *délicieux*   delicious
   3 *une couronne*   crown
   4 *une carte*   card
   5 *la religion hindoue* the Hindu religion

b 1 *le jour de l'An*   New Year's Day
   2 *des crêpes*   pancakes
   3 *Bonne Année!*   Happy New Year
   4 *des œufs*   eggs
   5 *la religion musulmane* the Muslim religion
   6 *des fleurs*   flowers
   7 *la nuit*   night
   8 *un feu d'artifice* fireworks

 **45**   **AT2; 7C2; AfL**

3   C'est quel mois?

Check that students know the greetings for each of the main festivals, e.g.

Qu'est-ce qu'on dit à Noël/Pâques/pour le nouvel an?
On dit «Joyeux Noël/Joyeuses Pâques/Bonne Année».

The pronoun *on* is used in tasks 1–4. Briefly explain its meaning here. It is taught more fully in *Unité 6*.

To give oral practice of saying the greetings and festivals, students work in pairs on this task. In turns, one student reads a statement and the other provides the answer. They can assess each other's performance in terms of pronunciation and the correct answers and give feedback. Agree the criteria before starting and remind students of the spread objectives.

Solution: **1** *en mars ou en avril,* **2** *en février ou en mars,* **3** *en décembre,* **4** *en janvier,* **5** *en janvier,* **6** *en mai*

 **45** AT2; 7C2; AfL

4 C'est quelle fête?

In pairs, students read out the short dialogue then, following the example, one student describes an event and the other has to guess the *fête*. Refer students back to task 3 for models and further ideas for this activity.

Review the spread objectives and assessment criteria and use this for peer assessment.

 **146 Au choix** AT3

3 Des annonces

Students read material based on events linked to festivals and decide whether the statements are true or false. As an extension activity, students could correct the false sentences.

> **Solution:** **1** *faux. C'est à Pâques.* **2** *vrai,*
> **3** *faux. C'est vendredi, samedi et lundi.* **4** *faux.*
> *C'est le 14 juillet.* **5** *vrai,* **6** *vrai,* **7** *faux. C'est le*
> *17, le 18 et le 19 décembre.*

Plenaries (pages 44–45)

 Fiche de travail (ws02)

1 Students make up a wordsearch (using the 10 x 10 square grid provided on the online worksheet) to include approximately 12 items of vocabulary from the unit so far. They then exchange these and find the words and write them down with their English meaning.

Follow this with reflection and discussion, e.g. did students all choose similar words and if so, why? Which sort of words were chosen (adjectives, nouns) and is this because they are easier to learn? Did certain groups of letters 'pop out' at them from the wordsearch?

2 Students could discuss what they have found most useful/difficult so far in the unit.

5C Mardi gras   pages 46–47

Aims and objectives	Grammar and skills	Resources
• talk about a Shrove Tuesday fancy dress party • practise using the verb *être* (to be)	**Grammar** Present tense of *être* **Pronunciation** The letters é, è, ê	**Key language:** see p85 **Online resource:** *Unité 5 ppt02, ws02/04* **Copymasters:** 5/2 **CD** 2 tracks 20–22 **GiA:** p13

Starters (pages 46–47)

 Fiche de travail (ws02)

1 **Chaque mot à sa place** Display the following task (see online worksheet). Give students a few minutes to read and work out the answers, then ask students collectively or randomly to give the number of the box. Answers are given in brackets.

Quelle est la bonne case pour chaque mot?

mars (2), un cahier (5), vingt (3), brun (4), une fille (1)

1	2	3	4	5
un homme	février	neuf	blanc	un livre
une femme	août	seize	vert	un crayon
un garçon	juillet	trente	jaune	un classeur

2 **Trouve les paires** Display the following text on the board, or print it out (see online worksheet). Students match up the two parts of each sentence, writing down each number and the corresponding letter. This can be checked by the teacher randomly selecting students to answer.

Exemple: **1**h	
1 J'habite dans	**a** *télévision.*
2 J'aime beaucoup les	**b** *est un perroquet.*
3 Télé est un	**c** *et très mignon.*
4 Il aime la	**d** *la radio.*
5 Blanco est	**e** *animaux.*
6 Il préfère	**f** *chien noir.*
7 Jules	**i** *un chat blanc.*
8 Il est petit	**h** *une ferme.*

> **Solution:** **1** h, **2** e, **3** f, **4** a, **5** i, **6** d, **7** b, **8** c

Singular paradigm of *être*

Revise the names of rooms in a house taught in *Unité 3* and use these to revise the singular forms of *être*.

Give printouts of the flashcards (13–17) to individual students and ask *Où es-tu?* for the reply *Je suis dans* (+ room).

Next, revise the third person singular by asking the class: *Où est-il/elle? Où est* (name)? for the reply *Il/Elle est dans* (+ room).

The singular paradigm could be written on the board for reference.

For more practice, see *Touché-coulé* (TB 22).

 Présentation (ppt02)   **AT3**

Le verbe être

This PowerPoint presentation provides an introduction to all parts of the present tense of *être*.

Plural paradigm of être

*   ***nous* form**

To present *nous sommes*, say some sentences which relate to the class as a whole, and get students to deduce the meaning, e.g.

Nous sommes dans la salle de classe.
Nous sommes au collège.
Nous sommes à (+ town).
Nous sommes en Angleterre/en Écosse etc.

Write these on the board for a game of *Effacez!* later (see TB 21).

Add *nous sommes* to the paradigm on the board.

*   ***vous* form**

Play a 'mind-reading game' (see TB 23). The teacher thinks of a French town from the map (SB 3). Students guess where the teacher is, using *Vous êtes* (+ place). Then two students consult together to think of a town and the rest of the class guess where they are. Continue for about six goes. Then write a few example sentences on the board for a game of *Effacez!* (see TB 21).

Add *vous êtes* to the paradigm.

*   ***ils* form**

Collect together several pencils and revise:

Qu'est-ce que c'est?
C'est un crayon.
Il y a combien de crayons? etc.

Then describe them:

Ils sont verts.
Ils sont sur la table.

Choose two other groups of objects, e.g. pens, books, exercise books, and get the class to think of a few ways to describe them.

Eventually, add *ils sont* to the paradigm.

*   ***elles* form**

The *elles* form can then be presented in a similar way, using *gomme, boîte, règle*, and added to the paradigm.

Paradigm of être

Use the paradigm of *être* on the board for a version of *Effacez!* now or after referring to the *Dossier-langue* (SB 47). Make up sentences, using one of the forms, and choose a student to point to or rub out the form used.

After a few parts of the verb have disappeared, replace them, getting members of the class to spell out the missing words to someone else, who writes them in the gap.

Where possible, get students to make up further sentences themselves.

 **46** **2 tr 20** **AT1, AT3; 7W5, 7L3**

1 Mardi gras

This presents examples of all forms of *être* in context. Before listening to the recording, read the brief English introduction to *Mardi gras*, then look at the picture and speech bubbles for task 2 as well as the text for task 1. Practise some of the strategies mentioned earlier, e.g. ask which words they know. What kind of word is *méchantes*? etc. Elicit the meaning of words like *les deux méchantes sœurs de Cendrillon* and *déguisée*. Write these on the board, e.g.

'Déguisé', qu'est-ce que c'est en anglais?

Et 'les deux méchantes sœurs' de Cendrillon?

Students should then listen to the recording and choose the correct answer, **a** or **b**.

Solution: 1 a, **2** b, **3** a, **4** a, **5** b, **6** a, **7** b, **8** a

 transcript

Mardi gras

*   Bonjour. Je m'appelle Luc. Aujourd'hui, c'est le 5 février.
*   Oui, c'est mardi 5 février et c'est mardi gras.
*   Nous sommes en boîte pour une grande soirée Carnaval.
*   C'est très amusant. Beaucoup de personnes en boîte sont déguisées.
*   Regarde le garçon là-bas. Il est déguisé en Dracula.
*   Et moi, je suis déguisée en perroquet.
*   Voilà les deux méchantes sœurs de Cendrillon. Vous êtes bien déguisées! Qui êtes-vous?
*   Tu ne sais pas? Nous sommes Anne-Marie et Suzanne. Nous sommes bien en deux méchantes sœurs, non?
*   Oui, vous êtes excellentes.
*   Mais regarde le fantôme là-bas. Qui est-ce?
*   C'est Sébastien?
*   Non, ce n'est pas Sébastien.
*   Alors, c'est Olivier. C'est toi, Olivier? Tu es le fantôme?
*   Oui, c'est moi, je suis le fantôme.

46 **AT3; 7W5, 7T1**

2 C'est qui?

This gives further examples of the verb *être* in use. Students read through the introduction and speech bubbles in order to identify the people in fancy dress.

Solution: 1 *Coralie,* **2** *Luc,* **3** *Sébastien,* **4** *Olivier,* **5** *Roseline,* **6** *Christophe,* **7** *Jean-Pierre,* **8** *Anne-Marie et Suzanne*

 47 Dossier-langue 7W5

Être (to be) – I am, you are, etc.

This explains the complete paradigm of *être*. If not done earlier, write *être* on the board with some gaps and ask the class to read it out, filling in the gaps.

 47 2 tr 21–22 AT1; 7W6, 7S8, 7L1

Prononciation

This activity focuses on the effect of accents on the letter e in French. Students first have to distinguish between the acute and grave accents.

Solution: **1** é, **2** è, **3** é, é, **4** è, **5** è, **6** é, **7** è, **8** é, é

Next there is pronunciation practice of words with ê.

 transcript

Prononciation: les lettres é et è

1	février	5	discothèque
2	mère	6	méchantes
3	déguisé	7	complète
4	frère	8	défilé

Prononciation: la lettre ê

1	êtes	4	fête
2	arrête	5	pêche
3	être	6	fenêtre

 5/2 AT3, AT4

être

This provides further practice in using *être* and can be used at any time after the full paradigm has been presented.

Solution:

1 Où est tout le monde?
1 *êtes,* **2** *suis,* **3** *est,* **4** *sommes,* **5** *sont,* **6** *est,* **7** *est*

2 Questions
1 *sommes,* **2** *est,* **3** *es,* **4** *sont,* **5** *Es,* **6** *est,* **7** *êtes,* **8** *est*

3 Réponses
a *suis,* **b** *suis,* **c** *est,* **d** *sont,* **e** *est,* **f** *est,* **g** *est,* **h** *sommes*

4 Trouve les paires
1 g, **2** f, **3** b, **4** d, **5** a, **6** e, **7** h, **8** c

 Fiche de travail (ws04) AT3, AT4

Être

This online worksheet provides open-ended writing practice using the correct form of *être*.

 47 AT3; 7W5

3 C'est moi!

Students match the subject with the correct part of the verb.

Solution: **1** g, **2** h, **3** d, **4** c, **5** i, **6** a, **7** f, **8** e, **9** b

 47 AT2, AT4; 7W5, 7T5; AfL

4 Des photos

Students complete the comments on the photos with parts of *être*. This can be done orally or by writing the complete part of *être*. Remind students of the spread objective relating to *être* and use this for peer assessment. Agree the criteria for success.

Solution: **1** *Vous êtes,* **2** *je suis,* **3** *Tu es,* **4** *Nous sommes,* **5** *je suis,* **6** *Il est,* **7** *Ils sont,* **8** *Elles sont,* **9** *Coralie est,* **10** *Roseline est*

 147 Au choix AT3, AT4

4 Notre famille

This task provides further practice of the different parts of *être*.

Solution: **1** *est,* **2** *suis,* **3** *est,* **4** *est,* **5** *est,* **6** *es,* **7** *est,* **8** *est,* **9** *sommes,* **10** *sont,* **11** *sont*

 1 p13

Using the verb *être* – to be

This provides further practice of *être*.

Plenaries (pages 46–47)

 Fiche de travail (ws02)

1 In pairs or small groups, students write down as many words as possible with accents on them. They discuss ways of remembering which accent to use and how it affects pronunciation.

2 In pairs or groups, students discuss different techniques they might use for learning verbs, then pool their results and discuss which they find most useful.

 **86 Dossier-langue** **7W5**

Aller (to go)

Students have already used several parts of *aller* in the unit. Revise the different pronouns and their meanings (*je, tu, il, elle, nous, vous, ils, elles*).

Encourage the class to produce different parts of *aller* from memory or by looking at earlier pages.

Gradually build up the whole verb on the board, e.g. using the flashcards, ask students:

Où vas-tu? for the reply *Je vais …*

Où va-t-il/elle? (*Il/Elle va…*)

Remind students about the idea of the paradigm, regular and irregular verbs, and that nouns are followed by the third person of the verb etc. Refer to the cartoons to explain this.

 **86** ● **3 tr 32** **AT1, AT3; 7W5, 7L3**

2 **Coralie est au lit**

Students practise the third person of *aller* singular and plural.

a Students listen to the recording and note down the [...]er, indicating who goes where. When checking orally, for the full sentences.

Solution:

1 *Sébastien va au cinéma Dragon.* c
2 *Luc va au parc.* f
3 *Anne-Marie va aux magasins.* d
4 *Vincent va au musée Maritime.* a
5 *Stéphanie et Mireille vont au club des jeunes.* e
6 *Christophe et Jean-Pierre vont à la discothèque Plaza. Mais le soir, ils vont tous chez Coralie.* b

b As an extension, students listen again to the recording and write down with whom each person goes out.

Solution:

1 *Sébastien va en ville avec son cousin.*
2 *Luc va en ville avec son frère.*
3 *Anne-Marie va en ville avec sa mère.*
4 *Vincent va en ville avec ses cousins.*
5 *Stéphanie va en ville avec Mireille.*
6 *Christophe va en ville avec Jean-Pierre.*

Coralie est au lit

– Allô!
– Salut, Coralie. Ça va?
– Ah, bonjour, Sébastien. Non, ça ne va pas. Je suis au lit. Où vas-tu aujourd'hui?
– Je vais au cinéma avec mon cousin.
– Ah oui. Alors, au revoir.
– Au revoir, Coralie.
  …
– Allô, oui?
– Bonjour, Coralie.

– Ah, bonjour, Luc. Qu'est-ce que tu fais ce soir? Tu viens chez moi?
– Euh, Coralie, je suis désolé, mais moi, je vais au parc avec mon frère – il y a un match de football.
– Ah bon. Alors, au revoir, Luc.
– Au revoir.
  …
– Salut, Coralie. C'est moi, Anne-Marie.
– Ah, bonjour, Anne-Marie, tu viens me voir?
– Ah … non. Je suis désolée, mais je vais aux magasins avec ma mère. Je vais te téléphoner ce soir, ça va?
– Ah, oui, oui, oui. Ça va!
  …
– Bonjour, Coralie. C'est Vincent ici.
– Ah salut, Vincent. Je me suis cassé la jambe, tu sais. Tu viens me voir?
– Non Coralie. Je vais au musée Maritime avec mes cousins. Je suis désolé!
– Moi aussi! Au revoir, Vincent.
  …
– Salut, Coralie. C'est Stéphanie ici.
– Bonjour, Stéphanie. Qu'est-ce que tu fais?
– Ben, je suis avec Mireille. Nous allons au club des jeunes. Tu viens?
– Ah non. Je suis au lit. Je me suis cassé la jambe.
– Ça alors! Quel désastre! Alors, au revoir, Coralie.
– Au revoir!
  …
– Bonjour, Coralie. C'est Christophe. Je vais à la discothèque avec Jean-Pierre. Nous allons au Plaza. Tu viens?
– Mais non Christophe, je me suis cassé la jambe!
– Oh pardon, Coralie. Je suis désolé!
  …

Coralie reste au lit, elle regarde la télé, elle dessine … mais ça ne va pas. Elle n'est pas contente.

– Zut alors! J'ai beaucoup d'amis, ils sont gentils, mais où sont-ils? … Qu'est-ce que c'est?
– Salut, Coralie!
– Surprise, surprise!
– Voilà, c'est nous!
– Oh, salut, bonjour … ça alors, mais c'est fantastique!

 **87** **AT4; 7W5**

3 **Allez!**

Grammar practice in matching correct pronouns with the different parts of *aller*.

Solution: **1** h, **2** e, **3** c, **4** a, **5** b, **6** g, **7** d, **8** f

 **87** AT2, AT4; 7W5; AfL

4 Ah non!

Students complete the conversation with the correct part of *aller*. They could then practise this short sketch in pairs, with some of them perhaps recording it. This links well with the spread objective and can be used for peer assessment.

> **Solution:** **1** *vais*, **2** *vais*, **3** *allons*, **4** *vais*, **5** *va, vas*, **6** *va, vais*, **7** *allons*

 87 AT2, AT4; 7S7, 7T5

5 Le week-end

Check the class remember the difference between the two words for 'you' and respective parts of *aller*.

Ask questions using *Où vas-tu le samedi?* and also *Où allez-vous?* and help them to make up some answers orally before they write their own six sentences.

Students should not feel restricted by the words listed and could invent their own phrases in a more creative way, if wished.

Students could work in small groups, seeing which group can make the most sentences in, say, ten minutes.

 **Fiche de travail (ws07)** AT1, AT4

Le week-end

This online worksheet provides practice in using *aller* to write about weekend activities.

 7/9

Aller

This provides practice of *aller* in the context of a cartoon strip.

1 aller – to go

Check that the paradigm has been correctly completed before students work on the comic strip, or ask students to check it themselves in *Grammaire* (SB 164).

2 Une erreur

> **Solution:** **1** *vais*, **2** *va*, **3** *va*, **4** *va*, **5** *allons*, **6** *vas*, **7** *vont*, **8** *va*, **9** *allons*, **10** *allez*

 1 pp24–25

Using the verb *aller* – to go (1) and (2)

This provides further practice of *aller*.

Plenary (pages 86–87)

 Fiche de travail (ws02)

Discuss other irregular verbs learnt so far, e.g. *avoir, être*, and ask: how do you know verbs are irregular, are they hard to learn, are there patterns you can learn for irregulars too? (There is a regular pattern of endings to most irregulars – *s/s/t ons/ez/ent*.) Discuss tips to learn irregular verbs – e.g. practice of most useful parts in key phrases.

Aims and objectives	Grammar and skills	Resources
• understand tourist information • listen to a longer text	**Skills** Understanding longer texts	**Key language:** see p128 **Online resource:** *Unité 7* int05/06/07/08, ppt05, ws02/08 **Copymasters:** 7/10, 7/11 **CD** 3 tracks 33–37

Starters (pages 88–89)

 Fiche de travail (ws02)

1 **Vrai/faux?** Make some true/false statements about La Rochelle. Students respond by showing their *vrai* or *faux* card. e.g.

> *Il n'y a pas beaucoup de touristes en été.*
> *C'est au bord de la mer.*
> *C'est à la montagne.*
> *Le centre-ville est une zone piétonne.*
> *Les vélos de La Rochelle sont verts.*
> *Il y a des musées mais il n'y a pas d'aquarium.*
> *Il y a trois tours.*
> *Il y a un vieux port intéressant.*

2 **C'est masculin ou féminin?** Display the following words, use flashcards, or say the words and ask students to hold up their *masculin* or *féminin* cards.

masculin: hôtel, centre sportif, aquarium, bateau, bowling, cinéma

féminin: mosquée, cathédrale, patinoire, rue, ville, bibliothèque

Introduction

Go through the objectives for this spread.

 **88 Stratégies** 7T1

Reading and listening to longer texts

This gives some tips to help with comprehension.

 **88** AT3; 7T1

1 Une fenêtre ouverte sur l'océan

This presents some information about the aquarium in La Rochelle.

Ask a few questions e.g. *Qu'est-ce qu'on trouve dans un aquarium? Des oiseaux? Des souris?*

Qui a visité un aquarium? Où ça?

Use the photos to explain *un requin, des étoiles de mer, une méduse.*

Students then practise reading strategies to find key information.

Solution:

a 1 a, **2** in the town centre, near the train station, **3** visit the café

b 1 *faux,* **2** *faux,* **3** *vrai*

Students could look at the website and see some of the fish.

www.aquarium-larochelle.com

 **88** **3 tr 33** AT1; 7L3; AfL

2 À l'office de tourisme

This provides structured practice of listening to a longer text. Students should listen to the recording several times in order to complete the tasks.

Solution: 1 c, **2** c, e, f, a, h, b, d, g, **3** various

transcript

À l'office de tourisme

Hasan, Alain et Caroline arrivent à l'office de tourisme de La Rochelle.

H – Bonjour, madame. Nous passons quelques jours à La Rochelle.Qu'est-ce qu'il y a à faire ici?

M – À La Rochelle, il y a beaucoup de choses. Il y a le vieux port avec les trois tours. On peut visiter les tours et monter en haut. La tour de la Lanterne, par exemple, était une prison autrefois et on peut voir les graffiti réalisés par les prisonniers.

Vous aimez les musées?

A – Ça dépend. Qu'est-ce qu'il y a comme musées ici?

M – Ah... bon, il y a beaucoup de musées différents. Il y a par exemple le musée Maritime, qui est très intéressant. C'est un musée flottant. On embarque sur deux bateaux, ou plutôt deux navires, dans le port. Un navire, le France 1, était utilisé pour les services de la météo, et l'autre était un bateau de pêche. La pêche est très importante à La Rochelle. Il y a le port de pêche et un marché aux poissons ici.

C – Ah bon. J'aime bien les poissons.

M – Ah, mais si vous aimez les poissons, allez visiter l'aquarium. C'est vraiment fantastique. Il y a des poissons de toutes sortes.

C – Et l'aquarium est près d'ici?

M – Oui, ce n'est pas loin.

H – Et pour circuler en ville, il y a des vélos?

M – Oui, il y a des vélos jaunes. C'est un très bon système. On trouve des vélos sur la place de Verdun.

H – C'est près d'ici?

M – Non, c'est assez loin, à 30 minutes environ, mais il y a un bus.

A – Est-ce qu'il y a des excursions en bateau?

M – Oui, il y a des excursions en bateau aux îles, par exemple l'Île de Ré. Il y a aussi le bus de mer qui va au port des Minimes, le port de plaisance. Là-bas, il y a beaucoup de bateaux et on fait des sports nautiques.

Voilà de la documentation. Il y a beaucoup à faire. Amusez-vous bien à La Rochelle.

H – Merci, madame.

C – Alors on va visiter d'abord l'aquarium, comme c'est tout près.

A – Et après on va prendre le bus de mer.

H – D'accord. On y va.

 151 Au choix AT3

6 Tu comprends?

Students could look at the adverts and spot any cognates or near-cognates, e.g. *une prison, graffiti, un prisonnier, flottant,* etc., then answer the comprehension questions.

Solution: 1 prison, **2** graffiti (made by prisoners), **3** under 18s, **4** *place de Verdun,* **5** no, **6** either the *vieux port (*near the tour *de la Chaîne)* or the *port des Minimes,* **7** 15–20 mins, **8** because it's on two ships (a weather ship and a fishing boat).

 Activité (int05) AT1, AT3

Rue Danton: En ville

Online activities to support the seventh episode of the 'video' soap.

Activité (int06) AT1, AT3

Vocabulaire de classe (7)

This online activity practises some more key classroom language.

 Fiche de travail (ws08)/Présentation (ppt05) AT3

Bienvenues à La Rochelle

This online book-fold reader provides extension reading material on La Rochelle.

Use the PowerPoint for whole-class presentation of the Reader.

7/10 ⊙ **3 tr 34–37** **AT1**

Tu comprends?

1 Qu'est-ce que c'est?

Simple practice, matching town vocabulary with pictures or symbols.

▌ **Solution: 1** b, **2** j, **3** h, **4** i, **5** e, **6** g, **7** f, **8** d, **9** a, **10** c

transcript

Qu'est-ce que c'est?

Nous sommes en ville.

1 – Voici la poste. C'est la poste principale.

2 – Où est l'hôtel de ville?
– L'hôtel de ville est ici.

3 – Et voilà la cathédrale. Elle est superbe, la cathédrale, non?

4 – Pardon, je cherche l'office de tourisme.
– L'office de tourisme est par là.

5 – Où est la piscine, s'il vous plaît?
– La piscine? Là-bas, à droite.

6 – Est-ce qu'il y a des toilettes par ici?
– Des toilettes? Oui, voilà les toilettes.

7 – Pour aller au centre-ville, c'est par là?
– Le centre-ville? Oui, c'est par là.

8 – Le camping, c'est loin?
– Le camping? Non, ce n'est pas loin.

9 – Est-ce que la gare est près d'ici?
– La gare? Oui, c'est près d'ici.

10 – Est-ce que l'auberge de jeunesse est loin d'ici?
– L'auberge de jeunesse? Oui, c'est assez loin.

2 C'est dans quelle direction?

Choosing directions to match each conversation.

▌ **Solution: 1** b, **2** c, **3** d, **4** a, **5** e, **6** f

transcript

C'est dans quelle direction?

1 Tournez à gauche.

2 Continuez tout droit.

3 Prenez la première rue à gauche.

4 Tournez à droite.

5 Prenez la première rue à droite.

6 Prenez la deuxième rue à gauche.

3 Où vas-tu?

Following directions and giving the destinations.

▌ **Solution: 1c** *à l'hôtel Royal,* **2a** *au parc,* **3f** *aux toilettes,* **4d** *au supermarché,* **5b** *à la piscine,* **6e** *au théâtre,* **7g** *à l'auberge de jeunesse*

transcript

Où vas-tu?

1 Allez tout droit et prenez la deuxième rue à droite.

2 Allez tout droit et prenez la deuxième rue à gauche. Puis c'est à gauche.

3 Allez tout droit et tournez à droite. C'est la première rue à droite.

4 Allez tout droit et prenez la première rue à gauche. C'est devant vous.

5 Tout droit, toujours tout droit, puis prenez la troisième rue à droite.

6 Allez tout droit, puis prenez la deuxième rue à gauche et c'est sur votre droite.

7 Allez tout droit, puis prenez la deuxième rue à gauche, puis la première rue à droite.

4 Ma ville

▌ **Solution: 1** V, **2** F, **3** V, **4** F, **5** V, **6** F, **7** V, **8** F

transcript

Ma ville

Salut. Je m'appelle Hugo. J'habite à Boulogne-sur-mer. C'est une ville de taille moyenne dans le nord de la France et c'est un port important. Mon quartier est près de la plage mais c'est assez loin du centre-ville. Dans mon quartier il y a de petits magasins, des maisons et une église. Au centre-ville, il y a une piscine, une bibliothèque, des cinémas, un aquarium et beaucoup de magasins. C'est très bien parce que j'adore le shopping. L'aquarium aussi est très intéressant. Il y a aussi un vieux quartier, la ville, où il y a un château. J'aime bien ma ville.

 89 **7/11**

Sommaire

A summary of the main language and structures of the unit, also on copymaster for ease of reference.

▌ **Activité (int07)** **AT3**

Vocabulaire (7)

An online game which tests the vocabulary of the unit.

▌ **Activité (int08)** **AT1, AT2, AT3**

Quiz – Unités 6–7

An online quiz which tests the language and content of units 6 and 7.

Plenaries (pages 88–89)

 Fiche de travail (ws02)

1 Students think about three things in the unit they have found useful/interesting and compare their choice with others.

2 Use the *Sommaire* to review the objectives of the unit and what has been learnt.

Unité 7 Consolidation and assessment

Épreuves Unité 7

These worksheets can be used for an informal test of listening, reading and writing or for extra practice, as required.

For general notes on the *Épreuves*, see TB 20.

 **7/12 Écouter** ⊙ **3 tr 38–40**　　　　　**AT1**

A Voici ma ville

Understanding of words.

Solution:　**1** b, **2** a, **3** f, **4** c, **5** d, **6** e, **7** h, **8** g

transcript

A Voici ma ville

1　Voici le musée. Le musée est sur la place principale.
2　Et voici la piscine. J'aime bien aller à la piscine.
3　Et ici, c'est un restaurant. C'est un très bon restaurant.
4　Ça, c'est la bibliothèque. La bibliothèque est ouverte le mercredi et le vendredi.
5　Puis il y a un supermarché. Voici le supermarché.
6　Et voici la poste. Là, c'est la poste.
7　Et voilà l'église. C'est l'église St. Pierre.
8　Et la gare est ici. Voici la gare SNCF.

(mark/7)

B Qu'est-ce qu'ils cherchent?

Students identify **a)** the correct symbol and **b)** note whether it's *près* (P) or *loin* (L)

Solution:　**1** b P, **2** h L, **3** e P, **4** a L, **5** d P, **6** g P, **7** f P, **8** c L (mark /7)

transcript

Qu'est-ce qu'ils cherchent?

1　– Est-ce que l'hôtel de ville est près d'ici?
　　– Oui, oui, l'hôtel de ville, c'est tout près.
2　– Le bowling, c'est loin?
　　– Le bowling? Ah oui, c'est assez loin.
3　– L'auberge de jeunesse c'est près d'ici?
　　– L'auberge de jeunesse? Oui, c'est assez près, c'est à dix minutes d'ici.
4　– Je cherche le camping 'Bon séjour'. C'est près d'ici?
　　– Le camping? Ah non, il est à cinq ou six kilomètres de la ville. Il est loin, le camping.
5　– Je vais au parc aujourd'hui. Tu viens?
　　– Au parc? Oui, je viens. Ce n'est pas loin.

6　– Où est l'hôpital, s'il vous plaît? C'est urgent!
　　– C'est tout près. Tournez à gauche et voilà l'hôpital.
7　– Je voudrais un plan de la ville.
　　– Alors, allez à l'office de tourisme.
　　– À l'office de tourisme. Oui, c'est tout près.
8　– Où allez-vous?
　　– Je vais à la mosquée.
　　– À la mosquée? Mais c'est très loin!

(mark/7)

C Sophie

Solution:　**1** V, **2** F, **3** V, **4** F, **5** V, **6** F, **7** V

transcript

– Où habites-tu, Sophie?
– J'habite dans un village près de Saint-Malo.
– Dans un village? Et qu'est-ce qu'il y a dans le village?
– Bof … Il n'y a pas grand-chose. Il y a deux ou trois magasins, un café … des maisons et une église.
– Alors, pour les jeunes, c'est bien? C'est comment pour les jeunes?
– Moi, je trouve que c'est ennuyeux. Il n'y a pas de piscine, il n'y a pas de cinéma. Oui, c'est vraiment ennuyeux, surtout pendant les vacances.
– Alors, tu vas à Saint-Malo quelquefois?
– Ah oui. Saint-Malo n'est pas loin et je vais quelquefois en ville avec mes parents. Saint-Malo, c'est super. Il y a un grand centre commercial avec beaucoup de magasins, c'est très bien pour le shopping. Il y a aussi un grand centre sportif avec une piscine et il y a une patinoire, des cinémas, etc. C'est vraiment bien. J'aime bien la ville.

7/13 Lire

A C'est où?

Solution:　**1** ←, **2** →, **3** ↑, **4** ←, **5** ←, **6** ↑
(mark /5)

B Le jeu des définitions

Solution:　**1** g, **2** d, **3** a, **4** f, **5** b, **6** c
(mark /5)

C C'est où, exactement?

Solution:　**1** b, **2** c, **3** a, **4** c, **5** b
(mark /4)

D Des vacances de Christelle

Solution:　**1** b, **2** a, **3** e, **4** d, **5** f, **6** c, **7** g
(mark /6)

7/14 Écrire et Grammaire AT4

A En ville

This is an open-ended task. (mark /4)

B Où va-t-on?

Solution:

1 *Je vais à l'église.*
2 *Je vais au collège.*
3 *Nous allons à la piscine.*
4 *Tous mes amis vont au cinéma ce soir.*
5 *Ils vont aux magasins.*

(mark /4)

C Des destinations

This is an open-ended task. (mark /6)

D Chez moi

This is an open-ended task. (mark /6)

Rappel 3

 **90–91**

This section can be used at any point after *Unité 7* for revision and consolidation. It provides reading and writing activities which are self-instructional and can be used by students working indiviudally for homework or during cover lessons.

 **90**

1 Au contraire

Solution: **1** e, **2** g, **3** a, **4** f, **5** h, **6** d, **7** c, **8** b

 **90**

2 Les mots en escargot

Solution:

a *église, gare, hôpital, poste, banque, tour*
b *printemps*

 **90**

3 Chasse à l'intrus

Solution:

a **1** *du sport,* **2** *travailler,* **3** *février,* **4** *un homme,*
5 *derrière,* **6** *méchant,* **7** *l'ami,* **8** *le printemps*
b **1** *Les autres sont des descriptions du temps.*
2 *Les autres sont des nombres.*
3 *Les autres sont des verbes.*
4 *Les autres sont des bâtiments.*
5 *Les autres sont des nombres.*
6 *Les autres sont des prépositions.*
7 *Les autres sont des saisons.*
8 *Les autres sont des sports.*

 **90**

4 Quel temps fait-il?

Solution:

1 *Il y a du soleil.* (C)
2 *Il fait froid.* (A)
3 *Il pleut.* (D)
4 *Il y a du brouillard.* (B)
5 *Il neige.* (E)
6 *Il fait chaud.* (F)

 **90**

5 Masculin, féminin

Solution:

masculin	féminin
un bureau	une brochure
un camping	une chaussette
un bateau	une chaussure
un parking	une calculatrice
un tableau	

 **90**

6 À la maison

Solution: **1** *neige,* **2** *reste,* **3** *téléphone,*
4 *travailles,* **5** *écoute,* **6** *dessine,* **7** *préparons,*
8 *rangez,* **9** *jouent,* **10** *regardent*

 **91**

7 Où est le lapin?

Solution:

1 *Le lapin est entre les livres.*
2 *Le lapin est sur l'ordinateur.*
3 *Le lapin est sous la chaise.*
4 *Le lapin est derrière la radio.*
5 *Le lapin est dans la boîte.*
6 *Le lapin est devant la télévision.*

 **91**

8 Le week-end

Solution: **1** c, **2** d, **3** b, **4** e, **5** h, **6** g, **7** a, **8** f

 **91**

9 À toi

This is an open-ended task.

 **91**

10 Tom et Jojo en ville

Solution: **1** *ville,* **2** *aux,* **3** *au,* **4** *à l',* **5** *à la,*
6 *à la,* **7** *chasse,* **8** *va,* **9** *tourne,* **10** *tout droit,*
11 *au,* **12** *tombe*

8A A quelle heure? pp92–93

- tell the time
- arrange a time to meet

Quelle heure est-il?
Il est une heure/deux heures/trois heures ...

... cinq	... moins vingt-cinq
... dix	... moins vingt
... et quart	... moins le quart
... vingt	... moins dix
... vingt-cinq	... moins cinq
... et demie	

Il est midi./Il est minuit/Il est midi et demi/Il est minuit et demi
Revision of numbers

Grammar
Telling the time

Attainment AT1 Level 1–4, AT2 Level 1–4, AT3 Level 1–3, AT4 Level 1–3
Framework 7S7, 7T1, 7L3/4/5
Languages ladder/Asset languages Grades 1–4
Assessment for learning ex 5

8B Une journée en semaine pp94–95

- talk about daily routine
- recognise some reflexive verbs

une journée typique
Le matin, je prends mon petit déjeuner à ...
J'arrive au collège à ...
Les cours commencent à ...
À midi, je mange à la cantine/des sandwichs.
Je rentre à la maison à ...
Je commence mes devoirs à ...
Le soir, on mange à ...
Je vais au lit à .../Je me couche à ...
un repas
le petit déjeuner/le déjeuner/le goûter/le dîner

Grammar
Reflexive verbs

Attainment AT1 Level 1–4, AT2 Level 1–4, AT3 Level 1–4, AT4 Level 1–4
Framework 7W5, 7T1/5/6, 7L2
Languages ladder/Asset languages Grades 1–3
Assessment for learning ex 5

8C Mon emploi du temps pp96–97

- talk about school subjects
- practise telling the time

anglais (m)/dessin (m)/EPS (éducation physique et sportive) (f)/français (m)/ géographie (f)/histoire (f)/informatique (f)/maths (f pl)/musique (f)/ sciences (f pl)/sport (m)/technologie (f)
Culture
The French school timetable

Pronunciation
The letters *oi* and *ui*
Skills
Comparing talking about school subjects in French and English
Recognising English/French spelling patterns: *y* and *ie*

Attainment AT1 Level 1–3, AT2 Level 1–3, AT3 Level 1–3, AT4 Level 1–3
Framework 7W2/3/4/5/6/7, 7S4/7, 7T1/5, 7L1/3/6
Languages ladder/Asset languages Grades 1–3
Assessment for learning ex 7

8D Qu'est-ce que vous faites? pp98–99

- use the verb faire
- say what you think of school subjects

Present tense of faire
C'est très/assez/un peu ...
amusant/difficile/ennuyeux/facile/intéressant/utile.
C'est vraiment ...
nul/super/sympa/génial.
Pourquoi? Parce que...

Grammar
Present tense of the verb faire
Skills
Adding more meaning with different qualifiers and adjectives

Attainment AT1 Level 1–4, AT2 Level 1–4, AT3 Level 1–4, AT4 Level 1–3
Framework 7W2/5/7, 7S2/4, 7L3/4/6, 7T7
Languages ladder/Asset languages Grades 1–4
Assessment for learning ex 6

8E Ma matière préférée pp100–101

- use quel to ask questions
- revise 'my' and 'your'
- say 'his', 'her' and 'its'

Quel (quelle, quels, quelles) + question
Son, sa, ses

Skills
Using *quel* to ask questions
Using possessive adjectives: my, your, his, her and its

Attainment AT1 Level 1–4, AT2 Level 1–4, AT3 Level 1–4, AT4 Level 1–4
Framework 7W2/4, 7S3/4, 7T2/5, 7L3/4
Languages ladder/Asset languages Grades 1–4

8F Notre collège pp102–103

- say 'our', 'your' and 'their'

notre, nos/votre, vos/leur, leurs
Notre collège .../Nos cours ...
Dans notre classe, il y a ...
le prof d'anglais
le club de judo
leur livre de géographie

Grammar
Using possessive adjectives: our, your and their
Skills
Different word order in French and English

Attainment AT1 Level 1–4, AT2 Level 1–3, AT3 Level 1–4, AT4 Level 1–3
Framework 7W2/4/7, 7S1/2, 7T5, 7L2/3
Languages ladder/Asset languages Grades 1–4
Assessment for learning ex 6

8G Au Sénégal pp104–105

- find out about a French-speaking country
- understand a longer text
- practise working out meanings of new words

Consolidation
Culture
Other French-speaking countries, especially in Africa

Skills
Working out the meaning of unfamiliar words
Pronunciation
The letter *r*

Attainment AT1 Level 1–4, AT2 Level 1–3, AT3 Level 1–4, AT4 Level 1–3
Framework 7W2/6/7/8, 7S4, 7T1/5, 7L1/2
Languages ladder/Asset languages Grades 1–4
Assessment for learning ex 4

8H Une présentation pp106–107

- learn more about a French school
- prepare a presentation about your school

Revision
Culture
A French college

Skills
Reading and listening comprehension
Giving a presentation

Attainment AT1 Level 1–4, AT2 Level 1–4, AT3 Level 1–4, AT4 Level 1–4
Framework 7T1, 7L5, 7C2
Languages ladder/Asset languages Grades 1–2
Assessment for learning ex 2

Other resources: Online resource *Unité 8*. Copymasters 8/1–8/12, 105, CD 4 tracks 2–26. Flashcards 43–60. 81, 90, 93 GIA pp.28–34

8A À quelle heure?

8A À quelle heure?   pages 92–93

Aims and objectives	Grammar and skills	Resources
• tell the time • arrange a time to meet		**Key language:** see p149 **Online resource:** *Unité 8* int01, ppt01, ws02/03 **Copymasters:** 8/1 **CD** 4 tracks 2–3 **Flashcards:** 43–60 **GiA:** pp28–29

Starters (pages 92–93)

 Fiche de travail (ws02)

1 **Numbers** Revise numbers 0–60 using a number game, e.g. *Effacez!*.

2 **Vrai ou faux/Masculin ou féminin + places in a town**

  a Display a selection of flashcards from 43–60. Say the correct or incorrect name and ask students to respond with their *vrai/faux* cards.

  b Display the following words or read them randomly and ask *C'est masculin ou féminin?* Students respond by showing a *masculin* or *féminin* card.

   A (*masc*): *collège, marché, parc, parking, supermarché*

   B (*fém*): *piscine, gare, poste, église, plage*

Introduction

Teaching the time

Go through the objectives for this spread.

It is useful to space out the teaching of the time, giving practice at each stage, as this helps to avoid confusion later on.

All times are presented in this section but practice can take place at various points in the unit so full competence can be built up gradually.

Once the time has been taught, remember to ask two or three students the time at some point in each lesson.

 Présentation (ppt01)   **AT1, (AT2), AT3**

L'heure

An online PowerPoint presentation of the time (not 24-hours).

Start by teaching the hours involving numbers that do not change in pronunciation, i.e. 4, 5, 7, 8 and 11.

Then add 2, 3, 6 and 10. Ask the class to listen for the *z* sound before *heures*. If appropriate, explain that this is called elision and occurs before a vowel – here the *h* is silent, so it is as if the word begins with *e*.

Next, teach 9 and 1, *midi* and *minuit* and then put them all together.

---

sb **92** **4 tr 2**   **AT1; 7S7, 7L3**

1 C'est à quelle heure?

Students listen to the recording and write down, in figures, the time mentioned in each conversation.

> **Solution:** **1** 3h00, **2** 8h00, **3** 2h00, **4** 9h00, **5** 10h00, **6** 11h00, **7** *midi*, **8** *minuit*

transcript

C'est à quelle heure?

1 – Salut, Guy!
  – Salut, Jean-Claude. Tu vas au match de football?
  – Oui.
  – C'est à quelle heure?
  – Le match commence à trois heures.

2 – Qu'est-ce que tu fais ce soir, Monique?
  – Je vais au cinéma. Il y a un bon film.
  – Ça commence à quelle heure?
  – À huit heures.

3 – Christophe, à quelle heure est-ce que tu joues au tennis avec Marc?
  – À deux heures.

4 – Bonjour, Anne-Marie. C'est Jean-Claude à l'appareil. Écoute, il y a une surprise-partie chez Robert samedi soir.
  – Ah, chouette! C'est à quelle heure?
  – Ça commence à neuf heures.

5 – Maman, tu vas en ville ce matin?
  – Oui, j'y vais à dix heures.

6 – Quand est-ce que papa va en ville?
  – Il va aux magasins à onze heures, puis il va jouer au golf.

7 – Vous allez en ville ce matin?
  – Oui, nous allons en ville, et à midi, nous allons au restaurant. Tu viens avec nous au restaurant?
  – Oui, je veux bien. À midi, alors.

8 – Le supermarché est ouvert jusqu'à quelle heure, le vendredi?
  – Le vendredi, c'est ouvert jusqu'à minuit.

 **92** AT2, AT3, AT4; 7S7

2 Le week-end

Revise the places illustrated then work through this task orally. Students can then complete it for homework.

Solution: **1** *à midi,* **2** *à onze heures,* **3** *à neuf heures,* **4** *à quatre heures,* **5** *à dix heures,* **6** *à sept heures,* **7** *à deux heures,* **8** *à minuit*

 Présentation (ppt01) AT1, (AT2), AT3

L'heure

Using the online PowerPoint presentation to teach the quarter and half hours.

Dictate some times to students, who write them down as Xh15, Xh30, etc. Students then read them back.

Write some times on the board for a game of *Effacez!*.

 **92** **4 tr 3** AT1; 7S7, 7L3

3 Rendez-vous à quelle heure?

Explain *une horloge* (large clock or clock tower). *La grosse horloge* is a well-known site in La Rochelle.

Students listen to the conversations and write down the time (in figures) of each meeting.

Solution: **1** *à 2h30,* **2** *à 11h,* **3** *à 3h15,* **4** *à 4h45,* **5** *à 7h30,* **6** *à 1h30,* **7** *à 8h15,* **8** *à 8h,* **9** *à 10h15,* **10** *à 10h30*

transcript

Rendez-vous à quelle heure?

1 – On va en ville samedi?
 – Oui, je veux bien, À quelle heure?
 – À deux heures et demie?
 – D'accord. Alors rendez-vous sous la grosse horloge à deux heures et demie.

2 – Tu es libre ce matin? On va au musée?
 – Oui, d'accord. À onze heures?
 – Oui, d'accord. Alors, rendez-vous devant le musée à onze heures.

3 – On va au marché cet après-midi?
 – Oui, d'accord.
 – Alors, rendez-vous derrière la cathédrale à trois heures et quart.
 – À trois heures et quart, d'accord.

4 – On va au café après?
 – Oui, d'accord.
 – Alors, rendez-vous au café à cinq heures moins le quart.
 – À cinq heures moins le quart, d'accord.

5 – On va au cinéma ce soir?
 – Oui, je veux bien. À quelle heure?
 – À sept heures et demie?
 – D'accord. Alors, rendez-vous devant le cinéma à sept heures et demie.

6 – On joue au tennis cet après-midi?
 – Oui, je veux bien.
 – Alors, rendez-vous dans le parc à une heure et demie.
 – D'accord, à une heure et demie dans le parc.

7 – Tu es libre vendredi? On va à Bordeaux?
 – À Bordeaux? Oui, je veux bien.
 – Alors, rendez-vous à la gare à huit heures et quart.
 – Bon, à huit heures et quart à la gare.
 – C'est ça. À vendredi alors.

8 – On va au restaurant ce soir?
 – Oui, bonne idée. À quelle heure?
 – À huit heures.
 – Alors rendez-vous devant le restaurant à huit heures.
 – C'est ça. À ce soir.

9 – On va à la piscine ce matin?
 – Oui, d'accord.
 – Alors, rendez-vous devant la piscine à dix heures et quart.
 – D'accord, à bientôt.

10 – Tu vas au supermarché, ce matin?
 – Oui, à dix heures et demie.
 – Alors, rendez-vous au supermarché à dix heures et demie.

 Présentation (ppt01) AT1, (AT2), AT3

L'heure

Use the presentation to introduce times past the hour: *Il est … heures cinq/dix/vingt/vingt-cinq.*

 Activité (int01) AT1, (AT2), AT3

L'heure du rendez-vous

An online animated activity to practise time and place of meeting.

 Présentation (ppt01) AT1, (AT2), AT3

L'heure

Use the presentation to introduce times to the hour.

 8/1 **mini-flashcards**

Quelle heure est-il?

Students draw in the hands so the clock face shows the correct time. When completed, the worksheet can be stuck on to card, cut up and used as a set of mini-flashcards. With two or more sets, various games can be played in pairs, e.g. dominos and Pelmanism (see TB 23). Students have to give the correct time on a matching pair of cards before they can keep them.

 **93** AT3; 7S7, 7T1

4 Quelle journée!

This provides practice of all forms of the time linked with places in a town.

Solution: **1** C, **2** F, **3** A, **4** H, **5** B, **6** E, **7** G, **8** D

 **93** AT2; 7S7, 7L4, 7L5; AfL

5 Conversations aux nombres

Students make up similar conversations in pairs to arrange a meeting place and time. Review the spread objectives and assessment criteria, then use this for peer assessment. Ask successful students to demonstrate their conversation to the class.

 Fiche de travail (ws03) AT2, AT3, AT4

Inventez des conversations

An online worksheet to practise arranging time and place to meet.

 152 Au choix AT3

1 Mlle Dupont

This task provides revision of times and *à* with places in a town.

> **Solution:**
>
> **1** *À six heures, elle va à la poste.*
> **2** *À sept heures et demie, elle va au collège.*
> **3** *À huit heures et quart, elle va à la piscine.*
> **4** *À neuf heures vingt, elle va au café.*
> **5** *À dix heures moins cinq, elle va au parc.*
> **6** *À dix heures vingt-cinq, elle va à la gare.*
> **7** *À midi moins vingt, elle va à l'hôtel.*
> **8** *À midi, elle va au cinéma.*

> **9** *À une heure et demie, elle va au restaurant.*
> **10** *À dix heures et quart, elle va au lit.*

 1 pp28–29

Telling the time (1) and (2)

This provides graded practice of all times.

Regular practice

From now on, spend a short time in each lesson of this unit, dictating some times which students take down in figures and then read back. This can gradually be taken over by the students themselves or developed as a pairwork or group activity.

When asking the time, use *Quelle heure est-il?* and *Il est quelle heure?* to familiarise students with both expressions.

Further revision of time

Time and the 24 hour clock is revised in *Unité 10*.

Plenary (pages 92–93)

 Fiche de travail (ws02)

1 Students work in pairs or groups to discuss what they find the easiest and the most difficult points to remember about telling the time in French and to share any tips for learning the time.

This can be discussed first in pairs or groups and then shared with the class.

2 A similar discussion can take place about numbers.

8B Une journée en semaine pages 94–95

Aims and objectives	Grammar and skills	Resources
• talk about daily routine • recognise some reflexive verbs	Reflexive verbs	**Key language:** see p149 **Online resource:** *Unité 8* int02, ws02/04 **Copymasters:** 8/2 **CD** 4 track 4 **Flashcards:** 81, 90, 93

Starters (pages 94–95)

Fiche de travail (ws02)

1 Chaque mot à sa place Display the following task. Give students one minute to read and work out the answers, then ask students collectively or randomly to give the number of the box.

Quelle est la bonne boîte pour chaque mot?

l'église(2), noir(4), le volley(5), entre(1), vingt(3)

1	2	3	4	5
devant	le temple	huit	blanc	le judo
derrière	la mosquée	quinze	vert	le hockey
sur	le synagogue	soixante	jaune	le basket

2 Quel verbe? Display the following:

a *Je ... à une amie.*
b *Tu ... au football?*
c *Nous ... en ville.*
d *Vous ... à la maison après l'école?*
e *Ils ... un sandwich à midi.*

1 rentrez **2** parle **3** mangent **4** allons **5** joues

Give students one minute to read and work out the answers, then ask students collectively or randomly for the answers.

Solution: 1 d, **2** a, **3** e, **4** c, **5** b

Introduction

Go through the objectives for this spread.

Time of day

Revise *la journée, le matin, l'après-midi, le soir* and teach *la nuit* perhaps by drawing a diagram on the board, representing *la journée*, and dividing it into parts shown by time ranges, e.g. 7h00–12h00, 12h01–18h00, 18h01–23h00; 23h01–6h59.

Les repas

Teach and practise *le repas, le petit déjeuner, le déjeuner, le goûter, le dîner*, e.g.

Le matin, on prend le petit déjeuner; à midi, on prend le déjeuner; l'après-midi, on prend le goûter et le soir, on prend le dîner.

Write the new vocabulary on the board for reference and/or for a game of *Effacez!* (TB 21).

Food

Flashcards (81, 90, 93) can be used to present and practise *du pain, du jus d'orange, un chocolat chaud*. These are used in the following item, but are not taught for active use until *Unité 9*.

 | 94 | 4 tr 4 | AT1; 7T1, 7L2

1 Une journée typique

Students listen to the recording and follow the text in their books.

Ask some questions to check comprehension, e.g.

C'est la journée d'un élève français, non?
Comment s'appelle-t-il?
C'est une journée scolaire ou c'est dimanche?
Qu'est-ce qu'il fait à midi? (Teach and practise *le déjeuner*)
Qu'est-ce qu'il fait pendant la journée? Il va au parc? Il va au collège?
Et quand il rentre à la maison, qu'est-ce qu'il fait?
Il joue au football? Il travaille? Il joue sur l'ordinateur? etc.

 transcript

Une journée typique

Olivier parle d'une journée scolaire.

– Le matin, je me lève à sept heures.

Je prends mon petit déjeuner à sept heures et demie. Je mange du pain avec du beurre et de la confiture et je bois du jus d'orange.

Je quitte la maison à huit heures et j'arrive au collège à huit heures vingt.

Les cours commencent à huit heures et demie. J'ai quatre cours le matin.

À dix heures et demie, il y a la récréation du matin. Ça dure dix minutes.

À midi, je mange à la cantine. Puis je vais dans la cour avec mes copains. Quelquefois, nous jouons au football.

L'après-midi, nous commençons à deux heures. J'ai cours jusqu'à quatre heures moins dix. Puis je rentre à la maison.

Pour mon goûter, je mange un sandwich et je bois un chocolat chaud.

À six heures, je commence mes devoirs.

Le soir, nous mangeons à sept heures. Après le dîner, je continue à travailler.

Puis je regarde la télé, j'écoute de la musique ou je joue sur l'ordinateur.

Et à neuf heures, je me couche.

 | Activité (int02) | AT3

Une journée typique

An online activity to practise the new vocabulary of schoolday routine.

 | 95 | Dossier-langue | 7W5

Reflexive verbs are briefly mentioned in connection with *je me lève* and *je me couche*. They are covered in more detail in Stage 2. Other examples used in Stage 1 which could be mentioned are: *je m'appelle, tu t'appelles, il/elle s'appelle; asseyez-vous, levez-vous.*

| 95 | | AT3; 7W5

2 La journée d'Olivier

These short follow-up tasks provide more vocabulary practice.

> **Solution:**
>
> **a** *La journée: le matin, l'après-midi, le soir, la nuit*
>
> *Les repas: le petit déjeuner, le déjeuner, le goûter, le dîner*
>
> **b**
>
> **4** *nombres:* various, e.g. *sept, huit, quatre, dix, deux, six, neuf*
>
> **3** *verbes:* various e.g. (–er verbs) *mange, quitte, arrive, commencent, dure, jouons, rentre, regarde, écoute*
>
> **2** *bâtiments: la maison, le collège*
>
> **1** *chose à manger:* various, e.g. *du pain, du beurre, de la confiture, un sandwich*
>
> **c 1** f, **2** a, **3** e, **4** b, **5** i, **6** g, **7** h, **8** c, **9** j, **10** d

| 95 | | AT3; 7T5

3 Ma journée

This task practises mealtimes and time of day. The times relate to a typical day in the UK rather than France.

> **Solution: 1** *matin,* **2** *petit déjeuner,* **3** *cours,* **4** *déjeuner,* **5** *après-midi,* **6** *goûter,* **7** *devoirs,* **8** *soir,* **9** *dîner*

 | Fiche de travail (ws04) | AT3

Des questions

An online worksheet to practise questions and answers. It provides preparation for the questionnaire that follows.

 95   AT1–4

4 Un questionnaire

Before interviewing their partner, students should write down their own answers to the questions. Some questions could be asked of the whole class, e.g. *Combien de personnes quittent la maison à sept heures du matin? Qui arrive au collège à huit heures?* etc.

Students just write the times of each answer. If fuller answers are required, revise how the verb would need to be written in the third person and write some examples on the board.

For extension, ask questions involving the third person, e.g. *Ton/Ta partenaire quitte la maison à quelle heure?* etc.

 152 Au choix   AT3

2 Notre journée au collège

For additional reading practice, students put the sentences in the correct order.

> **Solution:** *Le matin:* d, b, f, a, e, c
> *L'après-midi et le soir:* j, g, i, h, k, l

 95   AT3; 7W5, 7T6; AfL

5 Dossier personnel

Students describe their own day using the information from the questionnaire and earlier tasks. This relates closely to the spread objective. Discuss assessment criteria by giving examples of successful language, and use this for self-assessment.

 8/2   AT2

Qui est-ce?

Able students could work in pairs on this information gap activity to find out details about a person's day in order to identify the person. Additional forms of the reflexive verb *se coucher* are used (*tu te couches, il/elle se couche*). Perhaps two able students could demonstrate how this works, so everyone understands what is entailed.

Plenaries (pages 94–95)

 **Fiche de travail (ws02)**

1 **Learning nouns** Discuss what students find most difficult about learning nouns (gender, spellings, etc). Share useful tips, such as (Look, say, copy, spell, hide and repeat or similar). With gender, ask how students are learning this and whether their strategies are successful. Has anyone worked out any patterns that might help? Perhaps suggest some word endings which normally denote a specific gender (see SB 158).

2 **Using the *Sommaire*** Suggest students find 5 words that they have difficulty remembering in this area which are listed in the *Sommaire*. They should discuss in pairs how they can remember them. They should share ideas with another pair and a spokesperson then reports back to the class.

8C Mon emploi du temps   pages 96–97

Aims and objectives	Grammar and skills	Resources
• talk about school subjects • practise telling the time	**Pronunciation** The letters *oi* and *ui* **Skills** Comparing talking about school subjects in French and English Recognising English/French spelling patterns: *y* and *ie*	**Key language:** see p149 **Online resource:** *Unité 8* int03, ppt02, ws02/05 **Copymasters:** 8/3, 8/4 **CD** 4 tracks 5–11

Starters (pages 96–97)

 Fiche de travail (ws02)

1 **Times** Display a selection of times for students to write down in figures on mini-whiteboards or paper.

huit heures, neuf heures, midi, sept heures vingt, cinq heures moins le quart, six heures cinq, onze heures dix, dix heures vingt-cinq, trois heures et demie, une heure et quart.

Point to a time and ask students to say it in chorus and hold up their mini-whiteboard or paper.

2 **Cognates** Hand out a list of the following cognates in random order. Read them out and students mark 1, 2, 3, 4, etc. by the side of the word as they recognise it. Volunteers then read out the words. In this way,

students can work privately, change their minds and be passive and still learn.

géographie, musique, biologie, art, maths, histoire, technologie, double, éducation, fruit

Introduction

Go through the objectives for this spread.

Ask able students if they have a text book for different subjects, e.g.

(Name), *tu as ton livre d'anglais?* (Name) *tu as ton livre de maths?* etc.

Use these to teach the names for different subjects.

Write a list on the board for a game of *Effacez!*, then write some initial letters on the board and ask volunteers to complete the words, thereby recreating the list.

 96 • 4 tr 5   AT1; 7W2, 7W3, 7W4, 7L3

1 Les matières

a Students listen to the recording and write the appropriate letter.

Solution: 1 G, **2** C, **3** A, **4** E, **5** H, **6** F, **7** B, **8** I, **9** K, **10** D, **11** J

 transcript

Les matières

1	la technologie	7	la musique
2	l'anglais	8	les sciences
3	la géographie	9	l'informatique
4	les maths	10	le français
5	le sport	11	le dessin
6	l'histoire		

b Students then go through the symbols in order, giving the French for the subject. These can be written out, perhaps with the English equivalent.

Solution: A *la géographie,* **B** *la musique,* **C** *l'anglais,* **D** *le français,* **E** *les maths,* **F** *l'histoire,* **G** *la technologie,* **H** *le sport,* **I** *les sciences,* **J** *le dessin,* **K** *l'informatique*

 96   AT3; 7W2, 7W3, 7S7, 7T1

2 Trouve les paires

Revision of times, subjects and daily school events. Teach *la pause-déjeuner.*

Students match the sentences to the digital clocks. This includes some examples, using the 24-hour clock as widely used on school timetables.

Solution: 1 G, **2** D, **3** F, **4** B, **5** E, **6** H, **7** A, **8** C

 96 • 4 tr 6   AT1; 7W2, 7W3, 7L3

3 Dans la cour

This provides further practice of times and subjects. Explain EPS (éducation physique et sportive) which is used in item 4.

Solution: 1 *anglais* 8h30, **2** *technologie* 10h10, **3** *histoire* 11h05, **4** *EPS* 14h00, **5** *géographie* 09h15, **6** *maths* 15h00, **7** *sciences* 13h25, **8** *dessin* 16h20

transcript

Dans la cour

1 – Quel est ton premier cours aujourd'hui?
  – On a anglais à huit heures et demie.
  – Alors, anglais à huit heures et demie.
2 – Tu as technologie ce matin?
  – Oui, un cours de deux heures de technologie à dix heures dix.
3 – Tu as histoire mercredi?
  – Oui, on a histoire à 11h05.
4 – C'est bien, on a EPS cet après-midi.
  – Oui, EPS à deux heures.

5 – C'est quand, le cours de géographie?
  – On a géographie à neuf heures et quart.
6 – Les maths, c'est à quelle heure?
  – On a maths à trois heures.
7 – Tu as sciences à quelle heure?
  – Nous avons sciences à une heure vingt-cinq.
8 – Nous avons dessin cet après-midi.
  – Oui, nous avons dessin à quatre heures vingt. C'est le dernier cours.

 96 • 4 tr 7–8   AT1, AT2; 7W6, 7L1

Prononciation

Les lettres 'oi'/les lettres 'ui'

Students listen to the recording and write the letter by each word they hear.

Solution: *'oi':* **1** d, **2** e, **3** c, **4** a, **5** b
'ui': **1** c, **2** b, **3** e, **4** a, **5** d

transcript

Les lettres 'oi'

1	moi	4	soir
2	toi	5	histoire
3	soixante		

Les lettres 'ui'

1	huit	4	minuit
2	nuit	5	biscuit
3	fruit		

 97   AT3

4 Tu comprends?

Teach *un emploi du temps* and then use this for oral work, pointing out some of the differences of a French school e.g.

Regardez l'emploi du temps.
Est-ce qu'on a cours tous les jours de la semaine?
Et vous, vous avez cours le samedi aussi?
Et le mercredi? Souvent il n'y a pas cours le mercredi en France.
Qu'est-ce qu'on a comme cours, lundi à 8h30? Est-ce qu'on a sciences, lundi? Est-ce qu'on a histoire? etc.

The 24-hour clock is normally used on French timetables. This is taught for active use in *Unité 10.*

Fiche de travail (ws05)   AT3, AT4

Un emploi du temps

This online worksheet provides a blank timetable as support for work on this spread.

97 • 4 tr 9   AT1; 7L3

5 C'est quel jour?

Students listen to the recording and decide which day is being referred to.

Solution: **1** *samedi matin,* **2** *lundi après-midi,* **3** *jeudi matin,* **4** *mardi matin,* **5** *mardi après-midi,* **6** *lundi matin,* **7** *vendredi matin,* **8** *vendredi après-midi*

transcript

C'est quel jour?

1 Alors, je commence avec un cours de français, puis j'ai anglais. À dix heures vingt, c'est la récréation, et après la récré, j'ai musique.

2 Après le déjeuner, nous avons technologie. Ça c'est bien, c'est ma matière préférée.

3 Eh bien, nous commençons avec un cours de maths. Aprés on a anglais. Puis c'est la récré, et après la récré, on a français et informatique.

4 Je commence à huit heures et demie avec un cours de français, aprés ça c'est la géographie. Après la récré, nous avons maths, et puis dessin.

5 Après le déjeuner, nous avons un cours de deux heures, on a sciences, puis c'est la récré et après la récré, on a EPS (éducation physique et sportive).

6 On commence à huit heures et demie avec un cours d'anglais, puis on a histoire. Après la récréation, on a français et puis maths.

7 D'abord, on a éducation civique. Puis le deuxième cours, c'est français. Après la récréation, on a un cours de deux heures de maths.

8 Après le déjeuner, nous avons EPS de deux heures dix jusqu'à quatre heures. Et cette semaine, nous allons à la piscine. Ça, c'est bien.

 **Activité (int03)** **AT1**

Le matin ou l'après-midi?

An online animated activity to practise time of day and school subjects.

 **97 Stratégies** **7W5, 7W7**

This covers: *avoir* + subject without the use of *le/la/les*; the spelling pattern of a noun ending in *–ie* in French, often ending in *–y* in English. Other examples with some additional changes are: *économie, fantaisie, comédie,* etc.

 **97** **AT2; 7S4, 7L6**

6 On a quelle matière?

Students make up their own conversations with partners, based on the timetable.

 **97** **AT4; 7T5; AfL**

7 Dossier personnel

This could be done initially as a class activity with students volunteering information. Then review the spread objectives and discuss assessment criteria. Students could then write out their own timetable in French and evaluate their work.

 **Présentation (ppt02)** **4 tr 10–11** **AT1, AT2, AT3**

Chantez! Attention, c'est l'heure!

This online PowerPoint presentation provides the lyrics and music for a rap to practise time and daily routine.

For notes on using the songs and the words for the rap, See TB 25.

 **8/3** **AT3, AT4**

Jeux de vocabulaire: les matières

Some students could work on this worksheet, while others do CM 8/4. (See TB 157.)

Solutions:

1 Mots mêlés

Correct answers to be circled.

a	p	r	è	s	-	m	i	d	i
é	t	e	-	o	b	a	l	é	r
r	c	p	ê	i	a	t	à	j	o
n	o	a	t	r	t	i	p	e	s
u	u	s	-	m	o	n	f	u	t
i	r	l	c	a	n	t	i	n	e
t	s	c	o	l	l	è	g	e	r
c	a	l	d	e	v	o	i	r	s

1	school	*collège*
2	morning	*matin*
3	afternoon	*après-midi*
4	evening	*soir*
5	night	*nuit*
6	lesson	*cours*
7	meal	*repas*
8	lunch	*déjeuner*
9	canteen	*cantine*
10	homework	*devoirs*

2 Où sont les voyelles?

1 *l'informatique,* **2** *la musique,* **3** *l'éducation physique,* **4** *le dessin,* **5** *l'histoire,* **6** *la géographie*

3 Un serpent

Des opinions positives: *utile, amusant, facile.*

Des opinions négatives: *difficile, nul, ennuyeux.*

Le repas est dîner.

4 Un acrostiche

1 *technologie,* **2** *histoire,* **3** *sciences,* **4** *français,* **5** *anglais,* **6** *géographie,* **7** *dessin*

8/4 AT3, AT4

La vie scolaire
More able students could work on this worksheet or it could be used later for revision.

1 Mots croisés
Solution:
Horizontalement:
2 de, **3** maths, **4** tu, **7** histoire, **8** la, **9** je, **10** son, **12** géographie, **14** repas
Verticalement:
1 technologie, **2** dessin, **3** musique, **5** temps, **6** sciences, **11** jour, **13** pas

2 Un jeu
Students invent an acrostic puzzle, using school subjects.
This is a possible solution. Clues should be given in English.

 Solution:
1 sciences, **2** français, **3** géographie, **4** maths, **5** histoire, **6** musique, **7** informatique

Plenary (pages 96–97)

Fiche de travail (ws02)

1 Think, pair and share Students think about the topic of school life in France for a few minutes. Working in pairs, they have two minutes to come up with two differences between French and British schooling. They then report back to the class. Then they have one minute to come up with two things, which are the same, before reporting back. Ask for any further comments about school life in France.

8D Qu'est-ce que vous faites? pages 98–99

Aims and objectives	Grammar and skills	Resources
• use the verb *faire* • say what you think of school subjects	**Grammar** Present tense of the verb *faire* **Skills** Adding more meaning with different qualifiers and adjectives	**Key language:** see p149 **Online resource:** *Unité 8* int04, ws02 **Copymasters:** 8/5 **CD** 4 tracks 12–14

Starters (pages 98–99)

 Fiche de travail (ws02)

1 En groupes Display a list of words in random order or hand this out on slips of paper. Ask students to put these into 5 groups:

le déjeuner, le dîner, le goûter
les maths, l'histoire, le dessin
la chaussette, la jupe, le pantalon
as, ont, avons
grand, petit, long

2 Quel verbe? Display the following:

a Je ... à la bibliothèque.
b Tu ... à la cantine?
c Nous ... dans la salle d'informatique.
d Vous ... au gymnase pour EPS?
e Elles ... à la piscine ce matin.

1 allons, **2** vas, **3** vont, **4** vais, **5** allez

Give students one minute to read and work out the answers, then ask students collectively or randomly to read the sentence with the correct verb.

Solution: **1** c, **2** b, **3** e, **4** a, **5** d

Introduction
Go through the objectives for this spread.

 **98** **4 tr 12** AT1, AT3; 7W5, 7S2, 7S4, 7L3

1 Conversations au collège
Read through the conversation and ask the class to think about what kind of word is missing in each case. Students could try to guess the missing words first. Some clues could be given e.g. (1) c'est le nom d'une matière/d'un sport/d'une couleur/d'une saison? They can then listen to find the answers.

Solution: **1** EPS, **2** sport, **3** basket, **4** la piscine, **5** été, **6** judo, **7** le français, **8** l'informatique, **9** Le français, **10** L'informatique

transcript

Conversations au collège
– Qu'est-ce que tu aimes comme matières?
– Ma matière préférée est l'EPS. J'adore le sport.
– Qu'est-ce que vous faites comme sport au collège?
– En hiver, nous faisons de la gymnastique, du volley et du basket. On fait aussi de la natation. Nous allons à la piscine en ville le jeudi après-midi. Et en été, nous faisons de l'athlétisme.
– Est-ce qu'il y a des clubs de sports?

– Oui, il y a un club de judo. J'ai des amis qui font du judo, mais pas moi. Et toi, quelles sont tes matières préférées?

– Mes matières préférées sont le français et l'informatique.

– Pourquoi?

– Le français parce que j'adore la lecture et nous faisons aussi du théâtre. C'est amusant. Et j'aime l'informatique, parce que nous faisons des choses intéressantes.

---

sb 98 Dossier-langue 7W5

Students have been using parts of the singular of *faire* for some time. This brings together the complete present tense. It is further practised in *Unité 10*.

Discuss other irregular verbs taught and see if students can see any similarities with any parts, e.g. *ils font* (*ils vont/ils sont/ils ont*).

Look at the phrases listed in *Pour t'aider* and mention that *faire* is used in many useful expressions.

---

sb 98 AT3; 7W5

2 Trouve les paires

Practice in matching up all parts of the verb with English translations.

 **Solution:** **1** c, **2** e, **3** b, **4** h, **5** f, **6** d, **7** a, **8** g

---

sb 98 AT4; 7W5

3 Fais des phrases

Practice in writing the correct part of *faire* with each subject. Students can refer to the box to help with the phrases for the activities.

 **Solution:**

1 *Je fais du théatre.*
2 *Moi, je fais du dessin.*
3 *Tu fais de la natation.*
4 *Il fait des photos.*
5 *Elle fait de la gymnastique.*
6 *Nous faisons du vélo.*
7 *Vous faites du judo.*
8 *Ils font de l'athlétisme.*

Activité (int04) AT3

On fait ça

An online activity to practise activities and the verb *faire*.

---

cm 8/5 AT3, AT4

On fait beaucoup de choses

 Solutions:

1 Un acrostiche

 1 *faisons,* **2** *faites,* **3** *fait,* **4** *font,* **5** *fais*

---

2 Samedi après-midi

1 *elle fait*
2 *Vous faites*
3 *Tu fais*
4 *Je fais*
5 *Nous faisons*
6 *(Théo) fait*
7 *Elles font*
8 *(Les chats) font*

---

sb 99 ⊙ 4 tr 13 AT1, AT3; 7L3

4 Ils aiment ou ils n'aiment pas?

a Students listen and note down whether the person likes ♡, loves ♡♡, dislikes ⊠ or hates ⊠ ⊠ each subject and the names of the subject.

Solution: **1** ⊠ *h (l'histoire),* **2** ♡♡*(les sciences),* **3** ♡*(l'anglais),* **4** ⊠ ⊠ *(les maths),* **5** ♡♡*(la technologie),* **6** ♡*(l'éducation physique),* **7** ♡*(le dessin),* **8** ⊠ ⊠ *(la géographie)*

---

transcript

Ils aiment ou ils n'aiment pas?

1 – Je n'aime pas l'histoire.
– Pourquoi?
– Parce que c'est ennuyeux.

2 – J'adore les sciences.
– Pourquoi?
– J'adore les sciences parce que je trouve ça très intéressant.

3 – Tu aimes l'anglais?
– Oui, j'aime beaucoup l'anglais.
– Pourquoi?
– L'anglais, c'est super et c'est assez facile.

4 – Moi, je déteste les maths.
– Pourquoi?
– Parce que c'est difficile. Oh, les maths, je trouve ça très difficile.

5 – Tu aimes la technologie?
– Oui, j'adore la technologie. La technologie, c'est utile et amusant.

6 – Tu aimes l'éducation physique?
– Oui, j'aime ça.
– Pourquoi?
– J'aime l'éducation physique parce que je trouve ça amusant.

7 – Moi, j'aime beaucoup le dessin.
– Ah bon? Pourquoi?
– Le dessin, c'est génial.

8 – Tu aimes la géographie?
– Non je déteste la géographie, c'est nul.

---

b Students listen again and write down the adjectives under the correct heading: *des opinions positives*, *des opinions négatives*.

c They guess and then check the English translation and add that to the list.

Solution:

des opinions positives	des opinions négatives
amusant – fun *super* – great *facile* – easy *intéressant* – interesting *utile* – useful *sympa* – nice *génial* – brilliant	*difficile* – difficult *nul* – rubbish *ennuyeux* – boring

 **99 Stratégies**　　　　**7W2, 7W7, 7T7**

très, assez, vraiment

This suggests how students could enrich their use of language by using qualifiers such as *très*, *assez*, *vraiment*.

Ask students to practise in pairs adding more detail and complexity to a sentence. Give them a simple sentence, e.g. *J'aime le sport.* and challenge them to make it more interesting.

 **99**  **4 tr 14**　　**AT1, AT2; 7W2, 7W7, 7L3**

5 Six élèves

Start by doing some oral work, using *Qui aime le sport? Qui n'aime pas la géographie?* etc

Students could spend some time studying the preferences of the six young people, before listening to the recording.

a They note down who is speaking.

Solution: **1E** *Sylvie*, **2D** *Thomas*, **3A** *Sika*, **4C** *Marion*, **5F** *Tchang*, **6B** *Philippe*

b They listen again and note down details of the subjects mentioned and any adjectives used (none in 5).

Solution:

1 *les maths – très utile; le dessin – ennuyeux*

2 *les maths – très difficile; le sport – super*

3 *l'anglais – nul; les sciences – amusant*

4 *le français – intéressant et facile; l'histoire – pas intéressant*

5 *la musique; la technologie*

6 *l'informatique – super; la géographie – ennuyeux*

Six élèves

1 – Quelle est ta matière préférée?
　 – Les maths, j'adore les maths. C'est très utile et notre prof de maths est très gentil. Il explique tout très bien.
　 – Est-ce qu'il y a des matières que tu n'aimes pas?
　 – Oui, je déteste le dessin. C'est ennuyeux.

2 – Et toi?
　 – Moi, je n'aime pas les maths. Ça, c'est très difficile, mais j'aime le sport. Le sport, c'est super.

3 – Est-ce que tu aimes l'anglais?
　 – Ah non, je déteste ça. L'anglais, c'est nul.
　 – Alors, qu'est-ce que tu aimes, comme matières?
　 – J'aime les sciences. Les sciences, c'est amusant.

4 – Quelle est ta matière préférée?
　 – Le français, j'adore le français. Je trouve ça très intéressant et c'est facile.
　 – Est-ce qu'il y a des matières que tu n'aimes pas?
　 – Oui, je n'aime pas l'histoire. Ce n'est pas intéressant.

5 – Et toi, qu'est-ce que tu aimes comme matières?
　 – Moi, j'aime la musique. Oui, la musique, c'est ma matière préférée.
　 – Et qu'est-ce que tu n'aimes pas?
　 – Je n'aime pas la technologie.

6 – Et toi, quelle est ta matière préférée?
　 – L'informatique, j'adore l'informatique. C'est super.
　 – Et est-ce qu'il y a des matières que tu n'aimes pas?
　 – Oui, je n'aime pas la géographie. C'est ennuyeux.

 **99**　　　　**AT1, AT2; 7L4, 7L6; AfL**

6 Inventez des conversations

Students should now practise similar conversations in pairs. Review the spread objectives and assessment criteria. Ask volunteers to demonstrate a suitable conversation. Students could discuss how they could make their conversations more interesting by using qualifiers, e.g. *très, assez, un peu, vraiment*.

This can then be used for peer assessment.

Plenary (pages 98–99)

 Fiche de travail (ws02)

Irregular verbs Have a general discussion about the use of irregular verbs and mention that of the twenty most commonly-used French verbs, seventeen are irregular. Five of these are taught in Stage 1 (*être, avoir, faire, aller, prendre*). Discuss how many irregular verbs have been learnt so far. How you know when verbs are irregular? Are they hard to learn? Is it useful to learn irregulars in set phrases? Are there patterns you can learn for irregulars too – e.g. endings?

(There is a regular pattern of endings to most irregulars – *s/s/t ons/ez/ent* or *ont* – most irregulars share some of these endings, but not all.)

8E Ma matière préférée   pages 100–101

Aims and objectives	Grammar and skills	Resources
• use *quel* to ask questions • revise 'my' and 'your' • say 'his', 'her' and 'its'	Using *quel* to ask questions Using possessive adjectives: my, your, his, her and its	**Key language:** see p149 **Online resource:** *Unité 8* ws02/06/07 **Copymasters:** 8/6 **CD** 4 track 15 **GiA:** pp30, 31, 32

Starters (pages 100–101)

Fiche de travail (ws02)

1 C'est masculin ou féminin? Display the following list or hand it out on slips of paper. Ask students to work out whether each word is masculine or feminine. Students reply by holding up a *masculin* or *féminin* card or in chorus.

baladeur m	*jeu* m
cadeau m	*raquette* f
cahier m	*souris* f
casquette f	*stylo* m
chambre f	*trousse* f

2 Quel mot? Display the following. Give students one minute to read and work out the answers, then ask for them randomly or collectively.

a ... s'appelle le nouveau prof de dessin?

b *Tu n'aimes pas l'anglais – mais ...?*

c *C'est ..., le match de tennis?*

d *... va au club d'informatique ce soir?*

e *... est la bibliothèque?*

1 *Qui* **2** *quand* **3** *où* **4** *Comment* **5** *Pourquoi*

Solution:

a 4, **b** 5, **c** 2, **d** 1, **e** 3

Introduction

Go through the objectives for this spread.

 **100** ⏺ **4 tr 15**   **AT1; 7S4, 7L3**

Un nouvel élève

This task presents examples of different question forms, including *quel*, as well as examples of *ton*, *ta*, *tes* and *mon*, *ma*, *mes*. First read through the questions and check that students understand them, then play the recording.

Solution:

a *La question qu'on ne pose pas est la question* 6.

b a *le basket,* b *le sport et l'informatique,* c *douze ans,* d *l'histoire,* e *le 8 juillet*

c **1** c, **2** e, **3** d, **4** b, **5** a

 transcript

Un nouvel élève

– Karim, quel âge as-tu?

– J'ai douze ans.

– Et quelle est la date de ton anniversaire?

– C'est en juillet, le huit juillet.

– Quelle est ta matière préférée?

– Ma matière préférée? Bon, l'anglais, c'est utile, mais ce n'est pas ma matière préférée. Ma matière préférée, c'est l'histoire.

– Et quels sont tes passe-temps préférés?

– Mes passe-temps préférés sont le sport et l'informatique. J'adore faire du sport.

– Quel est ton sport préféré?

– Mon sport préféré est le basket.

 **100 Dossier-langue**   **7W4, 7S4**

'which?'/'what?'

Using *quel* to ask questions.

 **100**   **AT4; 7W4, 7S4**

2 Complète les questions

This gives practice in using the correct spelling of *quel*.

Solution:

1 *Quel,* **2** *Quelle,* **3** *Quelle,* **4** *Quels,* **5** *Quels,* **6** *Quelle,* **7** *Quel*

 **100**   **AT3, AT4; 7W4, 7S4, 7L4**

3 Mes choses préférées

Before students work in pairs on this task, ask how they can work out the gender of the noun in each question (by looking at the spelling of *quel/quelle* and *préféré/e*).

In part **a**, one student asks the question, supplying *ton/ta*, the other responds using *mon/ma*. After 3 questions, they could change roles. In part **b**, the questions are repeated, but students reply with their personal preferences. The answers to part **b** could be written and added to the *Dossier personnel*.

Solution:

a 1 *ton sport préféré/mon sport préféré,*
2 *ta couleur préférée/ma couleur préférée,*
3 *ta journée préférée/ma journée,* **4** *ton animal préféré/mon animal préféré* **5** *ta saison préférée/ ma saison préférée,* **6** *ta matière préférée/ma matière préférée.*

| Fiche de travail (ws06) | AT3, AT4 |

Mes préférences

An online worksheet to provide support for work on preferences, possessive adjectives (*mon, ton*) and general extension work.

| 100 | AT2; 7S4, 7L4 |

4 Inventez des conversations

Students practise in pairs asking and answering questions.

| 1 pp30–31 |

More practice of *mon, ma, mes/ton, ta, tes* (1) and (2).

Further practice of these possessive adjectives, if required.

| 152 Au choix | AT3 |

3 As-tu une bonne mémoire?

This optional task based on *Un nouvel élève* (SB 100) presents examples of *son, sa, ses* meaning 'his'.

Solution:

1 *Non, son sport préféré est le basket.*

2 *Non, ses passe-temps préférés sont le sport et l'informatique.*

3 *Non, sa matière préférée est l'histoire.*

4 *Non, son anniversaire est le 8 juillet.*

| 101 | AT3; 7W4, 7S3 |

5 Mes amis

This presents examples of *son, sa, ses* meaning his or her. Students should read through the text and then correct the statements.

Solution:

1 *Camille est française.*

2 *Son sport préféré est la gymnastique.*

3 *Elle aime les maths.*

4 *Ses grands-parents habitent au Sénégal.*

5 *Son frère s'appelle Noah.*

6 *Son anniversaire est le 15 avril.*

7 *Sa souris s'appelle Minnie.*

8 *Ses passe-temps préférés sont la natation et le football.*

| 101 | AT2; 7T2, 7T5 |

6 Jeu d'identité

Students could interview one another or make up descriptions of famous people for a 'guess the identity' game.

| 101 Dossier-langue | 7W2, 7W4 |

son/sa/ses (his, her, its)

Remind students of the earlier work on *mon, ma, mes* and *ton, ta, tes* and get them to work out the rule for *son, sa, ses*. Emphasise the importance of the adjective agreeing with the object, not the owner.

| 101 | AT3; 7W4 |

7 C'est quoi, en français?

Practice in linking the use of *son* and *sa* with the correct meaning. This could be done individually or in pairs.

Solution: 1 *son anniversaire,* **2** *son anniversaire,* **3** *sa sœur,* **4** *sa sœur,* **5** *son chat,* **6** *son chien,* **7** *son dîner,* **8** *son livre,* **9** *son livre,* **10** *son ami*

| Fiche de travail (ws07) | AT4 |

Des phrases au choix

An online worksheet to provide further practice of the correct use of *son, sa, ses.*

| 8/6 |

Mon, ton, son

Further practice of the singular possessive adjectives.

Solutions:

1 Fais des listes

Mots masculins: jour, livre, film

Mots féminins: matière, saison, ville

Mots féminins (avec voyelle): affiche, amie, équipe

Mots au pluriel: animaux, couleurs, sports

2 Remplis les blancs

1 *livre,* **2** *ville,* **3** *équipe,* **4** *sports,* **5** *film,* **6** *matière,* **7** *couleurs,* **8** *animaux,* **9** *jour,* **10** *saison*

3 Un questionnaire

This can be discussed in class and some suggestions written on the board.

| 153 Au choix |

4 À la maison

Students practise using *son, sa, ses* to mean 'his' or 'her'.

Solution:

a 1 *ses, sa,* **2** *Ses, sa, sa,* **3** *son, ses,* **4** *son, ses, son,* **5** *son, ses,* **6** *son,* **7** *son, ses,* **8** *son, son, ses,* **9** *son, son,* **10** *ses, sa, son,* **11** *son,* **12** *ses*

b *Luc:* 1, 2, 5, 6, 8, 9, 11

| 1 p32 |

The possessive adjectives *son/sa/ses*

This provides further practice of the third person singular possessive adjectives if required.

Plenaries (pages 100–101)

Fiche de travail (ws02)

Have a brainstorming session to see how many question words students remember. Do students find it easy or hard to make up questions in French?

Students work in pairs, then join a second pair to share findings, then one spokesperson from the foursome reports on the most common findings.

Mid unit review: Ask students how it's going so far and suggest they discuss the following in pairs/groups and then get a spokesperson to relay the most common answers back to the whole class.

> What over the last 2–3 spreads has proved most difficult/easiest?
>
> Where do you think your personal improvement has been?
>
> What is still a problem?

Use the discussion as an opportunity to discuss the spread objectives and assess what has been achieved.

8F Notre collège pages 102–103

Aims and objectives	Grammar and skills	Resources
• say 'our', 'your' and 'their'	**Grammar** Using possessive adjectives: our, your and their **Skills** Different word order in French and English	**Key language:** see p149 **Online resource:** *Unité 8* int05, ws02/08 **Copymasters:** 8/7 **CD** 4 track 16 **GiA:** pp33–34

Starter (pages 102–103)

Fiche de travail (ws02)

Chasse à l'intrus Display or print out the following lists and ask students to write down the odd word out in each list (shown in bold).

Students exchange answers for checking. Ask several students for the correct answer before confirming this.

1	2	3	4	5
le chat	lundi	treize	la salle	**quand**
le château	dimanche	**faites**	la bibliothèque	facile
le cheval	**difficile**	quinze	la cuisine	sympa
le chien	vendredi	cinq	**la nuit**	utile

Introduction

Go through the objectives for this spread.

 102   4 tr 16   AT1; 7L2, 7L3

1 Au collège

Mention that students won't understand all of the words in the interview, but can use skills previously learnt to work out the gist. Students could listen for *notre* and *votre* in the passage and suggest what they could mean.

After a second listening, students should note down the missing words. Use the pause button as required.

Solution: 1 *Jules Verne,* **2** *trente-huit,* **3** *la biologie,* **4** *le dessin,* **5** *maths,* **6** *technologie,* **7** *huit heures et demie,* **8** *mercredi,* **9** *samedi*

---

transcript

Au collège

Nos jeunes reporters, Robert et Cécile, visitent un collège et parlent à deux élèves, Marc et Anne.

– Bonjour, Anne et Marc, comment s'appelle votre collège?

– Notre collège s'appelle le Collège Jules Verne.

– Et vous êtes en quelle classe?

– Nous sommes en Sixième B.

– Il y a combien d'élèves dans votre classe?

– Il y a trente-huit élèves. C'est beaucoup.

– Oui, c'est vrai. Quelles sont vos matières préférées?

– Moi, j'aime beaucoup la biologie. Notre prof est très sympa.

– Moi, je préfère le dessin. Notre prof de dessin est très amusant.

– En général, est-ce que vos profs sont gentils?

– Oui, en général, ils sont assez gentils. Notre prof de maths, par exemple, est super. Il organise bien ses cours et il explique tout très bien.

– Oui, mais notre prof de technologie est un peu sévère.

– Vos cours commencent à quelle heure, le matin?

– À huit heures et demie, mais on n'a pas cours le mercredi, et le samedi, on finit à midi.

 **102 Dossier-langue** 7W2, 7W4

'our' and 'your'

This sets out the different forms of *notre* and *votre*. Ask students how these possessive adjectives differ from *mon*, *ma*, *mes*, etc. Students could work in pairs and see how many examples they can find in the interview in a given time, e.g. 5 minutes.

 **102** AT2, AT4

2 Notre voyage scolaire

Students practise using *notre* and *nos*.

> **Solution: 1** *notre*, **2** *Notre*, **3** *notre*, **4** *nos*, **5** *notre*, **6** *nos*, **7** *nos*, **8** *notre*

 **102** AT2, AT4

3 Vos affaires scolaires

Students practise using *votre* and *vos*.

> **Solution: 1** *votre sac*, **2** *votre gomme*, **3** *vos crayons*, **4** *votre calculatrice*, **5** *vos classeurs*, **6** *votre trousse*, **7** *vos cahiers*, **8** *vos stylos*

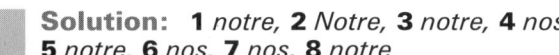 **8/7** AT3, AT4

Des questions et des réponses

Practice of *notre/nos* and *votre/vos*.

> **Solutions:**
>
> **1 Dans le bon ordre**
>
> Students write out the sentences in the correct order
>
> **1** *Comment s'appelle votre collège?*
> **2** *Il y a combien d'élèves dans votre classe?*
> **3** *Comment s'appelle votre prof de français?*
> **4** *Votre uniforme scolaire est de quelle couleur?*
> **5** *Vos cours commencent à quelle heure, le matin?*
> **6** *Quel est votre premier cours le lundi?*
> **7** *Quel est votre dernier cours le vendredi?*
>
> **2 Complète les réponses avec notre ou nos**
>
> **a** *Notre*, **b** *notre*, **c** *nos*, **d** *Notre*, **e** *Notre*, **f** *notre*, **g** *Notre*
>
> **3 Trouve les paires**
>
> Students match the completed answers to the questions in the correct order.
>
> **1** e, **2** b, **3** g, **4** a, **5** c, **6** f, **7** d
>
> **4 Un peu différent**
>
> **a** Students practise changing one detail in any 3 questions.
>
> **b** Students respond to any three questions on the worksheet.

 **102** AT4; 7T5

4 Notre collège

Students write a short article about their school, using *notre* and *nos*. This could be added to the *Dossier personnel*. Suitable articles could be displayed in the classroom or posted on the school network/website.

 Activité (int05) AT1, AT2, AT3

Une interview

An online role play activity which practises most of the language of the unit.

 **103** AT3; 7W2, 7W4

5 Une lettre de Dylan

This letter about French school life includes examples of *leur* and *leurs* in context. Students read the letter and correct mistakes in the sentences which follow it.

> **Solution:**
>
> **1** *Lucie et André vont au collège aujourd'hui.*
> **2** *Leur collège est assez loin.*
> **3** *Leur premier cours est anglais.*
> **4** *C'est assez intéressant.*
> **5** *Leur prof d'anglais est très sympa.*
> **6** *Ils ont des cours de sciences et de géographie.*
> **7** *À midi, ils mangent à la cantine.*
> **8** *L'après-midi, ils ont technologie et EPS.*
> **9** *Dylan adore le sport.*

 **103 Dossier-langue** 7W2, 7W4

'their'

This sets out the different forms of *leur*. Ask students to spot similarities with *notre/nos*. They then find some examples in Dylan's letter.

> **Solution:**
>
> *Leur collège est assez loin;Nous retrouvons leurs amis;Leur premier cours est anglais;Leur prof d'anglais;Leur livre de géographie*

 **103 Stratégies** 7W7, 7S1, 7S2

This covers differences in French and English regarding word order and in expressing possession. Ask students if they can think of further examples, e.g. adjectives usually follow the noun so physical education = *éducation physique*.

 **103** AT4; 7W2, 7W4; AfL

6 Une conversation

This task brings together practice of all the plural possessive adjectives. Review the spread objectives and use this for assessment.

> **Solution: 1** *nos grands-parents*, **2** *notre grand-mère*, **3** *vos cousins*, **4** *nos grands-parents*, **5** *Leur maison*, **6** *Leurs chiens*, **7** *leur cheval*

1 pp33–34

Using *notre/nos, votre/vos, leur/leurs* (1) and (2)

This provides further practice of the plural possessive adjectives.

 Fiche de travail (ws08)   **AT3, AT4**

La famille d'Enzo

An online worksheet with an extended reading text to practise all possessive adjectives.

Plenary (pages 102–103)

 Fiche de travail (ws02)

Think, pair and share What do students find to be the main grammatical differences between French and English? (Gender, different word order, prepositions e.g. *à* changing form) Which present the most difficulties?

8G Au Sénégal pages 104–105

Aims and objectives	Grammar and skills	Resources
• find out about a French-speaking country • understand a longer text • practise working out meanings of new words	**Skills** Working out the meaning of unfamiliar words **Pronunciation** The letter *r*	**Key language:** see p149 **Online resource:** *Unité 8* ppt03, ws02/09 **CD** 4 track 17–18

Starter (pages 104–105)

 Fiche de travail (ws02)

5-4-3-2-1 Display a list of words and ask students to find groups of 5,4,3,2,1 similar words.

e.g.

ennuyeux, facile, génial, intéressant, nul
fais, faisons, faites, font
matin, soir, nuit
lapin, souris
élève

Students could record their answers on a pre-printed grid and these can then be checked in the usual way. (See TB 10.)

Introduction

Go through the objectives for this spread.

 **104**   **4 tr 17**   **AT1, AT3; 7T1, 7L2**

1 Notre pays – le Sénégal

This presents information about the French-speaking African country, Senegal. Students should look through the photos and captions to aid comprehension before listening to the recording.

transcript

Jabu et Pirane habitent au Sénégal, en Afrique. Elles parlent de leur pays.

– Notre pays se trouve en Afrique de l'ouest.

La capitale s'appelle Dakar. C'est une grande ville au bord de la mer.

– De juin à octobre, il fait très chaud (30°C) et il pleut souvent. C'est la saison des pluies.

De novembre à mai, il fait moins chaud (17 à 27°C) et il pleut moins. C'est la saison sèche.

À Dakar il fait un peu moins chaud parce que la ville est sur la côte.

– Nous allons à l'école à Dakar. À l'école on parle français (c'est la langue officielle), mais à la maison on parle wolof.

– Ma matière préférée, c'est les sciences parce que c'est très intéressant. En plus, notre prof de sciences est très sympa.

– Et moi, j'aime beaucoup la musique.

– Comme sports, nous faisons du basket et du hand. Le football est un sport très populaire au Sénégal.

– Voici une photo de mardi gras à Dakar.

Sur la photo, il y a une mosquée. Nous sommes catholiques mais beaucoup de personnes sont musulmanes.

– Voici le marché de Sandaga au centre-ville. Moi, j'adore faire du shopping ici.

Quelquefois, il y a des touristes au Sénégal. Ils vont à la plage et ils visitent des parcs et des réserves. Ils aiment voir les hippopotames, les crocodiles et les dauphins.

À la campagne, il y a des serpents, comme des pythons, des cobras et des mambas, mais ils sont assez rares.

 **105**   **AT3; 7W2, 7W7, 7W8**

2 Tu comprends?

Ask the class about the various reading comprehension strategies they have learnt. They can then put them into practice with this task. Check they understand the terms cognate and near cognate.

> **Solutions:**
>
> **a** Some possibilities include: *Afrique*, *capitale*, *côte* (remind students that the circumflex often indicates the letter 's' in English), *officielle*, *sport*, *musique*, *photo*, *touristes*, *les hippopotames*, *des crocodiles*, *des pythons*
>
> **b 1** v, **2** a, **3** a, **4** n, **5** n
>
> **c** There are other possibilities for 1 and 4.
>
> **1** *De novembre à mai, il fait moins chaud (17-27C) et il pleut moins.* (less)
>
> **2** *À Dakar il fait un peu moins chaud parce que la ville est sur la côte.* (because)
>
> **3** *En plus, notre prof de sciences est très sympa.* (in addition, what's more)
>
> **4** *À la campagne, il y a des serpents, comme des pythons, des cobras et des mambas, mais ils sont assez rares.* (but)

 **105**   **AT3; 7S4, 7T1**

3 Que sais-tu du Sénégal?

The questions about Sénégal could be answered orally in pairs or written.

> **Solution:**
>
> **1** *En Afrique (de l'ouest)*
>
> **2** *Dakar*
>
> **3** *Il fait très chaud et il pleut souvent. C'est la saison des pluies.*
>
> **4** *le français*
>
> **5** *des hippopotames, des crocodiles et des dauphins.*

 **105**   **AT3; 7T5; AfL**

4 Une journée à Dakar

Review the spread objectives with the class and use this for assessment. Students complete the summary using words from the box. Display a model answer for constructive feedback.

> **Solution:**   **1** *collège*, **2** *cours*, **3** *parle*, **4** *récréation*, **5** *cantine*, **6** *quatre heures*, **7** *rentrent*, **8** *dîner*, **9** *mange*

5 Faites des recherches

Students could search the web or reference materials to find other French-speaking countries in Africa. The following are all members of *Afrique francophone*.

Bénin, Burkina Faso, Burundi, Cameroun, Congo (Brazzaville), Congo, République Démocratique (Kinshasa) (RDC), Côte d'Ivoire, Djibouti, Gabon, Guinée, Mali, La Mauritanie, Niger, République Centrafricaine, Rwanda, Sénégal, Tchad, Togo, Liban, Algérie, Maroc, Tunisie.

 Fiche de travail (ws09)/Présentation (ppt03) AT3

La Polynésie française

This online book-fold reader provides extension reading material on school and life in French Polynesia. Use the PowerPoint for whole-class presentation of the reader.

 **105**   ○   **4 tr 18**   **AT1; 7W6, 7L1**

Prononciation

La lettre 'r'

a Students listen to the words listed and note the correct letter.

> **Solution:**   **1** d, **2** c, **3** b, **4** f, **5** e, **6** a

b Students practise pronunciation and check with the recording.

 **transcript**

> ### Prononciation: la lettre r
>
> | a | 1 | repas | b | revoir |
> |---|---|-------|---|--------|
> | | 2 | rare | | rouge |
> | | 3 | récréation | | radio |
> | | 4 | risque | | rue |
> | | 5 | regarde | | réserve |
> | | 6 | rentre | | restaurant |

Plenary (pages 104–105)

 Fiche de travail (ws02)

Cognates Students brainstorm cognates, trying to find 3 for each topic: school subjects, animals, verbs.

Working in pairs, students use their knowledge of French pronunciation to work out how the following cognates are pronounced:

une girafe, un tigre, un éléphant, un lion, un crocodile, une gorille, un zèbre

8H Une présentation   pages 106–107

Aims and objectives	Grammar and skills	Resources
• learn more about a French school • prepare a presentation about your school	Reading and listening comprehension Giving a presentation	**Key language:** see p149 **Online resource:** *Unité 8* int06/07, ppt04, ws02 **Copymasters:** 8/8, 8/9 **CD** 4 tracks 19–23

Starter (pages 106–107)

Fiche de travail (ws02)

En groupes Display a list of words in random order or hand this out on slips of paper. Ask students to put these into 5 groups.

cinq, huit, onze
l'anglais, la géographie, la technologie
l'athlétisme, le basket, le badminton
fais, font, fait
vraiment, très, assez

Introduction

Go through the objectives for this spread.

Présentation (ppt04)   **AT1, AT3; 7C2**

Le Collège Missy

This online presentation about the Collège Missy provides a model for students' own work later.

 106  4 tr 19   **AT1, AT3; 7T1**

1   Le Collège Missy

Students should watch the presentation (see above) and find out the gist and any information they can.

Then they read through the text, perhaps with different students reading each caption aloud to practise pronunciation.

transcript

Le Collège Missy

Le Collège Missy est un collège mixte pour les élèves de onze à quinze ans.

Voici le logo du Collège. C'est un arbre aux feuilles colorées. C'est une élève du Collège qui a dessiné le logo.

Le Collège est dans la rue Missy à La Rochelle en France.

Il y a environ 500 élèves.

Les élèves de onze ans sont en classe de sixième. Je suis en 6ème B.

Comme matières, nous faisons histoire-géo, maths, français, SVT, technologie et arts plastiques.

Comme langues, on fait anglais ou espagnol. Les élèves de 4ème, qui ont treize ou quatorze ans, font aussi latin ou grec.

En EPS, on fait de l'athlétisme, du hand, du basket et du badminton. On fait aussi de la natation.

Les élèves de 6ème font un stage de voile. Ça dure une semaine. On va à l'Île de Ré. C'est vraiment bien.

Il y a des ordinateurs qui sont reliés au réseau du Collège et à Internet, Chaque personne a un code d'accès personnel.

Voici la cantine. On mange ici le lundi, le mardi, le jeudi et le vendredi.

La journée scolaire commence à huit heures vingt et finit à cinq heures de l'après-midi.

 106   **AT2; 7L5; AfL**

2   Une présentation

Students prepare a similar presentation about their own school, perhaps working in groups, with each group taking a different theme. Some students could give their presentation to the class, and assessment criteria can be discussed and later used for peer assessment.

Activité (int06)   **AT1, AT3**

Rue Danton: Les profs du collège

Online activities to support the eighth episode of the video 'soap'.

153 Au choix   **AT3**

5   Une belle journée

For consolidation of time and daily routine, students could answer questions about a typical day for the cat, *Mangetout*.

Solution:

1 *dans la cuisine,* **2** *il est neuf heures,*
3 *il mange,* **4** *il est midi,* **5** *le déjeuner,*
6 *l'après-midi,* **7** *il dort dans son panier,*
8 *le soir,* **9** *il est sept heures et demie,*
10 *il mange,* **11** *il est minuit,* **12** *il dort et il rêve.*

8/8 ● 4 tr 20–23

Tu comprends?

Solutions:

1 Quelle heure est-il?

1 9h00, **2** 8h00, **3** 12h00, **4** 11h30, **5** 2h15, **6** 2h45, **7** 1h30, **8** 5h15

transcript

Quelle heure est-il?

1 Il est neuf heures.
2 Il est huit heures.
3 Il est midi.
4 Il est onze heures et demie.
5 Il est deux heures et quart.
6 Il est trois heures moins le quart.
7 Il est une heure et demie.
8 Il est cinq heures et quart.

2 Samedi

The language needed for the speaking task in CM 8/8 is incorporated in this dialogue for practice.

Solution: **1** 7h15, **2a**, **3** 8h20, **4** 11h00, **5c**, **6b**, **7** 9h30

transcript

Samedi

– Tu prends le petit déjeuner à quelle heure le samedi?
– Normalement, je prends le petit déjeuner à sept heures et quart.
– À sept heures et quart? Et qu'est-ce que tu fais le matin?
– Eh bien, le matin, je vais au collège. J'ai cours le samedi matin.
– Ah bon, tu as cours le samedi matin? Les cours commencent à quelle heure?
– À huit heures vingt, comme les autres jours.
– Bon, le collège commence à huit heures vingt. Et les cours se terminent à quelle heure?
– À onze heures. Donc je rentre à la maison à midi.
– Et l'après-midi, qu'est-ce que tu fais?
– Pas grand-chose … je joue sur l'ordinateur, par exemple.
– Et le soir, qu'est-ce que tu fais le soir?
– Le samedi soir, je regarde la télévision ou une vidéo.
– Et le soir, tu te couches à quelle heure?
– À neuf heures et demie, normalement.

3 Comment ça s'écrit?

Solution: *Le mot qui ne va pas avec les autres est déjeuner (2).*

transcript

Comment ça s'écrit?

1 d–e–s–s–i–n
2 d–é–j–e–u–n–e–r
3 m–u–s–i–q–u–e
4 h–i–s–t–o–i–r–e
5 a–n–g–l–a–i–s
6 m–a–t–h–s
7 g–é–o–g–r–a–p–h–i–e

4 L'emploi du temps

Solution:

8h	maths	déjeuner	
9h	sciences	14h	français
récréation		15h	technologie
10h10	histoire	16h	EPS
11h10	anglais		

transcript

L'emploi du temps

– Qu'est-ce que tu as comme cours le lundi?
– Le lundi? Bon, le matin on a quatre cours. On commence avec maths.
– Alors, maths comme premier cours.
– Ensuite, nous avons sciences.
– Alors sciences, puis …
– Puis il y a la récréation.
– Et après la récréation?
– Nous avons histoire.
– Alors, histoire.
– Et ensuite, nous avons anglais.
– Alors, anglais, et puis c'est l'heure du déjeuner, je suppose.
– Oui, alors l'après-midi, on a trois cours. Pour commencer, il y a français.
– Alors, français.
– Puis nous avons technologie.
– Ensuite, technologie, et puis?
– Et puis nous avons EPS, c'est à dire éducation physique et sportive.
– Alors, EPS. Et ça, c'est le dernier cours?
– Oui, c'est ça.
– Alors, le lundi, tu as maths, sciences, histoire, anglais, français, technologie et EPS.
– Exactement.

 sb 107 cm 8/9

Sommaire

A summary of the main vocabulary and structures of the unit.

8H Une présentation

Activité (int07)   AT1, AT3

Vocabulaire de classe (8)

This online activity practises some more key classroom language.

Activité (int08)   AT3

Vocabulaire (8)

An online game which tests the vocabulary of the unit.

Plenaries (pages 106–107)

Fiche de travail (ws02)

Improving use of spoken and written French

1 Start with a very simple phrase and challenge students to suggest at least three ways it could be improved/made more interesting or complex.

2 Use the *Sommaire* to review the objectives of the unit and what has been learnt. Discuss how the language could be used in different contexts.

Unité 8 Consolidation and assessment

Épreuves Unité 8

  8/10 Écouter   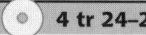 **4 tr 24–26**

A Quelle heure est-il?

Solution: **1** d, **2** c, **3** b, **4** g, **5** e, **6** a, **7** f
(mark /6)

transcript

Quelle heure est-il?

1 – On va au cinéma cet après-midi?
   – Oui, bonne idée.
   – Alors, rendez-vous à deux heures moins le quart?
   – À deux heures moins le quart. D'accord.
2 – Quelle heure est-il, s'il vous plaît?
   – Il est dix heures et demie.
   – Dix heures et demie, merci.
3 – Quand est-ce que Marc et Sophie arrivent à la gare?
   – Ils arrivent à trois heures et quart.
   – À trois heures et quart, bon.
4 – Quand est-ce que le film commence?
   – Il commence à huit heures moins le quart.
   – À huit heures moins le quart. Bon.
5 – Le concert commence à quelle heure?
   – Il commence à neuf heures et quart.
   – À neuf heures et quart. Bon, merci.
6 – Les cours se terminent à quelle heure le mercredi?
   – Ils se terminent à onze heures.
   – À onze heures?
   – Oui, c'est ça.
7 – Papa rentre à quelle heure ce soir, maman?
   – Il rentre très tard, à minuit.
   – À minuit, ah bon.

B On parle des matières

Solution: **1a** *difficile*, **2a** *facile*, **3b** *intéressant*, **4c** *ennuyeux*, **5c** *amusant*
(mark /8

transcript

On parle des matières

1 – Est-ce que tu aimes la géographie?
   – Non, je n'aime pas la géographie.
   – Pourquoi?
   – Parce que c'est difficile.
2 – Quelle est ta matière préférée?
   – La technologie. J'adore la technologie.
   – Pourquoi?
   – C'est facile.
3 – Tu aimes l'anglais?
   – Oui, j'aime beaucoup l'anglais. L'anglais, c'est très intéressant.
4 – Est-ce qu'il y a une matière que tu n'aimes pas?
   – Les maths. Je déteste les maths.
   – Pourquoi?
   – Parce que c'est ennuyeux. Oh, les maths, je trouve ça ennuyeux.
5 – Tu aimes le dessin?
   – Oui, j'adore le dessin. Le dessin, c'est amusant.

C Un jour de la semaine scolaire

Solution: **1** 6h50, **2** 6h55, **3** 7h40, **4** 8h20, **5** 10h25, **6** 5h10, **7** 7h00 (mark /6)

transcript

Un jour de la semaine scolaire

1 – Quand est-ce que tu te lèves, le matin?
   – Je me lève à sept heures moins dix.
   – À sept heures moins dix.

2 – Et tu prends ton petit déjeuner à quelle heure?

– Je prends mon petit déjeuner à sept heures moins cinq.

– Ah bon, tu prends le petit déjeuner à sept heures moins cinq.

3 – À quelle heure est-ce que tu quittes la maison?

– Je quitte la maison à huit heures moins vingt.

– Alors, à huit heures moins vingt, tu quittes la maison.

4 – Quand est-ce que les cours commencent?

– Les cours commencent à huit heures vingt.

5 – La récréation est à quelle heure?

– À dix heures vingt-cinq.

– La récréation est à dix heures vingt-cinq.

6 – Quand est-ce que tu rentres à la maison?

– Normalement, je rentre à la maison à cinq heures dix.

– Alors, tu rentres à la maison à cinq heures dix.

7 – Et le soir, vous mangez à quelle heure?

– Nous mangeons à sept heures, normalement.

– Alors, vous mangez à sept heures.

 8/11 Lire

A La journée

Solution: **1** b, **2** c, **3** e, **4** a, **5** d (mark /4)

B Les matières préférées

Solution:

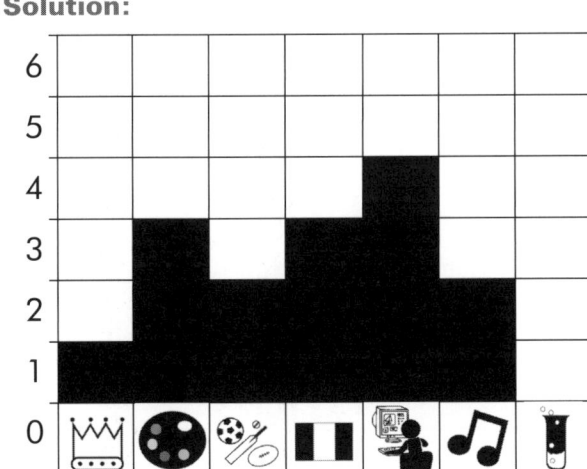

La matière préférée de la classe est l'informatique.

(mark /6: 5 for correct graph, 1 for correct statement)

C Questions et réponses

Solution: **1** e, **2** d, **3** a, **4** c, **5** b (mark /4)

D Une interview

Solution: **1** V, **2** F, **3** F, **4** V, **5** F, **6** F, **7** V (mark /6)

 **8/12 Écrire et grammaire**

A Les matières

For more able students, the words in the box could be blanked out.

This is an open-ended task. (mark /6)

B Des questions

Students complete the questions with the correct form of *quel*.

Solution: **1** *Quel*, **2** *Quel*, **3** *Quelles*, **4** *Quelle*, **5** *Quels* (mark /4)

C Des conversations

Solution:

a **1** *votre*, **2** *Notre*, **5** *Vos*, **6** *Nos*

b **1** *leur*, **2** *sa*, **3** *sa*, *son*, **4** *leurs*, **5** *leur*

(mark /4: 1/2 mark for each correct word)

D Des questions

This is an open-ended task. (mark /6: 2 marks per correct answer)

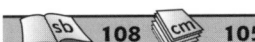 **108–109** **105** **AT3**

Presse-Jeunesse 3

These pages provide reading for pleasure. They can be used alone or with the accompanying worksheet. See the notes on TB 4.

108

Jeu-test
Es-tu un(e) élève modèle?

A personality quiz for fun.

108 **105**

Le sais-tu?

The worksheet tasks practise reading for more detail.

Solution:

A **1** b, **2** d, **3** g, **4** c, **5** a, **6** e, **7** h, **8** f

B **1** *par personne*, **2** *la vitamine C*, **3** *nécessaire*, **4** *minéraux*, **5** *du calcium*, **6** *résister*, **7** *originaires de*, **8** *mentionnée*, **9** *l'explorateur*, **10** *un ornement*

C **1** *oranges*, **2** *contient*, **3** *oranger*, **4** *froid*, **5** *bâtiment, hiver*, **6** *manger*

 **109** **105**

Tout est bien qui finit bien

Students read the story and do the true/false task and correct the false statements on the worksheet.

Solution:

A **1** *vrai*, **2** *faux*, **3** *vrai*, **4** *faux*, **5** *faux*, **6** *vrai*, **7** *faux*, **8** *vrai*, **9** *vrai*, **10** *vrai*

B There may be other possible answers.

2 *Sa famille n'est pas très riche.*

4 *Sandrine n'a pas d'ordinateur à la maison.*

5 *Il y a un grand Festival de l'informatique à Paris.*

7 *Sandrine est triste quand les autres préparent pour le Festival.*

Tricolore Total 1
Unité 9 C'est bon, ça!   pages 110–121

Aims and objectives	Key language/Culture	Grammar and skills	National criteria
9A Les repas en France pp110–111 • find out about meals in France • learn the words for things to eat and drink	le repas/le petit déjeuner/le déjeuner/le goûter/le dîner/un hors-d'œuvre/du jambon/du melon/du pâté/un plat principal/du poulet/de la viande/du poisson/de l'omelette/des légumes/des pommes de terre/des frites/des carottes/des petits pois/de la salade (verte)/du fromage/un dessert/un gâteau/une tarte aux pommes/un yaourt/des fruits/une pomme/une banane/des boissons/du vin/de l'eau/de la limonade **Culture** Eating habits in France	**Grammar** Some: du, de la, de l', des (introduction)	**Attainment** AT1 Level 1–5, AT2 Level 1–2, AT3 Level 1–4. AT4 Level 1 **Framework** 7W2/4, 7L3 **Language ladder/Asset languages** Grades 1–5
9B Le petit déjeuner pp112–113 • learn about breakfast in France • practise the words for 'some' • use the verbs manger and prendre	du café/du beurre/du jus de fruit/du lait/du pain/du sucre/du thé un chocolat chaud/un œuf (à la coque)/un yaourt de la confiture/de la confiture d'oranges/des céréales/des croissants/des fruits/des toasts/des tartines prendre (present tense)	**Grammar** Some: du, de la, de l', des (consolidation) Present tense of prendre **Skills** Identifying and explaining irregularities (nous mangeons) **Pronunciation** The letter g	**Attainment** AT1 Level 1–4, AT2 Level 1–4, AT3 Level 1–3, AT4 Level 1–3 **Framework** 7W2/4/5/6/7, 7S4, 7T5, 7L1/3, 7C2 **Language ladder/Asset languages** Grades 1–4 **Assessment for learning** Au choix ex 5
9C On mange sainement pp114–115 • learn words for fruit and vegetables • discuss healthy eating	des légumes (m pl) des brocolis/une carotte/un chou/un chou-fleur/des haricots verts/un oignon/des petits pois/une tomate des fruits (m pl) un ananas/une banane/une fraise/une framboise/un melon/une orange/une pêche/une poire/une pomme/des raisins (du raisin) le riz/le sel/des sucreries/des chips/des bonbons/une glace	**Grammar** Perfect tense – j'ai mangé, tu as mangé, il/elle a mangé **Skills** Working out unfamiliar language (consolidation) **Cross-curricular** Healthy eating	**Attainment** AT1 Level 1–5, AT2 Level 1–5, AT3 Level 1–5, AT4 Level 1 **Framework** 7W5/6/8, 7S4/7, 7T1, 7L2/3/4/5 **Language ladder/Asset languages** Grades 1–5 **Assessment for learning** ex 2, ex 6
9D Un repas en famille pp116–117 • discuss what you like to eat and drink • practise the negative and say 'not any' • learn what to say when having a meal with a French family	je n'aime pas (ça) je n'ai pas de/d' …/Il n'y a pas de/d' … s'il te/vous plaît merci Qu'est-ce que tu prends? pour commencer comme légumes Bon appétit C'est bon, ça. C'est délicieux Tu veux encore …? je veux bien/j'ai assez mangé/je regrette/je voudrais **Culture** Social conventions: mealtimes	**Grammar** The negative (ne … pas) **Skills** Please and thank you	**Attainment** AT1 Level 1–4, AT2 Level 1–4, AT3 Level 1–4, AT4 Level 1–3 **Framework** 7W2, 7S3/5, 7T1, 7L2, 7C5 **Language ladder/Asset languages** Grades 1–5
9E Des projets pp118–119 • discuss what you are going to do (using aller + infinitive) • plan some meals and some picnics	aller le pique-nique bon pour la santé	**Grammar** The future, using aller + infinitive	**Attainment** AT1 Level 1–5, AT2 Level 1–5, AT3 Level 1–4, AT4 Level 1–3 **Framework** 7W5, 7T1/5, 7L3 **Language ladder/Asset languages** Grades 1–5 **Assessment for learning** ex 2 follow-up. CM 9/6
9F La fête autour du monde pp120–121 • practise reading longer passages • learn about festival foods	**Culture** Religious and national celebrations	**Skills** Practising reading skills **Cross-curricular** Religious studies	**Attainment** AT1 Level 1–5, AT2 Level 1–5, AT3 Level 1–5, AT4 Level 1–3 **Framework** 7W8, 7T1, 7C2 **Language ladder/Asset languages** Grades 1–5

Other resources: Online resource Unité 9, Copymasters 9/1–9/11, CD 4 tracks 27–45, Flashcards 61–94, GIA pp35–42

9A Les repas en France   pages 110–111

Aims and objectives	Grammar and skills	Resources
• find out about meals in France • learn the words for things to eat and drink	**Grammar** Some: *du, de la, de l', des* (introduction)	**Key language:** see p170 **Online resource:** *Unité 9* ws02/03/04 **Copymasters:** 9/1 **CD** 4 track 27 **Flashcards:** 61–88

Starters (pages 110–111)

 Fiche de travail (ws02)

1 **C'est masculin ou féminin?** Reinforce the focus on masculine and feminine in preparation for the use of *du/de la/des*. Display the following words (see online worksheet), use flashcards (e.g. of places in town), or say the words and ask students to hold up their *masculin* or *féminin* cards.

   masculin: *bowling, château, cinéma, français, hôpital, magasin, marché, matin, restaurant, soir, sport*

   féminin: *banque, église, musique, nuit, patinoire, plage, poste, sciences, technologie*

2 Dictate a selection of times for students to write down in figures. As you check the answers, display them and use them for a game of *Effacez!* for reinforcement.

   Suggestion: 7h00, 12h00 (*midi*), 3h45, 5h30, 7h40, 9h20, 10h05, 3h25, 2h15, 1h10

   This will prepare students to talk about times of meals later.

Introduction

Go through the objectives for this spread.

Food

Use flashcards 61–88 to introduce and practise the new vocabulary for food and meals. Ensure plenty of oral practice before students look at the printed text.

With food, use the correct word for 'some', as this will familiarise the class with the different forms of the partitive article. This is explained fully later and practised throughout the unit.

Ask questions, such as *Qu'est-ce que c'est? Qu'est-ce que tu manges? Et comme boisson?* and prompt replies with the flashcards.

After plenty of oral practice, write some of the words on the board for a game of *Effacez!* later.

The words fall naturally into groups, such as the separate courses (as presented in SB 110–111).

At this stage, students can absorb a lot of vocabulary at once so long as they use it in plenty of enjoyable activities, e.g. *Jeu de mémoire, Morpion*, etc. (TB 22).

Ongoing activities

• Wall display

Students, perhaps working in pairs or small groups, could cut out pictures of food and drink from magazines. At the appropriate point, they could label them in French, using the words for 'some'.

They could make these into collages or simple wall displays, each featuring a particular meal or category of food, or their own favourite meal. As they learn more vocabulary, they can add to their displays. Several groups could combine to make their display into a complete meal, e.g.

Comme hors-d'œuvre, il y a/je préfère …
Comme plat principal, il y a …
Comme légumes, il y a …
Comme dessert, il y a …
Comme boisson, il y a …

Labels, short sentences in French and, perhaps, clip-art or other design features could be prepared on the computer and used in these displays.

• French food tasting

Brave teachers, or a school French club, could organise a French food-tasting session or a French meal with French bread, cheeses and pâté, etc.

French culture

During the following activities, encourage students to spot differences between French and British meals (e.g. cheese before or after dessert, vegetables with or after meat, etc.) and tell them about the general importance of food in French culture.

Mealtime arrangements are changing in France, e.g. the main meal is often not at lunchtime but in the evening, and the practice of two big meals daily is no longer the norm. Similarly, the habit of eating the vegetables separately from the meat or fish seems to be changing. However, practice varies and some agricultural areas may still have a long break at midday.

Students could also be given information on typical school dinners in France (how long students get, example of a menu).

Students could work in pairs/groups and report back what they have found out about meals in France. Some students could prepare visuals to describe different meals using the new vocabulary.

 **110–111** **AT2; 7W2**

1 Un repas typique

A lot of vocabulary is introduced in the first item, which is re-used and practised throughout the unit. Discuss the photos, and introduce and practise the vocabulary, e.g.

Le numéro neuf, qu'est-ce que c'est? (Des frites.)
Qu'est-ce qu'il y a comme hors-d'œuvre/desserts/boissons?
Le poulet, c'est un légume?

Explain the meaning of *prendre*, which is taught fully on pages 112–113.

 **111** **AT3; 7W2**

2 Trouve les paires

This simple matching activity reinforces the vocabulary for the different categories of food.

Solution: **1** b, **2** e, **3** a, **4** d, **5** f, **6** c

 **111 Dossier-langue** **7W2, 7W4**

some (1)

Introduce the partitive in stages, encouraging students to work out the rule for themselves. The full presentation is on SB 112.

 **111** **4 tr 27** **AT1; 7W2, 7L3; AfL**

3 Trois familles

Students listen to the recording, in which three families discuss what they are eating for their main meal, and then note down the number for each item mentioned. This can be used as an assessment task. Remind students of the spread objectives, and encourage them to self-evaluate their skills.

As follow-up, students can listen for and identify sequencers (*ensuite, puis, alors, pour commencer*). They can then use these in their own work.

Solution:

les Dubois: 2, 4, 11, 14, 15, 18, 19
les Martin: 1, 7, 9, 12, 16
les Lacan: 3, 6, 8, 10, 13, 17, 18, 20

transcript

Trois familles

La famille Dubois

– Chez la famille Dubois, on mange du pâté, comme hors-d'œuvre. Ensuite, comme plat principal, il y a du poulet avec des petits pois. Puis il y a des yaourts et des fruits. Comme boisson, il y a du vin et de l'eau.

La famille Martin

– La famille Martin est végétarienne. Alors, pour commencer, ils vont manger du melon. Puis, comme plat principal, ils vont manger de l'omelette avec des frites. Toute la famille aime ça. Puis ils vont prendre de la salade. Et comme dessert, ils vont manger un gâteau.

La famille Lacan

– Mme Lacan, qu'est-ce que vous mangez aujourd'hui pour le déjeuner?

– Comme hors-d'œuvre, nous mangeons du jambon. Puis comme plat principal, nous mangeons du poisson, avec, comme légumes, des pommes de terre et des carottes. Ensuite, on va prendre du fromage. Et comme dessert, il y a une tarte aux pommes.

– Et qu'est-ce que vous prenez comme boisson?

– Alors, comme boisson, il y a du vin et, pour les enfants, il y a de la limonade.

 **154 Au choix** **(AT2), AT3**

1 Qu'est-ce que c'est?

Students supply the vowels to identify items of food and drink. This could be done orally first.

Solution: **1** *de la viande,* **2** *de l'omelette,* **3** *du poulet,* **4** *des petits pois,* **5** *des pommes de terre,* **6** *une banane,* **7** *un yaourt,* **8** *de l'eau,* **9** *du melon*

 Fiche de travail (ws03) **AT3, AT4**

On prend …

This online worksheet provides extra practice of the food and drink vocabulary and the partitive.

 **111** **AT2, AT3; 7W2**

4 Un repas en morceaux

Students find the two parts of each word to make an item of food or drink for each category.

Check the answers orally, with students reading out the complete sentence.

Solution: **1** *jambon,* **2** *poisson,* **3** *carottes,* **4** *salade,* **5** *fromage,* **6** *gâteau,* **7** *limonade*

 Fiche de travail (ws04) **AT3, AT4**

Un repas typique

An online worksheet to practise writing about food and drink.

9/1 **AT3, AT4**

On mange et on boit

The mini-flashcards can be used for a number of games, e.g. *Le jeu des sept familles, Je pense à quelque chose*, etc. (see TB 23–24).

Plenaries (pages 110–111)

Fiche de travail (ws02)

1 **Think, pair and share** Students think about the topic of meals in France for a few minutes. They then discuss it in pairs for 5 mins, then share what they know with the class.

2 **Pronunciation** Students discuss which sounds they find most difficult (with particular regard to the vocabulary of this spread) and share ideas about how they can practise them.

9B Le petit déjeuner   pages 112–113

Aims and objectives	Grammar and skills	Resources
• learn about breakfast in France • practise the words for 'some' • use the verbs *manger* and *prendre*	**Grammar** Some: *du, de la, de l', des* (consolidation) Present tense of *prendre* **Skills** Identifying and explaining irregularities (*nous mangeons*) **Pronunciation** The letter *g*	**Key language:** see p170 **Online resource:** *Unité 9* int01, ws02 **Copymasters:** 9/2 **CD** 4 tracks 28–30 **GiA:** pp35–38

Starters (pages 112–113)

 Fiche de travail (ws02)

1 **En groupes** Display a list of words in random order or hand this out on paper (see online worksheet). Ask students to put these into four groups.

goûter, déjeuner, petit déjeuner
mange, est, avons
pomme, banane, melon
hors-d'œuvre, plat principal, dessert

2 **Chaque mot à sa place** Hand out the table below to students and display the following words on the board (see online worksheet):
cent, sont, grand, commencer, thé

Students write the correct word in each column. This can be done as a game to see who is fastest.

Solution:

A	B	C	D	E
eau	manger	quinze	suis	bon
café	aimer	soixante	sommes	vert
limonade	détester	trois	est	petit
thé	**commencer**	**cent**	**ont**	**grand**

Introduction

Breakfast food and drink

Introduce this topic by saying what you (and other members of the family) eat for breakfast and display an image each time one of the items of food and drink is mentioned, e.g.

À sept heures et demie, je prends le petit déjeuner. Je mange du pain avec du beurre et de la confiture. Quelquefois, je mange un fruit, par exemple une banane. Je bois du jus de fruit et un café au lait.

 112 ● 4 tr 28   AT1, AT3; 7W2, 7W4

1 Le petit déjeuner

a Students listen to the recording and look at the list of breakfast food and drink. They repeat each item and note down the appropriate letter. This could be done in two stages: listen and repeat; listen again and note down the letter.

Solution: **1** c, **2** o, **3** l, **4** e, **5** q, **6** h, **7** a, **8** n, **9** i, **10** p, **11** k, **12** r, **13** m, **14** f, **15** b, **16** j, **17** g, **18** d

transcript

Le petit déjeuner

1	du jus de fruit	10	des fruits
2	des croissants	11	un yaourt
3	de la confiture	12	des tartines
4	du Nutella®	13	de la confiture d'oranges
5	des toasts	14	du pain
6	du thé	15	du beurre
7	du café	16	un œuf à la coque
8	des céréales	17	du sucre
9	un chocolat chaud	18	du lait

b Go through the illustrations, asking students to repeat the names of the items illustrated. They then match the numbered items to the list of words in part **a**.

Solution: **1** n, **2** p, **3** a, **4** o, **5** e, **6** f, **7** l, **8** m, **9** c, **10** d, **11** k, **12** r, **13** g, **14** i, **15** j, **16** h, **17** q, **18** b

If not covered earlier, explain *des tartines*, *des croissants*, Nutella® and the custom of drinking hot chocolate, coffee, etc. in a *bol*. Encourage students to deduce the meanings by using reading strategies.

 112 ● 4 tr 29   AT3, AT4; 7L3

2 Qu'est-ce qu'ils prennent?

Next, students listen to the recording of what people have for breakfast. They note down the letters (from task **1a**) to indicate each item mentioned after the appropriate name.

Solution:

Nicole – f, b, l (or m), i
Marc – n, q, c
Claire – r (or f, b), e, h
Luc – o, f, b, l (or m), a (+ d), g
Des touristes – n, k, p, j, f, o, a, h

transcript

Qu'est-ce qu'ils prennent?

Nicole
– Normalement, je prends le petit déjeuner à sept heures du matin. Je prends du pain avec du beurre et de la confiture. Comme boisson, je prends un chocolat chaud.

Marc
– Moi, je prends le petit déjeuner à sept heures et quart. Je mange des céréales, par exemple des Corn Flakes, et des toasts et je bois du jus de fruit.

Claire
– Pendant la semaine, je prends le petit déjeuner à huit heures moins le quart. Je mange des tartines, c'est à dire, du pain avec du beurre. Quelquefois, je me fais des tartines avec du Nutella®. J'aime bien ça. Comme boisson, je prends du thé.

Luc
– Le dimanche, nous prenons le petit déjeuner plus tard, vers huit heures et demie. Nous mangeons souvent des croissants ou du pain avec du beurre et de la confiture. Moi, je bois du café au lait avec du sucre.

Des touristes
– Mes parents travaillent dans un grand hôtel. À l'hôtel, on prépare un petit déjeuner sous forme de buffet pour les touristes. Souvent, des touristes mangent des céréales ou des yaourts ou des fruits. Puis ils mangent un œuf à la coque avec du pain ou des croissants. Comme boissons, ils prennent du café ou du thé.

AT2

Au petit déjeuner, je prends …

Play a chain breakfast game with an ever-increasing list. This could be done as a whole-class activity or in groups.

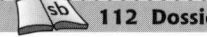 **Activité (int01)** | **AT1**

Je prends …

An online listening activity to practise talking about what people have for breakfast.

---

 112 Dossier-langue | **7W4, 7W7**

some (2)

Go through the explanation and encourage students to find other examples for 'some' from earlier in the unit. Emphasise the link between the correct word for 'some' and the gender of the noun.

If appropriate, explain that, in French, the word for 'some' is always used, whereas in English it is sometimes omitted, e.g. *Au petit déjeuner, je prends du pain et du beurre.* (For breakfast I have bread and butter.)

 **112** | **AT3, AT4; 7W4**

3 Complète les phrases

This gap-fill activity provides a useful summary of the partitive article.

> **Solution:** **1** *du,* **2** *du,* **3** *de la,* **4** *de la,* **5** *de l',* **6** *des*

---

 154 Au choix | **AT4**

2 Un mélange

Students write the names of food and drink for different courses, with the partitive article.

> **Solution:** **1** *du jambon, du pâté,* **2** *de la viande, de l'omelette,* **3** *des carottes, des oignons,* **4** *des tartes aux fruits, des yaourts,* **5** *de l'eau, du vin,* **6** *des bananes, des oranges*

 9/2 | **AT3, AT4**

C'est quel mot?

This copymaster provides practice of genders and the partitive with a slightly wider range of food and drink vocabulary.

1 Masculin/féminin

Practice in identifying genders.

> **Solution:**
> **a m:** *un repas, un yaourt, le petit déjeuner, le dîner, le goûter, le poisson*
> **f:** *une tarte, la pomme, la salade, une banane, la viande, une poire*
> **b** *une boisson (f), le petit pois (m), le légume (m), une banane (f), une carotte (f), un croissant (m), le sandwich (m), le gâteau (m)*

2 Un tableau

Students identify the gender, then complete a grid with the appropriate articles and possessive adjective.

3 Mon repas favori

Productive practice of the above language.

> **Solution:**
> **1** *Mon repas favori est **le** goûter. Je mange **du** pain avec **de la** confiture ou **un** fruit et je bois **un** chocolat chaud ou **un** jus de fruit.*
> **2** ***Mon** repas favori est **le** dîner. Je prends **du** pâté et comme plat principal, **du** poisson avec **des** petits pois. **Mon** dessert favori est **la** tarte aux pommes et **ma** boisson favorite est **le** jus d'orange.*

 **1 pp35–36** | **AT3, AT4**

Using *du, de la, de l', des* (1) and (2)

This provides practice of the partitive but would be best used later in the unit, when more food and drink vocabulary has been taught.

 **112** ◉ **4 tr 30** **AT1; 7W6, 7L1**

Prononciation: la lettre 'g'

Make sure students recognise the difference between the hard and soft 'g' sounds and when to use them. They then say the words aloud (individually or in pairs) and listen to check. If this is done in pairs, students could assess each other's pronunciation before listening to check. The word *garçon* could also be used to remind students of the hard and soft 'c' sounds.

 transcript

Prononciation: la lettre 'g'

garçon	orange
gâteau	garage
géographie	gerbille
galette	mangeons

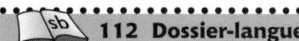 **112 Dossier-langue** **7W5, 7W7**

manger (to eat)

This looks at the slight difference in the *nous* form of *manger* (and other verbs ending in –*ger*).

 **154 Au choix** **AT3**

3 Le plat favori

This activity provides revision of animals and practice of the partitive article.

> **Solution:**
> **1** *La souris mange du fromage.*
> **2** *L'oiseau mange du pain.*
> **3** *Le cheval mange du sucre.*
> **4** *Le chien mange de la viande.*
> **5** *Le perroquet mange une tomate.*
> **6** *Le cochon d'Inde mange une pomme.*
> **7** *Le chat mange du poisson.*
> **8** *Le lapin mange des carottes.*

 **113** **AT2, AT4; 7W4, 7T5**

4 Un message

Read out the message and explain about the 'traditional British breakfast'. Discuss ideas and write some possible sentences on the board, before students work on this individually. Different parts of *prendre* are used here and this is explained more fully later in the unit.

 **113** **AT3; 7W2, 7C2**

5 Les repas en France

Revise the names of all meals, e.g. *Le matin, on prend quel repas? Et à midi, et le soir? Quand les enfants rentrent à la maison, ils prennent souvent quelque chose à manger et à boire, ça s'appelle …?*

This short quiz presents most parts of the verb *prendre*.

> **Solution:** **1** c, **2** b, **3** c, **4** a, **5** c

 1 p39 **AT3, AT4**

The verbs *manger* and *commencer*

Further practice of *manger*, and introduction of the similar pattern of *commencer*.

 113 Dossier-langue **7W5**

Prendre

Check that students understand the more common meaning of *prendre* – to take.

If students have compiled an individual verb table using a table facility on the computer, *prendre* could be added at this point.

113 **AT3; 7W5, 7S4**

6 Questions et réponses

Using the verb *prendre*, students have to first complete questions, then replies, then match them up.

> **Solution: 1** *prenez,* **e** *prenons,* **2** *prend,*
> **c** *prend,* **3** *prend,* **d** *prenons,* **4** *prends,* **a** *prends,*
> **5** *prennent,* **b** *prennent*

155 Au choix **AT2; AfL**

5 Mes repas

This pairwork game could be used to practise meals and food. It is suitable as an assessment task. Discuss spread objectives with students and emphasise that this task will allow them to demonstrate their skills.

a Each student writes down (secretly) three things to eat and one thing to drink for each meal, e.g. *Au petit déjeuner, je prends du lait, un croissant, du beurre et de la confiture.*

b Students take turns to ask each other questions to find out what they have chosen for one of their meals (see example). This could be done as a game to see who is first to discover their partner's choices.

Students who are not good at writing could draw pictures of the food and drink they choose or use some of the mini-flashcards made from CM 9/1.

1 pp37–38 **AT3, AT4**

Using the verb *prendre* – to take (1) & (2)

Further practice of *prendre*, if required.

Plenaries (pages 112–113)

Fiche de travail (ws02)

1 Discuss what students find most difficult about learning nouns (gender, spellings, etc.). Share useful tips, such as 'Look, say, copy, spell, hide and repeat', or similar.

With gender, ask how students are learning this and whether their approach has been successful and whether anyone has worked out any patterns.

2 Students think about three things in the unit so far that they have found useful/interesting and compare their choice with that of others.

9C On mange sainement

9C On mange sainement pages 114–115

Aims and objectives	Grammar and skills	Resources
• learn words for fruits and vegetables • discuss healthy eating	**Grammar** Perfect tense – *j'ai mangé, tu as mangé, il/elle a mangé* **Skills** Working out unfamiliar language (consolidation) **Cross-curricular** Healthy eating	**Key language:** see p170 **Online resource:** *Unité 9 int02*, ws02/05 **Copymasters:** 9/3 **CD** 4 tracks 31–33 **Flashcards:** 66–80

Starters (pages 114–115)

 Fiche de travail (ws02)

1 **Chasse à l'intrus** Students are given the six sets of words (see online worksheet) and have to find the odd one out, giving a reason for their choice. This could be done individually or in groups.

If required, give the first one as an example. For extra support, the 'reasons' could be written in jumbled order on the board (see Solution).

> **Solution:**
>
> **1** *le dîner, le déjeuner, le marché, le goûter (le marché – les autres sont des repas)*
>
> **2** *des carottes, des petits pois, des pommes de terre, des oranges (des oranges – les autres sont des légumes)*
>
> **3** *de la limonade, de l'eau, du vin, de la salade (de la salade – les autres sont des boissons)*
>
> **4** *du lait, de la viande, du poisson, de l'omelette (du lait – les autres sont des plats)*
>
> **5** *du melon, du jambon, des pommes, des bananes (du jambon – les autres sont des fruits)*
>
> **6** *des frites, une tarte aux pommes, des fruits, un gâteau (des frites – les autres sont des desserts)*

2 **Quel mot?** Students read the definitions and find the correct word in the box to complete each one. If required, give the first one as an example.

a *C'est une boisson alcoolisée. C'est rouge ou blanc. C'est du …*

b *C'est un fruit. Quelquefois, on mange ce fruit comme hors-d'œuvre. C'est du …*

c *C'est souvent un plat principal. Les végétariens ne mangent pas ça. C'est de la …*

d *C'est un plat de couleur jaune. C'est fait avec des œufs. C'est de l'…*

e *Ce sont des légumes. Ils sont oranges. Ce sont des …*

f *Ce sont des fruits. Ils sont verts, rouges ou jaunes. Ce sont des …*

(in the box) *omelette, pommes, melon, carottes, vin, viande*

> **Solution: a** *vin,* **b** *melon,* **c** *viande,*
> **d** *omelette,* **e** *carottes,* **f** *pommes*

1 Les fruits et les légumes

Teach the vocabulary orally first, using flashcards 66–80 and/or actual/plastic fruit and vegetables before commencing this task. Many students could already be familiar with fruit and vegetable language from primary French. Students match the text and pictures and then listen to check their answers.

Alternatively, get students (perhaps as a pairwork activity) to try to work out which item of fruit or vegetable is which, as follows:

* Start with the ones they know – *carottes, petits pois, melon, pommes, pommes de terre* (point out the link between these last two items).

* Next use similarity with English – *banane, orange, pêche, raisins* (dried grapes), *oignons*.

* They are then left with *ananas, fraises, poire* (which they might guess from the sound), *chou, chou-fleur, haricots verts* (might guess if they have heard of haricot beans). They will probably need to look these up in a dictionary/the glossary.

* List final words in French and English in vocab books.

* Finally play the recording for recognition and repetition practice.

> **Solution:** **1** i *du melon,* **2** g *une banane,* **3** o *un ananas,* **4** l *une pomme,* **5** h *une orange,* **6** m *une pêche,* **7** j *des raisins,* **8** n *une poire,* **9** p *des framboises,* **10** k *des fraises,* **11** e *un chou-fleur,* **12** d *un chou,* **13** f *des haricots verts,* **14** a *une carotte,* **15** b *des petits pois,* **16** c *un oignon*

 **transcript**

Les fruits et les légumes

1	du melon	**9**	des framboises
2	une banane	**10**	des fraises
3	un ananas	**11**	un chou-fleur
4	une pomme	**12**	un chou
5	une orange	**13**	des haricots verts
6	une pêche	**14**	une carotte
7	des raisins	**15**	des petits pois
8	une poire	**16**	un oignon

Fiche de travail (ws05)   AT3

C'est bon

This online worksheet provides further practice of the new vocabulary and structures.

Jeu   AT2

1 Qu'est-ce que c'est?

One student picks up a card, not showing it to the rest of the class. They can ask up to five 'yes/no' type questions to guess what it is, e.g.

C'est un fruit/un légume? C'est grand/petit?
C'est rouge/vert/orange/jaune/blanc?

2 J'adore les fruits et les légumes

A chain game in which one person says a fruit or vegetable that they eat and the next person adds another one, e.g.

Je mange une pêche.
Je mange une pêche et deux bananes.
Je mange une pêche, deux bananes et trois oignons, etc.

This can be played in various ways, e.g. alternating fruit and vegetables, with different subjects, e.g. *Mon chat mange …* etc.

3 Feely bag

Put items of fruit and veg (real or plastic, or both) in a bag. Students feel inside and guess what is in the bag.

9/3   AT3, AT4

Des jeux de vocabulaire

This copymaster provides a range of activities practising food and drink vocabulary. There is an incline of difficulty.

Solution:

1 Mots mêlés

o	p	ê	c	h	e	r	a
i	o	e	l	o	ç	b	i
g	i	e	a	u	v	a	m
n	r	a	i	s	i	n	è
o	e	u	t	ê	n	a	h
n	p	a	s	r	u	n	g
c	a	r	o	t	t	e	j
d	é	j	e	u	n	e	r

2 Un serpent

  a *potage, viande, pommes de terre, salade, yaourt*

  b *limonade*

3 Mots croisés

Horizontalement:

1 *délicieux,* **6** *le,* **8** *va,* **9** *eau,* **11** *viande,* **12** *sucre,* **14** *sel,* **16** *beurre,* **17** *un*

Verticalement:

1 *déjeuner,* **2** *légumes,* **3** *café,* **4** *un,* **5** *de,* **6** *la,* **7** *frites,* **8** *vin,* **10** *melon,* **13** *chou,* **15** *du*

sb 114   AT3; 7W8; AfL

2 L'alimentation

The exercises with this reading text take students through it in four stages:

1 Look at the text title with the teacher and predict what kind of advice they are going to get before doing more focused reading, e.g. they could find three pieces of advice and check what they found with a partner.

> **Solution:**
> **a** fruit, vegetables, **b** sugar and salt, **c** exercise

2 Work out the meaning of specific French words and expressions.

> **Solution:** **a** it's obvious/evident, **b** it's necessary, **c** to be fit, **d** sugary things

3 Work out the French expressions from the English.

> **Solution:** **a** *être en forme,* **b** *faites de l'exercice tous les jours,* **c** *L'important,* **d** *un peu de variété,* **e** *mais pas trop*

4 Complete sentences using information from the text.

The last stage can be used as an AfL task: students have to explain why/how they made their choices, thus showing evidence of reading and understanding.

With words like *sucreries* the teacher can do work on word families (e.g. we know that *sucre* means sugar…). There is also the opportunity to reinforce time phrases learnt in *Unité 6* (*quelquefois, souvent, normalement*).

sb 115 ● 4 tr 32   AT1, AT3; 7W5, 7S7, 7T1, 7L2

3 Lou Leroux et la bonne alimentation

Play the recording while students read the text. Then ask some general questions about the text, e.g. *Qui mange des fruits? Les fruits, c'est bon pour la santé? Manger du chocolat, c'est bon pour la santé?* This provides a model for the next speaking activity.

The expressions with *manger* in the perfect tense should be treated as vocabulary items here. In *Unité 10* there is an optional section on the perfect tense for teachers to use if they wish.

Point out a common *faux ami (les chips)*. The phrase *une pomme d'amour (toffee apple)* in the text could also provide scope for discussion.

transcript

Lou Leroux et la bonne alimentation

LL	Alors, Sophie, qu'est-ce que tu manges au goûter?
Girl	Au goûter, je mange une banane ou une poire, et quelquefois du chocolat aussi.
LL	Et toi, Thierry, qu'est-ce que tu prends normalement au déjeuner?
Boy	Au déjeuner, je mange un sandwich au fromage ou au jambon, avec beaucoup de chips et une tomate, puis un gâteau au chocolat.

LL Alors, les enfants, ce n'est pas très bien. Pour être en forme, mangez cinq portions de fruits et légumes par jour. Manger des chips et des gâteaux, ce n'est pas bon pour la santé.

Boy Monsieur! Hier j'ai mangé cinq portions de fruits et légumes.

LL Excellent, Sébastien! Qu'est-ce que tu as mangé?

Boy Au goûter, j'ai mangé une pomme, et le soir, au dîner, j'ai mangé des pommes de terre et des oignons. Puis comme dessert, j'ai mangé des fraises et des pêches.

LL Fantastique!

LL Votre fils a mangé cinq portions de fruits et légumes hier, c'est excellent!

Mum Voilà ce qu'il a mangé: une pomme d'amour ... un hamburger aux oignons et des frites ... et des fraises et des pêches avec beaucoup de crème.

LL Zut alors, Sébastien! La bonne alimentation, ce n'est pas ça!

 115   AT2; 7S4, 7L4

4 Travaillez à deux

In this pairwork activity students ask each other questions about the people in the cartoon and the food they eat.

115 4 tr 33   7L3

5 Ils mangent sainement?

This listening activity provides practice of the phrases needed to talk about healthy eating.

Solution: 1 *Karine – oui,* **2** *Noah – pas mal,* **3** *Nicolas – oui,* **4** *Valérie – non*

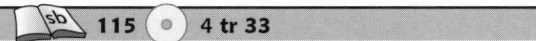

Ils mangent sainement?

1 – Karine qu'est-ce que tu manges au petit déjeuner?

 – Alors, pour le petit déjeuner, je mange des fruits et une tapour le rtine avec de la confiture d'oranges et, comme boisson, je prends un jus de fruits.

2 – Noah, tu déjeunes à la maison, non? Qu'est-ce qu tu manges, d'habitude?

 – Au déjeuner, je mange un hors-d'œuvre – par exemple, du melon avec du jambon. Puis de la viande avec des légumes comme des haricots verts, mais comme dessert, du gâteau ou une glace – j'adore ça!

3 – Nicolas, tu aimes être en forme, non, et tu manges bien?

 – Bien sûr. Aujourd'hui, on fait un pique-nique avec de la salade, des tomates et du fromage, puis après, du yaourt et un fruit.

4 – Valérie, c'est ton anniversaire aujourd'hui. Qu'est-ce que tu vas manger pour le goûter?

 – Euh, je ... alors, j'invite des amies à la maison et on va manger une grande glace au chocolat. Moi, je vais manger deux morceaux de mon gâteau favori. C'est mon anniversaire après tout!!

 Activité (int02)   AT1, AT2, AT3

Tu manges sainement?

Use this online role play activity as preparation for the following pairwork task.

115   AT2; 7L5; AfL

6 Tu manges sainement?

This pairwork activity draws together the discussion about healthy eating and food vocabulary. Some of the conversations could be recorded or presented to the class, with students giving feedback on the quality of the content and the accuracy of pronunciation. Remind them of the spread objectives and agree the criteria for success.

Plenaries (pages 114–115)

Fiche de travail (ws02)

1 Students write down two sentences summarising the lesson, then share these with the class. Discuss the key points to remember and what aspects might cause difficulties.

2 Students agree on (for instance) 10 words that they are going to find more difficult to remember from this unit so far. They then suggest and discuss things they are going to do to remember them.

9D Un repas en famille   pages 116–117

Aims and objectives	Grammar and skills	Resources
• discuss what you like to eat and drink • practise the negative and say 'not any' • learn what to say when having a meal with a French family	**Grammar** The negative (*ne ... pas*) **Skills** Please and thank you	**Key language:** see p170 **Online resource:** *Unité 9* int03, ppt01, ws02/06 **Copymasters:** 9/4, 9/5 **CD** 4 track 34 **GiA:** pp40–41

Starters (pages 116–117)

Fiche de travail (ws02)

1 **Qu'est que ça va être?** Display a random list of vocabulary items (food, drink, items from previous units such as animals, rooms, furniture – see online worksheet for suggestions). Begin to draw any one of the items. Students tell you as soon as they know what it is. Bad drawing makes this activity even more effective! Students can then continue in pairs.

2 **5-4-3-2-1** Display the grid and a list of words in random order (see online worksheet). Students find groups of similar words.

  5 fruits/légumes: *pêche, carotte, oignon, chou-fleur, fraise*

  4 adjectifs: *petit, jaune, bonne, délicieux*

  3 boissons: *café, eau, limonade*

  2 repas: *goûter, déjeuner*

  1 verbe: *mangeons*

116   **AT2, AT3; 7S5, 7T1**

1 Tu aimes ça?

Students read the two e-mails then work in pairs to ask questions and answer as Alex. Go over the text and check comprehension with a few questions. The online activity below could be used to consolidate work on the text.

Revise question forms if necessary and see how many different questions students can ask about the e-mails.

Remind students of words like *surtout* and as follow-up get them to make up sentences saying what they particularly like or dislike, e.g. *j'adore/j'aime/je déteste (les fruits), surtout (l'ananas)*.

116 Dossier-langue   **7S5**

The negative

Before looking for examples in the e-mails, remind students, if necessary, about negatives they have been using since *Unité 4*, e.g. *Je n'aime pas …, Je n'ai pas de …, Il n'y a pas …* and summarise the key points on the board, e.g.

  In English, the word .... is used to make a sentence negative.

  In French two words are used: ...... and ....

  (Use ...... before a vowel.)

  These two words go before and after the .... in a sentence.

116   **AT4; 7S5**

2 Je n'aime pas ça!

This short activity practises using the negative to say what students do not like (especially food, drink and activities).

Activité (int03)   **AT1, AT3, AT4**

Qu'est-ce qu'ils mangent?

This online activity provides practice in using the negative and revises animals, food, and the partitive.

117 Dossier-langue

pas de – not any

This explains the use of *de* instead of *du/de la/de l'/des* in the negative. The Mangetout cartoon on SB 116 presents several examples of *pas de/d'*. Do some oral work by displaying an item on the board and saying, e.g. *Il y a du fromage*. Then remove it and ask *Et maintenant? Il n'y a pas de fromage*. Gradually hand the activity over to students.

For further practice, display several items (this could be the online version of Kim's game below) then remove one or two items and ask *Qu'est-ce qu'il n'y a pas?*

Présentation (ppt01)   **AT2**

Jeu de mémoire: Il y a des frites?

A PowerPoint version of Kim's games to practise food and drink, including negative phrases.

9/4   **AT3, AT4**

La forme négative

This copymaster practises the negative.

  Solution:

  1 Des expressions utiles
    1 e, **2** a, **3** d, **4** c, **5** b

  2 À la cantine
    1 e, **2** d, **3** c, **4** a, **5** f, **6** g, **7** b

  3 Luc et Lucie
    1 d, **2** f, **3** h, **4** a, **5** b, **6** e, **7** c, **8** g

  4 Des phrases
    In this open-ended task, students make up their own sentences using some negative expressions.

117   **AT3; 7S5**

3 Complète les phrases

This activity provides further practice of the negative.

  Solution:
  Il n'y a pas <u>de farine</u>.
  Il n'y a pas <u>de margarine</u> et il n'y a pas d'<u>œufs</u>.

1 pp40–41

The negative (1) and (2)

Further practice of the negative.

154 Au choix   **AT3**

4 Le jeu de la carotte

First check that students recognise and remember the words for all the items illustrated.

The clues to the correct answers are in the negative. If some students need help, write the two alternatives on the board and work out one or two answers with them, letting them finish alone.

Solution: **1** *sucre*, **2** *fromage*, **3** *beurre*, **4** *poisson*, **5** *chocolats*, **6** *carotte*, **7** *viande*

 155 Au choix **AT3, AT4**

6 Les chiens et les chats

This sequencing task provides practice of the formation of negative sentences. If help is needed, suggest that students pick out the verb and then 'surround' it by *ne … pas*. The rest of the sentence should then be easily guessable.

Solution:

a **1** *Les chats ne jouent pas avec les enfants.*
 2 *Les chats ne sont pas intelligents.*
 3 *Les chats ne mangent pas bien.*
 4 *Les chats ne restent pas à la maison.*
 5 *Les chats n'aiment pas les enfants.*
b **1** *Les chiens ne sont pas indépendants.*
 2 *Les chiens ne sont pas intelligents.*
 3 *Les chiens ne mangent pas bien.*
 4 *Les chiens ne respectent pas les jardins.*
 5 *Les chiens n'aiment pas les autres animaux.*

 **117 Stratégies** **7W2, 7C5**

'Please' and 'thank you'

Remind students when to say *tu* and when to say *vous*, then ask them for some situations where they would use the different forms of 'please'.

Ask whether students are familiar with the letters RSVP at the bottom of an invitation. Can they work out what French words they stand for (*Répondez, S'il Vous Plaît*)?

 **117** 4 tr 34 **AT1, AT2, AT3; 7S3, 7L2**

4 À table

This item contains some key phrases and vocabulary, which are practised in part **b** and should be learnt by heart by the majority of students.

a Students listen to the recording without looking at the text. Ask a few general questions, e.g. *C'est quel repas? Est-ce qu'on prend un dessert?*

Then students listen with the text. To check understanding, ask what they would say (in French) in the following situations:

- say you'll have some water
- accept something you are offered
- say something is good
- say something is delicious
- say you don't like something very much
- say you've eaten enough of something
- say 'No thank you'
- say you'd like a banana

b Students vary the core conversation, which should help them to learn the key phrases and vocabulary.

 transcript

À table

Alex dîne chez une famille française.

- Assieds-toi là, Alex, à côté de Laurent.
- Oui, madame.
- Qu'est-ce que tu prends comme boisson? Il y a de l'eau minérale et de la limonade.
- De l'eau, s'il vous plaît.
- Pour commencer, il y a du potage aux légumes.
- Bon appétit, tout le monde.
- Mmm! C'est bon, ça.
- Tu veux encore du potage?
- Oui, je veux bien.
- Voilà. Maintenant, il y a du poisson. Et comme légumes, il y a des pommes de terre et du chou-fleur.
- C'est délicieux, madame.
- Tu veux encore du poisson?
- Non, merci, j'ai assez mangé.
- Tu prends de la salade?
- Non, merci, je n'aime pas beaucoup ça.
- Comme dessert, il y a des fruits. Qu'est-ce que tu prends?
- Je voudrais une banane, s'il vous plaît. Merci.

 Fiche de travail (ws06) **AT3, AT4**

Deux réponses possibles

This online worksheet provides a text reconstruction exercise based on the previous conversations.

 9/5 **AT2, AT3**

À table

This provides further practice of what to say when having a meal with a family. In task 2, students practise a dialogue with different variations.

1 Questions et réponses

Solution: **1** g, **2** e, **3** c, **4** d, **5** f, **6** a, **7** b

Plenaries (pages 116–117)

Fiche de travail (ws02)

1 Find out from students how they remember the gender, spelling and pronunciation of the items of food and drink. They work in pairs then report back to the whole class. If necessary, provide some ideas to start them off, e.g. *du chou* – both end in *u* – and cabbage can be tough/tasty as a 'shoe'?; *omelette* – spell it rhythmically *O–M–E … L–E … T–T–E.*

2 Mid-unit review: This is a suitable point for a Unit Review. Students shut their books and take stock of what they have learnt so far in this unit: vocabulary for food and meals, differences between *du/de la/de l'/des*, using the negative, discussing healthy eating.

9E Des projets   pages 118–119

Aims and objectives	Grammar and skills	Resources
• discuss what you are going to do (using *aller* + infinitive) • plan some meals and some picnics	**Grammar** The future, using *aller* + infinitive	**Key language:** see p170 **Online resource:** *Unité 9* int04, ppt02, ws02/07 **Copymasters:** 9/6 **CD** 4 tracks 35–36 **GiA:** p42

Starters (pages 118–119)

 Fiche de travail (ws02)

1 En groupes Display a list of words in random order or hand this out on slips of paper (see online worksheet). Ask students to put these into five groups:

le français, les mathématiques, la technologie
le déjeuner, le goûter, le dîner
des chaussures, une chemise, une veste
aime, adore, préfère
vert, petit, intéressant

2 Complète les phrases Display the following (see online worksheet). Give students a few minutes to read and work out the answers, then ask: *Le verbe numéro un va avec quelle phrase?* etc.

les verbes	*les phrases*
1 allons	**a** *Je … à Paris ce weekend.*
2 allez	**b** *Tu … au cinéma ce soir?*
3 vais	**c** *Mon frère … au bowling.*
4 vas	**d** *Nous … à la plage s'il fait beau.*
5 vont	**e** *Vous … aux magasins?*
6 va	**f** *Elles … au centre sportif.*

Solution: **1** d, **2** e, **3** a, **4** b, **5** f, **6** c

 **118**   **AT2, AT3; 7W5**

1 Deux e-mails

These two reading texts contain several examples of the future using *aller* + infinitive. Students should first read through the e-mails for gist and say what they think they are about. The online presentation below can be used to display the text initially and can accompany the *Dossier-langue* to highlight words like the infinitives and parts of *aller*.

Go through the true/false activity orally. To make it more interesting and involve all students, they could hold up a green card for *vrai* and a red one for *faux*. This also makes it easy to assess at a glance who has understood the text.

Solution: **1** *faux,* **2** *vrai,* **3** *vrai,* **4** *vrai,* **5** *faux,* **6** *faux*

 Fiche de travail (ws07)   **AT3, AT4**

Deux e-mails

This online worksheet provides support for task 1.

118 Dossier-langue   **7W5**

The future

Go through this, helping students to work out the structure and meaning of *aller* + infinitive. Check that they remember how to recognise an infinitive.

Présentation (ppt02)   **AT3**

aller + infinitif

This online PowerPoint presentation revises *aller* and introduces the future using *aller* + infinitive.

118   **4 tr 35**   **AT1, AT3; 7T1, 7L3**

2 Un pique-nique un peu spécial!

Go through the introductory text and make sure all students know what the conversations will cover. Ask questions such as *Est-ce qu'il va faire beau samedi prochain? Quel temps va-t-il faire dimanche?* etc.

Ask a few quick questions about the pictures, e.g. *Le jambon, c'est quel numéro? Le numéro 6, c'est quoi?* etc. Students then listen to the recording and note down the items each person brings.

Solution: *Léa 3, 5 (jambon + ananas), Dominique 7 (poulet), Chloé 2, 6 (tomates + oignons), Vivienne 1 (fromage), Hugo 8 (poisson/sardines), Noah 4 (petits pois)*

 transcript

Un pique-nique un peu spécial!

Chloé	Allô, c'est toi, Léa?
Léa	Oui, c'est moi. Salut, Chloé!
Chloé	Tu vas venir au pique-nique 'pizza'?
Léa	Oui, je vais venir. C'est une bonne idée.
Chloé	Qu'est-ce que tu vas apporter?
Léa	Euh, du jambon et de l'ananas pour une pizza hawaïenne. Ça va?
Chloé	Très bien! À samedi, alors.
	......
Chloé	Allô! C'est toi, Dominique?
Dom.	Oui, c'est moi, Chloé. Ça va?

Chloé	Oui, oui. Très bien. Dis-moi, Dominique, qu'est-ce que tu vas apporter pour le pique-nique?
Dom.	Ben, du poulet. Ça va, des morceaux de poulet?
Chloé	Des morceaux de poulet? C'est idéal!
Dom.	Et toi, Chloé? Qu'est-ce que tu vas mettre sur la pizza?
Chloé	Alors, moi, des tomates … et aussi des oignons.
Dom.	Ah bon! J'adore les oignons!
	……
Chloé	Salut! C'est Chloé à l'appareil. C'est Vivienne?
Viv.	Oui, oui, c'est moi, Vivienne. Tout va bien pour la pique-nique pizza?
Chloé	Oui, très bien.
Viv.	Moi, je vais apporter du fromage et Hugo va apporter du poisson.
Chloé	Ah, Hugo est là aussi? Génial! Alors toi, tu vas apporter du fromage, et Hugo du poisson. Quelle sorte de poisson?
Viv.	Je ne sais pas exactement. Des sardines, peut-être.
Chloé	Et ton frère, Noah, il vient aussi? Il va apporter quelque chose?
Viv.	Euh, oui. Il va venir! Mais il va apporter des petits pois!
Chloé	Des petits pois? C'est bon, sur les pizzas?
Viv.	Je ne sais pas. Mais Noah adore les petits pois, alors il pense que tout le monde les adore aussi.
Chloé	Ça va. À samedi, alors! Et bon appétit!
Viv.	Au revoir, Chloé. À samedi!

AT2; AfL

Follow-up for this activity could involve planning pizzas for different people, e.g. *une pizza pour les végétariens/carnivores*… Students work in pairs or groups and present their planned pizza to the class. This can be used as an opportunity for peer assessment, with students agreeing the criteria first (e.g. range of vocabulary, accuracy of French, use of future, suitability of content) then giving a score. This makes them listen carefully and critically to each presentation.

This could be followed by a pair work discussion planning what to put in a lunch box (*panier-repas*).

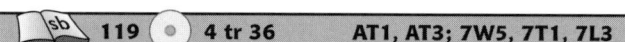
119 | **4 tr 36** | **AT1, AT3; 7W5, 7T1, 7L3**

3 Un repas «bon pour la santé»

This activity provides further practice of the future in the context of preparing healthy meals.

Part **a** is a reading text with structured questions using the future with *aller*.

Solution:

1 *Comme hors-d'œuvre, elle va manger **du potage aux légumes**.*

2 *Comme légumes, elle va prendre **des carottes et des oignons**.*

3 *Comme plat principal, Dylan va préparer **une grande omelette avec du jambon et des petits pois**.*

4 *Ses frères vont manger **des frites** avec l'omelette.*

5 *Ils vont manger du fromage **avant** le dessert.*

6 ***Ses frères** vont probablement manger du gâteau.*

7 ***Oui**, Marine va manger sainement.*

8 ***Non**, ses frères ne vont pas manger sainement.*

Part **b** gives an example of a healthy meal. Ask students questions similar to the ones in part **a** and discuss with them whether they think this is a healthy meal. *La salade, c'est bon pour la santé? Tu aimes les fruits? Est-ce que Max et sa sœur vont manger du fromage? Et de la viande? etc. Alors, le repas, c'est bon pour la santé?* Take a vote in the class.

Students then listen to the recording and complete the sentences.

Solution: **1** *de la salade,* **2** *des carottes, du chou et des brocolis,* **3** *des pommes ou des poires et peut-être du raisin,* **4** *viande/poisson,* **5** *des lapins*

---

transcript

Un repas «bon pour la santé»

– Alors Clémentine, félicitations! Ton repas, c'est vraiment très bon pour la santé. Tu vas préparer beaucoup de légumes, n'est-ce pas?

– Oui, c'est ça. Pour commencer, je vais préparer de la salade. Max adore ça.

– Oui, et comme plat principal?

– Alors, comme plat principal, Max et sa sœur vont manger des carottes, du chou et des brocolis.

– Mais il n'y a pas de viande et il n'y a pas de poisson?

– Ah non, ils n'aiment pas ça.

– Ah bon. Et comme dessert, ils vont manger des fruits, non?

– Oui. Je vais préparer une grande sélection de fruits: des pommes ou des poires et peut-être du raisin.

– Mais, dis-moi, Clémentine. Tu es sûre qu'ils vont manger tout ça, tous ces fruits et légumes?

– Oui, oui. Ils vont adorer tout ça.

– C'est qui, Max? C'est ton ami?

– Ah non. Max et sa sœur, ce sont mes deux lapins. Ils sont mignons!

 **119**   AT2, AT3; 7T5

4 Faites des projets

In this activity students discuss meals they would make for different people.

Read through the texts and explain any new vocabulary. They then work in pairs (or small groups) to discuss what they would offer for each course. Brainstorm suitable questions and display them as a reminder, e.g. *Qu'est-ce qu'on va manger comme hors-d'œuvre? Il/Elle va aimer le fromage? Le poisson, c'est bon pour la santé?*

Remind students that the answer to the question *Est-ce qu'il/elle va manger du fromage?* will require *de* rather than *du* because it is negative: *Non, il/elle ne va pas manger de fromage.*

 **9/6**   AT3, AT4; AfL

Qu'est-ce qu'on va faire?

1   aller *to go/to be going to*

Students revise the verb *aller* and complete the paradigm.

2   Chez la diseuse de bonne aventure

A   They then read the fortune teller's predictions and complete the *vrai ou faux* section.

> **Solution:**   **1** *vrai,* **2** *vrai,* **3** *faux,* **4** *vrai,* **5** *faux,* **6** *faux*

B   This time students complete the sentences about the future and underline the infinitives

> **Solution:**   **1** *va* <u>vivre</u>, **2** *vont* <u>aller</u>, **3** *va* <u>perdre</u>, **4** *vont* <u>avoir</u>, **5** *va* <u>gagner</u>, **6** *va* <u>arriver</u>

 Activité (int04)   AT1, AT3

On va manger

This online activity consolidates work on meals and *aller* + infinitive.

 **1 p42**   AT3, AT4

Verbs followed by an infinitive

Further practice of *aller* + infinitive.

Plenaries (pages 118–119)

 Fiche de travail (ws02)

1   Show visuals of some of the items of vocabulary that students have met in this unit (and also from earlier units). Which, if any, do students find hard to remember? Is it easy to remember the gender? Discuss as a class ways of memorising the more difficult words.

2   Discuss what students have been able to include in their *Dossier personnel* at this stage of the unit. Students could assess how far they have come in the last 3 units (before moving on to the final *Rappel* section of the book) and summarise what they now know.

9F La fête autour du monde   pages 120–121

Aims and objectives	Grammar and skills	Resources
• practise reading longer passages • learn about festival foods	**Skills** Practising reading skills **Cross-curricular** Religious studies	**Key language:** see p170 **Online resource:** *Unité 9* int05/06/07/08, ppt03, ws02/08/09 **Copymasters:** 9/7, 9/8 **CD** 4 tracks 37–42

Starters (pages 120–121)

 Fiche de travail (ws02)

1   **Vrai ou faux?** Display a series of statements (see online worksheet). When you read out each statement, students have to hold up a green card if it is true and a red card if it is false.

Statements:

Le chou est un fruit. [F]
Les carottes sont des légumes. [V]
Normalement, on mange le petit déjeuner l'après-midi, à cinq heures. [F]
Il n'y a pas de fruit dans une tarte aux pommes. [F]
La limonade est une boisson froide. [V]
Les lapins sont des légumes. [F]
Normalement, on prend le déjeuner à midi. [V]
Les végétariens mangent beaucoup de poulet. [F]
Manger beaucoup de chips, c'est bon pour la santé. [F]
Les Français prennent le dîner entre sept et huit heures du soir. [V]

2   **En groupes** Display a list of words (see online worksheet) in random order and ask students to put these into six groups:

un peu, beaucoup, pas trop
écris, lis, choisis
de l'eau, du jus, du lait
aller, manger, prendre
inventez, chantez, travaillez
des tartines, des croissants, des toasts

 **120**   AT3; 7W7, 7W8, 7T1

1 On parle des fêtes

This page practises reading harder texts and provides tips on how to approach longer texts. The descriptions cover three different festivals in the francophone world. Work through the various hints and strategies before students tackle each text and answer the questions in the online worksheet.

Students who are familiar with Eid, Thanksgiving and Diwali could give more information. The Islamic and Hindu calendars are different from the Gregorian calendar used in Europe, so the months do not entirely correspond. Ramadan can occur at various times of the year. Diwali is in October or November.

 Fiche de travail (ws08)   **AT3, AT4**

Autour du monde

This online worksheet provides writing follow-up based on the text *On parle des fêtes*.

 **155 Au choix**   **4 tr 37**   **AT1, AT3, AT4; 7C2**

7 On déjeune au Collège Missy

This item is based on authentic school dinner menus from the Collège Missy in La Rochelle, with students planning what they will have for lunch. If necessary, explain the use of *entrée* as an alternative to *hors-d'œuvre*.

Besides doing the linked tasks, pupils could discuss these menus, asking each other which they would choose.

Solution:

a 1 4, **2** starter, main course, cheese, dessert, **3** 1, **4** 4, **5** Wednesday (no school that day)

b 1 *une salade composée*, **2** *haricots (au beurre)*, **3** *poisson, lentilles*, **4** *mardi*, **5** *potage (aux légumes)*, **6** *mardi*, **7** *fruits*, **8** *jambon*

c 1 *jeudi*, **2** *jeudi*, **3** *lundi*, **4** *vendredi*, **5** *mardi*, **6** *vendredi*, **7** *vendredi*, **8** *jeudi*

transcript

On déjeune au Collège Missy

1 – Qu'est-ce qu'on va manger aujourd'hui?
  – Alors, de l'agneau comme plat principal – un kebab d'agneau. Et puis du fromage.

2 – On va manger un dessert aujourd'hui?
  – Bien sûr! On va manger de la mousse au chocolat.
  – Mmm! J'aime beaucoup ça!

3 – Qu'est-ce qu'on va manger comme plat principal?
  – Du poulet. Tu aimes ça?
  – Oui, j'aime beaucoup le poulet.

4 – Il fait froid ce matin. On va manger une entrée chaude?
  – Oui, il y a du potage au menu, du potage aux légumes.
  – Fantastique!

5 – Nous allons manger du poisson aujourd'hui?
  – Oui, c'est ça.
  – Avec des frites?
  – Ah non! Avec des lentilles.

6 – Ah bon! On va manger du steak aujourd'hui. J'adore ça.
  – Oui, oui, mais c'est du steak haché.
  – Oui, je sais. C'est avec quoi?
  – Avec des pommes de terre.

7 – J'adore les fruits. On va manger un fruit comme dessert aujourd'hui?
  – Regardons le menu … Ah oui, il y a des fruits. Moi, je vais choisir une banane. J'adore les bananes.
  – Excellent!

8 – On va nous servir de la charcuterie cette semaine?
  – Oui, regarde. Voilà!
  – Ah bon! Et des petits pois avec de la viande comme plat principal. Délicieux!

 **Présentation (ppt03)**   **4 tr 38–39**   **AT1, AT2, AT3**

Chantez! Pique-nique à la plage

This online PowerPoint presentation provides the lyrics and music for a song to practise language from the unit. It can be used at any convenient point, but now is a good time as it includes expressions with *aller* + infinitive. The song introduces some new vocabulary, e.g. *le panier, les petits pains, il ne faut pas, oublier*. This could be written on the board (or highlighted in the text) and students could be asked to check the words in the glossary. See TB 30 for words and music.

 **9/7**   **4 tr 40–42**   **AT1, AT3**

Tu comprends?

Students work alone on these listening activities.

1 Le déjeuner

Solution: **1** c, **2** b, **3** c, **4** b, **5** c, **6** b

transcript

Le déjeuner

– Qu'est-ce qu'on mange aujourd'hui au déjeuner?
– Pour commencer, il y a du jambon.
– Alors comme entrée, il y a du jambon.
– Oui, et comme plat principal, il y a du poisson.
– Mmm, j'aime bien le poisson. Et comme légumes?
– Comme légumes, il y a des petits pois.
– Des petits pois, oui.
– Et ensuite, il y a du fromage.
– Ah, j'aime bien le fromage. Et comme dessert?
– Comme dessert, il y a un gâteau au chocolat.
– Un gâteau au chocolat, chouette!
– Et comme boisson, il y a de l'eau minérale.
– De l'eau minérale, bien.

2 Qu'est-ce qu'ils prennent?

Solution: **A 1** b, **2** a, **3** g, **4** h, **5** d, **6** e
B 1 f, **2** d, **3** g, **4** b, **5** a, **6** c

transcript

Qu'est-ce qu'ils prennent?

A Des boissons

1 – Qu'est-ce que vous prenez, comme boisson?
– Je prends un café, s'il te plaît.
2 – Pour moi, un thé.
– Un thé, oui.
3 – Et Thomas, qu'est-ce qu'il prend?
– Alors pour Thomas, du lait, s'il te plaît.
– Un verre de lait, oui.
4 – Et toi, Nicole?
– Pour moi, un Coca, s'il te plaît.
– Un Coca, d'accord.
5 – Et toi, Luc?
– Un jus d'orange, s'il te plaît.
6 – Très bien, et pour moi, un chocolat chaud.

B Des fruits

– Comme dessert, il y a des fruits, alors qu'est-ce que vous prenez?
1 – Pour moi, des raisins, s'il vous plaît.
2 – Moi, je prends une pêche.
3 – Mmm, moi j'adore les fraises, alors je prends des fraises.
4 – Moi, je voudrais une poire.
5 – Pour moi, une pomme, s'il vous plaît.
6 – Et moi, je prends une banane.

3 Réponse positive ou négative?

Solution: 1 ✓, 2 ✗, 3 ✗, 4 ✗, 5 ✓, 6 ✗, 7 ✗, 8 ✗

transcript

Réponse positive ou négative?

1 – Est-ce qu'il y a du pain?
– Voilà le pain.
2 – Et avez-vous du beurre?
– Désolé, il n'y a pas de beurre.
3 – Est-ce qu'il y a de la confiture?
– Nous n'avons pas de confiture.
4 – Tu prends du chou-fleur?
– Désolé, mais je n'aime pas le chou-fleur.
5 – Est-ce qu'il y a du lait?
– Bien sûr, il y a du lait.
6 – Est-ce que Claire mange de la viande?
– Elle est végétarienne, alors elle ne mange pas de viande.
7 – Tu prends du sucre?
– Merci, je ne prends pas de sucre.
8 – Tu veux du fromage?
– Merci, mais je n'aime pas beaucoup le fromage.

Activité (int05)   AT1, AT3

Rue Danton: Les courses à l'hypermarché

Online activities to support the ninth episode in the ongoing soap story.

Activité (int06)   AT1, AT3

Vocabulaire de classe (9)

This online activity practises some more key classroom language.

Fiche de travail (ws09)/Présentation (ppt04) AT3

Métallo

This online book-fold reader provides extension fiction reading material. Use the PowerPoint for whole-class presentation of the reader.

sb 121 cm 9/8

Sommaire

A summary of the main language and structures of the unit, also provided on copymaster for reference.

Activité (int07)   AT3

Vocabulaire (9)

An online game which tests the vocabulary of the unit.

Activité (int08)   AT1, AT3

Quiz – Unités 8 et 9

An online quiz which tests the language and content of *Unités 8* and *9*.

Plenaries (pages 120–121)

Fiche de travail (ws02)

1 Students think about how they read for gist in understanding texts with unfamiliar language, e.g. *La fête autour du monde*. Discuss useful strategies, e.g. similarity to English, context, type of word, need to know etc.

2 Students produce a spider diagram of everything learnt in the unit. This could be in groups or as a whole-class activity with students contributing to the spider diagram on the board.

Unité 9 Consolidation and assessment

Épreuves Unité 9

These worksheets can be used for an informal test of listening, reading and writing or for extra practice.

For general notes on the *Épreuves*, see TB 20.

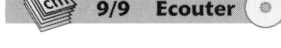 9/9   Écouter ○ 4 tr 43–45   AT1

A Le pique-nique

Solution: **1** f, **2** j, **3** b, **4** a, **5** h, **6** g, **7** c, **8** e (mark /7)

transcript

Le pique-nique

Qu'est-ce qu'il y a pour le pique-nique?

1 Il y a du pain, du pain,

2 du jambon, du jambon,

3 du fromage, du fromage,

4 des tomates, des tomates,

5 des œufs, des œufs,

6 des pommes, des pommes,

7 des raisins, des raisins.

8 Et comme boisson? Comme boisson, il y a de la limonade. Ah bon, j'aime bien la limonade.

B Le petit déjeuner

Solution: (mark /6: 1/2 mark per correct tick)

	bread etc.	cereal	juice	coffee	milk	choc	tea
1	✓			✓			
2	✓						✓
3	✓	✓	✓				
4		✓				✓	
5	✓				✓		
6	✓	✓		✓			

transcript

Le petit déjeuner

1 – Au petit déjeuner, je prends du café au lait et des tartines avec du beurre.
  – Alors, tu prends du café comme boisson et du pain avec du beurre, c'est tout?
  – Oui, c'est tout.

2 – Le matin, je prends des tartines avec du beurre et de la confiture et un bol de thé.
  – Tu prends du thé comme boisson et du pain avec du beurre et de la confiture, c'est ça?
  – Oui, c'est ça.

3 – Au petit déjeuner, je prends du jus de fruit et des céréales. Et je prends aussi des tartines beurrées.
  – Comme boisson, tu prends un jus de fruit, et avec ça tu prends des céréales et des tartines avec du beurre.

4 – Et moi, je prends un chocolat chaud comme boisson et je mange des céréales.
  – Alors, tu prends un chocolat chaud et des céréales, c'est tout?
  – Oui, c'est tout.

5 – Le matin, je prends des tartines avec du beurre et de la confiture et je bois du lait.
  – Bon, tu prends du lait comme boisson et tu manges du pain avec du beurre et de la confiture, c'est ça?
  – Oui, c'est ça.

6 – Au petit déjeuner, je mange des céréales et des tartines avec du beurre et je bois du café.
  – Alors, comme boisson, tu prends un café, et avec ça tu prends des céréales et des tartines avec du beurre.
  – Oui, c'est ça.

C À table

Solution: **1** a, **2** c, **3** b, **4** a, **5** b, **6** a, **7** b, **8** a (mark /7)

transcript

À table

– Assieds-toi là, Claire, à côté de Sophie.
– Oui, madame.
– Qu'est-ce que tu prends comme boisson? Il y a de la limonade et de l'eau.
– De la limonade, s'il vous plaît.
– Pour commencer, il y a de la salade aux tomates.
– Bon appétit, tout le monde.
– Mmm! C'est bon, ça.
…

– Voilà, maintenant, il y a de l'omelette au fromage. Et comme légumes, il y a des pommes de terre et du chou.
– C'est délicieux, madame.
– Tu veux encore de l'omelette?
– Non, merci, j'ai assez mangé.
…

– Tu veux de la salade?
– Oui, s'il vous plaît.
– Et comme fromage, il y a du Camembert. Tu veux du fromage, Claire?

La météo

- Ce week-end, il y a des matchs importants en Angleterre, en Écosse et au pays de Galles. Alors, quel temps fait-il là-bas ce week-end, Robert Legrand?

- Oui, eh bien, ce week-end le temps est assez variable. À Cardiff, par exemple, où il y a un grand match de rugby, la France contre le pays de Galles, il fait froid. La température est de 6 degrés.

- Oh, à Cardiff, il fait froid. Alors, bon courage à tous les supporters de l'équipe de France. Et à Birmingham?

- À Birmingham, il y a du vent assez fort, alors il ne fait pas beau non plus. Oui, à Birmingham, il y a du vent pour le match de football cet après-midi ... mais la température est de 10 degrés, une température normale pour la saison.

- Hmm, du vent à Birmingham. Et en Écosse?

- Eh bien, à Édimbourg, pour le grand match international de hockey, il fait beau. Alors, si vous allez à Édimbourg pour le match de hockey, vous avez de la chance, il fait beau. La température est de 12 degrés.

- Très bien, du beau temps à Édimbourg. Merci, Robert.

📖 **62 Dossier-langue**   **7W6**

Les accents

This extends the work on accents, covering grave and circumflex accents on other vowels, *c* cedilla and the trema.

Students should look for words with accents on the spread and these can be collected in groups and written on the board.

📖 **62** ● **3 tr 6**   **AT1**

3 Trouve le mot

Students listen to the spelling of each word, write it down and identify it.

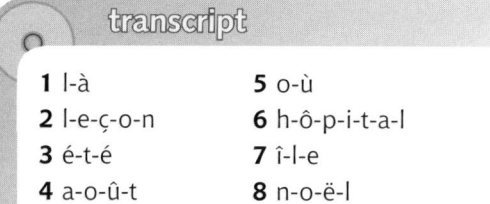

1 l-à	**5** o-ù
2 l-e-ç-o-n	**6** h-ô-p-i-t-a-l
3 é-t-é	**7** î-l-e
4 a-o-û-t	**8** n-o-ë-l

📄 **Fiche de travail (ws04)**   **AT3, AT4**

Les accents

An online worksheet to practise recognising and writing the correct accents.

📖 **63**   **AT3; 7T1**

4 Le climat en France

This could be introduced by referring to a map of France and talking briefly about the climate (in English, if necessary), mentioning such things as:

- the Mediterranean climate, with hot summers and mild winters, fruit such as peaches and grapes growing outside and people eating outdoors a lot;

- the Alps, where there is often snow for five months of the year, making skiing a popular sport;

- the Mistral, and how houses are built with no windows on the side it blows from;

- the effect of the warmer climate on people's homes – houses have shutters to keep out the strong sunlight, tiled floors in the kitchen to keep the house cool, fitted carpets are generally less common.

Students match each photo with the text.

> **Solution:** **1** d, **2** c, **3** a, **4** b

✏️ **Fiche de travail (ws05)**   **AT2, AT3, AT4**

En été, il fait beau

An online worksheet to practise describing the weather in more detail.

📖 **63 Dossier-langue**   **7W2, 7S2, 7S8, 7T7**

This covers clauses with *quand*. Able students could create longer sentences linking weather conditions and activities. Invite suggestions and display suitable sentences around the classroom.

📖 **63**   **AT4; 7T6**

5 Dossier personnel

The work on weather should be completed with students writing a few sentences describing the weather in their area.

📖 **63**   **AT2; 7W6, 7S4, 7S8, 7L1, 7L6; AfL**

6 C'est quel mot?

Working in pairs students take it in turns to ask and answer questions. Some students could make up additional questions for use in a pair or team game. If used for peer assessment, review the spread objectives and assessment criteria first. Share with students how work can be improved. Successful students could share their dialogue with the class.

> **Solution:** (suggestions) **1** *avril*, **2** *automne*, **3** *beau, brouillard*, **4** *chaud*, **5** *décembre*, **6** *été*, **7** *février*, **8** *hiver*, **9** *juin, juillet*, **10** *un parapluie*

64   Stratégies

Everyday sayings (idioms)

This mentions the use of idioms with the following French examples: *il pleut des cordes*; *il fait un temps de chien*. These sometimes give an insight into the culture. English is particularly rich in idioms, so if there is time for cross-curricular work, there could be more discussion about idioms in English.

Plenaries (pages 62–63)

Fiche de travail (ws02)

1   Ask students to think about words with accents and work in pairs to see how many they can recall of the different types mentioned. Ask whether they think the accent helps them with pronunciation. Students who have studied other languages could comment on whether there are accents in other languages and whether they think they would be useful in English.

2   If possible display a large map of France (ICT resource, **CM 128**) and ask students what they have learnt about the climate in France.

6C Le sport	pages 64–65	
Aims and objectives	**Grammar and skills**	**Resources**
• talk about sport • use the verb *jouer*	**Grammar** *je joue* **au** … Present tense of *jouer*	**Key language:** see p108 **Online resource:** *Unité 6* ppt03, ws02/06 **CD** 3 track 7 **Flashcards:** 37–42

Starters (pages 64–65)

 Fiche de travail (ws 02)

1   **Chasse à l'intrus** Display or print out the following lists. Students identify the odd word out in each list (shown in bold). Ask students collectively or randomly to give the '*intrus*'. Several students could be asked for their answer before the teacher gives the correct one. Ask for volunteers to explain why.

A	B	C	D	E	F
dimanche	suis	**du papier**	je	nous	deux
vendredi	êtes	du brouillard	**est**	ils	treize
froid	sont	du vent	tu	**avons**	vingt
samedi	**chaud**	du soleil	elle	vous	**mauvais**

2   **Ça commence avec …** Display or print the words in brackets below.

Students have to recognise and write down the word which fits each category. Ask students randomly or collectively for the correct answers.

Ça commence avec **c**
1   *un vêtement (une chaussette)*
2   *un animal (un chien)*
3   *une pièce à la maison (une cuisine)*
4   *un verbe (chanter)*
5   *quelque chose dans la salle de classe (un cahier)*
6   *une expression qui décrit le temps (chaud)*
7   *un nombre (cinquante)*

Ça commence avec **p**
1   *une saison (le printemps)*
2   *un oiseau (un perroquet)*
3   *un adjectif (petit)*
4   *un verbe (préférer)*

5   *une fête (Pâques)*
6   *un vêtement (un pantalon)*
7   *un prénom (Pierre)*

Introduction FC 38–40	**AT1, AT2**

Les sports

Go through the objectives for this spread.

List the names of sports, which are the same in English and French, e.g.

le badminton, le football, le golf, le hockey, le rugby, le tennis,

and read them out so students hear the correct pronunciation.

Then teach *le tennis de table, le basket* and *le volley* using the flashcards 38–40.

Practise the words orally e.g. through a chain question game:

- *Un sport qui commence avec b?*

- *le badminton.*

- *Très bien. Pose une question.*

- *Un sport qui commence avec h*, etc.

Introduce the photographs on SB 64 orally first, e.g.

Voilà un groupe de jeunes.

On fait beaucoup de sports.

Claire et Thomas jouent au volley. Le volley, qu'est-ce que c'est en anglais? C'est 'volleyball'.

On joue beaucoup au volley en France, et ici?

Est-ce que Claire et Thomas jouent au tennis?

Non, ils jouent au …

Et Sophie, elle joue au volley?

Paul et Yannick jouent à quel sport?

Qui joue au basket? etc.

1 Au club de sports

This task brings together the eight sports and the different forms of *jouer* which are explained and practised later. Students note down the correct photo for each speaker.

Solution: **1** A, **2** D, **3** B, **4** F, **5** H, **6** G, **7** E, **8** C

Au club de sports

1 – Bonjour Claire, bonjour Thomas. Qu'est-ce que vous faites aujourd'hui?
  – Bonjour. Aujourd'hui, nous jouons au volley.

2 – Et Marc, est-ce qu'il joue avec vous?
  – Non, Marc joue au basket.

3 – Et toi, Simon, tu joues au tennis, non?
  – Oui, moi, je joue au tennis.

4 – Tu aimes le sport, Ibrahim?
  – Oui, j'adore le sport, je joue aujourd'hui au hockey.

5 – Est-ce que Jonathan et Nicole jouent aussi au hockey?
  – Non, ils jouent au badminton.

6 – Et vous, Daniel et Luc, vous jouez au tennis de table, non?
  – Oui, nous jouons au tennis de table.

7 – Et Sophie, elle joue avec vous?
  – Non, Sophie joue au golf.

8 – Et Paul et Yannick, ils jouent au football, je suppose?
  – Oui, ils jouent au football.

2 C'est faux!

This task presents the third person, singular and plural, and should be done orally first. Point out that the third person singular and plural forms sound identical, although they are spelt differently.

Solution:

1 *Marc joue au basket.*
2 *Claire et Thomas jouent au volley.*
3 *Ibrahim joue au hockey.*
4 *Paul et Yannick jouent au football.*
5 *Simon joue au tennis.*
6 *Sophie joue au golf.*
7 *Daniel et Luc jouent au tennis de table.*
8 *Jonathan et Nicole jouent au badminton.*

Chain game

Play a quick class game, such as a cumulative list of sports or a game where each person has to mention a different sport, referring to the list on the board if necessary, e.g.

Je joue au tennis, et toi, (student A)?
Je joue au tennis et au football, et toi, (student B)? etc.

For other vocabulary games, see TB 21.

Ask: *les noms de ces sports sont-ils masculins ou féminins?*

This explains the use of *jouer au* + masculine sport and *jouer aux* + plural game. This point is covered in more detail in *Unité 10*.

3 Inventez des conversations

Students practise in pairs making up short conversations about sport. This could be done as an information gap activity in pairs, with each student first writing the names of three sports on a mini whiteboard. They take it in turn to guess the three sports listed, by asking:

- *Tu joues au football?*
- *Non, alors, c'est à moi. Tu joues au golf?*
- *Oui.*
- *Alors je continue. Tu joues au volley?*
- *Non, etc*

Les verbes réguliers

An online PowerPoint presentation of the present tense of regular –er verbs.

Jouer (to play) – a regular –er verb

This sets out the present tense of *jouer*, with key points that apply to all verbs. More work is done on –er verbs later.

Build on students' knowledge of the standard paradigm (following earlier work on *avoir* and *être*) and build up the pattern for a regular –er verb.

Use the ICT resource or write the verb on the board and give plenty of practice in deleting a few endings at a time or removing the stem or the pronoun from some parts and asking students to replace them. This could be played in teams, with students taking turns to delete or fill in missing parts.

4 Ils jouent bien?

Practice in selecting the correct part of the verb from three options.

Solution: **1** *Je joue,* **2** *Tu joues,* **3** *Ma fille joue,* **4** *Nous jouons,* **5** *Vous jouez,* **6** *Ils jouent*

5 Du sport pour tous

Students complete each sentence with the correct part of the verb and sport. This could be used for assessment. Revise the spread learning objectives with students and relate success criteria to these objectives.

> **Solution:**
>
> 1 *vous jouez au volley*
> 2 *nous jouons au basket*
> 3 *tu joues au badminton*
> 4 *je joue au badminton*
> 5 *il joue au hockey*
> 6 *ma sœur joue au hockey*
> 7 *mon frère joue au rugby*
> 8 *tes parents jouent au tennis*
> 9 *ils jouent au tennis*
> 10 *mon grand-père joue au golf*

FC 37, 41, 42

Vous n'aimez pas le sport?

Present the words for a few activities (with *jouer*) for non-sporty people, e.g.

Moi, je ne suis pas sportif/sportive, je joue aux cartes.
Mon frère n'est pas sportif, il joue aux jeux vidéo/sur l'ordinateur.
Mes parents ne sont pas sportifs. Quelquefois, nous jouons tous au Monopoly.

6 Dossier personnel

Prepare this in class with volunteers writing suggestions on the board to help students who need more support.

Fiche de travail (ws06)   AT4

Je joue ...

This online worksheet provides a writing frame to support the *Dossier personnel*.

Plenaries (pages 64–65)

Fiche de travail (ws02)

1 Students should discuss tips for remembering regular verb endings; for instance writing out a verb in a table and using colour to distinguish the stem and the ending. They could then use the find and replace function to change the stem of the verb. This could be tried using *jouer* and replacing *'jou'* with *'aim'* of *aimer*.

Applying the paradigm to other regular –*er* verbs is covered fully in the next area.

2 Students (perhaps in pairs) could think of a way to teach someone else the present tense of *jouer* and invent a suitable activity.

6D Des verbes   pages 66–67

Aims and objectives	Grammar and skills	Resources
• use some regular –*er* verbs	**Grammar** Conjugating regular –*er* verbs Using different subject pronouns	**Key language:** see p108 **Online resource:** *Unité 6* int03/04, ppt03, ws02 **CD** 3 tracks 8–9 **Flashcards:** 38–42 **GiA:** pp17–21

Starters (pages 66–67)

Fiche de travail (ws02)

1 **En groupes** Display or print out a list of words in random order and ask students to put these into 5 groups. Ask for volunteers to read out three words which form a group.

> *je, tu, elle*
> *Écoute, Regarde, Complète*
> *nous, vous, ils*
> *trouver, jouer, copier*
> *inventez, chantez, travaillez*

2 **Trouve les paires** Display or print out the following table. Students match up the two parts and note the pairs. Check these by asking the class collectively to read out the correct sentences.

1 *Tu*	**a** *regarde un film.*
2 *Est-ce qu'il*	**b** *jouons au golf.*
3 *Marie*	**c** *détestent les devoirs.*
4 *Nous*	**d** *aimez les animaux?*
5 *Vous*	**e** *aimes le football?*
6 *Elles*	**f** *joue au tennis?*

Solution: **1** e, **2** f, **3** a, **4** b, **5** d, **6** c

---

Introduction   AT1, AT2

Go through the objectives for this spread.

Teach *Qu'est-ce que tu fais?* and use this to ask for answers in the first person, e.g.

Je regarde la télévision.
J'écoute la radio/de la musique.

Je travaille.

Then play some miming or flashcard games using different persons of the verb (see TB 22). The flashcards using *jouer* (38–42) can also be used for further practice.

 Présentation (ppt03) | **AT3**

Les verbes réguliers

Presentation of *jouer* as a regular *-er* verb. Introduced earlier, this online presentation could also be used here to support this spread.

 Activité (int03) | **AT1, AT3**

Des activités

This online activity presents leisure activities and can be used at any suitable point from now on.

 **66** ⊙ **3 tr 8** | **AT1, AT3; 7T1, 7T2**

1 Un film avec Tom et Jojo

This presents several examples of verbs of action. Students listen to the recording and follow the text.

transcript

Un film avec Tom et Jojo

Jojo est une souris. Elle pense à quelque chose. C'est le fromage.

Tom est un chat. Il pense à quelque chose. C'est Jojo.

Voilà le fromage. Voilà Jojo.

Jojo mange le fromage.

Voilà Tom. Tom entre dans la cuisine.

Tom chasse Jojo. Est-ce qu'il mange Jojo? Jojo entre dans le salon.

Tom saute sur Jojo. Il attrape Jojo?

Aïe!! Non, il n'attrape pas Jojo.

Tom chasse Jojo dans la salle de bains. Il saute …

Pouf! Non! Il n'attrape pas Jojo dans la salle de bains.

Jojo rentre dans la cuisine. Voilà le fromage! Mais voilà Tom!

Et voilà Butch! Butch arrive. Butch n'aime pas Tom. Il chasse Tom … et Jojo mange le fromage.

 **66** | **AT3; 7T1**

2 Vrai ou faux?

Students read the sentences individually or in pairs and decide whether they are true or false.

> **Solution:** **1** *vrai,* **2** *faux,* **3** *vrai,* **4** *faux,* **5** *faux,* **6** *vrai,* **7** *vrai,* **8** *vrai,* **9** *vrai,* **10** *faux*

 Activité (int04) | **AT1, AT3, AT4**

Tom et Jojo

An online gap-fill activity based on the *Tom et Jojo* cartoon.

 **1 pp17–19**

Regular *-er* verbs – singular (1), (2), (3)

Further practice of the singular forms of regular *-er* verbs.

 **67** | **AT3; AfI**

3 Où est le verbe?

This task provides practice in identifying the verb in a sentence and can be used for assessment. Emphasise to students the process they should work through to achieve success. Students could also be asked for the meaning and/or infinitive.

> **Solution:** **1** *écoute,* **2** *habites,* **3** *clique,* **4** *parle,* **5** *surfons,* **6** *aimez,* **7** *cherchent,* **8** *détestent*

  **67 Dossier-langue** | **7W6**

Regular *-er* verbs

The pattern of regular *-er* verbs is applied here to other verbs. Use the example of the flower – the stem remains the same whilst the flower has different petals – just like the stem of a verb, which doesn't change whilst the endings do.

To reinforce the importance of learning the endings, explain to students that they can use these to form the present tense of all verbs in French which end in *-er* (except *aller*) and prove it by giving them one or two verbs they have never used before, e.g. *fabriquer, téléphoner, surfer, cliquer, danser* to conjugate.

Stress that, whilst the spelling changes for some endings, the pronunciation of all the parts is the same except for the *nous* and *vous* forms.

Another idea for learning verbs is to make verb cards. Make two slits in a large card and write the 3 singular persons + endings on one side and the plural persons + endings on the reverse.

Then on a strip of card the width of the slit, write the stem of some *-er* verbs with a good gap in between each. Weave the strip through the two slits. By moving the strip up and down the verbs can be read off.

If students created a verb table with *jouer,* they can now add other verbs.

Practice of verbs

There are a number of tasks to practise verbs and the teacher can select those that are most appropriate for the class. It is not necessary to do them all and some could be used later for revision. See also **Games for practising verbs** (TB 24).

 **148 Au choix** AT4

3 Devant la télé

This task gives practice in writing out different parts of the verb *regarder* and provides consolidation for all students.

Solution: 1 *regardes,* 2 *regarde,* 3 *regardent,* 4 *regardez,* 5 *regardent,* 6 *regardons,* 7 *regarde,* 8 *regardent,* 9 *regarde,* 10 *regardent,* 11 *regarde*

 **67** ● **3 tr 9** AT1; 7W5, 7T5

4 Pendant les vacances

Introduce this item by referring to the opening dialogue, e.g.

On va écouter des personnes qui parlent des vacances. Par exemple, voici François. Il aime les vacances et il adore le camping.

Discuss possible answers first and why – linking the subjects and appropriate endings.

Maintenant écoutez les conversations et trouvez les paires.

Play the conversations, pausing after each one for students to match up the two parts of the sentences, or play the whole recording twice, with shorter pauses. If used in a language laboratory, this task could be done on an individual basis.
Correct the task as a class activity, with students reading out the complete sentences as well as giving the matching numbers and letters.

Solution: 1 b, 2 c, 3 a, 4 e, 5 d, 6 g, 7 j, 8 f, 9 h, 10 i

 transcript

Pendant les vacances

1 – François, tu aimes les vacances?
 – Bien sûr.
 – Et qu'est-ce que tu fais pendant les vacances?
 – Je fais du camping avec mes amis. J'adore le camping.
2 – Et toi, Christine, qu'est-ce que tu fais?
 – J'habite à La Rochelle avec ma famille et en été, nous passons beaucoup de temps au soleil.
3 – Jean-Marc et Sandrine, qu'est-ce que vous aimez faire pendant les vacances?
 – Ça dépend. En hiver, nous aimons faire du ski.

4 – Et en été, qu'est-ce que vous faites?
 – En été, nous restons à la maison et nous invitons des amis à la maison.
5 – M. et Mme Duval, qu'est-ce que vous faites pendant les vacances?
 – Eh bien, au mois de juin, il y a la fête de la Musique. Alors nous écoutons toutes sortes de musique.
6 – Et votre fille Mathilde chante dans un groupe, non?
 – Oui, c'est ça. Notre fille Mathilde chante dans un groupe ici.
7 – Salut, Nicolas et Isabelle. Qu'est-ce que vous faites pendant les vacances?
 – Comme nous habitons à la ferme, nous restons ici, normalement. Ma sœur, Isabelle, et moi, nous travaillons à la ferme avec mon père.
8 – Tu aimes les animaux, Isabelle?
 – Ah oui, j'aime beaucoup les animaux.
9 – Et qu'est-ce que tu fais, le soir, Nicolas?
 – Le soir, je joue au football avec mes amis.
10 – Et quand il pleut?
 – Quand il pleut, je joue sur l'ordinateur.

g/a **1 pp20–21**

Regular –*er* verbs – singular and plural (1), (2)

Further practice of the full paradigm of regular –*er* verbs.

Plenaries (pages 66–67)

Fiche de travail (ws02)

1 Students practise several different techniques for learning verbs in pairs or groups, e.g. paradigm circle practice, chain verb game and then discuss which they find most useful.
2 Students work individually or in pairs to design a framework for learning verbs, e.g. flower with petals, Ollie the Octopus with 8 tentacles, chest of drawers, house with different person of the verb in each room.

6E En famille pages 68–69

Aims and objectives	Grammar and skills	Resources
• talk about family activities • say what you do at weekends • practise using –er verbs	**Grammar** Practising using –er verbs **Skills** Keeping a conversation going	**Key language:** see p108 **Online resource:** *Unité* 6 int05, ppt04, ws02/07 **Copymasters:** 6/4, 6/5, 6/6 **CD** 3 track 10

Starters (pages 68–69)

 Fiche de travail (ws02)

1 Chasse à l'intrus Display or print out the following lists. Students identify the odd word out in each list (shown in bold). Ask students collectively or randomly to give the 'intrus'. Several students could be asked for their answer before the teacher gives the correct one.

A	B	C	D	E	F
un frère	**février**	quatre	chantons	méchant	un lit
une sœur	préparer	onze	cherchez	petit	**un cahier**
une chambre	détester	**range**	parlent	**saute**	une table
un cousin	écouter	douze		grand	une chaise

2 Chaque mot à sa place Display the following task. Give students one minute to read and work out the answers, then ask students collectively or randomly to give the number of the box. Several students could be asked, before confirming the correct answer.

Quelle est la bonne boîte pour chaque mot?

quinze (C), regardons (D), bon (E), téléphoner (B), cahier (F), cousin (A)

A	B	C	D	E	F
frère	préparer	quatre	chantons	méchant	crayon
cousine	détester	onze	cherchons	petit	stylo
sœur	écouter	douze	parlons	grand	classeur

Introduction

Go through the objectives for this spread.

 **68** AT3; 7T6

1 Les frères, c'est difficile!

Check that students have understood the main points by asking a few questions, e.g.

Comment s'appelle le frère d'Alain? (Henri)
Henri, quel âge a-t-il? (4 ans)
Henri, est-il méchant ou mignon?
Alain, qu'est-ce qu'il pense?
Et sa mère?
Et vous, que pensez-vous/Et toi, que penses-tu?

a This could be prepared orally and the missing words written on the board in random order.

Solution: **1** *frère*, **2** *chambre*, **3** *méchant*, **4** *saute*, **5** *dessine*, **6** *mange*, **7** *écoute*, **8** *travaille*, **9** *chante*, **10** *danse*

b This task involves recognition of a range of verbs, including parts of *avoir* and *être*.

Solution: Any ten verbs from the following:
J'ai, Il s'appelle, Il a, il partage, Il est, Il saute, il dessine, il écoute, il mange, je travaille, il chante, il danse, je raconte, elle dit, il est, il est, pensez-vous

Further work on this topic is given in *Au Choix* task 5 (SB 149), *Une petite sœur difficile* (see later).

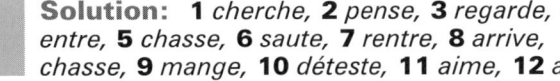 **6/4** AT4; 7W5

Tom et Jojo

1 Un petit lexique

This gives the vocabulary required for the next item. Students write down the English meanings.

 Solution:

adorer	to love	entrer	to come/go in
aimer	to like	manger	to eat
arriver	to arrive	penser	to think
chasser	to chase	regarder	to look at/watch
chercher	to look for	rentrer	to return
détester	to hate	sauter	to jump

2 Tom et Jojo

Practice of the *il* and *je* forms of the *–er* verbs in the previous list.

 **Solution:** **1** *cherche*, **2** *pense*, **3** *regarde*, **4** *entre*, **5** *chasse*, **6** *saute*, **7** *rentre*, **8** *arrive*, *chasse*, **9** *mange*, **10** *déteste*, **11** *aime*, **12** *adore*

 Présentation (ppt04) AT2, AT3

Les Paresseux

An online presentation of the text *Les Paresseux* showing the appropriate changes to the infinitives.

 **68** AT3; 7W5

2 Les Paresseux

This gives practice of the *nous* and *ils* forms of regular *–er* verbs.

Solution: **1** *nous organisons*, **2** *les Paresseux surfent*, **3** *nous jouons*, **4** *les Paresseux regardent*, **5** *nous dansons*, **6** *ils écoutent*, **7** *nous travaillons*, **8** *ils restent, ils consultent*, **9** *nous chantons*, **10** *ils écoutent*, **11** *nous fêtons*

For follow-up ask some questions, e.g.
Est-ce que les Paresseux jouent au tennis?
Et les Actives, est-ce qu'ils jouent?
Et dans ta famille, vous jouez au tennis ou vous regardez le tennis à la télé?

Extra practice

Students work in groups of 6, with each person making up a sentence for one person of a different *–er* verb.

 Activité (int05) AT3, AT4

La vie des Paresseux

An online writing activity to support *Les Paresseux*.

 **69** AT3, AT4; 7W5

3 Le week-end

Practice of all forms of the present tense with a range of *–er* verbs.

Solution: **1** *Je prépare*, **2** *Tu chantes*, **3** *Il déteste*, **4** *Elle travaille*, **5** *Nous surfons*, **6** *Vous travaillez*, **7** *Ils aiment*, **8** *Elles regardent*

6E En famille

Les verbes

This provides further practice of the present tense of *–er* verbs.

> **Solution:**
>
> **1 Sept verbes**
>
> **1** *chantons,* **2** *regardez,* **3** *préparent,*
> **4** *travaille,* **5** *écoutes,* **6** *dansent,* **7** *travaillent*
>
> **2 Qu'est-ce qu'on dit?**
>
> **1** *joue,* **2** *travailles,* **3** *prépare,* **4** *joue,*
> **5** *dansons,* **6** *aimez,* **7** *regardent*

4 Deux interviews

This listening task provides some examples for students to use in their own conversations in task 5.

For task **b**, discuss possible answers with the class first.

> **Solution: a 1** b, **2** a, **3** b, **4** a, **5** a, **6** b
> **b 1** c, **2** a, **3** d, **4** e, **5** b

transcript

Deux interviews

Anne

– Bonjour. Comment t'appelles-tu?

– Je m'appelle Anne.

– Est-ce que tu aimes le sport, Anne?

– Non, je n'aime pas le sport.

– Qu'est-ce que tu fais, normalement, le week-end?

– Ça dépend. Quelquefois, je retrouve des amis. Nous discutons ensemble. Nous écoutons de la musique.

– Et quand tu n'es pas avec tes amis, qu'est-ce que tu fais?

– Alors, je joue à la console ou je regarde une vidéo.

Marc

– Et toi, comment t'appelles-tu?

– Je m'appelle Marc.

– Et qu'est-ce que tu fais, normalement, le week-end, Marc?

– Eh bien, moi, j'adore le sport. Alors, je joue au football avec des amis. Quelquefois, je joue au tennis dans le parc.

– Et quand il fait mauvais, qu'est-ce que tu fais?

– Quand il fait mauvais, je regarde du sport à la télé.

– Est-ce que tu aimes la musique?

– Non, je n'aime pas beaucoup la musique.

5 Une longue conversation

Students work in pairs to pose questions about week-end activities and to develop the conversation for as long as possible. Review the spread objectives and assessment criteria, then use this task for peer assessment. A successful conversation could be shared with the class as a model answer.

This mentions the use of *souvent, normalement* and *quelquefois* and the need to ask questions to keep a conversation going.

Fiche de travail (ws07)   AT3, AT4

Phrases au choix

An online worksheet providing a 'dictate and create' activity based on the verbs used in this unit.

148 Au choix   AT2, AT4

4 Des phrases au choix

Students throw a dice or write down numbers randomly to create different sentences.

This can be done initially as a speaking activity (pair or groupwork), then written. Students could compete to make up the silliest sentence.

149 Au choix   AT3

5 Une petite sœur difficile

This letter, in response to the earlier letter from Alain (SB 68, 1 *Les frères, c'est difficile!*), provides further practice of verbs in the context of family life.

a *Vrai/faux* task. For extension, students could correct the false statements.

> **Solution:** **1** *vrai,* **2** *faux (Elle a une sœur.)*
> **3** *vrai,* **4** *faux (Elle a sept ans.)* **5** *vrai,* **6** *faux*
> *(Sophie porte les vêtements de Julie.)* **7** *vrai*

b Students complete a summary of the letter. The missing words could be written in jumbled order on the board.

> **Solution:** **1** *sœur,* **2** *Elle,* **3** *chambre,* **4** *pulls,*
> *chaussures,* **5** *écoute, danse,* **6** *travaille,* **7** *jouent*

c Students complete sentences about a difficult younger sister.

> **Solution:** **1** *travaille, mange,* **2** *joue,* **3**
> *dessine,* **4** *regarde*

6/6

Des activités

Further practice of sport, *–er* verbs and adverbs of time.

1 J'adore le sport

Solution:

2 Chaque jour, un sport différent

Various answers are possible.

3 Un acrostiche

Solution:

1 *téléphonent*, **2** *retrouve*, **3** *cliques*,
4 *préfère*, **5** *écoutez*, **6** *tapent*, **7** *restons*

4 Les verbes

Solution:

Students complete the table as follows:

anglais		français	phrases
1	to draw	dessiner	dessine
2	to sing	chanter	chantes
3	to listen to	écouter	écoute
4	to dance	danser	danse
5	to play	jouer	jouons
6	to watch	regarder	regardez
7	to type	taper	tapent
8	to prepare	préparer	préparent

Plenaries (pages 68–69)

 Fiche de travail (ws02)

1 Students could reflect on techniques for developing speaking skills, such as the ways they used to keep the conversation going in the earlier task.

2 Students could discuss what they have found most useful/difficult so far in the unit.

6F On s'amuse   pages 70–71

Aims and objectives	Grammar and skills	Resources
• use *on* + verb • talk about different activities according to the weather	**Grammar** *On* **Skills** Reading French handwriting Writing a postcard **Pronunciation** Nasal sounds	**Key language:** see p108 **Online resource:** *Unité 6* ws02/08 **Copymasters:** 6/7 **CD** 3 tracks 11–13

Starters (pages 70–71)

 **Fiche de travail (ws02)**

1 **En groupes** Display or print out a list of words in random order and ask students to put these into 5 groups. Ask volunteers to read out three words in a group or circle them on the board.

chanter, danser, écouter
hiver, printemps, automne
juin, janvier, juillet
Pâques, Noël, Eid
beau, mauvais, chaud

2 **Vrai ou faux cards** Make true/false statements, using the weather/activity flashcards and ask students to hold up a *vrai* or *faux* card.

Introduction

Go through the objectives for this spread.

70   AT3

1 La fête de la science

La fête (Faites) de la science is a programme of free scientific events for the general public. It is part of the Europe-wide Festival of Science, which aims to increase the links between professional scientists, researchers and the public. It usually takes place in October/November and comprises workshops, exhibitions, visits to laboratories and industrial organisations, etc. Some towns set up a marquee to house a *village de science* during the fête.

For further details, see the website:
www.fetedelascience.fr

Solution:

1 October

2 exhibitions, laboratory visits, industrial and natural sites, lectures, films, shows

3 No, it's free to the public.

4 More than 1 million

 **70   Dossier-langue**   **7W2**

On

Explain that *on* is used a lot in French and can be translated in different ways (one, they, we, you, people in general, etc.).

 **70**   **AT3; 7S9**

2   C'est quoi en anglais?

Students translate sentences into English. This demonstrates the different ways in which *on* is used. They could do this individually first then the answers can be checked in class. There may be several possible versions.

Solution:

1 Shall we watch the film on TV?
2 It's raining so shall we surf the net?
3 At Easter, people eat Easter eggs.
4 At Eid, people organise a big meal.
5 At Diwali, we light lamps.
6 You don't play football in the kitchen.
7 The weather's good; shall we play tennis?
8 They don't speak English in France.

 **70**   **AT2; 7S4, 7L5**

3   Qu'est-ce qu'on fait?

Practice in pairs using *on* to make suggestions.

 **71   3 tr 11**   **AT1; 7T5, 7L3**

4   Au téléphone

These two conversations bring together the themes of weather and leisure activities.

a Discuss possible answers with students before they listen to the recording. They could also guess the answers first then listen to check.

Solution: 1 *Bordeaux*, 2 *basket*, 3 *beau*, 4 *La Rochelle*, 5 *mauvais*, 6 *chambre*

b In this task, students have to answer questions in French.

Solution: 1 *Max*, 2 *Nicole*, 3 *Max*, 4 *Nicole*, 5 *Il fait très froid.*

---

transcript

Au téléphone

a   Suzanne et Luc

– Allô?
– Salut, Suzanne. C'est Luc à l'appareil.
– Ah bonjour, Luc. Ça va?
– Oui, ça va bien. Je suis à Bordeaux.
– Ah bon, et qu'est-ce que tu fais là-bas?
– Je suis avec l'équipe de basket. Nous jouons un match aujourd'hui.
– Et est-ce qu'il fait beau?
– Oui, il fait beau, mais pas très chaud. C'est bien. Et toi, qu'est-ce que tu fais aujourd'hui?
– Ben, ici à La Rochelle, il fait très mauvais. Alors, je reste à la maison et je range ma chambre.

b   Nicole et Max

– Allô?
– Bonjour, Nicole. C'est Max à l'appareil.
– Ah, bonjour, Max. Ça va?
– Oui, merci. Et toi?
– Oui, ça va bien.
– Qu'est-ce que tu fais aujourd'hui?
– Je travaille sur l'ordinateur. Je regarde mes e-mails et je tape des messages.
– Mais on joue au tennis dans le parc. Tu aimes le tennis? Viens jouer avec nous.
– Merci, mais il fait très froid aujourd'hui. Je préfère rester à la maison.

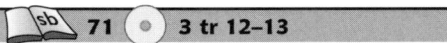 **71   3 tr 12–13**   **AT1, 7W6**

Prononciation

This gives practice in nasal sounds: *on* and *om*, followed by *in*, *ain*, and *im*.

Students listen to each word and write the corresponding letter.

Solution: 1 c, 2 d, 3 a, 4 b

---

transcript

Prononciation: words with 'on' and 'om'

Écoute et écris la bonne lettre.

1 sont
2 computer
3 combien
4 conquête

Solution: 1 b, 2 c, 3 a, 4 d

Prononciation: words with '*in*', '*ain*', and '*im*'

Écoute et écris la bonne lettre.

1 juin
2 important
3 printemps
4 américain

 **71**   AT2; 7S3, 7S4, 7T2, 7L4, 7L6

5 Inventez des conversations

Students practise conversations about the weather and related activities.

 71   AT3, AT4; 7W5, 7T3, 7T6; AfL

6 Des cartes postales

Students practise reading then writing a postcard.

Solution: a 1 *janvier*, **2** *passe*, **3** *mauvais*, **4** *il*, **5** *On*, **6** *jouent*, **7** *regarde*, **8** *prépare*

b Prepare this orally first, writing suggestions on the board.

Review the objectives and assessment criteria, then use this task for assessment. A model of successful work can be used as a focus for improvement once the task has been completed.

 **Fiche de travail (ws08)**   AT3, AT4

Des cartes postales

This online activity provides a writing frame to support the Student's Book activity.

 **71   Stratégies**

Writing a postcard

Tips for writing cards and messages.

6/7   AT3, AT4

Des cartes postales

This provides further practice of weather, leisure and verbs for use here or later for revision.

1 À lire

Solution:

1 ~~un mois~~ – une semaine
2 ~~août~~ – octobre
3 ~~beau~~ – mauvais
4 ~~volley~~ – tennis de table

2 À compléter

Solution:

> *Bordeaux, le 12 **avril***
> *Nous **passons** un week-end ici, dans un hôtel.*
> *C'est pour fêter l'anniversaire de mon père.*
> *Il fait **chaud**. Il y a du **soleil**. C'est fantastique.*
> *Aujourd'hui, nous **jouons** au tennis.*
> > *À bientôt,*
> > *Alex*

3 À écrire

Students can now write their own postcards based on the details given.

 **149   Au choix**   AT4

6 Ça dépend du temps

An open-ended task in which students complete the sentences with an appropriate activity.

 **149   Au choix**   AT4

7 Mon journal de vacances

Students describe the weather and activities for different days.

Plenary (pages 70–71)

 Fiche de travail (ws02)

Students could reflect on writing French; what they find easy and difficult, whether they find writing words and phrases helps to reinforce learning.

6G On invente des conversations   pages 72–73

Aims and objectives	Grammar and skills	Resources
• practise and improve speaking skills	**Skills** Using familiar language to work out unfamiliar phrases Improving your spoken work using adverbs, connectives and extra detail	**Key language:** see p108 **Online resource:** *Unité 6* int06/07/08/09. ppt05, ws02/09 **Copymasters:** 6/8, 6/9 **CD** 3 tracks 14–18

Starters (pages 72–73)

Fiche de travail (ws02)

1 **5-4-3-2-1** Display a list of words and students find groups of 5,4,3,2,1 similar words.

e.g. *aimer, chercher, écouter, regarder, travailler*
froid, chaud, beau, mauvais
printemps, hiver, été
volley, tennis de table
souvent

A sheet with a printed grid for this could be distributed for students to record their answers.

2 **C'est comme l'anglais mais le son est différent**
Give out a list of cognates or near cognates.

a	*animal*	**e**	*juin*
b	*automne*	**f**	*message*
c	*chocolat*	**g**	*région*
d	*iPod*	**h**	*rugby*

Read them out in a different order, as below. Students note the number by the word they hear. When checking, ask for volunteers to say the words in French.

1	*animal*	**5**	*juin*
2	*iPod*	**6**	*message*
3	*rugby*	**7**	*chocolat*
4	*automne*	**8**	*région*

Introduction

Go through the objective for this spread.

In the following sequence of tasks, students work individually until the final conversation, but this could be varied. There are strategy boxes to help students with the different tasks.

 72 | AT4; 7S3, 7S4

1 Des questions

Students write any three questions, using three different structures.

 72 | AT2, AT4; 7S3

2 Des réponses

Working individually, students write answers for their three questions.

Alternatively they could work in pairs, asking a partner a question and responding in turn.

 72 | 3 tr 14 | AT1; 7W2, 7L3

3 Deux personnes

Students listen to two people in conversation using similar questions and answers and complete the gaps in their text.

Solution: **1** *le week-end*, **2** *amis*, **3** *mauvais*, **4** *badminton*, **5** *basket*, **6** *télé*, **7** *musique*

– Qu'est-ce que tu fais le week-end?
– Je joue souvent au foot avec mes amis. Quand il fait mauvais, je surfe sur Internet.
Est-ce que tu joues au foot?
– Non, je ne joue pas au foot, mais quelquefois, je joue au badminton avec ma sœur.
Tu aimes le sport?
– Oui, j'adore le sport. Je joue au foot et au basket et je regarde souvent des matchs à la télé. Et toi?
– Le sport, ça va, mais je préfère écouter de la musique ou surfer sur Internet.

 72 | AT2; 7L4, 7L5; AfL

4 Une conversation

Working in pairs, students make up a conversation with at least three exchanges. This can be used for peer assessment. Relate success criteria to spread objective and encourage students to demonstrate their skills.

Activité (int06) | AT1, AT2, AT3

On discute des vacances

An online role play activity to practise asking and answering questions about holiday leisure and sport activities.

6/8 | 3 tr 15–18

Tu comprends?

1 Les numéros de téléphone

Solution:
le cinéma Rex:	03.24.13.42.50
le café Robert:	03.15.56.37.60
le collège:	03.39.68.12.41
la famille Laurent:	03.75.80.16.23

Les numéros de téléphone

1 – Tu as le numéro de téléphone du cinéma Rex?
– Oui, le voilà. C'est le zéro trois, vingt-quatre, treize, quarante-deux, cinquante.
– Alors, je répète: zéro trois, vingt-quatre, treize, quarante-deux, cinquante.

2 – Le numéro du café Robert, qu'est-ce que c'est?
– C'est le zéro trois, quinze, cinquante-six, trente-sept, soixante. Je répète: zéro trois, quinze, cinquante-six, trente-sept, soixante.

3 – Le numéro du collège, qu'est-ce que c'est?
– C'est le zéro trois, trente-neuf, soixante-huit, douze, quarante et un.
– Alors, je répète: zéro trois, trente-neuf, soixante-huit, douze, quarante et un.

4 – Vous avez le numéro de téléphone de la famille Laurent?

– Oui, le voilà. C'est le zéro trois, soixante-quinze, quatre-vingts, seize, vingt-trois. Je répète: zéro trois, soixante-quinze, quatre-vingts, seize, vingt-trois.

2 La météo

Solution: **1** b, **2** b, **3** a, **4** a, c, **5** b, a, **6** b, b

transcript

La météo

– Bonjour mesdames et messieurs. Aujourd'hui, nous sommes le jeudi quinze janvier. Il fait froid. Est-ce que ça va continuer, Claire Artaud?

– Oui, en effet, il fait froid et il va continuer à faire froid dans toute la France. La température est de trois degrés. À Paris, il pleut et il y a du vent.

– Alors de la pluie et du vent à Paris. Et dans les Alpes, est-ce qu'il y a de la neige?

– Oui, dans les Alpes, il y a de la neige et il y a aussi du brouillard. Alors, faites très attention, si vous êtes en montagne.

– Alors, dans les Alpes, de la neige et du brouillard. Et le beau temps, est-ce qu'il y a du beau temps aussi?

– Oui, dans l'ouest, à Bordeaux, il y a du soleil et il fait assez beau, mais il fait toujours froid.

– Alors, voilà, pour trouver le beau temps, il faut aller à Bordeaux. Merci, Claire.

3 Comment ça s'écrit?

Solution: 4 (*cahier*) is the odd word out.

transcript

Comment ça s'écrit?

1 c–h–a–n–t–e–r
2 j–o–u–e–r
3 a–i–m–e–r
4 c–a–h–i–e–r
5 é–c–o–u–t–e–r
6 p–r–é–p–a–r–e–r
7 t–r–a–v–a–i–l–l–e–r

4 Un sondage sur le sport

Solution:

	bad'ton	basket	hockey	football	tennis	volley
1 Anne					✓	✓
2 Marc		✓		✓		
3 Nicole						✓
4 Paul	✓		✓			
5 Lucie	✓				✓	✓
6 Robert				✓		
Total	2	1	1	2	2	3

Le sport le plus populaire est: le volley

transcript

Un sondage sur le sport

1 – Bonjour, Anne. Est-ce que tu fais du sport?

– Oui, je fais beaucoup de sport. Je joue au volley et je joue au tennis.

2 – Bonjour, Marc. Est-ce que tu aimes le sport?

– Oui, j'aime le sport. Je joue au football et au basket.

3 – Bonjour, Nicole. Est-ce que toi aussi tu aimes le sport?

– Non, pas beaucoup, mais je joue quelquefois au volley.

4 – Tu es Paul, c'est bien ça?

– Oui, c'est moi.

– Alors, Paul, est-ce que tu fais du sport?

– Oui, je fais beaucoup de sport. Je joue au badminton et au hockey. J'aime bien ça.

5 – Lucie, est-ce que tu aimes le sport?

– Le sport? Oui, j'adore le sport.

– Qu'est-ce que tu fais comme sports?

– Je joue au badminton et au tennis et je joue aussi au volley.

6 – Et toi, Robert, est-ce que tu aimes le sport?

– Un peu. Je joue quelquefois au football, mais c'est tout.

 **73** **6/9**

Sommaire

A summary of the main vocabulary and structures in the unit.

 **Activité (int07)** **AT3**

Rue Danton: Le sport préféré de Manon

Online activities to support the sixth episode of the video 'soap'.

6G On invente des conversations

Activité (int08)   **AT3**

Vocabulaire de classe (6)

An online activity to present and practise more key phrases for use in the classroom.

Fiche de travail (ws09)/Présentation (ppt05) AT3

Le blog de Sébastien

This online book-fold reader provides extension material on the language and topics of this unit.

Use the PowerPoint for whole-class presentation of the reader.

Activité (int09)

Vocabulaire (6)

An online game which tests the vocabulary of the unit.

Plenaries (pages 72–73)

Fiche de travail (ws02)

Reflect on the importance of correct pronunciation when speaking French.

Give students some cognates to practise saying in French. See if students are beginning to grasp spelling and pronunciation patterns.

e.g.
1	*danger*	5	*nature*
2	*excellent*	6	*table*
3	*intelligent*	7	*imagination*
4	*incident*	8	*important*

Use the *Sommaire* to review the objectives of the unit and what has been learnt. Discuss how the language learnt could be useful in other contexts.

Unité 6 Consolidation and assessment

Épreuves Unité 6

 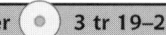 **6/10 Écouter** ⬤ **3 tr 19–21**   **AT1**

A Le temps et les saisons

Solution: **1** f, **2** d, **3** i, **4** h, **5** e, **6** g, **7** b, **8** a, **9** c

(mark /4: 1/2 mark per correct item)

transcript

Le temps et les saisons

1. – Il neige.
   – Ah oui, il neige.
2. – Il fait chaud.
   – Pff, comme il fait chaud.
3. – Il y a du vent.
   – Oui, quel vent.
4. – Il pleut.
   – Oui, il pleut beaucoup.
5. – Il fait froid.
   – Oui, il fait très froid.
6. – Il y a du brouillard.
   – Oui, il y a du brouillard.
7. – C'est l'hiver.
   – On est en hiver.
8. – Moi, je préfère le printemps. Le printemps, c'est ma saison préférée.
9. – Il y a du soleil.
   – Oui, j'adore le soleil.

B À la maison

Solution:

	musique	ord'teur	cartes	dessiner	télé	console
1 Sanjay			✓			
2 Claire				✓		
3 Jonathan						✓
4 Magali					✓	
5 Daniel	✓					
6 Sika		✓				

(mark /5)

transcript

À la maison

1. – Qu'est-ce que tu fais quand il fait mauvais, Sanjay?
   – Moi, je joue aux cartes avec mes amis.
   – Tu joues aux cartes. C'est bien.
2. – Et toi, Claire, qu'est-ce que tu fais?
   – Moi, je dessine. J'aime beaucoup dessiner.
3. – Jonathan, qu'est-ce que tu fais, normalement, quand tu es à la maison?
   – Je joue à la console. J'adore les jeux vidéo.
   – Alors, toi, tu joues à la console.
4. – Et toi, Magali, qu'est-ce que tu fais?
   – Moi, je regarde la télévision.
   – Tu regardes la télévision.

5 – Et toi, Daniel, qu'est-ce que tu fais quand il fait mauvais?

– J'écoute de la musique sur mon baladeur. J'adore la musique.

6 – Et toi, Sika, qu'est-ce que tu fais à la maison?

– Je travaille sur l'ordinateur. J'écris des messages électroniques à mes amis.

– Alors, toi, tu travailles sur l'ordinateur.

C Une interview

Solution:

Nom: *Hériot*   (1 mark)

Prénom: *Claire*

Adresse: *81 rue Saint-Pierre*   (1 mark)

Numéro de téléphone: *13 67 90 75 42* (5 marks)

Sports préférés: hockey ✓; volley ✓   (2 marks)

Autres loisirs: drawing ✓; listening to music ✓ (2 marks)

(mark /11: the name Claire is given and is not awarded a mark)

transcript

Une interview

– Bonjour. Comment t'appelles-tu?

– Je m'appelle Claire Hériot.

– Hériot. Comment ça s'écrit?

– H–É–R–I–O–T.

– Alors, c'est H–É–R–I–O–T.

– C'est exact.

– Et ton adresse, Claire?

– Alors, mon adresse, c'est quatre-vingt-un, rue Saint-Pierre.

– Quatre-vingt-un, rue Saint-Pierre. Très bien. Et ton numéro de téléphone?

– Mon numéro de téléphone c'est le 13, 67, 90, 75, 42.

– Alors, je répète, c'est le 13, 67, 90, 75, 42. Et quels sont tes sports favoris?

– Mes sports favoris sont le hockey et le volley.

– Alors, tes sports favoris sont le hockey et le volley. Très bien. Et est-ce que tu as d'autres loisirs, à part le sport?

– Oui, j'écoute souvent de la musique et je dessine.

– Bon, tu écoutes de la musique et tu dessines. Très bien. Merci, Claire.

6/11 Lire   **AT3**

A Des activités

Solution: **1** f, **2** e, **3** h, **4** b, **5** c, **6** g, **7** d, **8** a

(mark /7)

B Samedi

Solution: **1** c, **2** g, **3** d, **4** e, **5** a, **6** b, **7** f

(mark /6)

C Une lettre de Bordeaux

Solution: **1** *faux*, **2** *vrai*, **3** *vrai*, **4** *faux*, **5** *vrai*, **6** *vrai*, **7** *vrai*, **8** *faux*

(mark /7)

6/12 Écrire et grammaire   **AT4**

A Le temps

Solution: **1** *mauvais*, **2** *beau*, **3** *chaud*, **4** *froid*

(mark /3)

B Quel temps fait-il?

Solution: **1** *Il neige.* **2** *Il pleut.* **3** *Il y a du soleil.* **4** *Il y a du vent.* **5** *Il y a du brouillard.*

(mark /4)

C À Dieppe

Solution: **1** *passe*, **2** *habitent*, **3** *travaille*, **4** *jouons*, **5** *aimes*, **6** *chantent*, **7** *rentrez*

(marks/6)

D Une carte postale

Solution: (mark /7: 1 mark for each meaningful sentence + 2 marks for style/accuracy)

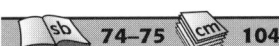

74–75   **104**   **AT3**

Presse-Jeunesse 2

These pages provide reading for pleasure. They can be used alone or with the accompanying worksheet. See the notes on TB 4.

74–75   **104**

Tom et Jojo

The worksheet task focuses on verbs and provides practice in gist comprehension of the cartoon story.

Solution:

1 *adore*, **2** *il n'y a pas de fromage*, **3** *il y a du fromage*, **4** *n'est pas*, **5** *n'est pas*, **6** *est*, **7** *Jojo*

Le sais-tu?

L'origine des coutumes de Noël

Solution: **1** *La crèche*, **2** *une bûche en chocolat*, **3** *une bûche traditionnelle*, **4** *le Père Noël*, **5** *le Saint Nicolas*, **6** *le Père Janvier*

Le nouvel élève

Task A gives practice in gist comprehension. Task B requires more detail.

Solution:

A 3 is the correct summary.
B **1** a, **2** b, **3** b, **4** a, **5** a, **6** b, **7** a, **8** b

Tricolore Total 1
Unité 7　En ville　pages 76–89

Aims and objectives	Key language/Culture	Grammar and skills	National criteria
7A La Rochelle pp76–77 • learn about a town in France • learn some town vocabulary	Locations: aquarium (m)/auberge de jeunesse (f)/camping (m)/hôtel de ville (m)/marché (m)/musée (m)/office de tourisme (m)/parc (m)/piscine (f)/restaurant (m)/tour (f) vieux festival **Culture** Finding out about a French town, La Rochelle	**Pronunciation** The letter h	**Attainment** AT1 Level 1–3, AT2 Level 1–2, AT3 Level 1–3, AT4 Level 1–2 **Framework** 7W6/7, 7T2, 7L1/2 **Languages ladder/Asset languages** Grades 1–4 **Assessment for learning** ex 2
7B Qu'est-ce qu'il y a en ville? pp78–79 • learn more town vocabulary • ask about places	More locations : un hôpital/une banque/un centre sportif/un centre commercial/une école/un parking/un bowling/la poste/un supermarché/les toilettes (f pl)/le château/ un vélo/une voiture un bâtiment vieux/vieille Il y a .../Il y a beaucoup de ... **Culture** History of les vélos jaunes in La Rochelle	**Grammar** vieux/vieille **Pronunciation** Words ending in –t and –te	**Attainment** AT1 Level 1–3, AT2 Level 1–3, AT3 Level 1–4, AT4 Level 1–4 **Framework** 7W2/4/6, 7S4/9, 7T1/5, 7L1/3 **Languages ladder/Asset languages** Grades 1–4 **Assessment for learning** Oral practice
7C C'est près d'ici? pp80–81 • ask for directions and information • understand directions	la cathédrale/la gare/le théâtre/l'église (f) sur la place le bus Directions: Pour aller... Est-ce qu'il y a (un café) près d'ici? Où est ....? C'est loin? C'est à (+ distance) à gauche, à droite, tout droit premier(ère), deuxième, troisième		**Attainment** AT1 Level 1–4, AT2 Level 1–4, AT3 Level 1–4, AT4 Level 1–2 **Framework** 7S4, 7T1, 7L2/3/4/6 **Languages ladder/Asset languages** Grades 1–4 **Assessment for learning** ex 2 consolidation, ex 7
7D Où exactement? pp82–83 • use the preposition 'à' • say where things are using other prepositions	Prepositions : au, à la, à l', aux devant/dans/sur/derrière/entre/sous + à côté de, en face de	**Grammar** The preposition à – au, à la, à l', aux Other prepositions: devant, entre, derrière, à côté de, en face de + revision of dans, sur, sous	**Attainment** AT1 Level 1–3, AT2 Level 1–3, AT3 Level 1–3, AT4 Level 1–3 **Framework** 7W2/4/6, 7S2/4, 7T2, 7L3/6 **Languages ladder/Asset languages** Grades 1–3 **Assessment for learning** ex 2
7E C'est comment, ta ville? pp84–85 • talk about the area where you live • use longer sentences	Dans mon quartier, il y a ... mais il n'y a pas de ... Près d'ici il y a ... Au centre-ville, il y a ... C'est bien pour les jeunes? Oui, c'est bien/C'est assez bien/Non, c'est nul une mosquée/une synagogue/un temple/une patinoire/un terrain de football/une bibliothèque	**Skills** Extending sentences using connectives	**Attainment** AT1 Level 1–4, AT2 Level 1–4, AT3 Level 1–4, AT4 Level 1–4 **Framework** 7W2/4, 7S1/5, 7T5/7, 7L3/4/5/6 **Languages ladder/Asset languages** Grades 1–4 **Assessment for learning** ex 5, ex 7
7F Allez, on y va pp86–87 • use the verb 'aller'	Present tense of aller : je vais　　　nous allons tu vas　　　vous allez il/elle/on va　ils vont	**Grammar** Present tense of aller	**Attainment** AT1 Level 1–4, AT2 Level 1–3, AT3 Level 1–3, AT4 Level 1–3 **Framework** 7W4/5, 7S7, 7T5, 7L3 **Languages ladder/Asset languages** Grades 1–4 **Assessment for learning** ex 4
7G Une ville touristique pp88–89 • understand tourist information • listen to a longer text	Consolidation	**Skills** Understanding longer texts	**Attainment** AT1 Level 1–4, AT2 Level 1–3, AT3 Level 1–4, AT4 Level 1–3 **Framework** 7T1, 7L3 **Languages ladder/Asset languages** Grades 1–4 **Assessment for learning** ex 2

Other resources: Online resource *Unité 7*, Copymasters 7/1–7/14, CD 3 tracks 22–40, Flashcards 8–12, 43–60, GIA pp22–27

La Rochelle

This unit contains information that will be useful when visiting any French town, but La Rochelle was selected as the setting for this unit for a variety of reasons:

- it is an attractive place to visit and a holiday resort, but also very much a working town; a university was opened in 1992.

- it is a major centre for marine and nautical activities (Aquarium opened in 2000).

- it combines old and new areas and has both picturesque buildings and modern developments; it is big enough to contain many interesting features, but not too big to visit on foot.

- it has been at the forefront in developing initiatives to protect the environment and has pioneered recycling schemes, pedestrian zones in the town centre (1975), the municipal bikes scheme (1976) and the use of electric cars. Michel Crépeau was elected mayor in 1971 and later became Minister for the Environment (1981–1983). An earlier councillor was nicknamed *Monsieur Imagination*.

- the festival of French music, *Les Francofolies*, set up in 1984, attracts many musicians in July.

- it is easy to reach by rail, road and air and welcomes school parties!

For more information about La Rochelle, see
http://www.ville-larochelle.fr
http://www.larochelle-tourisme.com.

7A La Rochelle pages 76–77

Aims and objectives	Grammar and skills	Resources
• learn about a town in France • learn some town vocabulary	**Pronunciation** The letter *h*	**Key language:** see p128 **Online resource:** *Unité 7* ppt01, ws02 **CD** 3 tracks 22–23 **Flashcards:** 43–51

Starters (pages 76–77)

 Fiche de travail (ws02)

1 **5-4-3-2-1** Play in small groups or as a class. Display the following words in random order or partially group them with 1 or 2 word(s) to be added to each group.

5 *bâtiments:* une maison, un café, un cinéma, un appartement, un magasin
4 *points du compas:* nord, sud, est, ouest
3 *saisons:* hiver, printemps, été
2 *prépositions:* dans, à
1 *endroit où se trouvent les bâtiments:* une rue

A sheet with a printed grid could be distributed for students to record their answers. This could then be checked and completed as a class activity.

2 Display the following words and ask students if they can guess how they would be pronounced in French. They could practise in pairs and then volunteers could demonstrate their French pronunciation.

un hôpital, un hôtel, horrible, le horizon, une histoire

Introduction

Go through the objectives for this spread. Mention that the French town of La Rochelle provides the background for the unit. It has been linked with Tricolore for about 30 years and has become increasingly popular as a tourist destination (the 3rd most visited town in France); 25% are foreign tourists, of which the majority are English. The town is also known for its many environmental initiatives.

 Présentation (ppt01) | **AT1, AT3**

La Rochelle

An online PowerPoint presentation of some of the new vocabulary for places in town in the context of La Rochelle.

Town vocabulary

Teach the following: *l'auberge de jeunesse, le camping, l'école, le marché, le musée, l'office de tourisme, la piscine, le restaurant, l'hôtel de ville* (this will need a brief explanation in English to prevent confusion with *hôtel*).

- Ask students to guess the following cognates (writing them on the board): *l'hôtel, le parc, le parking, la tour.*

- Do some question and answer practice, e.g. distribute flashcards (43–51), ask *Où est* (+ noun)?

The student with the appropriate flashcard returns it, saying *Voici* (+ noun).

- Play some flashcard games and spelling games, e.g. *Effacez!* (using flashcards or words), *Je pense à quelque chose dans une ville* and *Jeu de mémoire* (see TB 22).

 **76** ● **3 tr 22**　　　　**AT1, AT3; 7T2, 7L2**

1 Voici La Rochelle

Look at the photos with the class and discuss what they show about the town.

Students then listen to the recording and match the text with the pictures, either individually or in pairs.

■ **Solution: 1** I, **2** B, **3** K, **4** G, **5** A, **6** F, **7** L, **8** H, **9** D, **10** J, **11** C, **12** E

transcript

Voici La Rochelle

1 – Salut! Je m'appelle Marine, et voici mon frère, Noah.

– Nous habitons à La Rochelle. C'est une ville dans l'ouest de la France.

2 – La Rochelle est au bord de la mer, alors on fait beaucoup de sports nautiques,

3 – Dans le centre-ville, il y a beaucoup de magasins et de cafés.

4 – Et il y a un marché dans les rues le mercredi et le samedi.

5 – En été, il fait très beau ici et beaucoup de touristes visitent la ville.

Ils vont au vieux port et ses trois tours. Quelquefois, il y a des acrobates et des clowns, c'est amusant.

6 – Moi, je vais souvent à la piscine.

7 – Pour aider les touristes, il y a un office de tourisme. Il y a des touristes français, mais aussi beaucoup de touristes britanniques.

8 – Les touristes logent à l'hôtel, au camping ou à l'auberge de jeunesse.

9 – Voici l'hôtel de ville avec son drapeau tricolore.

10 – En ville, il y a des jardins et des parcs.

11 – Il y a aussi des musées et un aquarium.

12 – Et, au mois de juillet, il y a un grand festival de musique avec beaucoup de concerts. Ça s'appelle les Francofolies.

　　　　　　　　　　　　　　　　　　　　AT2

C'est quelle image?

The class could be divided into two teams. Someone from each team in turn says something about one of the pictures and the other team has to identify the appropriate picture, e.g.

– Ça, c'est le vieux port.

– C'est l'image A. Voici l'hôtel de ville. C'est joli, non?

– C'est l'image D. Ça, c'est le parc.

 **76**　　　　　　　　**AT3; 7W7; AfL**

2 Trouve les paires

Students match French and English translations to consolidate vocabulary. This could be done in pairs, with one student saying the French and the other finding the English. This links with the objective of learning some town vocabulary and can be used for peer assessment.

To develop the skill of learning about words, discuss tips for memorising spelling, sound and meaning – see later plenary. Words could be added to students' vocabulary books or electronic word lists.

■ **Solution: 1** e, **2** c, **3** g, **4** f, **5** d, **6** a, **7** h, **8** b

 **76** ● **3 tr 23**　　　　**AT1; 7W6, 7L1**

Prononciation: la lettre 'h'

a Students listen to the words and match them with the printed version.

■ **Solution: 1** d, **2** c, **3** a, **4** e, **5** b

b Students pronounce the words and check their pronunciation.

c The silly sentence helps fix the sound for students.

transcript

Prononciation: la lettre h

a 1 hamster

　　2 hiver

　　3 hôtel

　　4 huit

　　5 habitons

b homme hôpital horrible histoire horizon

c Huit hamsters habitent en haut de l'hôtel en hiver.

Plenaries (pages 76–77)

　Fiche de travail (ws02)

1 Develop the discussion about learning about words, spelling, gender and meaning. Discuss useful tips for remembering these, such as colour-coding, writing masculine words and feminine words in clearly different lists or in a different place (either right/left or opposite sides of the page), learning with a phrase or adjective which clearly denotes feminine gender e.g. *grande/petite*.

2 Practise some of these ideas with a brainstorming session in which one half of the class thinks of masculine town vocabulary and the other half thinks of feminine words. These are then listed on the board in two sections, using blue and red to denote gender.

7B Qu'est-ce qu'il y a en ville? pages 78–79

Aims and objectives	Grammar and skills	Resources
• learn more town vocabulary • ask about places	**Grammar** *vieux/vieille* **Pronunciation** words ending in -t and -te	**Key language:** see p128 **Online resource:** *Unité 7* int01, ppt02, ws02 **Copymasters:** 7/1 **CD** 3 tracks 24–25

Starters (pages 78–79)

Fiche de travail (ws02)

1 Display the following words and ask students for the English meaning and for volunteers to pronounce the words in French. After several suggestions, give the correct pronunciation for repetiton by the whole class.

une banque	*la poste*
un centre sportif	*un supermarché*
un centre commercial	*le théâtre*
un parking	*le château*
un bowling	

2 **Nouns and adjectives** To practise nouns and adjectives, display the following table and ask one half of the class to make up 5 phrases using an adjective which goes before the noun and the other half to make up 5 phrases with an adjective which follows the noun. After a few minutes, ask each team in turn for a phrase and award one point for each correct phrase.

If preferred, students could do this in pairs, with one person using the adjectives which precede and the other using adjectives which follow the noun.

avant le nom exemple *un grand parking*	les noms	après le nom exemple *une maison moderne*
grand petit nouveau (nouvel, nouvelle) bon (bonne)	un hôpital un hôtel un parking un supermarché un musée une piscine	moderne énorme historique horrible rouge (autres couleurs) etc

Introduction

Go through the objectives for this spread.

 78   AT2, AT4; 7W2

1 As-tu une bonne mémoire?

As an individual or group activity, students look back at the photos for a few minutes, then close their books and try to recall as many different places as possible. This can be built up as a cumulative list on the board. Prompt as necessary or give initial letters, e.g. *des m…, le p…, des r…*, etc.

As follow-up, ask how students remembered the words and whether some were easier than others.

   Présentation (ppt02)   AT1, AT3

En ville

An online PowerPoint presentation of new vocabulary for places in town.

 78   AT3; 7W2, 7T1

2 Qu'est-ce que c'est?

Students match the correct text to each symbol.

Solution:

A *une banque*	**F** *un supermarché*
B *un centre sportif*	**G** *un bowling*
C *un hôpital*	**H** *un château*
D *un parking*	**I** *le centre commercial*
E *une poste*	**J** *la plage*

 78   3 tr 24   AT1; 7W2, 7S4, 7L3

3 Où vont-ils?

Students listen to the eight items and write the letter by the matching symbol.

Solution: 1 E, **2** F, **3** D, **4** C, **5** J, **6** H, **7** B, **8** G

transcript

1 Pardon, madame, est-ce que la poste est près d'ici?

2 Je vais au supermarché pour acheter des provisions pour un pique-nique.

3 Les touristes cherchent un parking au centre-ville.

4 Est-ce qu'il y a un hôpital en ville?

5 Nous allons à la plage. La plage, c'est loin?

6 Il y a un château historique dans la ville. Où est le château exactement?

7 Mes amis vont au centre sportif pour un cours de judo.

8 C'est bien, il y a un bowling en ville. On va au bowling samedi.

 78 AT2, AT3; 7W2, 7S9

4 Complète les phrases

Further practice of reading and new vocabulary. When checking, ask students to read the full sentence aloud to practise pronunciation.

> **Solution:**
>
> 1 *Pour les touristes, il y a des* **hôtels**, *une* **auberge** *de jeunesse et un* **camping**.
> 2 *Si vous aimez le shopping, allez aux* **magasins** *au* **centre commercial**.
> 3 *Pour acheter des provisions, allez au* **supermarché**.
> 4 *Il y a beaucoup de bateaux au vieux* **port**.
> 5 *Il y a des* **musées** *intéressants et un vieux* **château**.
> 6 *Pour les sportifs, il y a une* **piscine** *et un* **centre sportif**.
> 7 *Pour les personnes en voiture, il y a un grand* **parking** *près de la place*.
> 8 *C'est amusant d'aller au* **bowling** *et au* **théâtre**.

 7/1

En ville (1) – mini-flashcards

This worksheet could be used now or later. Students could just fill in the words, colour the pictures and stick them in their books. The completed sheets could also be mounted on card and used as mini-flashcards for additional practice in pairs or groups.

See TB 23 for ideas for using mini-flashcards.

> **Solution: 1** H, **2** B, **3** F, **4** A, **5** C, **6** D, **7** K, **8** L, **9** J, **10** I, **11** G, **12** E

 78 ⊙ 3 tr 25 AT1; 7W6, 7L1

Prononciation

Students should work out the rule for pronunciation of the final –*t* in a word.

a Students listen to the words and match them with the printed version.

> **Solution: 1** a, **2** c, **3** d, **4** b

b Students then listen to three more words ending in –*e*, where the final consonant is pronounced.

 transcript

Prononciation:

a	**1** un port	**b**	une carte
	2 un restaurant		une visite
	3 le concert		la poste
	4 le sport		

Every Wednesday etc. (le + day)

Encourage students to deduce the rule about using *le* with a day of the week to mean 'on' or 'every'. Students could practise making further sentences based on the examples given.

 79 AT3; 7T1

5 La Rochelle – ville du vélo

A short reading text about the La Rochelle bike initiative, with comprehension questions in English.

> **Solution:**
>
> 1 It's historical with many old buildings and houses and is now a pedestrian zone. There are no cars, but bikes (and pedestrians) are permitted.
> 2 yellow
> 3 to reduce pollution

 79 Dossier-langue 7W4

Vieux/vieille

Revise adjective forms and explain that *vieux* is irregular but has some features of regular adjectives (feminine ends in –*e*, plural ends in –*x*)

Practise the pronunciation, e.g. *vieux: c'est le contraire de moderne*, and give more examples: *une vieille voiture, un vieux vélo*. For more oral practice, ask e.g.

Dis le contraire:

C'est une maison moderne? C'est un appartement moderne? C'est une voiture moderne?

Ask students whether *vieux* precedes or follows the noun.

Students meet *vieux* in texts but do not need to use it productively. For able students, explain the form *vieil* before a vowel.

 79 AT4; 7T5

6 Des cartes postales

Students choose the correct words to complete the two postcards and then write their own postcard on similar lines. This could be prepared on the board. Able students could invent a gapped task for others to complete.

> **Solution:**
>
> **a A 1** *l'auberge de jeunesse*, **2** *ville*, **3** *port*, **4** *tours*, **5** *musées*, **6** *chaud*, **7** *piscine*
>
> **B 1** *passons*, **2** *camping*, **3** *touristes*, **4** *beau*, **5** *marché*, **6** *parc*, **7** *restaurant*

Une carte postale virtuelle

Many websites offer the chance of selecting and e-mailing a 'virtual' postcard. Students could look at various websites and choose a photo to send as a virtual postcard to a friend.

Possible websites:

http://www.ville-larochelle.fr

http://www.charente-maritime.org

AT2; AfL

Oral practice

Summarise all the town vocabulary taught so far with a class game e.g. a chain game listing places that may be found in any town, not necessarily in La Rochelle: *En ville, il y a un cinéma et ...*

Link this activity with the spread objective and use for assessment. Afterwards discuss what has been achieved and what needs more practice. If time, students could then practise this in pairs for peer assessment.

 Activité (int01)   **AT3, AT4**

Un week-end en ville

An online activity to practise town vocabulary taught so far.

 150 Au choix   **AT3, AT4**

1 La Rochelle – ville touristique

For reading and writing practice, students complete the publicity material.

> **Solution:** **1** *ville,* **2** *port,* **3** *tours,* **4** *magasins,* **5** *restaurants,* **6** *vélo,* **7** *musées,* **8** *aquarium*

Plenaries (pages 78–79)

Fiche de travail (ws02)

1 **Think, pair and share** Students discuss in pairs which 3 town words they find most difficult and consider ways for learning them. They share their ideas with another pair and then a spokesperson relays the findings to the rest of the class.

2 Students brainstorm tips for reading strategies.

7C C'est près d'ici?   pages 80–81

Aims and objectives	Grammar and skills	Resources
• ask for directions and information • understand directions		**Key language:** see p128 **Online resource:** *Unité 7* int02, ppt03, ws02/03 **Copymasters:** 7/2, 7/3 **CD** 3 tracks 26–29 **Flashcards:** 8–12, 43–56

Starters (pages 80–81)

 Fiche de travail (ws02)

1 **Quelle est la question?** Display the following incomplete questions and answers and ask students to note down the correct question word on mini-whiteboards if available. To check the answers, ask students to hold up their white board or ask for spoken responses by individuals or the whole class.

1 – ... est la Rochelle?
 – C'est dans l'ouest de la France, au bord de la mer.
2 – ... temps fait-il?
 – Il fait beau.
3 – ... de touristes visitent La Rochelle par an?
 – Plus de 3 millions – c'est beaucoup!
4 – ... habite à La Rochelle?
 – Marine et Noah habitent là.
5 – ... il y a au centre-ville?
 – Il y a le port, des musées et un aquarium.
6 – ... un théâtre?
 – Oui, il y a un théâtre et des cinémas.

> **Solution:** **1** *Où,* **2** *Quel,* **3** *Combien,* **4** *Qui,* **5** *Qu'est-ce qu',* **6** *Est-ce qu'il y a*

2 **Revise numbers** Ask easy questions or sums for students to write down a number. Check the answers as above. e.g.
Il y a combien de jours dans une semaine?
Il y a combien de mois dans l'année?
Deux plus trois, ça fait combien?

Introduction

Go through the objectives for this spread.

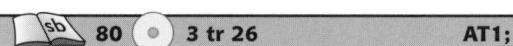 **80** **3 tr 26**   **AT1; 7S4, 7L3**

1 Où vont les touristes?

Go through the symbols to make sure students understand what they represent.

Students listen to the questions and find the correct picture for each destination.

> **Solution:** **1** D, **2** F, **3** H, **4** I, **5** E, **6** B, **7** G, **8** J, **9** A, **10** C

transcript

1 Pardon, monsieur, pour aller au théâtre, s'il vous plaît?

2 Pardon, madame, est-ce qu'il y a un supermarché près d'ici?

3 Pardon, monsieur, le centre-ville, c'est loin?

4 Pardon, madame, pour aller à l'église Notre Dame, s'il vous plaît?

5 Pardon, madame, est-ce qu'il y a des toilettes près d'ici?

6 Pardon, monsieur, le marché, c'est près d'ici?

7 Pardon, monsieur, pour aller à la gare, s'il vous plaît?

8 Pardon, madame, pour aller aux magasins, s'il vous plaît?

9 Pardon, madame, est-ce qu'il y a une piscine près d'ici?

10 Pardon, monsieur, l'office de tourisme, c'est loin?

 Activité (int02)   AT1, (AT2), AT3

Des touristes

An online activity to consolidate town vocabulary.

 **80**   AT2, 7S4, 7L4

2 Pose des questions

Students practise asking questions either in pairs or as a class activity.

> **Solution:**
>
> **a 1** *Pour aller au cinéma, s'il vous plaît?*
>
> **2** *Pour aller au port, s'il vous plaît?*
>
> **3** *Pour aller à l'hôpital, s'il vous plaît?*
>
> **b 1** *Est-ce qu'il y a un parking près d'ici?*
>
> **2** *Est-ce qu'il y a un hôtel près d'ici?*
>
> **3** *Est-ce qu'il y a un camping près d'ici?*
>
> **c 1** *La plage, c'est loin/c'est près d'ici?*
>
> **2** *Le parc, c'est loin/c'est près d'ici?*
>
> **3** *La gare, c'est loin/c'est près d'ici?*

Consolidation   AfL

Chain game

Play a chain question game, with students asking a different question each time, e.g.

Student A   *Le port, c'est loin, (Student B)?*

Student B   *Oui/Non/Je ne sais pas. Est-ce qu'il y a un camping près d'ici, (Student C)? etc.*

This could be done in groups with three students keeping the chain going and a fourth acting as referee and listening to each phrase to make sure it is correct. As it links to the spread objective, it could be used for peer assessment. At the end, discuss what was achieved and what needs extra practice.

Flashcard games

If students need extra practice of these structures, use flashcards to cue further questions or play some games, e.g.

Flashcard noughts and crosses

Stick nine 'town' flashcards to the board. Students play this in two teams, with each team in turn asking the way to a place (*Pour aller au .../Est-ce qu'il y a ... près d'ici?*). The card representing the place is then removed and replaced with a cross or a nought. The object of the game is to get three in a row.

80   **3 tr 27**   AT1, AT2, AT3; 7T1, 7L2

3 On arrive en ville

Play the recording first, without the text, and ask students to get the gist of what happens. Then go through the text, encouraging students to ask in French if there is anything they don't understand.

Students eventually practise reading the conversations aloud, in groups of six (three students, three passers-by).

transcript

On arrive en ville

Hassan et ses amis, Alain et Caroline, passent les vacances à La Rochelle. Ils arrivent à la gare de La Rochelle. C'est le cinq juillet et il fait très chaud.

– Pardon, madame. Le centre-ville, c'est loin?

– Le centre-ville? Oui, c'est loin!

– Est-ce qu'il y a un bus?

– Oui, prenez le bus numéro 1 devant la gare.

– Merci, madame.

– De rien.

Les trois amis arrivent au centre-ville. Ils descendent, place de Verdun.

– Alors, on va à l'office de tourisme?

– Bonne idée!

– Pardon, monsieur, est-ce que l'office de tourisme est près d'ici?

– L'office de tourisme? Oh, c'est loin! C'est sur le quai du Gabut.

– C'est où, ça?

– C'est près de la mer et c'est assez près de la gare.

– C'est près de la gare, oh non! Ça alors!

– Zut alors! L'office de tourisme est très loin!

– Pfff! Il fait très chaud, n'est-ce pas?

– Oui, c'est vrai. Alors, on cherche un café?

– Bonne idée. ... Pardon, madame. Est-ce qu'il y a un café près d'ici?

– Bien sûr! Il y a le café de la Paix dans la rue Chaudrier. Ce n'est pas loin.

b This provides practice in accurate reading. Students find the errors in the sentences and correct them.

Solution:

1 ~~janvier~~ juillet
2 ~~froid~~ chaud
3 ~~piscine~~ gare
4 ~~port~~ centre-ville
5 ~~l'auberge de jeunesse~~ l'office de tourisme
6 ~~piscine~~ gare
7 ~~marché~~ café

 Présentation (ppt03) or FC 8–12, 43–56
AT1, AT2, AT3

Trouver son chemin

An online PowerPoint presentation to introduce and practise directions and way finding.

À gauche, à droite, tout droit

To introduce the expressions *à gauche*, *à droite* and *tout droit*, draw three arrows on the board pointing to the left, right and straight on. Hold or attach flashcards on the left and right, and talk about them, e.g.

Où est le cinéma?
Le cinéma est à gauche.
La piscine est à droite.

Repeat this, and introduce *tout droit*.

Gradually encourage students to ask and answer the questions and add:

Pour aller au cinéma, s'il vous plaît?
Tournez à gauche etc.

Some students in this age group are not too confident, even in English, about the concepts of left and right. They may need extra practice in reacting quickly to *gauche* and *droite*.

📖 **81** ⊙ **3 tr 28** **AT1; 7L3**

4 Dans quelle direction?

Students write down the numbers 1 to 10 in their books and listen to find out whether the places mentioned are to the right, to the left or straight on. They can write their answers in English or draw arrows.

Solution: 1 left, **2** straight on, **3** right, **4** straight on, **5** left, **6** right, **7** straight on, **8** right, **9** left, **10** straight on

Dans quelle direction?

1 – Pardon, madame, la piscine, c'est où, s'il vous plaît?
 – C'est à gauche, monsieur.

2 La cathédrale, c'est où, s'il vous plaît?
 – C'est tout droit.

3 – L'hôtel de ville, c'est loin, monsieur?
 – Non, c'est tout près, c'est à droite.

4 – Pour aller au supermarché, s'il vous plaît?
 – C'est tout droit, madame.

5 – Où est le camping, s'il vous plaît, monsieur?
 – C'est là-bas, à gauche.

6 – Où est l'hôpital, s'il vous plaît, madame?
 – C'est ici, à droite, monsieur.

7 – Le vieux port, c'est loin, madame?
 – Non, c'est tout droit.

8 – Pour aller au marché, s'il vous plaît?
 – C'est là-bas, à droite, madame.

9 – Où est le bowling, s'il vous plaît?
 – Le bowling? C'est tout près, à gauche.

10 – Pardon, je cherche le restaurant, Le Perroquet Vert?
 – Le restaurant, Le Perroquet Vert? Hmm – Ah oui, ce n'est pas loin. Allez tout droit.

 Fiche de travail (ws03) **AT2, AT3, AT4**

À gauche, à droit?

An online worksheet to practise directions and way finding.

📖 **81** **AT3; 7L3**

5 À gauche, à droite ou tout droit?

Students consult the signposts to find the answers.

Solution: 1 *à gauche,* **2** *à droite,* **3** *tout droit,* **4** *à droite,* **5** *tout droit,* **6** *tout droit,* **7** *à droite,* **8** *à gauche*

 **7/2** **AT3, AT4**

Vocabulaire: les endroits

These word games and activities can be used at any convenient point to consolidate vocabulary.

Solution:

1 Mots mêlés

a

â	p	é	s	t	u	w	h	l
m	a	r	c	h	é	y	n	p
o	r	l	è	é	d	o	b	i
é	k	c	h	â	t	e	a	u
t	i	d	f	t	g	u	n	s
î	n	d	a	r	j	q	q	p
k	g	f	h	e	i	s	u	o
t	o	i	l	e	t	t	e	s
e	r	s	u	h	c	â	m	t
h	ô	p	i	t	a	l	b	e

b **Écris le mot**

1 market *le marché,* **2** car park *le parking*
3 theatre *le théâtre,* **4** castle *le château,*
5 bank *la banque,* **6** post office *la poste,*
7 hospital *l'hôpital,* **8** toilets *les toilettes*

2 Dans l'ordre alphabétique

1 *auberge de jeunesse* = youth hostel
2 *bowling* = bowling alley
3 *cinéma* = cinema
4 *église* = church
5 *hôtel* = hotel
6 *magasin* = shop
7 *place* = square
8 *tour* = tower

3 Un panneau

A 1 *Ex. plage*, 2 *camping*,
   3 *auberge de jeunesse*, 4 *port*, 5 *gare*,
   6 *centre sportif*, 7 *piscine*, 8 *bowling*,
   9 *centre commercial*, 10 *parc*

B 1 *Le bowling, c'est à droite*
   2 *La piscine, c'est tout droit*
   3 *Le camping, c'est à gauche*
   4 *La plage, c'est à gauche*
   5 *La gare, c'est tout droit*
   6 *Le parc, c'est à droite*

Premier(ère), deuxième, troisième

Introduce the idea of *premier/première, deuxième, troisième*, by describing where students are sitting in class (*au premier/deuxième rang* etc.), or draw a simple town plan on the board and describe the turnings in order. (*Voici la première rue à gauche* etc.).

 **81**   **AT2, AT3; 7S4, 7T1**

6 Par ici!

First use the map to give directions to students, who follow these and discover where they are going, e.g. *Prenez la première rue à gauche. Puis c'est tout droit. Où êtes-vous?* (*À la poste.*) Students could also practise giving each other directions in pairs.

The task involves matching each question with the correct directions.

■ **Solution:** **1** b, **2** d, **3** a, **4** c, **5** e

 **81** ● **3 tr 29**   **AT1, AT2, AT3; 7S4, 7L6; AfL**

7 Conversations en ville

a Students complete the two conversations.
b They listen to the recorded version to check their answers.
c They practise the conversations in pairs.

■ **Solution: a1** *à la piscine, aller, droit, deuxième, gauche, Merci, loin*
a2 *château, tout droit, la première rue à gauche, Merci, loin*

Explain how the task reflects the spread objectives and demonstrate a successful conversation to indicate assessment criteria. This could then be used for peer assessment with students awarding two stars (for what is done well) and a wish for what could be improved.

transcript

Conversations en ville

1 – On va à la piscine?
   – Oui, d'accord.
   – Pardon, monsieur, pour aller à la piscine, s'il vous plaît?
   – Continuez tout droit, puis prenez la deuxième rue à gauche. Descendez la rue et voilà!
   – Merci, monsieur. C'est loin?
   – Non, c'est tout près.

2 – Pardon, madame, pour aller au château, s'il vous plaît?
   – Continuez tout droit, puis prenez la première rue à gauche.
   – Merci, madame. C'est loin?
   – Oui, c'est assez loin.

 7/3   **AT3**

C'est quelle direction?

This provides practice of understanding directions using a simple plan.

Solution:

1 Une petite ville

A 1 *vrai*, **2** *faux*, **3** *vrai*, **4** *faux*, **5** *vrai*, **6** *vrai*, **7** *faux*, **8** *vrai*

B 1 *première*, **2** *première*, **3** *deuxième*, **4** *deuxième*, **5** *troisième*, **6** *troisième*, **7** *gauche*, **8** *droite*

2 Pour arriver chez moi

*En sortant de la gare, tourne à gauche, puis prends la deuxième rue **à droite** et continue **tout droit**. (c'est la rue de l'Église). Notre maison est **à gauche**. C'est le numéro 5, **près de** l'église. Ce n'est pas **loin**.*

Plenary (pages 80–81)

Fiche de travail (ws02)

Conduct a mid-unit review. Ask: How's it going so far? What over the last 2–3 spreads has proved most difficult/ easiest? Where do you think your personal improvement has been? What is still a problem?

Students discuss these questions in groups and then a spokesperson gives group feedback to the whole class.

7D Où exactement? pages 82–83

Aims and objectives	Grammar and skills	Resources
• use the preposition *à* • say where things are using other prepositions	The preposition *à* – *au, à la, à l', aux* Other prepositions: *devant, entre, derrière, à côté de, en face de* plus revision of *dans, sur, sous*	**Key language:** see p128 **Online resource:** *Unité 7* int03/04, ws02/04/05 **Copymasters:** 7/5 **CD** 3 track 30 **Flashcards:** 43–56 **GiA:** pp22–23 and 26–27

Starters (pages 82–83)

 Fiche de travail (ws02)

1 Chasse à l'intrus Display the following words or print them out so students can circle the odd word out (shown in bold). If using the board, the answers can be checked as a whole class activity. If students are using the printed grid, they can exchange papers with a partner for marking.

un magasin	**mardi**	*aller*	*la plage*	*nous*	*cinq*
un vélo	*brouillard*	*continuer*	*la mer*	*ils*	**sous**
un château	*soleil*	**janvier**	*le port*	*vous*	*cent*
un théâtre	*vent*	*tourner*	**le chat**	**dans**	*soixante*

2 C'est masculin ou féminin? Display the following words, use flashcards, or say the words and ask students to hold up their *masculin* or *féminin* cards.

masculin: *parking, château, musée, marché, magasin, camping, théâtre*

féminin: *auberge de jeunesse, gare, plage, piscine, poste banque, église*

Introduction

Go through the objectives for this spread.

FC 43–56

Preposition à/au etc

Using the flashcards, demonstrate how to say where you are or where you're going, using *à, au, à la, à l'* and *aux* (which could be written on the board with suitable nouns).

Distribute the flashcards to students, saying *Où vas-tu?*

They reply *À la piscine* or *J'arrive à la piscine*, then return the flashcard.

 **82** **AT3; 7W2**

1 Questions sur la ville

This short quiz includes many examples of the preposition *à* in use. Ask students to spot these and say what they have noticed about how *à* changes form.

Solution: **1** c, **2** b, **3** c, **4** b, **5** a, **6** c

 **82** **AT2, AT3; 7W2, 7W4, 7S4, 7T2, 7L6; AfL**

2 On va en ville?

Students read through the dialogue then practise it in pairs, changing the destinations etc., using the substitution table (*Pour t'aider*) to help them. Explain how the task reflects the spread objective and demonstrate a successful conversation to indicate assessment criteria. This could then be used for peer assessment.

 **82** **Dossier-langue** **7W2, 7W4, 7W6**

au/à la/à l'/aux (to, at)

This summarises the different forms of *à*. Ask students to look out for other examples as they work through the unit.

 **82** **AT4; 7W4**

3 Une semaine de vacances

Students follow the lines to find the destinations and complete the sentences, practising the different forms of *à*.

Solution: **1** *au bowling*, **2** *au musée*, **3** *à la plage*, **4** *à l'aquarium*, **5** *à la piscine*, **6** *au château*

 Fiche de travail (ws04) **AT2, AT3**

C'est loin?

An online worksheet with further practice of the preposition *à* with places.

7/4   **AT3, AT4**

Où va-t-on?

Extra practice of different forms of *à*.

> **Solution:**
>
> **1 La semaine de Charles**
>
> **1** *au cinéma,* **2** *au parc,* **3** *à la plage,* **4** *à la piscine,* **5** *aux magasins,* **6** *à l'auberge de jeunesse,* **7** *au lit*
>
> **2 Où vont-ils?**
>
> **1** *au camping,* **2** *à la gare,* **3** *à la poste,* **4** *au restaurant,* **5** *à l'hôpital,* **6** *à la plage*

 **1 pp22–23**

Using *au, à la, à l', aux* (1) and (2)

This provides further practice, if required.

 Activité (int03)   **AT1, AT3**

Dans la rue

An online activity to practise places and their position.

 Fiche de travail (ws05)   **AT2, AT3, AT4**

La ville

This online worksheet provides further practice of places in town and finding out where they are.

 150 Au choix   **AT4**

2 Attention aux accents!

Practice in completing town vocabulary with vowels and accents.

> **Solution:**
>
> **1** *une cathédrale*   **5** *un hôpital*
>
> **2** *un bâtiment*   **6** *un musée*
>
> **3** *un château*   **7** *un supermarché*
>
> **4** *une église*   **8** *un théâtre*

 150 Au choix   **AT4**

3 Quelle est la destination?

Further practice in using the correct form of *à*.

> **Solution:**
>
> **1** *Ils vont au terrain de football.* B
>
> **2** *Il va au centre sportif.* A
>
> **3** *Elles vont aux magasins.* H
>
> **4** *Elle va à l'aquarium.* G
>
> **5** *Ils vont à la gare.* F
>
> **6** *L'ambulance va à l'hôpital.* D
>
> **7** *ils vont à l'office de tourisme.* E
>
> **8** *Ils vont à l'auberge de jeunesse.* C

FC 10–12, 43–56

Presentation and practice of prepositions

Teach *devant*, *derrière*, *à côté de* and *entre* by describing where students are sitting and where things are in the classroom.

Use the flashcards for various places in a town. Prop them against the board or hold them one behind another and describe where certain places are located, e.g.

La piscine est derrière le parc.
L'hôtel est entre la poste et le cinéma.

 **83**   **3 tr 3**   **AT1; 7S4, 7L3**

4 On va où?

Students listen and note the place mentioned and any further details.

> **Solution:**
>
> **1** castle, quite far, after supermarket
>
> **2** café, nearby, between cinema and supermarket
>
> **3** youth hostel, next to campsite, take bus
>
> **4** aquarium, not far, near station
>
> **5** car park, behind hotel
>
> **6** toilets, in the square
>
> **7** bike, in front of the swimming pool
>
> **8** bowling alley, in the shopping centre, next to cinema

transcript

On va où?

1 – Pour aller au château, s'il vous plaît?
 – Le château? C'est assez loin. Continuez tout droit. C'est après le supermarché.

2 – Est-ce qu'il y a un café près d'ici?
 – Oui, il y a un café tout près, entre le cinéma et le supermarché.

3 – L'auberge de jeunesse, c'est loin?
 – Ah oui, c'est loin. C'est à côté du camping. Prenez le bus là-bas.

4 – Pour aller à l'aquarium, s'il vous plaît?
 – Ah, l'aquarium, ce n'est pas loin, c'est près de la gare.

5 – Est-ce qu'il y a un parking à l'hôtel?
 – Oui, il y a un parking derrière l'hôtel.

6 – Pardon, madame, est-ce qu'il y a des toilettes près d'ici?
 – Oui, il y a des toilettes sur la place.

7 – Où est ton vélo?
 – Mon vélo? Il est là-bas, devant la piscine.

8 – Pardon, monsieur, je cherche le bowling. C'est près d'ici?
 – Le bowling, c'est dans le centre commercial. C'est à côté du cinéma.

 **sb** 83 AT3; 7W2

5 Trouve les paires

Solution: **1** b, **2** e, **3** g, **4** c, **5** f, **6** d, **7** a

 **sb** 83 AT2, AT3; 7W2, 7S2

6 Dans la rue

Start with some oral work on the illustration, e.g.

Où est le café? Entre le supermarché et …?

Then students can work on the true/false task.

Solution: **1** faux, **2** vrai, **3** faux, **4** vrai, **5** faux, **6** faux, **7** faux, **8** vrai, **9** faux, **10** vrai

 Activité (int04) AT1, AT2

Des conversations

This online role play activity practises asking the way and giving directions.

 **sb** 83 AT3; 7W2

7 Où?

This item is for further practice of *entre*, *devant* and *derrière* and revision of the prepositions *sur*, *dans* and *sous* learnt earlier.

a Students complete each sentence with the correct preposition.

Solution: **1** entre, **2** derrière, **3** sur, **4** sous, **5** devant, **6** sur, **7** entre, **8** dans

b Students could produce a similar cartoon to illustrate prepositions, perhaps on a computer using clip art.

Extra practice

Students make true/false statements about the location of objects in the classroom. The class have to decide whether it's true or false, e.g. *Il y a des livres sur la table. Il y a un vélo sous la table. Il y a un lion derrière la porte*, etc.

 cm 7/5

C'est où?

Further practice of prepositions in the context of animals hiding in a room.

Solution:

1 Un petit lexique

a *dans* in, **b** *derrière* behind, **c** *entre* between, **d** *sur* on, **e** *sous* under, **f** *devant* in front of

2 Attention! Le vétérinaire arrive!

A **1** V, **2** V, **3** F, **4** V, **5** F, **6** F, **7** V, **8** F

B **1** devant, **2** entre, **3** sur, **4** sous, **5** dans, **6** sous

C This is an open-ended task.

 gra 1 pp26–27

Using prepositions (1) and (2)

These pages provide additional practice of prepositions if required.

Plenaries (pages 82–83)

 Fiche de travail (ws02)

1 Students could reflect on how prepositions are used in French and English. Do they find the different forms of *à* hard to remember; what might help – learning some key phrases, e.g. *au collège, aux magasins*.

2 How easy do they find the other prepositions? Are there any tips for remembering them, e.g. visualising animals in/behind/on/under a box etc. and remembering key phrases.

7E C'est comment, ta ville? pages 84–85

Aims and objectives	Grammar and skills	Resources
• talk about the area where you live • use longer sentences	**Skills** Extending sentences using connectives	**Key language:** see p128 **Online resource:** *Unité 7* ppt04, ws02/06 **Copymasters:** 7/6, 7/7, 7/8 **CD** 3 track 31 **Flashcards:** 57–60

Starters (pages 84–85)

 Fiche de travail (ws02)

1 **En groupes** Display a list of words in random order or print these out and ask students to put them into 5 groups. This could be done as class activity with students taking it in turns to find a group of words – each group could be underlined in a different colour. If students are working on the printed lists, they could do this individually, then exchange lists with a partner for marking.

sur, sous, dans
je, tu, il
un château, un musée, un théâtre
vieux, petit, jaune
Prenez, Tournez, Visitez
une rue, une avenue, une place

2 **Chaque mot à sa place** Display the following lists of words and then, for each individual word, ask: *Quelle est la bonne boîte?*

derrière (E), un poisson (C), aux (D), une piscine (A), un vélo (F), habiter (B)

Students could write the appropriate letter on mini-whiteboards or on a piece of paper and display it when asked.

A	B	C	D	E	F
un bowling	*visiter*	*une souris*	*au*	*devant*	*un bus*
un centre sportif	*chercher*	*un oiseau*	*à la*	*entre*	*une voiture*

Introduction

Go through the objectives for this spread.

FC 57–60

Use the flashcards (57–60) to teach and practise: *une mosquée, une patinoire, un terrain de football, une bibliothèque.*

 **7/6**

En ville (2) – mini-flashcards

Students could just fill in the words, colour the pictures and stick them in their books. The completed sheets could also be mounted on card and used as mini-flashcards for additional practice in pairs or groups.

See TB 23 for ideas for using mini-flashcards.

Solution:

1 F *la plage*, 2 C *la gare*, 3 J *le supermarché*,
4 L *le théâtre*, 5 B *la cathédrale*,
6 I *le centre sportif*, 7 A *la bibliothèque*,
8 H *le camping*, 9 K *le terrain de football*,
10 D *la mosquée*, 11 G *le bowling*,
12 E *la patinoire*

 **84**   **AT3; 7W2**

1 Un jeu 5-4-3-2-1

This is a game to reinforce the new vocabulary.

Solution:

5 la religion
une cathédrale
une église
une mosquée
une synagogue
un temple

4 le sport
une patinoire
un centre sportif
un terrain de football
une piscine

3 le logement
un hôtel
un camping
une auberge de jeunesse

2 on mange là
un café
un restaurant

1 on trouve des livres là
une bibliothèque

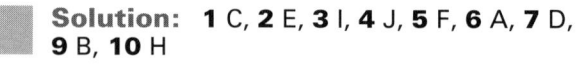 **84**   **3 tr 31**   **AT1; 7W2, 7L3**

2 Mon quartier

Students should listen first for the location and note the appropriate letter.

Solution: 1 C, 2 E, 3 I, 4 J, 5 F, 6 A, 7 D, 8 G, 9 B, 10 H

They can then listen again and note any further information in English.

transcript

1 Dans mon quartier, il y a un grand parc avec un terrain de football. J'aime bien jouer au football au parc.

2 Le mercredi, après l'école, je vais à la bibliothèque. Il y a des ordinateurs et je surfe sur le Net. Je regarde des livres aussi.

3 En ville, il y a un centre sportif. Je vais souvent au centre sportif pour jouer au basket et au badminton. J'adore le sport.

4 Pendant le week-end, je vais quelquefois au bowling avec mes amis.

5 Le dimanche, je vais à l'église avec ma mère.

6 Pour ma fête, je vais à la patinoire. J'aime bien ça.

7 Il y a une piscine dans mon quartier et en été, nous allons à la piscine le samedi.

8 J'aime bien ma ville parce qu'il y a beaucoup de magasins et un grand centre commercial – et moi, j'adore le shopping.

9 Le vendredi, ma famille va à la mosquée.

10 À Diwali, nous allons au temple.

 **150 Au choix** AT2, AT4

4 Trouve des endroits en ville

This provides more practice of town vocabulary.

Possible solution:

c	h
la cathédrale	l'hôpital
le centre commercial	l'hôtel de ville
le centre sportif	un hôtel
le cinéma	**m**
le château	le musée
le collège	le magasin
un café	le marché
	la mosquée
	une maison
p	**des lettres différentes**
une piscine	une auberge de jeunesse
une patinoire	la gare
un parc	un office de tourisme
la poste	un restaurant
un parking	un théâtre

L'A, B, C en ville

As an alternative, students could work in pairs or groups to think of places in a town beginning with as many different letters of the alphabet as possible. They can then check their answers by looking at the *Sommaire*.

 **84 Dossier-langue** 7W2, 7S1

This gives examples of the two useful phrases: *Il y a ...* and *Il n'y a pas de ...* Check that students notice that *un/une* change to *de* after *pas*. This is explained more fully in *Unité 9*.

 **84** AT4; 7W4

3 Qu'est-ce qu'il y a?

Students complete the sentences as indicated, taking care to get the genders correct.

Solution:

1 *Dans le centre-ville, il y a **un centre sportif**.*
2 *Dans ma ville, il y a **une patinoire** et **une bibliothèque**.*
3 *Près d'ici, il y a **un centre commercial** avec beaucoup de magasins.*
4 *J'aime bien mon quartier parce qu'il y a **un bowling** et **un cinéma**.*
5 *Dans mon quartier, il y a **un parc** avec **une piscine** et **un terrain de football**.*

 **84** AT4; 7S5

4 Et qu'est-ce qu'il n'y a pas?

Practice in using *il n'y a pas de...*

Solution: 1 *Il n'y a pas de bowling.* **2** *Il n'y a pas de piscine.* **3** *Il n'y a pas de bibliothèque.* **4** *Il n'y a pas de cinéma.* **5** *Il n'y a pas de supermarché.* **6** *Il n'y a pas de parc.* **7** *Il n'y a pas de patinoire.* **8** *Il n'y a pas de centre commercial.*

 Présentation (ppt04) AT2

Jeu de mémoire: En ville

This online version of Kim's game can be used to revise and practise town vocabulary. It provides good follow-up for the negative phrases used in task 4 above.

Notre ville

Discuss a local town/area, which is familiar to everyone and build up a description on the board. This could lead on to further productive work, perhaps creating a mini-town guide for French-speaking visitors using DTP software.

 **85** AT2; 7L5; AfL

5 Faites des phrases

Tasks 5 and 7 could be used for assessment as they link well with spread objectives. Discuss this with students and demonstrate a successful conversation to guide peer assessment.

Students work in pairs to make up different sentences to describe their town/area.

 **85** AT2; 7L4

6 C'est bien pour les jeunes?

Students work in pairs to make up conversations.

 **85 Stratégies** 7W2, 7T7, 7L6

Making longer sentences

Encourage students to make up sentences using *et* or *mais*, following the examples given.

 **85** AT4; 7T5; AfL

7 Ma ville/mon quartier

Students write a few sentences about their town or area referring to the example given.

This links well with the spread objective and can be used for self-evaluation. Prepare this by building up a suitable description on the board so students understand the criteria.

 Fiche de travail (ws06) AT3, AT4

Ma ville et mon quartier

This online worksheet provides a writing frame to support task 7 and the work done on this spread.

 7/7

Ma ville/mon village

This writing frame provides further support for writing about a town/area.

 7/8 AT2, AT4

Un plan à compléter

This worksheet provides extra oral practice of prepositions and places in a town.

Cut the sheet in half so that each partner has a different set of information. Each student asks questions to fill in the missing places on their plan.

 **151 Au choix** **AT3, AT4**

5 Un message

This provides more practice of reading and writing about a town.

Solution:

a Students correct the errors.

1 *C'est bientôt les vacances de <u>printemps</u>.*

2 *Hugo et Élodie vont souvent à <u>Saint-Malo</u> pendant les vacances.*

3 *Hugo trouve que c'est <u>super</u> à Saint-Malo.*

4 *La sœur de Hugo s'appelle <u>Élodie</u>.*

5 *Élodie <u>adore</u> le shopping.*

6 *En <u>été</u> il y a beaucoup de touristes à Saint-Malo.*

b Students answer the questions.

1 *Il va à Saint-Malo.*

2 *Il pense que c'est super.*

3 *Il y a un grand centre sportif et une piscine olympique.*

4 *Élodie aime la ville parce qu'il y a beaucoup de magasins et elle adore le shopping.*

5 Several possible answers, e.g. *Il y a un château, un fort, des musées et la plage.*

c Students write their own message to Hugo, describing a town they like.

Plenary (pages 84–85)

 Fiche de travail (ws02)

As there is a large amount of vocabulary in this unit, one plenary should be spent talking about how to memorise genders of words. How do students do this? Have their approaches been successful? Have they noticed any patterns to help, e.g. spelling. If appropriate, refer to the lists of word endings, which often denote a specific gender (SB *La Grammaire*, 1.2).

7F Allez, on y va   pages 86–87

Aims and objectives	Grammar and skills	Resources
• use the verb *aller*	Present tense of *aller*	**Key language:** see p128 **Online resource:** *Unité 7 ws02/07* **Copymasters:** 7/9 **CD** 3 track 32 **GiA:** pp24–25

Starters (pages 86–87)

 Fiche de travail (ws02)

1 Trouve les paires Display different subjects and verb endings on the board for students to match up, or print these on slips of paper and give out for individual work. This can be checked by the teacher randomly selecting students to answer. Some variations are possible.

1 *Tu*	a *visite un vieux château*
2 *Sa passion, c'est le sport – elle*	b *allons souvent au cinéma*
	c *regardent les poissons*
3 *Pour mon cours d'histoire, je*	d *cherches la patinoire?*
	e *travaille à la bibliothèque*
4 *Nous*	f *jouez au tennis?*
5 *Vous*	g *arrivent à l'école à 8 heures.*
6 *Les chats sont méchants, ils*	h *habite à Edimbourg.*
7 *Mon ami écossais*	i *joue au football ce soir.*
8 *Ma mère aime les livres – elle*	
9 *Les élèves*	

Solution: **1** d, **2** i, **3** a, **4** b, **5** f, **6** c, **7** h, **8** e, **9** g

2 Complète les phrases Display the following. Give students a few minutes to read and work out the answers, then ask:

Le verbe numéro un va avec quelle phrase?

les verbes:

1 *aimez* **2** *cherche* **3** *continues* **4** *écoutons* **5** *habitent* **6** *passe*

a *Je ... le week-end ici.*

b *Tu ... tout droit.*

c *Elle ... le bowling.*

d *Nous ... le CD.*

e *Vous ... le camping?*

f *Ils ... à La Rochelle.*

Solution: **1** e, **2** c, **3** b, **4** d, **5** f, **6** a

Introduction

Go through the objectives for this spread.

 **86** **AT3; 7W4, 7W5**

1 Où vont-ils?

This revises the correct form of à with places in a town and introduces different parts of the present tense of *aller*.

Solution: 1 *au concert,* **2** *à la piscine,* **3** *à la poste,* **4** *à l'église,* **5** *au camping,* **6** *au collège*

5D Ton anniversaire, c'est quand? pages 48–49

Aims and objectives	Grammar and skills	Resources
• talk about birthday dates and presents • practise using adjectives	**Grammar** Adjective agreement **Skills** Learning irregular adjectives	**Key language:** see p85 **Online resource:** *Unité 5 int02, ws02* **CD** 2 tracks 23–24 **GiA:** p14

Starters (pages 48–49)

 Fiche de travail (ws02)

1 5-4-3-2-1 Display a list of words in random order and ask students to find groups of 5, 4, 3, 2, 1 similar words. Students could record their answers on a pre-printed grid (see online worksheet) and these can then be checked by asking individual students to read out a group of words.

Suggestion:
février, avril, août, octobre, novembre
trois, huit, douze, quinze
mon, ma, mes
lundi, samedi
quand

2 C'est quel mois? Display the following text on the board, or print it out (see online worksheet). Students match up the two parts, writing down each number and the corresponding letter. This can be checked by the teacher randomly selecting students to answer.

Exemple: **1** f		
1 *la rentrée*	**a**	*juin*
2 *la fête nationale*	**b**	*décembre*
3 *Noël*	**c**	*janvier*
4 *la fête des Rois*	**d**	*juillet*
5 *la fête de la musique*	**e**	*mai*
6 *la fête des Mères*	**f**	*septembre*

Solution: 1 f, **2** d, **3** b, **4** c, **5** a, **6** e

Introduction

C'est quand, ton anniversaire?

First teach orally how to ask and reply about birthday dates. Then ask a few students *C'est quand, ton anniversaire?*

Eventually develop this into a chain game where each person asks someone else the date of their birthday.

 48 2 tr 23 **AT1, AT3; 7L3**

1 L'anniversaire de Marc

This conversation is used initially for listening comprehension and then as a model for three dialogues which students practise in pairs. Explain *une raquette de tennis* if necessary.

Solution: 1 a, **2** c, **3** b

---

transcript

L'anniversaire de Marc

– Salut, Marc!
– Salut, Claire!
– C'est quand ton anniversaire?
– C'est aujourd'hui, le premier février.
– Ah! Bon anniversaire. Quel âge as-tu?
– Aujourd'hui, j'ai treize ans.
– Qu'est-ce que tu as reçu comme cadeaux?
– J'ai reçu un t-shirt et une raquette de tennis.
– Il est de quelle couleur, le t-shirt?
– Il est vert.
– Et la raquette?
– Elle est noire.

AT2, AT4

Un sondage

Conduct a birthday survey to see how many students have their birthday in each month and whether any two or more students have a birthday on the same day.

Students could work in groups and then report back the results for their group to the class as a whole, e.g.

Dans notre groupe, il y a (number) personnes qui ont un anniversaire au mois de … etc.

Or students could work in pairs to find out the date of their partner's birthday and could then report back this information to a group leader or the teacher, e.g.

Robert, c'est quand, ton anniversaire?
C'est le 18 janvier.

Qui a un anniversaire au mois de janvier?
L'anniversaire de Robert est le 18 janvier.

The results could be put on a bar graph or database, showing the distribution of birthdays throughout the 12 months. This could be done using ICT.

AT2

J'ai reçu …

A chain game with an ever-increasing list could be played using vocabulary for presents. These could include classroom items, pets and other vocabulary learnt earlier.

This activity uses the perfect tense, but it can be treated purely as a vocabulary item. Further examples are given in *Unité 10*, but the perfect tense is not taught systematically until Stage 2.

 48 AT2; 7W4, 7S3, 7S4, 7T2, 7L6; AfL

2 Inventez des conversations

Students read the conversation based on the previous activity, then they make up further conversations, changing some details. They can use the suggestions in the coloured boxes or ones of their own choosing. The previous chain game is good preparation for this.

These conversations provide a good opportunity for peer assessment. Review the spread objectives and agree assessment criteria.

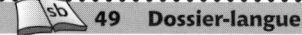 **Activité (int02)** AT2

Bon anniversaire

This online role play activity provides speaking practice of birthday present vocabulary.

 **48** AT3; 7S2, 7S6

3 Des cadeaux de Noël

Students match up written descriptions with packages.

Solution: **1** C, **2** A, **3** D, **4** E, **5** B

 **49 Dossier-langue** 7W4

Using adjectives (singular and plural)

Briefly revise adjectives previously taught, e.g. colours, *petit*, *grand*. Teach *content* and *nouveau/nouvelle*.

This *Dossier-langue* revises and summarises the agreement of adjectives, including some irregulars. Remind students what an adjective is by writing examples on the board and asking *Trouvez des adjectifs*, e.g.

- *Les perruches sont bleues.*
- *Les chevaux sont grands.*
- *Les souris sont petites.*

Students could reply orally or could underline the adjective.

Then go through the *Dossier-langue*, pronouncing the examples so that students realise that the final *–s* is not pronounced.

 **49 Stratégies** 7W7

Encourage students to learn irregular adjectives in phrases, preferably ones they have invented themselves.

 **49** AT3; 7W4

4 Merci pour les cadeaux

Students choose the appropriate adjective ending.

Solution: **1** *amusants,* **2** *modernes,* **3** *intéressant,* **4** *contente,* **5** *petits,* **6** *utiles,* **7** *mignonne,* **8** *nouveau*

 **49** AT3; 7W4, 7W8

5 Cherche des adjectifs

Remind students about the plural endings, e.g.

Quand l'adjectif est au pluriel, il y a un -s ou un -x à la fin du mot.

> **Solution:** **1** (possible examples on SB 49)
> *amusants, français, françaises, grands, grandes, mignonnes, modernes, nouveaux, nouvelles, petits, utiles, vertes*
>
> **2** *blanche, bonne, contente, française, grande, grise, grosse, intéressante, mignonne, nouvelle, petite, utile, verte*

 **49** ◉ **2 tr 24** AT1; 7W4, 7L3

6 C'est quel mot?

In this listening discrimination task, students have to choose the correct form of the adjective they hear repeated.

▓ **Solution:** **1** a, **2** b, **3** b, **4** a, **5** a, **6** b

transcript

C'est quel mot?

1 blancs, blanches – blancs
2 vert, verte – verte
3 petit, petite – petite
4 grands, grandes – grands
5 gris, grise – gris
6 gros, grosse – grosse

 1 p14

Singular and plural – nouns and adjectives

This provides additional practice and consolidation of the singular and plural and could be used by students working independently.

Plenaries (pages 48–49)

Fiche de travail (ws02)

1 Using a spider diagram with the word *Anniversaire* in the middle (see online worksheet), students note down as many French words as possible to do with birthdays. This could include days, months, dates, presents, people, likes, dislikes, etc.

2 Conduct a mid-unit review. Ask: How's it going so far? What over the first half of the unit has proved most difficult/easiest? Where do you think your personal improvement has been? What is still a problem? What 'repair strategies' need putting in place?

5E Des cadeaux pour tout le monde pages 50–51

Aims and objectives	Grammar and skills	Resources
• learn the words for some more presents • learn some higher numbers and prices	**Skills** Working out meanings **Grammar** Number patterns from 69 to 100s. **Pronunciation** The letters *qu* **Cross-curricular** Numeracy	**Key language:** see p85 **Online resource:** *Unité 5* ws02/05 **Copymasters:** 5/3 **CD** 2 tracks 25–28

Starters (pages 50–51)

 **Fiche de travail (ws02)**

1 C'est masculin ou féminin? Display the following words in random order, or say the words and ask students to hold up their *masculin* or *féminin* cards.

Masculin		*Féminin*	
père	*stylo*	*mère*	*jupe*
frère	*livre*	*sœur*	*calculatrice*
baladeur	*cinéma*	*cuisine*	*chaussette*
lapin	*sac*	*souris*	*trousse*

2 Revise numbers up to 70. Play some number games e.g. *Onze*, Fizz-Buzz and Backwards Bingo and/or others from TB 21.

 **50** **AT1, AT2**

Idées cadeaux

Begin with plenty of oral work based on the items pictured.

 50 ⦿ **2 tr 25** **AT1; 7W2, 7L3**

1 Vous cherchez un cadeau?

Students listen to the recording and note down the letter for each of the eight items mentioned.

▮ **Solution:** **1** J, **2** A, **3** L, **4** I, **5** C, **6** K, **7** F, **8** O

transcript

Vous cherchez un cadeau?

C'est l'anniversaire d'un ami? Vous cherchez un cadeau un peu spécial? Nous avons sélectionné pour vous un grand choix de cadeaux de toutes sortes:

1 Pour les enfants, il y a des chaussettes amusantes dans toutes les couleurs.

2 Pour les jeunes à l'école, le matériel scolaire est nécessaire et utile mais ça peut être amusant aussi. Nous avons, par exemple, une trousse avec un cahier et un stylo dans des couleurs très jolies.

3 Pour les personnes qui aiment le soleil, achetez des lunettes de soleil – très jolies et très utiles aussi.

4 Pour les jeunes qui aiment les vêtements, il y a des casquettes de tous les styles.

5 Pour les sportifs, il y a une montre sport qui est vraiment fantastique.

6 Pour toutes les personnes qui aiment lire, il y a un grand choix de livres de poche.

7 Pour les jeunes filles, il y a des bracelets en métal argenté. Très chic, non?

8 Et si vous n'avez pas encore trouvé un cadeau, pourquoi ne pas acheter des billets pour le cinéma? Bonne idée, non?

 50 **AT3; 7T1**

2 Les cadeaux

This presents the written form of each gift. Students should note down the letter for each item listed.

▮ **Solution:** **1** P, **2** M, **3** O, **4** F, **5** B, **6** I, **7** G, **8** J, **9** A, **10** N, **11** D, **12** K, **13** L, **14** C, **15** H, **16** E

Stratégies **AT1, AT3**

To provide further practice in working out the meaning of new words, refer students back to the tips on SB 45, then ask the following questions:

• What does the word *poche* mean?

• Why does it occur in numbers 11 and 12?

• Find any four plural nouns in the list of presents. How can you tell they are plural?

• Say them aloud – is the final letter sounded?

▮ **Solution:** plural nouns: *billets, bracelets, chaussettes, poches, lunettes, tennis* (**NB different from the others because singular also ends in –*s*)

Finally ask students to look at the list of presents and spot the words which are written the same or almost the same as in English. Read out the list of words below – students should see how different they sound in each language. The list could be displayed so students can compare the written and spoken word.

ballon, foot, cinéma, bracelets, métal, chic, fantaisie, collection, DVD, Spécial, danse, jean, sport, parfum, tennis

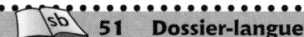 **51**   **AT3; 7T1**

3 Un cadeau idéal

Students choose an appropriate gift for each person. First ask for suggestions and write these on the board. The task could then be completed in writing.

> **Solution:** **1** K, **2** B, **3** N, **4** D, **5** H, **6** M, **7** O, **8** L, **9** P, **10** (open-ended)

      AT2

Memory game

At a suitable point, the class could play a memory game. They look at the selection of gifts in *Idées cadeaux*, close their books and try to recall as many items as possible. To help jog memories, write the initial letter of the items on the board.

Numbers 0–100

Use some of the number games to revise numbers 0–70 (see Starters). Teach 71–100 using the *Dossier-langue* item below and practise them using number games, e.g. *Continue!*, *Comptez comme ça!*, *Effacez!* (TB 21).

 **51**   **Dossier-langue**   **7W2, 7W7**

Numbers

This item presents the numbers 70–100 and numbers over 100. If appropriate for the class, explain that there is no –s on *cent* when combined with other numbers (e.g. *deux* **cents**, but *deux* **cent** *cinquante*).

There are some questions to help students remember the different combinations of the numbers 70–100.

You could also ask these questions:

Which numbers end in *–ante*? (40, 50, 60) What is the equivalent in English? (-ty).

Which numbers below 100 contain the word *et*? (21, 31, 41, 51, 61, 71)

Which numbers between 60 and 100 have hyphens? (all except 60, 61, 71)

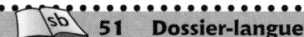 **51**   **2 tr 26**   **AT1, AT2, AT3; 7W6, 7L1**

Prononciation

Les lettres 'qu'

a   Students listen and identify words with *qu* in them, including some numbers.

> **Solution:** **1** d, **2** a, **3** c, **4** e, **5** b

b   Students practise pronouncing words correctly then listen to check.

 **transcript**

Prononciation: les lettres 'qu'

a   1   quarante   4   qu'est-ce que c'est?
      2   quel   5   quand
      3   quatre-vingts

Prononciation: les lettres 'qu'

b   quelle, quatre, question, quatorze, quatre-vingt-dix

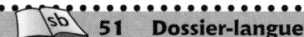 **51**   **2 tr 27**   **AT1; 7L3**

4 La tombola

Check that students can recognise and name the prizes illustrated. They then listen to the recording and match the numbers they hear with each prize.

> **Solution:** **1** *un ordinateur de poche*, **2** *un stylo*, **3** *une trousse*, **4** *des crayons*, **5** *un CD*, **6** *une calculatrice*, **7** *un poisson rouge*, **8** *un classeur*, **9** *un DVD*, **10** *un sac à dos*

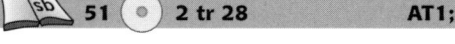 **transcript**

La tombola

1   J'ai le quatre-vingt-seize.
2   J'ai le soixante-sept.
3   J'ai le cinquante.
4   J'ai le trente-huit.
5   J'ai le soixante-treize.
6   J'ai le cent.
7   J'ai le soixante-quinze.
8   J'ai le quatre-vingt-dix.
9   J'ai le quatre-vingts.
10   J'ai le quatre-vingt-un.

5/3   **AT3**

Les numéros

These five tasks practise numbers.

1   **C'est la loterie**

> **Solution:** **1** i, **2** f, **3** b, **4** e, **5** l, **6** j, **7** m, **8** a, **9** g, **10** c

2   **Un message secret**

> **Solution:** ~~sept~~ rendez-vous ~~onze~~ ce ~~treize~~ soir ~~douze~~ au ~~quatorze~~ café ~~seize~~

3   **Continue comme ça**

For an extension activity, students could make up similar sequences.

> **Solution:** **1** *huit*, **2** *sept*, **3** *douze*, **4** *quarante*, **5** *cent*, **6** *quatre-vingts*

4   **Écris le bon nombre**

> **Solution:** **1** *soixante-trois*, **2** *quatorze*, **3** *quatre-vingt-huit*, **4** *quinze*, **5** *quarante*

5   **Calcule**

> **Solution:** **1** *neuf*, **2** *quinze*, **3** *treize*, **4** *seize*, **5** *dix-huit*, **6** *onze*, **7** *sept*, **8** *cent*, **9** *douze*, **10** *huit*

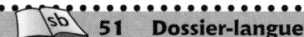 **51**   **2 tr 28**   **AT1; 7L3, 7L2; AfL**

5 C'est combien?

Practice in recognising numbers in prices. Students refer to the presents on SB 50.

Use this task for peer assessment: review the spread objectives and agree the criteria for success.

> **Solution:** **1** H, **2** G, **3** N, **4** J, **5** M, **6** F, **7** C, **8** K, **9** B, **10** O

C'est combien?

1 – C'est combien?
– Ça fait 42 euros, la petite bouteille.

2 – C'est combien?
– 16 euros 50, s'il vous plaît.

3 – Voilà. C'est combien, s'il vous plaît?
– C'est 19 euros 45.

4 – J'aime bien les rouges. Et toi?
– Oui, oui, pour ma petite sœur, c'est très bien.
– Combien?
– 2 euros 05.
– Voilà.

5 – Alors, ça, c'est pour mon frère. C'est combien?
– 17 euros.

6 – Oh, regarde! Très joli, non?
– Oui, pas mal. Ça coûte combien?
– 12 euros les trois, c'est tout!

7 – Regarde! Pour le cadeau de Christophe, c'est idéal.
– Oui, mais c'est combien?
– 39 euros 90.
– 39 euros 90 ... hmmm! C'est beaucoup!

8 – Pour Noah, c'est bien. Il adore les livres.
– C'est combien, alors?
– C'est 4 euros 99.

9 – C'est combien, ça?
– 5 euro 30. C'est amusant, non?

10 – C'est combien?
– 8 euros pour une personne.
– Alors deux, s'il vous plaît.
– Deux ... ça fait 16 euros.
– 16 euros. Voilà.

Fiche de travail (ws05)　　　　　　　**AT2, AT3**

Combien?

This online worksheet gives extra practice of presents, prices and higher numbers.

Plenaries (pages 50–51)

Fiche de travail (ws02)

1 Students summarise the different methods they have found for working out the meaning of unfamiliar words (refer back to SB 45 if necessary). They could make a list of words which fall into each category.

2 Students discuss in pairs or groups the numbers they have learnt on this spread. Which numbers did they find easy/difficult to remember? Why? What tips can they think of to remember the patterns (especially 70–99)?

5F Des vêtements pages 52–53

Aims and objectives	Grammar and skills	Resources
• learn the French for some clothes • practise plurals	**Grammar** Plurals **Skills** Identifying nouns, verbs and adjectives **Pronunciation** Pronunciation of clothes vocabulary (cognates and plurals)	**Key language:** see p85 **Online resource:** *Unité 5* int03, ppt03, ws02/06/07 **Copymasters:** 5/4, 5/5, 5/6 **CD** 2 tracks 29–30

Starters (pages 52–53)

Fiche de travail (ws02)

1 **En groupes** Display a list of words in random order or hand this out on paper (see online worksheet). Ask students to put these into 5 groups.

une maison, un appartement, une ferme
le salon, la chambre, la cuisine,
rouge, jaune, vert
nous, vous, ils
grand, petit, long

2 **Trouve les paires** Display the following text on the board (see online worksheet), or print it and hand out for individual work. Students should match up the two parts of the sentence. This can be checked by the teacher randomly selecting students to read out each pair.

1	*Aujourd'hui, c'est*	a	*sont déguisées.*
2	*Nous*	b	*es un fantôme, non?*
3	*Beaucoup de personnes*	c	*est déguisé comme un perroquet.*
4	*Un garçon*	d	*suis un chat.*
5	*Anne et Suzanne, vous*	e	*mardi gras.*
6	*Et toi, Olivier, tu*	f	*sommes au club des jeunes.*
7	*Et moi, je*	g	*êtes les deux méchantes sœurs.*

Solution: 1 e, **2** f, **3** a, **4** c, **5** g, **6** b, **7** d

Introduction AT2

Precede work on this spread by revising colours and teaching clothes orally, perhaps using the PowerPoint presentation (below) or actual garments or looking up French websites, e.g. **www.promod.com**.

Write new clothing vocabulary on the board for a game of *Effacez!*. Students then copy these into their books.

Flashcards for clothing can be made by using pictures from magazines or the internet, particularly of well-known personalities. Distribute visuals to students who then describe one or more item of clothing worn by the person illustrated.

Présentation (ppt03) AT1, (AT2), AT3

Les vêtements

This PowerPoint presentation introduces items of clothing.

52 **2 tr 29** AT1, AT3; 7W2, 7T1, 7L2

1 Lou Leroux. Chic: oui ou non?

This item introduces items of clothing and adjectives. Students listen to the recording and follow the text.

transcript

Lou Leroux. Chic: oui ou non?

Narrator	Lou Leroux fait beaucoup d'interviews pour la télé. Cette semaine, sa sœur, Léa, et son amie, Charlotte, sont avec Lou. Il choisit attentivement ses vêtements pour être chic!
Narrator	jeudi
	Aujourd'hui, il porte une chemise noire, un pantalon blanc, une cravate rouge, des chaussettes noires et des baskets blanches. Sa sœur, Léa, porte un pantalon brun et une chemise jaune et Charlotte, son amie, porte un short noir et un t-shirt blanc.
Narrator	vendredi
Lou Leroux	Ça va, Léa? Il est chic, mon pull, non?
Léa	Tu rigoles!
Narrator	Lou adore son pull vert et jaune et son pantalon vert. Avec ça, il porte des chaussettes jaunes et des chaussures marron. Léa est très chic. Elle porte une chemise blanche, une jupe noire et des chaussures noires.
Narrator	samedi
	Aujourd'hui, Lou et Léa sont au match de foot. Le joueur de foot porte un maillot rouge et blanc et un short noir. Léa porte une robe bleue et blanche et des sandales blanches. Lou porte un jogging gris, une casquette violette, un sweat orange et des tennis blanches. Est-il chic: oui ou non?
Narrator	dimanche
	Aujourd'hui, Lou est à la maison. Il porte un t-shirt et son jean favori.
Léa	Très bien, Lou!
Charlotte	Aujourd'hui, tu es très chic!

Activité (int03) AT1, AT3

On parle des vêtements

This online activity with animation practises clothing and colours.

52 AT4; 7W2

2 Des vêtements

Students complete the list of clothing, perhaps copying them into their vocabulary books.

53 Stratégies AT3

Remind students of the different parts of speech. From Lou's story, they have to find 4 nouns, 4 verbs and 4 adjectives. They could work in pairs and do this against the clock, reporting back their findings to the class.

53 Dossier-langue AT2, AT3; 7W4

Plurals

Several plural words have been introduced earlier, but this table summarises the basic plural forms. After students have read through the explanation, ask them to form plurals orally, using known vocabulary, e.g. *un livre, le garçon, la fille, l'appartement, un t-shirt, une robe*, etc. Emphasise that the plural does not normally sound any different from the singular in French (unlike in English).

In the final part students look at the Lou Leroux story to find four items of clothing which are plural in English, but singular in French.

> **Solution:** *un short, un jean, un pantalon, un jogging* (tracksuit bottoms)

 **AT2**

Describing clothing

For further practice of the new vocabulary and colours, play a chain game where each student describes one item of clothing that they are wearing and then names another student, e.g.

Je porte des chaussures noires. Philippe.
Je porte un pantalon gris. Suzanne … etc.

 5/4 **AT4**

Des vêtements

These mini-flashcards can be used here (to practise clothing) or later (to practise adjectives). See TB 23 for suggestions for use.

 53 **AT3; 7W4**

3 C'est au pluriel?

Students find five words in the plural.

> **Solution:** **2** *mes lunettes,* **3** *les baskets,* **5** *des chaussures,* **6** *des animaux,* **8** *des casquettes*

 Fiche de travail (ws06) **AT3, AT4**

Au pluriel

This online worksheet practises writing the correct gender and plural of nouns and determiners.

 53 ● 2 tr 30 **AT1, AT2, AT3; 7L1**

Prononciation

This item focuses first on the different pronunciation of items of clothing in French and English, then on the plural. Students should be able to work out that *des* or *les* helps them recognise plural words.

transcript

Prononciation: anglais ou français?

a un short, des baskets, un jean, un pull, un pantalon, des tennis, un jogging, un t-shirt, un sweat, une robe.

b 1 Voici des chaussettes.
   2 Lou porte des baskets.
   3 Léa porte des sandales.
   4 Regarde les chaussures de Léa.
   5 Les tennis de Lou sont blanches.
   6 Voici des t-shirts.

53 **AT2; 7W2, 7L5; AfL**

4 Vrai ou faux?

Pairwork practice of items of clothing and adjectives. Review objectives and assessment criteria and use this for peer assessment of pronunciation and intonation.

 Fiche de travail (ws07) **AT3**

Des adjectifs

This online worksheet practises adjectival agreement.

 147 Au choix **AT4**

5 Les chaussettes de Jacques

Students write out the missing words in the picture strip.

> **Solution:** **1** *Bon,* **2** *cadeau,* **3** *merci,*
> **4** *anniversaire,* **5** *beaucoup,* **6** *gentil,* **7** *rien,*
> **8** *petit,* **9** *chaussettes,* **10** *rouge,* **11** *aime*

 5/5

Jeux de vocabulaire

This consists of four vocabulary tasks based on the themes of the unit so far and could be used as an alternative to the other tasks by students who need more support.

> **Solution:** **1** Mots mêlés

j	a	n	v	i	e	r	l	d	o
u	b	d	o	c	l	i	a	é	m
i	f	h	n	v	r	p	o	c	a
l	é	è	t	v	e	j	û	e	i
l	v	o	a	y	h	m	t	m	t
e	r	s	j	u	i	n	b	b	u
t	i	s	o	c	t	o	b	r	e
s	e	p	t	e	m	b	r	e	e
y	r	g	m	a	r	s	k	u	x

2 Sept vêtements
1 *chaussettes,* **2** *casquette,* **3** *baskets,*
4 *short,* **5** *jupe,* **6** *pantalon,* **7** *chaussures*

3 Qu'est-ce qu'on dit?
1 d, **2** a, **3** e, **4** f, **5** b, **6** c

4 Un jour important
1 *anniversaire,* **2** *cadeau,* **3** *gentil,* **4** *cravate,*
5 *Merci,* **6** *beaucoup,* **7** *rien*

 5/6 **AT2, AT3, AT4**

Des cadeaux et des vêtements

This copymaster provides consolidation for all students.

1 Questions et réponses

This involves matching questions and replies.

> **Solution:** **1** f, **2** d, **3** a, **4** e, **5** b, **6** c

2 Conversations au choix

This provides a framework for a short conversation and could be used in pairs in class or written out for homework.

3 Qu'est-ce qu'il y a dans la valise?

This provides practice of the plural forms of clothing and colours.

> **Solution:** *Il y a deux t-shirts, deux pulls, deux pantalons, deux cravates, deux chaussures et deux jupes.*

 **147 Au choix**   **AT3, AT4**

6 Une lettre illustrée

a Students complete the 'thank you' letter by writing the names of the presents (and colours, if possible).

> **Solution: 1** *les lunettes de soleil rouges,* **2** *un t-shirt bleu,* **3** *un short blanc,* **4** *une casquette rouge,* **5** *une raquette de tennis verte,* **6** *des chaussettes bleues,* **7** *deux balles de tennis jaunes,* **8** *une (petite) souris blanche*

b For extension, students write a similar letter, describing four presents received.

Plenaries (pages 52–53)

 Fiche de travail (ws02)

1 Students discuss different techniques they can use to help remember the items of clothing and how to spell them, e.g. visualising the words spelt out in the shape of the item, identifying an item with a particular colour, etc.

2 In small groups, students think of as many adjectives as possible which they have learnt in French (colours, size, appearance etc.).

5G Les descriptions personnelles   pages 54–55

Aims and objectives	Grammar and skills	Resources
• describe yourself and other people • practise using the verb *avoir*	**Grammar** Present tense of *avoir*	**Key language:** see p85 **Online resource:** *Unité 5* int04, ppt04/05, ws02/08 **Copymasters:** 5/7, 5/8 **CD** 2 track 31 **GiA:** pp15–16

Starters (pages 54–55)

 Fiche de travail (ws02)

1 **Chaque mot à sa place** Display the following task (see online worksheet). Give students one minute to read and work out the answers, then ask them collectively or randomly to give the number of the box. Answers are in brackets.

Quelle est la bonne case pour chaque mot?
elles (2), *noir* (4), *grand* (1), *est* (5), *un pantalon* (3)

1	2	3	4	5
petit	je	un short	bleu	suis
gros	il	un sweat	vert	es
énorme	nous	une jupe	brun	sont

2 **Trouve six noms au pluriel** Display the following list of words (see online worksheet) and ask students to find six nouns in the plural. Answers in bold.

gros, **animaux**, *dans, sous,* **chevaux**, **lunettes**, *suis,* **baskets**, *mars,* **chaussettes**, **chaussures**, *faux*

Introduction

Les descriptions personnelles

First teach personal descriptions orally in class (just colour of eyes and colour, length and style of hair) and get pupils to deduce that the verb *avoir* is used for these personal descriptions.

Then ask general questions such as *Qui a les cheveux châtains/blonds?* getting people to put up hands. A class survey could be undertaken: *x élèves ont les cheveux courts; x élèves ont les yeux bleus,* etc.

 Présentation (ppt04)   **AT2, AT3**

Ils sont comment?

This PowerPoint presentation introduces and practises personal descriptions.

 **54**   **2 tr 31**   **AT1; 7L3**

1 Des photos d'identité

Students listen to descriptions and match to the correct person.

> **Solution: 1**B *Bruno,* **2**A *Marine,* **3**F *Victorien,* **4**D *Sonia,* **5**E *Zac,* **6**C *Julie*

After they have heard the recording and matched speakers to pictures, play it again and discuss why each description does or does not match, e.g. (C) *Elle a les cheveux assez longs, mais roux, pas blonds,* etc.

The table presents the written version of the vocabulary for descriptions, much of which is already familiar. Go through the new words and look for cognates, near cognates and ways of remembering the words (e.g. *frisé* is like 'frizzy'). If necessary, give further examples of the invariable adjective *marron*. Note also that *châtain(s)* is semi-invariable – it agrees in number but not gender.

Des photos d'identité

1 J'ai les cheveux châtains et les yeux marron.

2 Moi, j'ai les cheveux longs, très longs, et blonds. Et j'ai les yeux bleus.

3 Alors moi, j'ai les cheveux blonds et les yeux bleus. Mais je n'ai pas les cheveux longs. J'ai les cheveux courts et frisés.

4 J'ai les cheveux très courts, noirs et frisés. J'ai les yeux marron et je porte des lunettes.

5 Je ne porte pas de lunettes, contrairément à ma sœur, mais j'ai les cheveux très courts, noirs et frisés, comme elle. J'ai les yeux marron aussi. Aujourd'hui, je porte mon t-shirt favori – j'adore le foot!

6 Moi, j'ai les yeux verts et les cheveux roux, frisés et assez longs. Je porte des lunettes.

 54 AT2; 7L5

2 C'est qui?

This speaking activity is best done in groups, but it can also be done in pairs or as a whole class game. Make sure students know which verb to use for different aspects of description (*avoir* or *être*). Be aware of the danger of unflattering or insensitive descriptions of some students. Limiting to colour and style of hair and eyes should be fairly safe! Building up the description one characteristic at a time gives extra practice in using these constructions.

 **Fiche de travail (ws08)** AT3, AT4

Des descriptions

This online worksheet provides support for writing descriptions in the third person, followed by a writing frame as support for task 3 (first person).

 54 AT2, AT4; 7S9

3 Une description personnelle

Prepare this activity by getting individuals to describe themselves orally. They could play a chain game where they describe their hair, then pass on to the next person who describes their own eyes, etc.

They should then write their description and keep it in their *Dossier personnel*.

For more able students this could be developed to include height, garments worn, even likes and dislikes.

 Activité (int04) AT1

Des jeunes

This is an online listening activity on personal descriptions.

 Présentation (ppt05) AT3

Le verbe avoir

This PowerPoint presentation provides a visual introduction to all parts of the present tense of *avoir*. It can be used in conjunction with the suggestions below.

Singular paradigm of *avoir*

Using a collection of classroom objects or clothing, revise the singular paradigm of *avoir*, e.g.

Moi, j'ai une gomme, un livre, etc.

Distribute the objects to students and ask

(Nom), qu'est-ce que tu as? for the reply *J'ai … (une gomme/un livre).*

Then ask another student *Est-ce que (nom) a … (une gomme/un livre)?* for the reply *Oui/Non, il/elle a …*

Write the singular paradigm on the board.

Alternatively, ask about personal possessions, perhaps including some ridiculous ones for fun using props or homemade flashcards, e.g.

Est-ce que tu as un baladeur/un ordinateur/un perroquet/une tarentule/un dragon/un éléphant dans ta chambre?

Plural paradigm of *avoir*

To present the *nous* and *vous* forms, ask four able students to come to the front, and say they represent *la famille Lafitte*. Give each pupil pictures of two animals.

Explain to the rest of the class that the Lafittes have lots of pets, and the class have to ask them questions about them, e.g. *Est-ce que vous avez un chien?*

The student with the appropriate picture should reply *Oui, nous avons un chien* and show the picture.

Add the *nous* and *vous* forms to the paradigm on the board then make up some sentences about the Lafittes, using the *ils* form, e.g.

Ils ont beaucoup d'animaux.
Ils ont un chien, un cheval, un chat, des lapins.

Then complete the paradigm on the board.

Make up sentences using the present tense of *avoir* and get students to point to the form used and/or to repeat the sentences. Alternatively, make this into a game of *Effacez!* (TB 21).

 55 Dossier-langue 7W5

Avoir (to have)

This sets out a gapped version of the full paradigm of *avoir*. Students read the message in task 4 then complete the paradigm in their exercise books.

 **54** (AT2), AT3, AT4; 7W5, 7S2, 7T3

4 Un message de Nicole

This message presents all parts of the verb *avoir* and provides the vocabulary for the task which follows.

> **Solution: 5 adjectifs:** any five from: *longs, blonds, verts, noirs, petit, mignon, blancs, brun, grand, grise, nouveau*
>
> **4 animaux:** any four from: *un hamster, deux lapins, un cochon d'Inde, un chien, une chatte*
>
> **3 meubles:** *un lit, une table, une chaise*
>
> **2 membres de la famille:** *des frères, une sœur*
>
> **1 appareil électrique:** any one from: *un baladeur, un ordinateur*

This could be followed by pairwork practice, with students talking about their pets, home and room. Able students could then write a similar message, perhaps to send by e-mail to another class in the UK or in France.

 **55**   AT3; 7W5

5 Chez nous

Students choose the correct part of the verb *avoir* from three options.

> **Solution: 1** *Nous avons,* **2** *nous avons,*
> **3** *Nous avons,* **4** *vous avez,* **5** *j'ai,* **6** *ma sœur a,*
> **7** *mes frères ont,* **8** *tu as*

 **5/7**   AT3, AT4

avoir

This provides further practice of *avoir.*

1 *avoir* **– to have**

Students complete the paradigm for future reference.

> **Solution:**
>
> **2 En classe**
> **1** e, **2** f, **3** d, **4** a, **5** c, **6** b
>
> **3 Des questions et des réponses**
> **A 1** *as,* **2** *as,* **3** *ont,* **4** *a,* **5** *avez,* **6** *a*
> **B a** *ont,* **b** *a,* **c** *a,* **d** *avons,* **e** *ai,* **f** *ai*
> **C 1** e, **2** f, **3** a, **4** b, **5** d, **6** c
>
> **4 Mots croisés**
> **Horizontalement: 1** *avons,* **3** *ai,* **5** *tu,* **7** *a,*
> **8** *elles*
> **Verticalement: 1** *avez,* **2** *ont,* **4** *ils,* **6** *il,* **7** *as*

 **55**   AT4; 7W2, 7T5; AfL

6 Un e-mail

Students write an e-mail describing their house and their room. This revises much of what has been learnt in *Unités 3–5* and can become part of their *Dossier personnel.* This is a good opportunity for AfL. Remind students of the appropriate objectives in all three units and agree the criteria for success.

 **55**   AT2; 7L5; AfL

7 Une conversation

As consolidation of the work on *avoir* and descriptions, students talk in pairs about themselves. Encourage them to use a range of structures and put in adjectives where possible.

Review the spread objectives and assessment criteria and use this for peer assessment.

 **5/8**   AT4; AfL

Des descriptions

This is a writing frame for students to complete and retain as part of their *Dossier personnel.*

It would be suitable for peer assessment, students deciding if they think their partner's description of themselves is correct. Review the spread objectives and agree the assessment criteria.

As a follow-up students could describe each other.

 **1 p15–16**   AT3, AT4

Using the verb *avoir* – to have

These pages could be used for further practice of *avoir.*

Plenaries (pages 54–55)

    Fiche de travail (ws02)

1 Display a spider diagram with *MOI* at the centre (see online worksheet). Students fill in as many French words as they can in different categories. This could be done as a team game to see who can get the most entries in a set time.

2 Students should discuss tips for remembering the verb *avoir,* e.g. writing it out in a table and highlighting key differences from other verbs.

5H Écoutez bien!   pages 56–57

Aims and objectives	Grammar and skills	Resources
• develop and practise your listening skills	**Skills** Improving listening skills	**Key language:** see p85 **Online resource:** *Unité 5* int05/06/07/08, ppt06, ws02/09 **Copymasters:** 5/9, 5/10 **CD** 2 tracks 32–39

Starters (pages 56–57)

 Fiche de travail (ws02)

1 **5-4-3-2-1** Display a list of words in random order and ask students to find groups of 5, 4, 3, 2, 1 similar words. Students could record their answers on a pre-printed grid (see online worksheet) and these can then be checked by asking individual students to read out a group of words.

Suggestion:
un pantalon, une chemise, un jean, une jupe, un short
quarante, cinquante, soixante, cent
ton, ta, tes
avons, avez
un lapin

2 **Trouve les paires** Display the following lists for students to match up, or print these out and give out for individual work (see online worksheet). This can be checked by the teacher randomly selecting students to answer.

Exemple: **1** e *Un élève,*		*c'est... une personne*	
1	*un élève*	**a**	*un oiseau*
2	*une souris*	**b**	*une couleur*
3	*mars*	**c**	*un nombre*
4	*blanc*	**d**	*un vêtement*
5	*un perroquet*	**e**	*une personne*
6	*quatre-vingts*	**f**	*un jour*
7	*une cravate*	**g**	*un mois*
8	*dimanche*	**h**	*un animal*

■ **Solution:** **1** e, **2** h, **3** g, **4** b, **5** a, **6** c, **7** d, **8** f

56 ● **2 tr 32** AT1, AT3; 7W6, 7L1

1 Trouve le bon mot

This spread concentrates on developing and practising listening skills.

Students read through the six words listed, then listen to the recording and write down the letter for each word.

■ **Solution:** **1** f, **2** c, **3** a, **4** b, **5** d, **6** e

 **transcript**

Trouve le bon mot

1	oui, oui	4	famille, famille
2	livre, livre	5	ville, ville
3	fille, fille	6	fils, fils

Ask which letter represents the sound that all these words have in common. (i)

Discuss how this sound is usually spelt in English. (ee or ea)

56 ● **2 tr 33** AT1, AT3; 7W6, 7L1

2 C'est quelle image?

This task is similar, but uses unfamiliar words. Go through the words and pictures with the students first, perhaps getting them to work out correct pronunciation before

you teach it. They should then study the new words and read the listening tip, before listening to the recording.

■ **Solution:** **1** D, **2** A, **3** F, **4** B, **5** E, **6** C

transcript

C'est quelle image?

Exemple – une maison, une maison, un maçon, un maçon

1 un croissant, un croissant
2 la pluie, la pluie
3 un pharmacien, un pharmacien
4 un parapluie, un parapluie
5 une pharmacie. une pharmacie
6 une boisson, une boisson

56 ● **2 tr 34** AT1, AT3; 7W6, 7L1

3 C'est quel mot?

This item demands very careful listening. Two similar words are heard, then one of them is repeated and students have to spot which this is.

■ **Solution:** **1** b, **2** b, **3** a, **4** a, **5** b, **6** a

transcript

C'est quel mot?

1	je, j'ai – j'ai	4	trois, toi – trois
2	j'ai, j'aime – j'aime	5	sous, sur – sur
3	je, j'aime – je	6	sœur, sur – sœur

56 ● **2 tr 35** AT1; 7S4, 7L3

4 Questions ou réponses?

In this task the emphasis is on tone of voice. Students have to decide if they hear a question or a reply.

Some teachers might like to play this item again, this time for dictation.

■ **Solution:** **1** Q, **2** Q, **3** R, **4** Q, **5** R, **6** Q, **7** R, **8** Q, **9** R

transcript

Questions ou réponses?

1 Comment t'appelles-tu?
2 Tu as quel âge?
3 J'ai deux frères.
4 Tu as des frères?
5 Je m'appelle Alex.
6 C'est le quatorze juillet?
7 C'est le quatorze juillet.
8 Le chat est noir?
9 Il est noir et blanc.

sb 56 • 2 tr 36 **AT1, AT3; 7L3; AfL**

5 L'histoire de Suzanne

Students read through the tips, then listen to the recording three times, each time answering the questions.

Any or all of the three stages can be used as peer assessment. After looking again at the spread objective, students should agree the criteria for success (which might be slightly different each time).

Solution:

1 Suzanne's birthday

2 a No, **b** All her presents were CDs of the same group

3 c 29th January, **d** 14, **e** pop (singing) group

transcript

L'histoire de Suzanne

Le 29 janvier, c'est l'anniversaire de Suzanne. Elle a quatorze ans.

L'après-midi, ses amis et moi, nous arrivons à la maison avec des cadeaux et des cartes. Suzanne aime beaucoup le groupe Citron Pressé. C'est son groupe favori, alors moi, j'ai un CD de ce groupe pour elle. Mais quel désastre! Les cadeaux de tous ses amis sont aussi des CD. Pauvre Suzanne. Maintenant, elle a beaucoup de CD, mais tous de la même musique!

 5/9 • 2 tr 37–39 **AT1**

Tu comprends?

1 C'est quand?

This worksheet provides independent listening practice. The first task could be used at any time after learning the months and the date.

Solution: **1** août, **2** juin, **3** avril, **4** mai, **5** mars, **6** octobre

transcript

C'est quand?

1 – C'est quand le film sur les animaux?
  – C'est le 6 août.
  – Le 6 août, bon.

2 – C'est quand, le concert de musique?
  – C'est le 19 juin.
  – Ah bon, c'est le 19 juin.

3 – C'est quand, la fête d'anniversaire?
  – C'est le 21 avril.
  – Le 21 avril, c'est ça?
  – Oui.

4 – Le match de basket, c'est quand?
  – C'est le 14 mai.
  – Le 14 mai, d'accord.

5 – La soirée carnaval, c'est quand?
  – C'est le 2 mars.
  – Le 2 mars, bon.

6 – Le feu d'artifice, c'est quand?
  – C'est le 28 octobre.
  – Alors, le 28 octobre.

2 Carine et Max

This practises clothing and colours and can be used at any time after SB 52.

Students listen to the recording and colour the pictures of the boy and girl according to the descriptions.

Solution:

Carine: long blond hair, blue eyes, yellow T-shirt, red jumper, blue skirt, grey shoes, black baseball cap

Max: short black curly hair, brown eyes, green shorts, green socks, orange and white shirt, black trainers

transcript

Carine

Je m'appelle Carine. J'ai les cheveux longs et blonds, et les yeux bleus. Aujourd'hui, je porte un t-shirt jaune avec un pull rouge et une jupe bleue. J'ai des chaussures grises et je porte aussi une casquette noire.

Max

Je m'appelle Max. J'ai les cheveux noirs, courts et bouclés et les yeux marron. Je porte un short vert et des chaussettes vertes avec une chemise orange et blanche. Je porte aussi mes baskets noires. J'aime bien mes basket noires – elles sont vraiment cool!

3 Des cadeaux de Noël

Students listen to the recording and write the correct letter for each present.

Solution: 1 f, **2** d, **3** a, **4** c, **5** h, **6** b, **7** e, **8** g

transcript

1 – Qu'est-ce que c'est? Ah, un DVD. C'est bien; j'adore ce film.

2 – Qu'est-ce que tu as?
  – Une raquette de tennis. C'est fantastique; j'aime bien le tennis.

3 – Et toi?
  – Des baskets! Génial! Elles sont très chic!

4 – Mmm, une boîte de chocolats. Délicieux.

5 – Moi, j'ai des balles de tennis. Ça, c'est toujours utile.

6 – Qu'est-ce que c'est?
  – Un livre, ah! une bande dessinée. J'aime bien ça.

7 – Et toi, qu'est-ce que tu as?
  – Un ballon de football.

8 – Et moi, j'ai un nouveau stylo noir. Regarde, il est très chic.

 Activité (int05) **AT1, AT3**

Rue Danton: L'anniversaire de Manon

This is a suitable point to use the fifth episode in the ongoing soap story. It is accompanied by two matching activities.

Activité (int06) AT1, AT3

Vocabulaire de classe (5)

This online activity practises some more key classroom language.

 Présentation (ppt06)/Fiche de travail (ws09) AT3

Une année de fêtes

This reader provides extension material on festivals through diary extracts.

Use the PowerPoint for whole-class presentation of the reader.

 **sb 57** **cm 5/10**

Sommaire

A summary of the main language and structures of the unit, also provided on copymaster for reference.

 Activité (int07) AT3

Vocabulaire (5)

An online game which tests the vocabulary of the unit.

 Activité (int08) AT1, AT3, AT4

Quiz – Unités 4 et 5

An online quiz which tests the language and content of *Unités* 4 and 5.

Plenaries (pages 56–57)

 Fiche de travail (ws02)

1 Students think about how they listen for gist in understanding texts with unfamiliar language. Discuss useful strategies, e.g. similarity to English, context, type of word, need to know, etc.

2 **Think, pair and share** In pairs, students choose one of the objectives for the unit (these could be allocated so that they are all covered), they discuss it for five minutes in pairs, then they share their findings with the class.

Unité 5 Consolidation and assessment

Épreuves Unité 5

These worksheets can be used for an informal test of listening, reading and writing or for extra practice, as required.

For general notes on the *Épreuves*, see TB 18.

 cm 5/11 Écouter ◉ **2 tr 40–42**

A Les vêtements

Students listen and write the correct letter.

Solution: **1** e, **2** d, **3** a, **4** f, **5** c, **6** g, **7** b
(mark /6)

transcript

Les vêtements

1 J'ai un short. Voici mon short.

2 Je porte un jogging. J'aime bien ce jogging.

3 Sylvie porte une robe. Elle est jolie, la robe.

4 Marc a une cravate. La cravate est dans sa poche.

5 – Où sont mes baskets?
  – Tes baskets sont ici.

6 Lucie porte une jupe. La jupe est grise.

7 – Où sont mes chaussettes?
  – Voici tes chaussettes.

B C'est quelle date

Students listen and write the correct letter.

Solution: **1** c, **2** b, **3** g, **4** f, **5** a, **6** d, **7** e
(mark /6)

transcript

1 – Richard, c'est quand, ta fête?
  – Ma fête, c'est le trois avril.
  – Ah bon, la Saint-Richard, c'est le trois avril.

2 – Pâques, c'est quand cette année?
  – Le dimanche de Pâques, c'est le 29 mars.
  – Alors, c'est le 29 mars.

3 – Tu vas au match de football, Lille contre Strasbourg?
  – Je ne sais pas. C'est quand?
  – C'est le trois octobre.
  – Le trois octobre, alors oui, je veux bien.

4 – Il y a un bon concert à La Rochelle, tu sais.
  – Ah bon, c'est quand?
  – C'est le 13 novembre.
  – Le 13 novembre? Bon, je vais voir.

5 – Isabelle, c'est quand ta fête?
  – La Sainte-Isabelle, c'est le 22 février.
  – Ah bon, alors, ta fête, c'est le 22 février.

6 – C'est quand, le film sur le Canada?
  – C'est le cinq juin.
  – Ah bon, le cinq juin. Et c'est au club des jeunes, non?
  – Oui, c'est ça.

7 – Quelle est la date de ton anniversaire?
  – Mon anniversaire? C'est le 18 février.
  – Le 18 février, bon.

C Des cadeaux

Students listen to spot the correct presents and then write the adjective describing each one.

> **Solution:**
>
> **1 a** *petit,* **2 b** *vert,* **3 b** *rouge,* **4 b** *amusant,* **5 a** *mignon*
>
> (mark /8: 1 mark for correct present, 1 mark for adjective; ignore misspellings)

 transcript

Des cadeaux

1 J'ai reçu un petit lapin. Il est très petit, le lapin.
2 Alors moi, j'ai reçu un sac de sport, un sac de sport vert. J'adore le sport et le vert, c'est ma couleur préférée.
3 Et moi, j'ai reçu des chaussures, des chaussures rouges. J'aime bien la couleur rouge.
4 J'ai reçu une bande dessinée. C'est très amusant. J'adore les bandes dessinées.
5 – Alors moi, j'ai reçu un chien. Il est mignon, mon chien. J'adore les chiens.
   – Oui, il est très mignon.

5/12 Lire

A Pierre

Students read the description and colour the picture.

> **Solution:** red T-shirt, green jumper, grey trousers, blue socks, black shoes, yellow cap, brown sports bag (mark /6)

B Les fêtes

Students read the sentences and find the pairs.

> **Solution:** **1** b, **2** e, **3** a, **4** d, **5** f, **6** c, **7** g, **8** h (mark /7)

C Une conversation

Students match the questions and answers.

> **Solution:** **1** d, **2** g (allow h), **3** h (allow g), **4** f, **5** b, **6** e, **7** c, **8** a (mark /7)

5/13 Écrire et grammaire

A C'est quand?

Students complete the date.

> **Solution:** **1** *avril,* **2** *janvier,* **3** *février,* **4** *juillet,* **5** *décembre* (mark /4)

B Une liste de cadeaux

Students choose suitable gifts for everyone.

> **Solution:** Give one mark each for any five of the following presents that are reasonably appropriate and spelt recognisably:
>
> *(un cédérom), une cravate, un pull, un livre, des baskets, une raquette de tennis, un t-shirt, un DVD, un sac de sport*
>
> (mark /5)

C À la maison

Students complete the sentences.

> **Solution:** **1** *avons,* **2** *ont,* **3** *avez,* **4** *sont,* **5** *est,* **6** *sommes* (mark /5)

D Un message électronique

Students write their own replies

> **Solution:** (mark /6: 2 marks for correct date, 2 marks for each present correctly described)

Rappel 2

 58–59

This section can be used at any point after *Unité 5* for revision and consolidation. It provides reading and writing activities which are self-instructional and can be used by students working individually for homework or during cover lessons.

58 AT3

1 5-4-3-2-1

> **Solution:**
>
> **5** *blanc, jaune, noir, rouge, vert*
> **4** *un cochon d'Inde, un hamster, une souris, un lapin*
> **3** *une cravate, une jupe, une robe*
> **2** *grand, mignon*
> **1** *Pâques*

58 AT3, AT4

2 Chasse à l'intrus

> **Solution:**
>
> **1** *une carte – les autres sont des choses à manger*
> **2** *une chaussure – les autres sont des animaux*
> **3** *un lapin – les autres sont des vêtements*
> **4** *une cravate – les autres sont des affaires scolaires*
> **5** *bleu – les autres sont des mois*
> **6** *méchant – les autres sont des jours de la semaine*
> **7** *mardi – les autres sont des nombres*
> **8** *petit – les autres sont des jours de la semaine*
> **9** *le perroquet – les autres sont des pièces*
> **10** *ma maison – les autres sont des membres de la famille*

 **58** AT3

3 Masculin, féminin

Solution:

masculin	féminin
un cadeau	une casquette
un gâteau	une jupe
un oiseau	une gomme
	une salle
	une trousse
	une ville

 **58** AT3, AT4

4 Ça commence avec c

Solution:

une calculatrice   des chaussettes
un cartable   des chaussures
une carte d'anniversaire   un cheval
une casquette   un chien
un classeur   un cédérom
un cochon d'Inde   une chaise
des crayons

59 AT3, AT4

5 L'année en France

Solution:

1 janvier, **2** juin, **3** mars, avril, **4** avril,
5 mai, **6** février, mars, **7** juillet, **8** décembre,
9 août, **10** septembre, **11** octobre,
12 novembre

59 AT4

6 Beaucoup de cadeaux

Solution:

1 Le pull est vert.
2 Le sac est gris.
3 La casquette est rouge.
4 Les chaussettes sont jaunes.
5 Les baskets sont noires.
6 Les chaussures sont blanches.
7 Les hamsters sont bruns.
8 Le perroquet est bleu, vert et jaune.
9 La trousse est bleue.
10 Les stylos sont rouges.

59 AT3, AT4

7 Questions et réponses

Solution:

a 1 ton, **2** ton, **3** ta, **4** ta, **5** tes, **6** tes
b a ma, **b** Mes, **c** Mon, **d** mes, **e** Ma, **f** Mon
c 1 c, **2** f, **3** e, **4** a, **5** b, **6** d

59 AT3, AT4

8 Charles

Solution:

1 Je suis, **2** Mon père est, ma mère est,
3 J'ai, **4** J'ai, **5** Mon frère a, **6** Il est,
7 Ma sœur a, **8** Elle est, **9** Nous avons,
10 Ils sont, ils sont, **11** Mes amis sont,
12 Nous sommes

Aims and objectives	Key language/Culture	Grammar and skills	National criteria
6A Quel temps fait-il? pp60–61 • talk about the weather • say what the temperature is	*Quel temps fait-il?* *Il fait beau/chaud/froid/mauvais.* *Il y a du brouillard/du soleil/du vent.* *Il pleut./Il neige.* *Il fait (moins) X degrés.* **Culture** Geography of France	**Grammar** Revision of numbers 0–40 **Skills** Identifying word patterns (para ...) **Cross-curricular** Geography	**Attainment** AT1 Level 1–4, AT2 Level 1–3, AT3 Level 1–4. AT4 Level 1–3 **Framework** 7W2/8, 7S2, 7T1, 7L3/5 **Languages ladder/Asset languages** Grades 1–4 **Assessment for learning** ex 4
6B Les saisons pp62–63 • talk about months †and seasons • understand more about accents	*le printemps, au printemps/l'été (m), en été/l'automne (m), en automne/l'hiver (m), en hiver* *le ciel est bleu* *souvent/quelquefois/normalement* **Culture** Different climates in France	**Grammar** Prepositions for 'in' + season: *en/au* *Quand il fait ...., je ...* Accents – grave, acute, circumflex, cedilla, trema **Skills** Adverbs of frequency (*souvent, quelquefois, normalement*) Everyday sayings (idioms)	**Attainment** AT1 Level 1–4, AT2 Level 1–3, AT3 Level 1–4. AT4 Level 1–3 **Framework** 7W2/6, 7S2/4/8, 7T1/6/7, 7L1/6, 7C4 **Languages ladder/Asset languages** Grades 1–4 **Assessment for learning** ex 6
6C Le sport pp64–65 • talk about sport • use the verb *jouer*	Sports: *jouer au badminton/basket/golf/hockey/football/rugby/tennis/tennis de table/volley*	**Grammar** *J'ai joue au ...* Present tense of *jouer*	**Attainment** AT1 Level 1–3, AT2 Level 1–3, AT3 Level 1–3. AT4 Level 1–3 **Framework** 7W2/4/5/6, 7S3/4, 7T6, 7L3/6 **Languages ladder/Asset languages** Grades 1–3 **Assessment for learning** ex 5
6D Des verbes pp66–67 • use some regular –er verbs	*Qu'est-ce que tu fais?/Je reste à la maison./J'écoute de la musique./Tu aimes ... ?/Il/Elle mange .../Nous surfons sur le Net./Nous chantez?/Ils passent les vacances .../Elles travaillent.*	**Grammar** Conjugating regular –er verbs Using different subject pronouns	**Attainment** AT1 Level 1–3, AT2 Level 1–3. AT3 Level 1–3. AT4 Level 1–3 **Framework** 7W5/6, 7T1/2/5 **Languages ladder/Asset languages** Grades 1–3 **Assessment for learning** ex 3
6E En famille pp68–69 • talk about family activities • say what you do at weekends • practise using –er verbs	*Qu'est-ce que tu fais normalement, le week-end?* Some regular –er verbs *adorer, aimer, arriver, chercher, cliquer, détester, écouter, entrer, habiter, jouer, penser, regarder, rentrer, rester, surfer, taper, téléphoner, travailler*	**Grammar** Practising using –er verbs **Skills** Keeping a conversation going	**Attainment** AT1 Level 1–4, AT2 Level 1–4. AT3 Level 1–4. AT4 Level 1–4 **Framework** 7W5, 7S4, 7T5/6, 7L3/5/6 **Languages ladder/Asset languages** Grades 1–4 **Assessment for learning** ex 5
6F On s'amuse pp70–71 • use on + verb • talk about different activities according to the weather	*On regarde un film?/On joue aux jeux vidéo/On joue aux cartes./On joue au Monopoly./Qu'est-ce que tu fais quand il fait mauvais?* **Culture** *La fête de la science* French handwriting	**Grammar** *On* **Skills** Reading French handwriting Writing a postcard **Pronunciation** Nasal sounds	**Attainment** AT1 Level 1–3, AT2 Level 1–3. AT3 Level 1–4. AT4 Level 1–3 **Framework** 7W2/5/6, 7S3/4/9, 7T2/3/5/6, 7L3/4/5/6 **Languages ladder/Asset languages** Grades 1–4 **Assessment for learning** ex 6
6G On invente des conversations pp72–73 • practise and improve speaking skills	Consolidation	**Skills** Using familiar language to work out unfamiliar phrases Improving your spoken work using adverbs, connectives and extra detail	**Attainment** AT1 Level 1–3, AT2 Level 1–4. AT3 Level 1–3. AT4 Level 1–3 **Framework** 7W2, 7S3/4, 7L3/4/5 **Languages ladder/Asset languages** Grades 1–4 **Assessment for learning** ex 4

Other resources: Online resource *Unité 6*. Copymasters 6/1–6/2, 104, 128, CD 3 tracks 2–21, Flashcards 27–33/37–42. GIA pp17–21

<table>
<tr><td colspan="3">6A Quel temps fait-il? pages 60–61</td></tr>
<tr><th>Aims and objectives</th><th>Grammar and skills</th><th>Resources</th></tr>
<tr>
<td>
<ul>
<li>talk about the weather</li>
<li>say what the temperature is</li>
</ul>
</td>
<td>
Grammar
Revision of numbers 0–40
Skills
Identifying word patterns (para …)
Cross-curricular
Geography
</td>
<td>
Key language: see p108
Online resource: Unité 6 int01/02, ppt01, ws02/03
Copymasters: 6/1, 128
CD 3 track 2
Flashcards: 27–33
</td>
</tr>
</table>

Starters (pages 60–61)

 Fiche de travail (ws02)

1 Revise numbers 0–40 orally using *Effacez!* (see TB 21).

2 **Où est la ville?** Display the following towns on the board and ask students to match them to the appropriate country/region:

Édimbourg, Dublin, Grenoble, Cardiff, Londres, Paris, Sydney, Belfast

en Écosse, en Angleterre, en France, au pays de Galles, en Irlande, en Australie, en Irlande du Nord, dans les Alpes

Introduction	AT1, AT2

The weather

Go through the objectives for this spread.

Then start with the PowerPoint presentation (see below) or flashcards (27–33) to teach the following expressions. To help make the meaning clear, mime appropriate gestures, e.g. shivering, wiping brow. Ask which two words appear in many expressions and help students to identify *il fait*.

Quel temps fait-il? Il fait chaud/froid.

For *il fait beau*, use the sunny flashcard.

For *il fait mauvais*, use a combination of two or more of the rain, cold, foggy and windy flashcards.

Il pleut/neige. Il y a du soleil/vent/brouillard.

Use games to practise these expressions, e.g. *Effacez!* (where students point to or take the flashcard) and *Jeu de mémoire* (Kim's game – see below). See TB 21–22.

 Activité (int01) AT1, AT3

Le temps qu'il fait

An online activity to present and practise weather phrases.

 Présentation (ppt01) AT2

Jeu de mémoire: Le temps

A PowerPoint version of Kim's game to practise weather phrases.

 **60** AT3; 7S2

1 Le temps en France

Introduce the French weather map, checking that the symbols are clearly understood and referring to the *Légende*.

La France est un grand pays. Dans le nord de la France, il fait mauvais. À Lille il pleut. À Dieppe il y a du brouillard. À Strasbourg, il fait froid.

Mais à La Rochelle, il fait beau. Il y a du soleil.

Et dans les Alpes, à Grenoble, quel temps fait-il? Est-ce qu'il pleut? Est-ce qu'il fait chaud?

Et à Nice? Et à Bordeaux? etc.

a Students then complete the *vrai/faux* task. Able students could correct the wrong weather descriptions.

> **Solution: 1** *faux (Il fait mauvais.),* **2** *vrai,* **3** *faux (Il fait chaud.),* **4** *vrai,* **5** *faux (Il y a du brouillard.),* **6** *faux (Il fait beau.),* **7** *vrai,* **8** *faux (Il fait froid.)*

b Students refer to the table or the map to complete the weather descriptions.

> **Solution:**
> **1** *À Dieppe, il y a du brouillard.*
> **2** *À Strasbourg, il fait froid.*
> **3** *À Paris, il fait mauvais.*
> **4** *À Nice, il fait chaud.*
> **5** *À Toulouse, il y a du soleil.*
> **6** *À Grenoble, il neige*
> **7** *À Lille, il pleut.*

Weather forecasts

Students could work in groups to give their own weather forecast, using visuals and symbols in the style of a TV presentation.

The map on **CM 128** could be used for this.

 Fiche de travail (ws03) AT1, AT4

Est-ce qu'il fait beau?

An online worksheet to practise describing weather from maps.

 **148 Au choix** AT4

1 Quel temps fait-il?

Further practice of writing weather descriptions.

Solution:

1 À Brighton, il fait mauvais.
2 À Exeter, il fait chaud.
3 À Bristol, il y a du soleil.
4 À Bangor, il pleut.
5 À Dublin, il y a du vent.
6 À Belfast, il fait beau.
7 À Glasgow, il fait froid.
8 À Aberdeen, il neige.
9 À Leeds, il y a du brouillard.
10 À Ipswich, il fait beau.

 **60** AT1, AT2; 7W2

2 Les températures

Look at the thermometer and teach *assez chaud*, *assez froid* and *moins* (+ number). Draw a simplified thermometer on the board, e.g.

Quand il fait 35 degrés, est-ce qu'il fait froid?
Non, il fait chaud.
Est-ce qu'il fait assez chaud?
Non, il fait très chaud.
Et quand il fait moins cinq degrés, est-ce qu'il fait chaud?
etc.

Introduce the table of temperatures to the class, using the example to show what to say.

Students could then practise this orally in pairs.

For further practice, write a list of towns (perhaps local or well known ones) on the board, each with a different temperature.

Give the name of the town or the temperature, or invite a volunteer to do so.

A student then has to give the other item and prompt the next student, and so on, e.g.

Teacher:	*Quelle température fait-il à Strasbourg?*
Student A:	*(Il fait) 9 degrés. À Paris? …*
Student B:	*(Il fait) 18 degrés. À Londres? …*

To maintain pace, set a time limit of, say, five seconds for each reply.

 Activité (int02) AT1; AT2

Quel temps fait-il?

An online role play activity to practise talking about the weather (including temperatures).

 **61** ● **3 tr 2** AT1, 7L3

3 Voici la météo

Teach *parapluie* and write it on the board. The recording could be played with pauses after each town for students to note down their answers. To make it easier, students could work in pairs or the class could be divided into two groups. One pair or group just notes down the weather, and the other notes down the temperatures.

Solution: **1a** C, **1b** 7°C, **2a** F, **2b** 12°C, **3a** A, **3b** 13°C, **4a** I/G, **4b** 19°C, **5a** G/B, **5b** 21°C, **6a** E, **6b** –4°C, **7a** H, **7b** 5°C, **8a** D, **8b** 8°C, **9a** A/F, **9b** 9°C

 **transcript**

Voici la météo

– Bonjour, mesdames et messieurs.

Aujourd'hui, nous sommes le cinq mars. Est-ce qu'il va faire beau aujourd'hui? Écoutons la météo avec Daniel Dubois.

– Eh bien, voici la météo.

Commençons par la capitale. À Paris, il fait froid pour la saison; la température est de sept degrés.

Dans l'ouest de la France, à Rennes, il pleut. Alors, prenez votre parapluie si vous êtes à Rennes. La température à Rennes est de douze degrés.

À Bordeaux, sur la côte atlantique, il y a du brouillard. Température: treize degrés.

Dans le sud de la France, il fait beau. À Toulouse, il fait beau et la température est de dix-neuf degrés. Alors, du beau temps à Toulouse.

Et à Nice et partout dans la région méditerranéenne, le ciel est bleu. Il y a du soleil et il fait chaud. Température: vingt et un degrés.

Par contre, à Grenoble et dans les Alpes, il neige. C'est bien pour les skieurs, mais la température est de moins quatre degrés.

À Strasbourg et dans l'est de la France, il y a du vent. Oui, du vent assez fort et la température à Strasbourg est de cinq degrés.

Passons maintenant au nord du pays. À Lille, il fait mauvais en général. Température: huit degrés.

Et à Dieppe, sur la côte nord, il y a du brouillard et il pleut. Température maximum de neuf degrés.

 **6/1** AT3, AT4

Le temps

Students copy the correct caption for each weather picture. The cards can then be cut up and used for speaking or matching activities, e.g.

Tu fais la météo

Students work in pairs. The weather cards are spread out face down. One asks about the weather in a town and the other turns over a weather card and decribes the weather.

e.g. *Quel temps fait-il à Reading?*
Il fait beau aujourd'hui.

61 AT2; 7L5; AfL

4 Inventez des conversations

This brings together towns, weather and temperatures and is suitable for peer assessment. Review the spread objectives and assessment criteria. Students work in pairs to make up a short conversation with three exchanges.

For further practice/peer assessment, consequences could be played in groups.

Each student has a piece of paper and writes the name of the town at the top. The paper is folded over and passed to another student, who adds a weather symbol. The paper is folded again and passed to a third student who writes a number for the temperature.

The next student unfolds the paper and reads the weather forecast according to the prompts.

 **61** AT3; 7T1

5 La météo aujourd'hui

If not used earlier, the map on **CM 128** could be used for revision of places in France and compass points. The map could also be used for follow-up work on the weather – recording weather details for different towns on particular days, perhaps using sticky notes.

Teach *nord* and *sud* by referring to towns on the map, e.g.

Lille est dans le nord de la France.
Nice est dans le sud de la France.
Et Dieppe? Et Toulouse?

Students look at the weather map (SB 60) and read the weather descriptions to find the correct one. This can be done as a group activity, with each group looking at one description in order to find out whether it is correct or not.

Explain the noun *pluie*, which is used here (rather than *il pleut*) for the sake of authenticity.

 Solution: 2 is the correct description.

61 Stratégies 7W8

Encourage students to look at similarities between words as a clue to meaning. Parachute could also be mentioned, with students guessing the meaning of *une chute*. Mention that prefixes can be helpful in decoding meaning and discuss others in English or French (e.g. in/im – impossible; un – unsure/unfriendly, unpleasant; dis – displeased, discontent, etc).

Plenaries (pages 60–61)

Fiche de travail (ws02)

1 Students work in pairs to group weather expressions, e.g. *il fait* + adjective, *il y a* + noun, *il* + verb. They see how many weather expressions they can remember and share tips on how to learn them.

2 Students think about how they read for gist in understanding texts with unfamiliar language, e.g. *La météo aujourd'hui*. Discuss useful strategies e.g. similarity to English, context, type of word, need to know, etc.

6B Les saisons   pages 62–63

Aims and objectives	Grammar and skills	Resources
• talk about months and seasons • understand more about accents	**Grammar** Prepositions for 'in' + season: *en/au* *Quand il fait …, je …* Accents – grave, acute, circumflex, cedilla, trema **Skills** Adverbs of frequency (*souvent, quelquefois, normalement*) Everyday sayings (idioms)	**Key language:** see p108 **Online resource:** *Unité 6* ppt02, ws02/04/05 **Copymasters:** 6/2, 6/3, 128 **CD** 3 tracks 3–6 **Flashcards:** 27–33

Starters (pages 62–63)

 Fiche de travail (ws02)

1 **Complète les mois** Display or give out the following task and ask students to complete the months, by inserting the missing vowels. Ask students randomly for the answers.

1	*s_pt_mbr_*	7	*m_ _*
2	*_vr_l*	8	*_ct_br_*
3	*j_ _ ll_t*	9	*m_rs*
4	*d_c_mbr_*	10	*j_ _n*
5	*f_vr_ _r*	11	*n_v_mbr_*
6	*j_nv_ _r*	12	*_ _ _t*

2 **Vrai/Faux cards** Make true/false statements about the weather flashcards (27–33) or use a PowerPoint presentation (see 6A) and ask students to indicate whether the statements are true or false by holding up their *vrai* or *faux* card.

Introduction FC 27–33 AT1, AT2

Seasons

Go through the objectives for this spread.

Teach the names of the seasons and practise related weather conditions, using the flashcards 27–33 or the picture in the Student's Book (SB 62), e.g.

Il y a quatre saisons dans l'année: le printemps, l'été, l'automne et l'hiver.

Le printemps commence le 21 mars.
Quel sont les mois de printemps? (mars, avril, mai)
Au printemps, quel temps fait-il?
Normalement il fait beau et il y a du soleil.
En été, il fait chaud et le ciel est bleu.
En automne, il y a du vent et quelquefois, il y a du brouillard.
Et en hiver, quel temps fait-il en hiver?
Il fait froid et quelquefois il neige.

 **62**   **AT3, AT4; 7W2**

1 Les quatre saisons

This presents the names of the seasons and some related vocabulary, e.g. *le ciel, la pluie, quelquefois.*

a   Students relate months, events, etc. to specific seasons.

> **Solution:**
> **1** *le printemps,* **2** *l'automne,* **3** *l'été,* **4** *l'hiver,* **5** *l'automne,* **6** *l'été,* **7** *le printemps,* **8** *l'hiver*

b   Students complete the sentences describing typical weather for each season.

> **Solution:**   **1** *beau,* **2** *soleil,* **3** *pleut,* **4** *chaud,* **5** *bleu,* **6** *vent,* **7** *brouillard,* **8** *froid,* **9** *mauvais,* **10** *neige*

Weather chain game

One student says a season and a weather condition and the next student repeats this and adds another appropriate weather condition up to a maximum of three or four, e.g.

En hiver/automne, il pleut et il y a du brouillard ... et il y a du vent ... et il fait froid.

En été, il fait chaud et il y a du soleil ... et le ciel est bleu ... et il fait beau.

This could also be played in teams and timed to see which team can say four items the fastest.

For variation, towns and countries could be changed, e.g.
À Glasgow il fait froid, mais à Nice ...

For practice of seasons, countries in northern and southern hemispheres could be contrasted, e.g.
En Angleterre, c'est l'hiver, mais en Australie ...

    Présentation (ppt02)   **3 tr 3–4**
AT1, AT2, AT3; 7C4

Chantez! Le premier mois

This online PowerPoint presentation provides the lyrics and music for a song to practise the weather, months and seasons. The song can be used at any convenient point in the unit. For the words and music see TB 29. For notes on using songs, see TB 25.

62   Dossier-langue/Stratégies   **7W2, 7T7**

Check that students have worked out that *en* is used before a vowel or mute 'h'.

Discuss with students other contexts where *souvent, quelquefois* or *normalement* could be used and mention that these are useful 'high frequency words'.

 **62**   **AT2, AT4; 7W2**

2 Des mots utiles

Invite suggestions from the class or display suitable sentences around the classroom.

---

e.g. *En hiver, il fait souvent froid. En Angleterre il pleut souvent.*
Au printemps, normalement il fait beau.
En été il y a souvent du soleil.
En automne, il y a quelquefois du brouillard.

 **6/2**

Vocabulaire: la météo et les saisons

Further practice of vocabulary linked to spreads 6A and 6B.

> **Solution:**
>
> **1 Des mots en serpent**
> **1** *mauvais,* **2** *froid,* **3** *beau,* **4** *chaud,* **5** *le printemps*
>
> **2 Complète les mots**
> Le ciel est **bleu.** Il fait **chaud.**
> Il fait **beau.** Il y a du **soleil.**
> Il fait **mauvais.** Il **neige.** Il **pleut.**
> Il y a du **vent.**
>
> **3 Complète les conversations**
> **A** – *Quel* **1** *temps fait-il en général dans les Alpes?*
> – *En hiver et au* **2** *printemps il* **3** *neige. Les hivers sont longs. Il fait* **4** *froid mais souvent il y a du* **5** *soleil.*
> **B** – *Et dans le Midi?*
> – *Bon, chez nous, à Nice, il fait* **1** *beau toute l'année. En été, il fait très* **2** *chaud et il ne* **3** *pleut pas souvent, mais il y a du* **4** *vent.*
>
> **4 Voici la météo**
> **1** *juin,* **2** *dix-huit,* **3** *chaud,* **4** *pleut,* **5** *vent,* **6** *température,* **7** *degrés*

 **6/3**   **AT2**

La météo

In this information-gap activity, students exchange details about the weather in different towns in order to complete a weather map.

 **148 Au choix**   **3 tr 5**   **AT1**

2 La météo

To extend their listening skills, students listen to a radio broadcast about events and weather in the UK and note down the details.

> **Solution:**   **a** *il fait froid,* **b** 6°, **c** *rugby,* **d** *(il y a du) vent,* **e** 10°, **f** *football,* **g** *il fait beau,* **h** 12°, **i** *hockey*

– Non, merci, désolée mais je n'aime pas beaucoup ça.
– Comme dessert, il y a des fruits. Qu'est-ce que tu prends?
– Je voudrais une pêche, s'il vous plaît. Merci.

 9/10 Lire   AT3

A Le déjeuner

Solution: **1** a, **2** f, **3** b, **4** d, **5** c, **6** h, **7** g, **8** e
(mark /7)

B Mon repas idéal

Solution: **1** F, **2** V, **3** F, **4** F, **5** F, **6** F, **7** F
(mark /6)

C Une conversation

Solution: **1** d, **2** h, **3** a (accept e), **4** f, **5** b
(accept e), **6** e (accept b), **7** c, **8** g (mark /7)

 9/11 Écrire et grammaire   AT4

A Une liste

Solution: **1** du pain, **2** du beurre, **3** de la
confiture, **4** des carottes, **5** de l'eau (minérale),
6 des pommes
(mark /5: 1/2 mark for correct partitive, 1/2 mark
for correct noun)

B Qu'est-ce qu'on prend?

Solution: **1** prenez, **2** prenons, **3** prennent,
4 prend, **5** prends, **6** prends
(mark /5: 1 mark per correct answer)

C Ça ne va pas!

Solution: **1** Il ne fait pas beau. **2** Nous ne
mangeons pas de viande. **3** Mes amis n'ont pas
d'animaux à la maison. **4** Je ne suis pas content.
(mark /6: 1 for correct verb, 1 for correct ne …
pas)

D Mon repas idéal

Solution: This is an open-ended task.
(mark /4: give 1 mark for each item listed)

Rappel 4

 **122–123**

This section can be used at any point after Unité 9 for
revision and consolidation. It provides reading and
writing activities which are self-instructional and can be
used by students working individually for homework or
during cover lessons.

 **122**   AT3, AT4

1 Où sont les voyelles?

Solution:

1 juillet, **2** novembre, **3** septembre, **4** avril,
5 mai, **6** l'anglais, **7** l'histoire, **8** la géographie,
9 la musique, **10** la technologie, **11** vert,
12 rouge, **13** jaune, **14** noir, **15** blanc,
16 le jogging, **17** la chemise, **18** le pantalon,
19 les chaussettes, **20** la cravate

 **122**   AT3, AT4

2 Des listes

Solution: **1** mercredi, **2** le soir, **3** il est une
heure et quart, **4** troisième, **5** l'hiver,
6 le déjeuner

122   AT3, AT4

3 Masculin, féminin

Solution:

masculin		féminin	
le matin	le fromage	une carotte	une omelette
le dessin	un lapin	une heure	une pomme
le potage	un village	la confiture	la salade
		une galette	
		la limonade	

122   AT3, AT4

4 C'est quel verbe?

Solution: **1** J'ai, **2** j'aime, **3** Je vais,
4 je prends, **5** je suis, **6** j'aime, je vais,
7 je prends, je suis, **8** j'ai

122   AT3, AT4

5 Un e-mail

Solution: **1** mon, **2** mes, **3** ma, **4** mes, **5** leur,
6 leurs, **7** nos, **8** ton, **9** ta, **10** mon

123   AT3, AT4

6 La journée de Mangetout

Solution:

a **a** entre, **b** reste, **c** commence, **d** mange,
   e retourne, **f** cherche, **g** pense, **h** chasse

b **1** b, **2** a, **3** f, **4** c, **5** h, **6** g, **7** d, **8** e

123   AT3

7 Questions et réponses

Solution: **1** c, **2** g, **3** e, **4** b, **5** a, **6** j, **7** d, **8** f,
9 h, **10** i

123   AT2, AT4

8 À toi!

This is an open-ended task.

Tricolore Total 1
Unité 10 Amuse-toi bien! pages 124–137

Aims and objectives	Key language/Culture	Grammar and skills	National criteria
10A On fait du sport? pp124–125 • talk about sport • revise the verb *faire*	*Je fais de la gymnastique/du cyclisme/du VTT/de l'équitation/de la natation/de la planche à voile/du ski/de la voile/du roller/du skate*	**Grammar** Revision of *faire* and different meanings of it	**Attainment** AT1 Level 1–3. AT2 Level 1–3. AT3 Level 1–3. AT4 Level 1–3 **Framework** 7W2/5/8. 7S2/4. 7T1/2. 7L3 **Languages ladder/Asset languages** Grades 1–3 **Assessment for learning** ex 3
10B Tu aimes la musique? pp126–127 • talk about music and other leisure activities • use *jouer de* + instrument	*Est-ce que tu aimes la musique? J'aime la musique.* *Je joue ...* *du clavier/du piano/du trombone/du saxophone/du violon/du violoncelle/de la batterie/de la clarinette/de la flûte/de la flûte à bec/de la guitare/de la trompette* *Je ne joue pas d'un instrument.* *J'aime écouter ...* **Culture** *Fête de la musique*	**Grammar** *Jouer de* + musical instrument **Skills** Understanding new language (revision)	**Attainment** AT1 Level 1–4. AT2 Level 1–3. AT3 Level 1–4. AT4 Level 1–3 **Framework** 7W2/7. 7S4. 7T1/2. 7L3/4. 7C2 **Languages ladder/Asset languages** Grades 1–4 **Assessment for learning** ex 4
10C Mes passe-temps pp128–129 • talk about leisure activities • use *jouer à* + sport/games • practise letter writing	*Est-ce que tu fais autre chose?* *Je fais du dessin/de la peinture/de la lecture/du théâtre/des photos.* *Je joue à l'ordinateur/aux cartes/aux échecs/aux jeux vidéo.* *C'est + adjective*	**Grammar** *Jouer de, jouer à* and *faire de* **Skills** Writing a letter to a friend	**Attainment** AT1 Level 1–3. AT2 Level 1–4. AT3 Level 1–4. AT4 Level 1–4 **Framework** 7W2/5/7. 7S2/3/4. 7T5/7. 7L3/6. 7C2 **Languages ladder/Asset languages** Grades 1–4 **Assessment for learning** ex 5
10D La semaine dernière pp130–131 • recognise the past tense • use some phrases in the past tense	*La semaine dernière* *Samedi dernier* *Qu'est-ce que tu as fait?* *J'ai joué au ...* *Et toi? Moi, j'ai fait ...* **Culture** Astérix and the *Parc Astérix*	**Grammar** Recognising and using some phrases in the past tense (*j'ai joué, j'ai fait*) **Skills** Knowledge about nouns and adjectives Adding extra detail to conversation	**Attainment** AT1 Level 1–5. AT2 Level 1–5. AT3 Level 1–5. AT4 Level 1–5 **Framework** 7W2/4/5/7. 7S1/3/4/7. 7T5. 7L3/4 **Languages ladder/Asset languages** Grades 1–5 **Assessment for learning** ex 7
10E Au parc d'attractions pp132–133 • find out about Astérix and the *Parc Astérix* • use the 24-hour clock	*le Parc Astérix* *un personnage* *une bande dessinée* *une attraction* *ouverture/fermeture/entrée* *treize/quatorze/quinze/seize/dix-sept/dix-huit/dix-neuf/vingt/vingt et un/vingt-deux/vingt-trois/vingt-quatre* **Culture** *Astérix* and the *Parc Astérix*	**Skills** Looking at related nouns and verbs Using the 24-hour clock	**Attainment** AT1 Level 1–3. AT2 Level 1–3. AT3 Level 1–4. AT4 Level 1–3 **Framework** 7W8. 7S3/7. 7T1. 7L3/6. 7C2 **Languages ladder/Asset languages** Grades 1–4 **Assessment for learning** ex 2, ex 4
10F Un bon week-end pp134–135 • revise places • learn how to say 'I went' • understand and use sequencing words • write about a special day	*Tu as passé un bon week-end?* *je suis allé* *le matin/l'après-midi /le soir* *d'abord/puis/ensuite/finalement/en plus*	**Grammar** Recognising and using some phrases in the past tense (*je suis allé(e)*) Sequencing words	**Attainment** AT1 Level 1–5. AT2 Level 1–5. AT3 Level 1–5. AT4 Level 1–5 **Framework** 7W2/5/7. 7S3/4/7. 7T1/5/7. 7L2/3/4 **Languages ladder/Asset languages** Grades 1–5 **Assessment for learning** ex 4
10G Les loisirs pp136–137 • talk about leisure in general • write questions	Consolidation of *Unité 10*		**Attainment** AT1 Level 1–5. AT2 Level 1–5. AT3 Level 1–5. AT4 Level 1–5 **Framework** 7W5. 7S4. 7T1/5. 7L5 **Languages ladder/Asset languages** Grades 1–5

Other resources: Online resource *Unité 10*. Copymasters 10/1–10/12. 106–107. CD 5 tracks 2–20. GIA pp43–49

10A On fait du sport? pages 124–125

Aims and objectives	Grammar and skills	Resources
• talk about sport • revise the verb *faire*	**Grammar** Revision of *faire* and different meanings of it	**Key language:** see p188 **Online resource:** *Unité 10* int01, ws02/03 **Copymasters:** 10/1 **CD** 5 track 2 **GiA:** p43

Starters (pages 124–125)

 Fiche de travail (ws02)

1 Chaque mot à sa place Display the following task. Give students one minute to read and work out the answers, then ask several students to give the number of the box before confirming the correct answer.

Quelle est la bonne boîte pour chaque mot?

le jour (4), juin (5), jouez (2), jeudi (1), jaune (3)

1 dimanche lundi	2 joues jouent	3 vert rouge	4 le mois la semaine	5 janvier juillet

2 Quel verbe? Display the following:

a *Je ... mes devoirs.*

b *Il ... beau aujourd'hui.*

c *Nous ... de l'informatique.*

d *Vous ... du shopping?*

e *Ils ... du sport.*

1 *faisons* **2** *fait* **3** *font* **4** *fais* **5** *faites*

Give students one minute to read and work out the answers, then ask for them collectively or randomly, e.g.

- *Le verbe numéro un va avec quelle phrase?*

- *Nous faisons de l'informatique.*

- *Oui, c'est ça. C'est la phrase 'c'.*

▌ **Solution: 1** c, **2** b, **3** e, **4** a, **5** d

Introduction

Go through the objectives for this spread.

 Activité (int01) AT1, AT3

Les loisirs

An online activity to present and practise the vocabulary for the leisure activities introduced in spreads A–C.

 **124** AT3; 7W2, 7S4, 7T2

1 Qu'est-ce qu'on fait?

Go through the article, reading the captions and teaching the new words (*faire de la voile/de la planche à voile/du VTT/des promenades*) and asking questions, e.g.

Qu'est-ce qu'on fait comme sport dans la photo D?

Ask volunteers to read out different captions and ask a question of the class.

For reinforcement, play a game such as *Jeu de mémoire* (this could be a group activity, each group being asked in turn to name one of the activities described until all have been mentioned), *Effacez!* or *Le jeu des mimes* (see TB 21).

124 ● **5 tr 2** AT1; 7L3

2 Faites-vous du sport?

Students listen and write down the letter of the photo illustrating the sport mentioned.

▌ **Solution: 1** G, **2** F, **3** C, **4** A, **5** H, **6** E, **7** D, **8** B

Faites-vous du sport?

1 – Qu'est-ce que vous faites comme sport, monsieur?

– Moi, je fais des promenades, euh, des promenades avec mon chien.

2 – Qu'est-ce que vous faites comme sport, mademoiselle?

– Je fais de l'équitation. J'adore les chevaux, mais je ne suis pas très sportive!

3 – Et toi, Christine, toi et ton frère, vous faites du sport?

– Oui, oui. En été, nous faisons de la planche à voile.

– Il y a un grand lac près d'ici où on fait de la planche à voile.

4 – Est-ce que vous faites du sport, mademoiselle?

– Oui, je fais de la natation. Je vais à la piscine tous les samedis.

5 – Est-ce que vous faites du sport, les garçons?
 – Oui, nous faisons du skate.
 – Du skate. Où faites-vous ça?
 – Au centre sportif, c'est très populaire.

6 – Qu'est-ce que tu fais comme sports, Lucie?
 – Je fais du roller avec mes copines.
 – Ah, le patin à roulettes, tu aimes ça?
 – J'adore ça. On va très vite, c'est fantastique!

7 – Est-ce que vous faites du sport en famille, madame?
 – Nous faisons du vélo. Ça, c'est un sport qu'on fait ensemble. C'est bien.

8 – Quel est ton sport préféré, Richard?
 – Pour moi, c'est la voile. J'aime beaucoup faire de la voile avec mes cousins. C'est amusant!

 **125** AT3; 7W5, 7S2, 7T1; AfL

3 Qu'est-ce qu'ils font?

Students match up captions and pictures. Check the answers orally to give practice of the different parts of *faire* as well as names of sports. As it links with the spread objectives, it could be used for assessment. Discuss with students how they can achieve the learning objectives.

 Solution: **1** c, **2** b, **3** f, **4** e, **5** a, **6** d

 **125 Dossier-langue** 7W5, 7W8

faire (different meanings)

Students will be familiar with using parts of the verb *faire* (presented in full in *Unité 8*). This focuses on the many expressions using *faire* and how these are best translated into English. It can be linked with the framework objective 'that words do not always carry their literal meaning'.

 **125** AT3; 7W5

4 Trouve les paires

Students match French and English meanings.

 Solution: **1** b, **2** g, **3** h, **4** f, **5** c, **6** a, **7** d, **8** e

 **125** AT3, AT4; 7W5

5 On fait de la voile

Students supply the missing parts of *faire*. The text could then be read aloud by groups of three students and acted like a short sketch.

 Solution: **1** *fais*, **2** *fais*, **3** *fait*, **4** *font*, **5** *fait*, **6** *fait*, **7** *faisons*, **8** *faites*, **9** *faisons*, **10** *fais*, **11** *faites*

 **156 Au choix** AT3

1 Qu'est-ce qu'on fait?

Students match questions and answers. If needed, give guidance in looking for the right pronoun in the answer to match with the noun in the question. Students can jot

down the matching numbers and letters, but, for more practice, they should read out the questions and answers in pairs like short conversations.

 Solution: **1** b, **2** g, **3** c, **4** f, **5** a, **6** e, **7** h, **8** d

 Fiche de travail (ws03) AT3, AT4

Questions et réponses

This online writing worksheet practises all forms of *faire* with leisure activities in the present tense. It provides a harder extension of the *Au choix* activity.

 10/1

faire

This gives practice of *faire*, with some incline of difficulty.

 Solution:

 1 Faire – to do, make
 Students complete the paradigm:
 je fais, tu fais, il/elle/on fait, nous faisons, vous faites, ils/elles font.

 2 Des questions
 1 *fait*, **2** *faites*, **3** *font*, **4** *fais*, **5** *fait*, **6** *fait*, **7** *fait*, **8** *font*

 3 Des réponses
 a *fait*, **b** *fait*, **c** *fait, fait*, **d** *faisons*, **e** *fait*, **f** *font*, **g** *fais*, **h** *fait, fait*

 4 Trouve les paires
 1 c, **2** d, **3** f, **4** g, **5** a, **6** b, **7** e, **8** h

 5 Mots croisés
 Horizontalement:
 1 *faisons*, **4** *il*, **6** *un*, **8** *fais*, **10** *font*, **11** *elles*
 Verticalement:
 1 *faites*, **2** *il*, **3** *nous*, **5** *la*, **7** *fait*, **8** *faire*, **9** *vous*

 **1 p43**

Using the verb *faire* – to do, to make

This provides further practice of *faire*, if required.

Plenaries (pages 124–125)

 Fiche de travail (ws02)

1 Students could have a brainstorming session to think of the many contexts in which the verb *faire* is used.

2 There could also be a short discussion about how meaning is expressed in different languages and the challenge of translation. Mention that the way foreigners construct sentences in English often indicates the way the same meanings are expressed in their own language, such as Yoda in *Star Wars*.

10B Tu aimes la musique? pages 126–127

Aims and objectives	Grammar and skills	Resources
• talk about music and other leisure activities • use *jouer de* + instrument	**Grammar** *Jouer de* + musical instrument **Skills** Understanding new language (revision)	**Key language:** see p188 **Online resource:** *Unité 10* int01, ws02/04 **Copymasters:** 10/2 **CD** 5 track 3

Starters (pages 126–127)

 Fiche de travail (ws02)

1 **Understanding cognates** Display visuals for the following instruments and say the names in French. As these are *vrais amis*, students need to listen to the pronunciation and then call out the number of the correct visual.

le piano, la flûte, le violon, la guitare, la trompette, la clarinette, le trombone, le saxophone.

Remind students that *le trombone* has an alternative meaning and ask them what it is.

2 **Quel verbe?** Display the following:

a *Je ... du piano*

b *Tu ... de la guitare?*

c *Nous ... de la flûte.*

d *Vous ... du trombone?*

e *Ils ... du violon.*

1 *jouez* 2 *joue* 3 *jouent* 4 *jouons* 5 *joues*

Give students one minute to read and work out the answers, then ask for them collectively or randomly.

Solution: **1** d, **2** a, **3** e, **4** c, **5** b

 Activité (int01)   AT1, AT3

Les loisirs

An online activity to present and practise the vocabulary for the leisure activities introduced in spreads A–C.

Introduction

Teaching musical instruments

There are activities requiring productive use of all instruments in this area, but some teachers may prefer to adopt a modified approach as follows.

Students should be able to recognise all pronunciations and meanings, so the main emphasis should be on those, which do not look like English, e.g. *la flute à bec, le clavier, la batterie*. For some students, production could be limited to those instruments that are personal to them for use in personal conversation and their *Dossier personnel*.

 126   7W2, 7W7

1 Les instruments de musique

Teach or practise the new vocabulary using flashcards, actual instruments or the photos.

Teach the six masculine words, then the six feminine ones. Revise *jouer* (*Unité 6*) and introduce *jouer de* + instrument with questions, e.g.

Regardez la photo. C'est quel instrument? Qui joue d'un instrument de musique? (Student A), *tu joues de quel instrument?* etc.

Teach the names of any additional instruments that students actually play, e.g. double bass – *une contrebasse*.

Solution: **1** D, **2** H, **3** J, **4** C, **5** F, **6** E, **7** G, **8** L, **9** A, **10** I, **11** B, **12** K

 126 ⊙ 5 tr 3   AT1; 7L3

2 La musique, c'est ma passion

Students listen and note the letter corresponding to each instrument mentioned.

Solution: **1** F, **2** G, **3** B, **4** K, **5** I, **6** D, **7** H, **8** L

transcript

La musique, c'est ma passion

1 – J'aime beaucoup la musique et je joue du violon dans l'orchestre du collège.

2 – Je joue de la batterie dans un groupe. Nous jouons le samedi après-midi.

3 – J'adore la musique et je joue de la guitare.

4 – Moi, j'aime bien écouter de la musique, mais je ne joue pas d'un instrument. Mon ami joue de la trompette.

5 – Je joue de la flûte à bec. Beaucoup d'élèves apprennent la flûte à bec dans ma classe.

6 – Moi, j'aime beaucoup la musique, surtout le jazz. Je joue du clavier. Le clavier, c'est mon instrument préféré.

7 – Je joue du piano. C'est très bien parce que nous avons un piano à la maison. Ma sœur aussi apprend le piano et quelquefois nous jouons ensemble.

8 – Moi, je ne joue pas d'un instrument mais mon frère joue de la clarinette. Je vais aussi apprendre à jouer de la clarinette un jour.

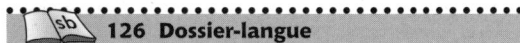

126 Dossier-langue   **7W7**

jouer de + musical instrument

Students work out the rule for the correct form of *de* by referring to the table.

Solution: **1** masculine, **2** feminine, **3** *pas*

126   **AT2; 7S4, 7L4**

3 Quel instrument?

Students work in pairs. One person thinks of an instrument or mimes playing it and the other has to ask questions for yes/no answers in order to identify the instrument.

127   **AT3, AT4; 7W2, 7T1; AfL**

4 Les jeunes musiciens

Students complete the text with the correct preposition and instrument.

Review the spread objectives and assessment criteria, this can then be used for assessment.

Solution: **1** *de la flûte à bec,* **2** *du piano,* **3** *du violon,* **4** *de la batterie,* **5** *de la guitare,* **6** *d'un instrument*

127   **AT3; 7T1, 7T2, 7C2**

5 Fête de la musique (Faites de la musique)

This musical festival is a great event in France and in other cities around the world. Students should read the article, using reading strategies to work out the gist and new language.

a Students could work on this in pairs and read out the French phrases to one another for checking.

Solution:
1 *un jeune sur deux*
2 *Quelques semaines plus tard*
3 *la journée la plus longue*
4 *une très grande manifestation culturelle*
5 *On fait de la musique partout*
6 *tous les concerts sont gratuits*

b

Solution:
1 The fact that one young person in two played an instrument.
2 21st June, summer solstice/longest day
3 Any of streets, parks, gardens, squares; cafés, theatres, schools, churches, prisons, hospitals
4 more than one hundred
5 All events are free to the public

Fiche de travail (ws04)   **AT3, AT4**

Faites de la musique ...

An online worksheet to provide extension work on the *Fête de la musique* article.

10/2

Grands mots croisés: la musique

Students interested in music could do this optional crossword at a convenient point.

Solution:

Horizontalement:

1 *violon,* **6** *ne,* **7** *concert,* **10** *sa,* **11** *ou,* **12** *le,* **13** *la,* **15** *du,* **16** *un,* **18** *et,* **20** *clarinette,* **23** *ta,* **24** *flûte,* **25** *piano,* **28** *jouent,* **29** *en,* **30** *trombone*

Verticalement:

1 *violoncelle,* **2** *on,* **3** *les,* **4** *en,* **5** *groupe,* **7** *clavier,* **8** *ce,* **9** *tu,* **14** *guitare,* **17** *batterie,* **19** *trompette,* **21** *il,* **22** *salle,* **26** *ne,* **27** *ont*

Plenary (pages 126–127)

Fiche de travail (ws02)

Think, pair and share Students think about how they can practise pronouncing cognates so they sound French. Have they noticed any spelling patterns which help with pronunciation, e.g. *...ette* (*clarinette, trompette*), *...on* (*violon, ballon*)?

They could discuss this in pairs, then share what they know with the class.

10C Mes passe-temps   pages 128–129

Aims and objectives	Grammar and skills	Resources
• talk about leisure activities • use *jouer à* + sport/games • practise letter writing	**Grammar** *Jouer de, jouer à* and *faire de* **Skills** Writing a letter to a friend	**Key language:** see p188 **Online resource:** *Unité 10* int01/02/03, ppt01, ws02/05 **Copymasters:** 10/3, 10/4 **CD** 5 track 4 **GiA:** pp44–45

Starter (pages 128–129)

Fiche de travail (ws02)

1 **Chasse à l'intrus** Display or print out the following lists. Students should write down the odd word out in each list. Ask several students for the answers, before confirming the correct one, then ask if anyone can explain why.

1	2	3	4	5
la natation	fais	le clavier	*mais*	les baskets
l'équitation	**fête**	la batterie	rouge	les chaussures
le violon	fait	**le vélo**	noir	les chaussettes
la voile	faites	la trompette	blanc	**les lunettes**

Introduction

Go through the objectives for this spread.

Other activities

Teach the words for other activities, not previously taught: *jouer aux jeux vidéo/aux cartes/aux échecs/à l'ordinateur, faire de la peinture/du dessin/des photos/du théâtre/de la lecture/de la cuisine.*

Practise with oral question and answer work.

Activité (int01) AT1, AT3

Les loisirs en France

An online activity to present and practise the vocabulary for the leisure activities introduced in spreads A–C.

128 AT3; 7W2, 7W5

1 On s'amuse

Read the introductory text, then students match the text and photos. Check this orally asking for complete sentences. Develop a wider discussion by asking who in the class does/likes/dislikes the activities shown here.

Solution: 1 B, **2** C, **3** A, **4** D, **5** E, **6** F

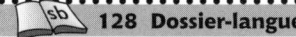
128 Dossier-langue 7W2, 7W7

jouer de … jouer à … faire de

This summarises the use of prepositions after *faire* and *jouer* with music, sport and other activities.

128 AT4; 7W2

2 C'est quelle activité?

Prepare this orally, then students write captions for the pictures. When checking this, ask students to read out their answers to practise pronunciation.

Solution:

1 *Il joue du violon.*
2 *Elles jouent de la flûte.*
3 *Ils jouent de la guitare.*
4 *Elle joue de la batterie.*
5 *Elles jouent au football.*
6 *Ils jouent aux échecs.*
7 *Il joue de la trompette.*

Activité (int02) AT1, AT2, AT3

L'interview d'Éloïse

An online role play activity practising sport, leisure and musical activites.

128 5 tr 4 AT1, AT2, AT4; 7W5, 7S3, 7S4, 7L3, 7L6

3 Des interviews

a Students read the questions then listen to the short interviews and note the question asked and the response.

Solution:

1 e *du sport – football, natation*
2 b *préfère la musique*
3 c *du clavier – cours le mercredi*
4 d *du théâtre - club au collège*
5 a *(s'il fait beau) promenade, (s'il pleut) jouer aux échecs/à des jeux vidéo*

b Students choose three questions and write their responses.

c Students interview one another in pairs.

transcript

Des interviews

1 – Tu as des passe-temps?
  – Oui, j'adore le sport. Je fais beaucoup de sport le week-end, surtout du football et de la natation. La natation, c'est super.

2 – Et toi, qu'est-ce que tu fais comme sport?
  – Pas grand-chose. Je ne suis vraiment pas sportive. Je préfère la musique.

3 – Est-ce que tu joues d'un instrument de musique?
  – Oui, je joue du clavier. J'ai un cours de clavier le mercredi après l'école.

4 – Et toi, est-ce que tu fais d'autres activités?
  – Oui, quelquefois je fais du théâtre. Il y a un club de théâtre au collège et j'aime bien ça.

5 – Et le week-end, qu'est-ce que tu fais le week-end normalement?
  – Ça dépend. S'il fait beau, j'aime faire une promenade avec mes amis. S'il pleut, j'aime jouer aux échecs ou à des jeux vidéo sur l'ordinateur.

AT1, AT2, AT3

Group identity game

Able students could write up the interview in the third person and this could be collected in and used for a group identity game, if the replies are sufficiently different, e.g. *Il adore le sport. Il fait beaucoup de sport le week-end, surtout le football et la natation. Qui est-ce?*

No names are given and the descriptions for each group are handed out to that group. Students have to interview other people in the group to identify the person fitting each description.

 **129** AT3; 7S2

4 Deux lettres

Students read through the letters and identify the person in the comprehension task. Ask for two volunteers to read the letters aloud for practice in pronunciation.

> **Solution: 1** *Léa,* **2** *Théo,* **3** *Théo,* **4** *Léa,*
> **5** *Théo,* **6** *Léa,* **7** *Théo*

129 Stratégies 7W2, 7W7, 7T7, 7C2

Writing a letter to a friend

This summarises some useful points when writing informal letters.

Reading French handwriting

French schoolchildren are taught a distinctive style of handwriting at school. This used to be a baroque style, but in 2002, the education minister, Jack Lang, said it was time France had a much clearer, more business-like handwriting for the 21st century.

However, most handwriting seen will still be in the traditional baroque style as shown here.

For more examples, see **http://www.momes.net/ education/ecriture/graphismes.html.**

Adding detail to personal speaking and writing

Demonstrate how students can make sentences more interesting by adding extra detail. Start with a simple sentence:

Je fais du judo.

Add *quand*

Le mercredi soir, je fais du judo.

Add *où*

Le mercredi soir, je fais du judo au centre sportif.

Add *avec qui*

Le mercredi soir, je fais du judo au centre sportif avec mon ami.

Add an opinion in a follow-up sentence

C'est vraiment bien.

 Activité (int03) AT3

Le mail de Sylvain

Multiple-choice activity on leisure activities and opinions. This can be used before tackling the writing activity in the SB or the worksheet 'Mes loisirs' (see below – ws05)

 Fiche de travail (ws05) AT3, AT4

Mes loisirs

An online writing worksheet practising leisure activities.

 **129** AT4; 7T5, 7T7; AfL

5 Une lettre

Review the spread objectives and discuss how this task could be used for assessment of progress. Perhaps give a model answer to demonstrate what is required. Students write a short letter about leisure activities, adding extra detail such as opinions, friends and asking some questions. Finish with a discussion about what was well done and what could be improved.

 Présentation (ppt01) AT2

Jeu de mémoire: Les activités

A PowerPoint version of Kim's game to practise leisure activities.

 156 Au choix AT3

2 Mes loisirs

a In this reading task, students find the correct words to complete the text.

> **Solution: 1** *ville,* **2** *piscine,* **3** *natation,*
> **4** *football,* **5** *super,* **6** *surfe,* **7** *lecture,* **8** *livres,*
> **9** *flûte,* **10** *fais*

b Students can then adapt the text by changing at least six details, and copy out their new version. Students could read out their new version in pairs and comment on one another's work.

For additional oral practice, play one of these games.

1 Chain game

There are several possible versions of this, e.g.

* the first person says *Je joue de la flûte.* The next repeats this and adds another instrument etc.
* as above, but alternating sports and musical activities
* as above, but adding days of the week, e.g. *Le lundi, je joue de la flûte; le mardi, je fais du dessin,* etc.

2 Qu'est-ce que tu fais?

Students write symbols for an activity or activities that they do (possibly in the form of a diary) and then take it in turns to guess what their partner does. The winner is the first to guess the activity or activities of their partner.

 10/3 AT3

Les loisirs

This provides a selection of word games to practise leisure vocabulary.

> **Solution:**
>
> **1 Mots mêlés**
>
> a
>
> | o | r | d | i | n | a | t | e | u | r |
> |---|---|---|---|---|---|---|---|---|---|
> | d | à | h | s | u | i | l | l | b | é |
> | p | e | i | n | t | u | r | e | o | m |
> | h | t | s | é | c | h | e | c | s | c |
> | o | q | u | s | k | i | a | t | v | a |
> | t | ç | a | n | i | k | j | u | é | r |
> | o | m | l | c | è | n | y | r | l | t |
> | s | a | i | d | u | g | f | e | s | e |
> | t | h | é | â | t | r | e | é | o | s |
> | p | r | o | m | e | n | a | d | e | s |

> **b 1** *J'aime faire des **promenades** avec nos chiens.*
>
> **2** *Je n'aime pas jouer aux cartes, mais j'aime jouer aux **échecs**.*
>
> **3** *Je vais faire des **photos** avec mon nouvel appareil.*
>
> **4** *En hiver, j'adore faire du **ski** à la montagne.*
>
> **5** *Quand il fait mauvais, je joue souvent sur l'**ordinateur**.*

2 Dans l'ordre alphabétique

1 *l'athlétisme* = athletics
2 *la batterie* = drums
3 *la chorale* = choir
4 *la danse* = dancing
5 *l'équitation* = horseriding
6 *la flûte* = flute
7 *la guitare* = guitar
8 *le hockey* = hockey
9 *le judo* = judo
10 *la natation* = swimming

3 Trouve les paires

1 e, **2** f, **3** d, **4** c, **5** a, **6** b

4 Ça ne m'intéresse pas du tout!

Students complete these sentences as they wish.

 10/4   **AT2**

Manon et Clément

Students work in pairs on this information gap activity. The teacher and an able student could demonstrate the activity first.

 1 pp44–45

Using *jouer à* and *jouer de* – to play (1) and (2)

These pages of graded activities could be used now or later, for revision.

Plenary (pages 128–129)

 Fiche de travail (ws02)

Using the *Sommaire*, suggest students find 5 words related to leisure that they have difficulty remembering. They should focus on each of the five words, and collect suggestions from round the class as to how to remember them. If few ideas are forthcoming, suggest perhaps linking each word to a finger, practise each word during the day and seeing if they can recall them in the next lesson.

10D La semaine dernière   pages 130–131

Aims and objectives	Grammar and skills	Resources
• recognise the past tense • use some phrases in the past tense	**Grammar** Recognising and using some phrases in the past tense (*j'ai joué, j'ai fait*) **Skills** Knowledge about nouns and adjectives Adding extra detail to conversation	**Key language:** see p188 **Online resource:** *Unité 10* ppt02, ws02/06 **Copymasters:** 10/5 **CD** 5 tracks 5–6 **GiA:** pp48–49

Note: This optional spread introduces some examples of the perfect tense with *avoir* to enable students to understand and talk about events in the past, using the *je* and *tu* forms.

Very little new vocabulary is introduced and the spread can be omitted if preferred. The perfect tense is taught systematically in Stage 2.

Starters (pages 130–131)

 Fiche de travail (ws02)

1 **Chaque mot à sa place** Display the following task. Give students one minute to read and work out the answers, then ask several individual students to give the number of the box, before confirming the correct answer.

Quelle est la bonne boîte pour chaque mot?

mardi (2), *la casquette* (5), *le dessin* (4), *la planche à voile* (1), *intéressant* (3)

1	2	3	4	5
le ski	lundi	génial	la peinture	la chemise
la natation	mercredi	amusant	la cuisine	le pantalon
le roller	jeudi	super	la photographie	la jupe

2 **Quel verbe?** Display the following:

a *J'... un petit chat.*
b *Tu ... un animal à la maison?*
c *Nous ... un chien et un lapin.*
d *Vous ... technologie aujourd'hui?*
e *Ils ... deux cours de géographie par semaine.*

1 *ont* **2** *ai* **3** *avez* **4** *as* **5** *avons*

Give students one minute to read and work out the answers.

Solution: 1 e, **2** a, **3** d, **4** b, **5** c

Introduction

Go through the objectives for this spread.

 **130 Stratégies**   **7W2, 7W4, 7W7, 7S7**

This explains the use of *dernier* as a pointer to an action in the past. Students should be able to adapt the pattern to other days. With able students, you could also ask them to predict how to say last summer, last winter, etc.

 **130** **5 tr 5** **AT1; 7S7, 7L3**

1 Samedi dernier

Look at the symbols and check that these are recognised and understood.

Students then listen to the recording and note the letter by each activity mentioned. The transcript introduces examples of the following phrases in the perfect tense: *j'ai fait, tu as fait; j'ai joué.*

> **Solution:** **1** C, **2** G, **3** E, **4** D, **5** I, **6** A, **7** F, **8** H, **9** J, **10** B

transcript

Samedi dernier

1 – Qu'est-ce que tu as fait samedi dernier?
– J'ai joué au badminton.

2 – Et toi, qu'est-ce que tu as fait?
– J'ai fait de la natation.

3 – Qu'est-ce que tu as fait samedi dernier?
– J'ai fait de la voile.

4 – Moi, j'ai joué au rugby.

5 – Et toi, qu'est-ce que tu as fait?
– J'ai fait du vélo au parc.

6 – Qu'est-ce que tu as fait?
– J'ai joué aux échecs avec mon ami.

7 – Moi, j'ai joué de la guitare.

8 – Qu'est-ce que tu as fait samedi dernier?
– J'ai fait du judo au centre sportif.

9 – Moi, j'ai fait de l'équitation.

10 – Et toi, qu'est-ce que tu as fait?
– J'ai joué du violon avec l'orchestre.

 **Présentation (ppt02)** **AT3**

Présent et passé

An online PowerPoint presentation of *je* and *tu* forms in perfect tense (*faire* and *jouer* only).

 **130 Dossier-langue** **7W5**

Recognising the past tense (1)

Explain that this just introduces a few examples (*j'ai joué* and *j'ai fait*) so that students can talk more fully about their free time. Explain that the perfect tense will be taught in full in Stage 2.

 **Fiche de travail (ws06)** **AT3, AT4**

C'est au passé?

Use this online worksheet to practise recognition of past and present tense verbs.

130 **AT3; 7W5, 7S7**

2 Présent ou passé?

Read the sentences aloud. Students decide whether they are past or present.

Then in pairs, one student could read the sentences in the present and the other those in the past.

> **Solution:**
>
> | présent | passé |
> |---------|-------|
> | 1, 2, 6, 8 | 3, 4, 5, 7 |

 **131** **AT2, AT4; 7W5, 7S1, 7S7**

3 Deux jours actifs

Students should not attempt to use other verbs, only those in the examples here.

> **Solution:**
>
> **a** *J'ai fait du vélo, etc.*
>
> **b** *J'ai joué de la batterie, etc.*

10/5 **AT3, AT4**

La semaine dernière

This provides a range of activities to practise recognition of the perfect tense and controlled practice.

1 Qu'est-ce que c'est en anglais?

> **Solution:**
>
> **a** **1** c, **2** e, **3** g, **4** i, **5** b, **6** f, **7** d, **8** j, **9** a, **10** h
>
> **b** Sentences in the perfect tense: 1, 3, 5, 8, 10

2 Trois jours actifs

This involves productive practice.

> **Solution:**
>
> **1** *Lundi matin, j'ai fait de la natation.*
>
> **2** *Lundi après-midi, j'ai fait du vélo.*
>
> **3** *Lundi soir, j'ai fait du roller.*
>
> **4** *Mardi matin, j'ai fait de la voile.*
>
> **5** *Mardi après-midi, j'ai fait une promenade avec le chien.*
>
> **6** *Mardi soir, j'ai joué au badminton.*
>
> **7** *Mercredi matin, j'ai joué au football.*
>
> **8** *Mercredi après-midi, j'ai joué de la guitare.*
>
> **9** *Mercredi soir, j'ai joué aux échecs.*

3 Un détail en plus

Students copy and complete the sentences and add a further detail of their choice.

131 **AT2; 7S4, 7S7, 7L4**

4 Inventez une conversation

Students work in pairs to develop a short conversation about past activities, using only *faire* and *jouer à/de.*

131 **5 tr 6** **AT1; 7S7, 7L3**

5 La semaine dernière

Students listen to the recording and note some additional details. Depending on ability, students could aim to note down 1–4 details for each item.

Solution:

	quand	quoi	avec qui	où
1	sam	danse	sœur	club des jeunes
2	ven	badminton	amis	centre sportif
3	dim	promenade	chien	parc
4	lun	clavier	frère	maison
5	jeu	foot	équipe	parc
6	mer	théâtre	club	collège
7	mar	échecs	grand-père	jardin
8	dim	camping	grand-mère	St-Malo

 transcript

La semaine dernière

1 Samedi dernier, j'ai fait de la danse avec ma sœur au club des jeunes.

2 Vendredi dernier, j'ai joué au badminton avec mes amis au centre sportif.

3 Dimanche dernier, j'ai fait une promenade dans le parc avec le chien.

4 Lundi dernier, j'ai joué du clavier avec mon frère à la maison.

5 Jeudi dernier, j'ai joué au football au parc avec l'équipe.

6 Mercredi dernier, j'ai fait du théâtre au collège avec le club.

7 Mardi dernier, j'ai joué aux échecs avec mon grand-père dans le jardin.

8 Dimanche dernier, j'ai fait du camping avec ma grand-mère à Saint-Malo.

 156 Au choix   **AT3, AT4**

3 Dans le bon ordre

Students copy the sentences in the correct word order.

Solution:

1 *Mercredi dernier, j'ai joué aux cartes avec mes amis.*

2 *Samedi dernier, j'ai fait de la danse au club des jeunes.*

3 *Dimanche dernier, j'ai fait une promenade avec mon chien.*

4 *Mercredi après-midi, j'ai joué aux échecs avec ma grand-mère.*

5 *Jeudi soir, j'ai fait du judo au centre sportif.*

6 *Mardi matin, j'ai fait du vélo au parc.*

7 *Vendredi dernier j'ai joué du violon dans un concert.*

8 *Lundi dernier, j'ai joué au tennis dans un match.*

 **131 Stratégies**

Adding more detail

A reminder about making written work more interesting.

 **131**   **AT2, AT4; 7S3**

6 Phrases aux nombres

Students practise forming sentences according to numbered options. This could also be played using just two or three numbers.

 **131**   **AT4; 7S7, 7T5; AfL**

7 Dossier personnel

Students could now write a few sentences about last week's activities for their *dossier*.

Remind students of the spread objective and indicate that this task will be ideal for them to demonstrate their skills. Discuss what a successful piece of work should include.

 1 pp48–49

Recognising the past tense (1) and (2)

This provides more explanation and practice of the perfect tense with *avoir* and regular *–er* verbs (*je* and *tu* forms only). Time phrases are also practised, including *hier*.

Plenary (pages 130–131)

 Fiche de travail (ws02)

Recognising and using the past tense Ask students how they've found this introduction to using the past tense. What do they find most difficult?

Ask them how often they use the past tense when they're speaking in English. Different ways of expressing the past in English could also be discussed, e.g. played, have played, did play.

10E Au parc d'attractions   pages 132–133

Aims and objectives	Grammar and skills	Resources
• find out about *Astérix* and the *Parc Astérix* • use the 24-hour clock	**Skills** Looking at related nouns and verbs Using the 24-hour clock	**Key language:** see p188 **Online resource:** *Unité 10* int04, ws02 **Copymasters:** 10/6 **CD** 5 tracks 7–8 **GiA:** p46

10E Au parc d'attractions

Starters (pages 132–133)

Fiche de travail (ws02)

1 **Times** Write a selection of times on the board for a game of *Effacez!*, e.g. 5h00, 6h05, 9h10, 11h20, 12h00 (*midi*), 1h25, 2h15, 3h30, 4h50, 7h30, 8h25, 9h45

2 **Chaque mot à sa place** Display the following task. Give students one minute to read and work out the answers, then ask students collectively or randomly to give the number of the box.

Quelle est la bonne boîte pour chaque mot?

samedi (5), *seize* (3), *la piscine* (4), *janvier* (1), *la batterie* (2)

1	2	3	4	5
février	le violon	quartorze	la patinoire	mardi
juillet	la guitare	vingt	le bowling	mercredi
août	le piano	cinquante	le stade	vendredi

Introduction

Go through the objectives for this spread.

sb 132 AT3; 7S3, 7T1, 7C2

1 Astérix le Gaulois

Ask students about comic strip characters in simple French. If possible show the class a comic strip book.

e.g. *Voici une bande dessinée. C'est un livre avec beaucoup d'images. On appelle un livre comme ça, une bande dessinée, ou une BD.*

Les Français aiment beaucoup les bandes dessinées – ou des BD. Il y a même un festival de la bande dessinée.

Qui sont les personnages de BD? Il y a Tintin, Lucky Luke et Astérix.

Astérix, qu'est-ce que c'est? C'est un animal? C'est une ville?

Non – c'est une personne imaginaire – un personnage de bande dessinée.

Qui connait Astérix? Il y a des livres d'Astérix en anglais. On trouve souvent les livres d'Astérix en anglais à la bibliothèque.

Then read through the text and check that students understand. Do some more oral work on the photos.

Corrige les phrases

Students could read out the corrected sentences.

Solution:
1 *Asterix habite dans **un village**.*
2 *Obélix est **l'ami** d'Astérix.*
3 *Obélix a un **chien** qui s'appelle Idéfix.*
4 *Panoramix fait des **potions** magiques.*
5 *Astérix et ses amis résistent aux invasions des **Romains**.*

Date and time (revision)

Revise orally the date and the time, using the 12-hour clock. There are several suitable games to help with this, e.g. *Et après?* (write on the board or say a day, month or number and the class have to say the one that follows), *Loto!* (students write down, say, three months and three days), *Le jeu du pendu* (see also TB 21–24).

sb 132 AT3; 7T1, 7C2; AfL

2 Le Parc Astérix

Find out if anyone has visited the *Parc Astérix* or knows about it and use this for discussion. Talk through the details and discuss the photos, identifying characters, etc.

Relate the task to the spread objectives and discuss how it can be used for self-assessment.

a Students match the captions to the photos of rides. This involves understanding some unfamiliar language so encourage the class to use appropriate strategies.

Solution: **1** A, **2** E, **3** C, **4** D, **5** B

b Students answer questions about visiting the *parc* (opening times, location, entry tarifs, etc)

Solution:
1 *Le Parc ferme à 18 heures.*
2 *À 19 heures.*
3 *Le Parc est ouvert le week-end en octobre.*
4 *Non, le Parc est fermé à Noël.*
5 *Le Parc, c'est près de Paris.*
6 *L'entrée, c'est combien 26 euros pour un jour ou 46 euros pour deux jours.*
7 *Et c'est gratuit pour un enfant de deux ans.*
8 *Pour les adultes, c'est 35 euros pour un jour ou 66 euros pour deux jours.*

sb 133 Stratégies 7W8

This encourages students to look for the meaning of a noun through linking it to a similar verb.

Solution:
1 *l'entrée* = entrance
2 *la fermeture* = closing
3 *l'ouverture* = opening
4 *la sortie* = exit

Other examples could be given e.g. *la danse – danser, le travail – travailler, une chanson – chanter*, etc

sb 133 Stratégies 7L6

The 24-hour clock

Explain that the 24-hour clock is used more widely on the continent, for television and radio programmes, on posters and timetables.

- Draw two columns on the board and, using figures, write a time after noon in the left-hand column, using the 24-hour clock. Then ask a student to write the equivalent time using the 12-hour clock in the right-hand column. Begin with hours only and then add in 30, 15, 45, and eventually other times, until you have a list of about twelve times. Say all the times in French as they are written up.

- Next, rub out the original times and do the whole thing again in reverse, this time seeing if the students can supply the times in French.

- Leave the times on the board and play a game of *Effacez!* (TB 21).

- For further practice, divide students into teams. Someone from each team in turn says a time in French, using the 24-hour clock, and someone from the other team has to write it on the board in figures.

Activité (int04)   **AT1, AT3**

C'est quand?

An animated online activity to practise the 24-hour clock.

---

133   **5 tr 7**   **AT1; 7S7, 7L3**

3 24 heures

Revise *ouvert* and *fermé* and explain *à partir de*. Students listen and note the time in figures. This task uses times on the hour only.

Solution:

1	15h00	**6**	16h00
2	13h00	**7**	14h00
3	20h00	**8**	18h00
4	21h00	**9**	20h00
5	17h00	**10**	22h00

transcript

Vingt-quatre heures

1 Le match de rugby commence à 15 heures.
2 Le déjeuner est à 13 heures.
3 Le film commence à 20 heures.
4 Le concert commence à 21 heures.
5 Le match de football commence à 17 heures.
6 La banque est ouverte jusqu'à 16 heures.
7 L'épicerie est ouverte à partir de 14 heures.
8 Le restaurant est ouvert à partir de 18 heures.
9 L'épicerie ferme à 20 heures.
10 Le match finit à 22 heures.

---

133   **AT3; 7T1; AfL**

4 Attention, c'est l'heure!

Students match up the times in words and numbers using the full range of times. This can also be used for self-assessment of understanding the 24-hour clock.

Solution: **1** B, **2** G, **3** D, **4** F, **5** C, **6** A, **7** E, **8** H

---

157 Au choix   **5 tr 8**   **AT1**

4 C'est quand?

Students listen and choose the correct time from the three options. For extra practice, the answers could be checked orally with students reading out all three possible times listed, then stating the correct one.

Solution: **1** b, **2** c, **3** c, **4** a, **5** b, **6** a

transcript

C'est quand?

1 – Allô! Ici le cinéma Dragon.
   – Bonjour, madame. Le film commence à quelle heure, s'il vous plaît?
   – À 20 heures 15, monsieur.
2 – Salut, Jacques. C'est à quelle heure, le match de football?

   – À 14 heures 30.
   – Ah bon.
3 – Le spectacle 'son et lumière' finit à quelle heure, s'il vous plaît, madame?
   – Il finit à 22 heures 30.
   – À 22 heures 30. Bon, merci, madame.
4 – Pardon, madame. Le concert commence à quelle heure?
   – À 20 heures 45, monsieur.
5 – La patinoire ferme à quelle heure le lundi soir?
   – Le lundi on ferme à 21 heures.
   – À 21 heures. Merci.
6 – La piscine ouvre à quelle heure aujourd'hui, s'il vous plaît?
   – À 14 heures, madame.

 10/6

24 heures

This provides further practice if required. The first two tasks involve matching times in figures and words (24-hour clock and ordinary time). The third task is harder, involving finding out opening and closing times from posters.

Solution:

1 Quelle heure est-il?
   1 b, **2** e, **3** f, **4** h, **5** g, **6** a, **7** d, **8** c

2 Autrement dit
   1 e, **2** c, **3** b, **4** a, **5** d, **6** f

3 Ça ouvre … ça ferme
   1 *dix heures, dix-huit heures*
   2 *quatorze heures trente, vingt heures*
   3 *dix heures, vingt-deux heures*
   4 *midi, dix-neuf heures trente*
   5 *dix-sept heures, vingt et une heures*
   6 *huit heures, treize heures*

---

1 p46

The 24-hour clock

Further practice of time using the 24-hour clock.

Chantez! Attention, c'est l'heure!

For revision and for fun, sing again the rap from *Unité 8* (see TB 25).

Plenaries (pages 132–133)

Fiche de travail (ws02)

1 **Think, pair and share** Students could discuss the 24 hour clock and its benefits and whether they find it easy to use and would like to see it more widely used in the UK.
2 Students could work in pairs or groups to suggest their top three tips for reading/getting the gist of a text in French. If ideas are slow to emerge, refer them to the reading strategies introduced earlier.

10F Un bon week-end   pages 134–135

Aims and objectives	Grammar and skills	Resources
• revise places • learn how to say 'I went' • understand and use sequencing words • write about a special day	Recognising and using some phrases in the perfect tense (*je suis allé(e)*) Sequencing words	**Key language:** see p188 **Online resource:** *Unité 10* int05, ws02/07/08 **Copymasters:** 10/7 **CD** 5 tracks 9–10 **GiA:** p 47

This optional section introduces additional phrases in the perfect tense, including *je suis allé(e)* and *tu es allé(e)*. The perfect tense is taught fully in Stage 2 with detailed explanations.Teachers who do not wish to cover the perfect tense could just use the final items in this spread and the practice of regular and irregular verbs in the present tense (Grammar in Action 1 p47).

Starters (pages 134–135)

 Fiche de travail (ws02)

1 **En groupes** Display a list of words in random order or hand this out on slips of paper. Ask students to put these into 5 groups:

le hockey, le basket, le rugby
faire, avoir, aller
le trombone, le violoncelle, le clavier
quinze, vingt-cinq, cinquante
les échecs, les cartes, les jeux vidéo

Give students a few minutes to work out the groups then ask for volunteers to read out one group each.

2 **Masculin ou féminin** Give out the following list on slips of paper or display the words and ask students to work in pairs to decide whether the words are masculine or feminine. Ask them to show a *masculin* or *féminin* card when checking.

Genders have been added for checking purposes.

bibliothèque f	*musée m*
bowling m	*parc m*
centre sportif m	*patinoire f*
château m	*piscine f*
cinéma m	*plage f*
club des jeunes m	*synagogue f*
mosquée f	*temple m*

Introduction
Go through the objectives for this spread.

 **134** 5 tr 9   AT1; 7W5, 7S7, 7L3

1 Tu as passé un bon week-end?
This introduces the phrase: *Je suis allé(e)* with destinations.

Students listen and write down the destinations. Able students could note any additional details.

Solution: **1** *à la plage,* **2** *au château,* **3** *au cinéma,* **4** *à la patinoire,* **5** *au parc,* **6** *aux magasins,* **7** *à l'aquarium,* **8** *à l'église,* **9** *au bowling,* **10** *au centre sportif*

transcript
1 – Je suis allé à la plage.
2 – Je suis allée au château.
3 – Lundi dernier, je suis allé au cinéma.
4 – Mardi dernier, je suis allée à la patinoire.
5 – Mercredi dernier, je suis allé au parc avec mon frère.
6 – Samedi dernier, je suis allée aux magasins avec mes copines.
7 – Vendredi dernier, je suis allé à l'aquarium avec le collège.
8 – Dimanche dernier, je suis allée à l'église avec ma famille.
9 – Jeudi dernier, je suis allé au bowling avec ma sœur.
10 – Et moi, je suis allée au centre sportif pour jouer au badminton.

 **134 Dossier-langue**   **7W5**

Recognising the past tense (2)
Ask students about the differences with *je suis allé(e)* and whether the two forms of *allé(e)* sound different.

134   AT2, AT4; 7W5

2 Je suis allé(e) en ville
Students practise forming sentences on this model.

Solution:
1 *Je suis allé(e) à la bibliothèque.*
2 *Je suis allé(e) à la patinoire.*
3 *Je suis allé(e) à la piscine.*
4 *Je suis allé(e) à la plage.*
5 *Je suis allé(e) au bowling.*
6 *Je suis allé(e) au château.*
7 *Je suis allé(e) au cinéma.*
8 *Je suis allé(e) à l'auberge de jeunesse.*
9 *Je suis allé(e) à l'aquarium.*
10 *Je suis allé(e) au centre commercial/aux magasins.*

 134 • 5 tr 10 | AT1; 7L2

3 Une journée à Paris

Students could read through the gapped text first and think about what the missing words might be, then listen to the recording and note down the missing words.

Solution:
1 b, **2** f, **3** c, **4** h, **5** e, **6** g, **7** a, **8** d

 transcript

Une journée à Paris

– Tu as passé un bon week-end?

– Ah oui, j'ai passé un excellent week-end. Je suis allé à Paris.

– Paris, c'est bien?

– Ah oui, il y a beaucoup de choses à faire. D'abord, le matin, je suis allé à la tour Eiffel. C'est vraiment impressionnant. Puis à midi, on a fait un pique-nique près de la Seine.

– Et l'après-midi?

– Ensuite, l'après-midi, je suis allé à la Cité des Sciences. C'est un grand musée avec beaucoup d'activités scientifiques et il y a aussi un planétarium et un grand cinéma IMAX. C'est très intéressant.

 Fiche de travail (ws07) | AT3, AT4

Une carte postale

An online worksheet to revise plural possessive adjectives (*notre, votre, nos, vos*) and activities.

 134 Stratégies | 7W2, 7W7, 7T7

Sequencing words

Ask students to look for examples of the sequencing words and phrases on the page.

 135 | AT2; 7S4, 7S7, 7L4; AfL

4 Inventez des conversations

Students practise a short conversation using the perfect tense phrases about the previous week or weekend. Two able students could demonstrate this first.

As this links well with the spread objectives, it could be used for assessment. Discuss the criteria for a successful conversation and, when students have completed the task, discuss any areas for improvement.

10/7 | AT3, AT4

Qu'est-ce que tu as fait?

A sequence of activities to practise *je suis allé(e)* + other details.

1 Dans le bon ordre

Students copy sentences in the correct order.

Solution:
1 *Vendredi dernier je suis allé au Parc Astérix avec mon collège.*

2 *D'abord je suis allé au village d'Astérix.*

3 *À midi, j'ai fait un pique-nique avec mes amis.*

4 *Puis, l'après-midi, j'ai fait une promenade en bateau au grand SPLATCH.*

5 *Finalement je suis allé au magasin de souvenirs.*

2 Où es-tu allé(e)?

Students follow the lines to find the correct destination.

Solution:

a

1 *D'abord, je suis allé au marché.*

2 *Puis, je suis allé au terrain de football.*

3 *Ensuite, je suis allé au port.*

4 *Finalement je suis allé au restaurant.*

b

1 *Samedi dernier, je suis allée à l'office de tourisme à 10 heures.*

2 *Puis, je suis allée à l'auberge de jeunesse avec mes amis.*

3 *Dimanche matin je suis allée à la cathédrale en ville.*

4 *Lundi soir je suis allée au théâtre avec mes parents.*

3 Où'es-tu allé(e) en ville?

This is an open-ended task.

 157 Au choix | AT3

5 Des cartes postales

Reading practice using a mixture of verbs in the past tense.

Students read through the postcards and do the tasks.

a Comprehension questions in English.

Solution:
1 La Rochelle
2 went sailing, went to aquarium
3 It was very good.
4 She went to *Parc Astérix* with her brother and mother.
5 Really cool.
6 Went horseriding, went to the village, watched a DVD, played football with his cousins
7 Had a picnic
8 a huge chocolate ice cream

b

Solution:
1 *Le week-end dernier*
2 *Samedi matin*
3 *l'après-midi*
4 *Dimanche*
5 *j'ai fait de la voile*
6 *je suis allé au village*
7 *j'ai joué au football*
8 *j'ai mangé une grande glace*

 **135**   **AT3; 7S3, 7T1**

5 Une journée idéale

The final items of this spread use the present tense but are more suited to able students. Students read the article about an ideal day, then read the ten sentences and correct the mistakes.

Solution:

1 *Lucie fait du **ski**.*

2 *C'est au mois d'**avril**.*

3 *Elle prend son déjeuner à **midi**.*

4 *Elle **adore** les pizzas.*

5 *Comme boisson, elle prend une **limonade**.*

6 *Elle mange une glace à la **vanille**.*

7 *À cinq heures, elle prend le **goûter**.*

8 *Elle mange du **gâteau**.*

9 *Puis, elle fait **du shopping**.*

10 *Le soir, elle dîne **au restaurant**.*

 Activité (int05)   **AT3**

Une journée un peu différente

An online activity to practise talking about daily activities, as well as opinions. Use this interactive activity before moving on to the writing activity. It provides a model for the kind of text pupils could produce.

 **Fiche de travail (ws08)**   **AT3, AT4**

Ma journée idéale

This online worksheet practises describing a holiday.

 **135**   **AT4; 7S7, 7T5**

6 Dossier personnel

Students write a short description of a special day, based on the outlines provided and with reference to the previous item. Part **a** is about their own ideal day and part **b** about a day which is definitely not ideal.

This could be prepared initially as a class activity.

 1 p47

Using regular and irregular verbs

This provides further practice of the present tense of a range of regular and irregular verbs.

Plenaries (pages 134–135)

 Fiche de travail (ws02)

Working in pairs or groups, students see how many sequencing words they can remember and discuss ways of memorising these. Students could also practise in turn making up sentences using a different sequencing word each time.

10G Les loisirs   pages 136–137

Aims and objectives	Grammar and skills	Resources
• talk about leisure in general • write questions		**Key language:** see p188 **Online resource:** *Unité 10* int06/07/08, ppt03/04, ws02/09 **Copymasters:** 10/8, 10/9 **CD** 5 tracks 11–16

Starters (pages 136–137)

 Fiche de travail (ws02)

1 **5-4-3-2-1** Display the following words in random order; students find groups of 5,4,3,2,1 similar words.

le ski, le judo, la natation, la danse, la voile
suis, est, sont, êtes
le piano, la batterie, la flûte
février, août
les vacances

Students could record their answers on a pre-printed grid and these can then be checked in the usual way.

2 **Quel mot?** Display the following or print them out. Give students a few minutes to read and work out the answers, then ask for them collectively or randomly.

a *... ça va?*

b *Tu n'aimes pas la gymnastique– mais ...?*

c *C'est ..., la visite au Parc Astérix?*

d *... va au club de natation, mercredi?*

e *... est le concert de musique du collège ?*

1 *qui* 2 *quand* 3 *où* 4 *comment* 5 *pourquoi*

Solution: **1** d, **2** c, **3** e, **4** a, **5** b,

Introduction

Go through the objectives for this spread.

 **136**   **AT3; 7W5, 7T1**

1 Un jeu-test: Comment passes-tu tes loisirs?

This is a light-hearted personality quiz based on leisure activities for pair or individual work.

 **136**   AT4; 7S4, 7T5, 7L5

2 Un sondage

Students prepare three questions which require *oui/non* responses. Start this as a class activity, then let students continue individually or in pairs. The completed questions can be put together for a *sondage* on leisure. Students then complete the full questionnaire themselves and the results can be analysed using a spreadsheet and graphs to give a class profile.

 Activité (int06)   AT1, AT3

Rue Danton: En musique

Online activites to support the final episode of the video 'soap'. The video clip includes some new language on household tasks.

 Présentation (ppt03) **5 tr 11–12**
AT1, AT2, AT3

Chantez! Samedi, on part en vacances

This online PowerPoint presentation provides the lyrics and music for a song about going on holiday.

With holidays and leisure in mind, students could listen to the song or sing along.

Teach *une valise* and *un maillot de bain*.

See TB 31 for words and music.

 Activité (int07)   AT1, AT3

Vocabulaire de classe (10)

This online activity practises some more key classroom language.

 Fiche de travail (ws09)/Présentation (ppt04) AT3

Les vacances de Margot

This online book-fold reader provides extension reading material in the form of a short story with a twist about preparations for a holiday.

Use the PowerPoint for whole-class presentation of the reader.

 10/8 **5 tr 13–16**

Tu comprends?

1 On fait du sport

Solution: **1** c, **2** h, **3** b, **4** f, **5** g, **6** a, **7** e, **8** d

---

transcript

On fait du sport

1 – Tu fais du sport, Sophie?
  – Oui, bien sûr. Je fais de l'équitation tous les dimanches.
2 – Et vous, Marc et Luc, est-ce que vous faites du sport?
  – Oui, nous faisons du VTT. Ça, c'est super.
3 – Et Sika, est-ce qu'elle fait du sport?
  – Oui, elle fait de la gymnastique, le mercredi.
4 – Et Claire et Nicole, qu'est-ce qu'elles font comme sport?
  – En été, elles font de la planche à voile. C'est bien, ça.
5 – Est-ce que tu fais du ski en hiver, Charles?
  – Oui, j'adore faire du ski.
6 – Et toi, Karim, qu'est-ce que tu fais comme sport?
  – Pas grand-chose, mais je fais de la natation de temps en temps. J'aime bien la natation.
7 – Et toi, Lucie, qu'est-ce que tu aimes faire comme sport?
  – Moi, j'adore faire du roller avec mes amis. C'est très amusant.
8 – Et Paul et Sanjay, est-ce qu'ils font du sport?
  – Oui, ils font de la voile avec le club de voile, ici à La Rochelle.

2 Enquête loisirs

Solution:

	painting	drama	chess	drums	flute	violin	computer
1			✓				
2				✓			
3					✓		
4		✓					
5	✓						
6						✓	
7							✓

---

transcript

Enquête loisirs

1 – Qu'est-ce que tu aimes faire, à part le sport?
  – Moi, j'aime jouer aux échecs. C'est très intéressant.
2 – Et toi, Charles, tu as d'autres loisirs?
  – Oui, j'aime bien la musique et je joue de la batterie.
3 – Nicole, toi aussi tu joues d'un instrument de musique?
  – Oui, moi, je joue de la flûte. J'aime bien cet instrument.

4 – Et vous, Paul et Sanjay, est-ce que vous avez d'autres loisirs?

   – Oui, nous aimons faire du théâtre. Ça, c'est toujours amusant.

5 – Magali, qu'est-ce que tu as comme loisirs?

   – Moi, je fais de la peinture. J'adore ça.

6 – Marc, est-ce que tu aimes la musique?

   – Oui, j'aime la musique et je joue du violon.

7 – Et vous, Lucie et Paul, est-ce que vous faites autre chose à part le sport?

   – Oui, nous jouons à des jeux vidéo sur l'ordinateur. Ça, c'est vraiment bien.

3 Le week-end dernier

Solution:

	Activité	Détails
1	Ex. e	*au concert*
2	c	*avec des amis*
3	a	*samedi matin*
4	f	*avec ma grand-mère*
5	b	*sur la plage*
6	d	*avec son frère*

transcript

Le week-end dernier

1 – Qu'est ce que tu as fait le week-end dernier?

   – Moi, j'ai joué du violon avec l'orchestre au concert.

2 – Et toi, tu as passé un bon week-end?

   – Oui, moi j'ai fait de la natation avec des amis.

3 – Est-ce que tu as passé un bon week-end?

   – Oui, j'ai fait du dessin samedi matin. J'adore le dessin.

4 – Et toi, qu'est ce que tu as fait le week-end dernier?

   – Moi, je suis allée chez mes grands-parents et j'ai joué aux cartes avec ma grand-mère.

5 – Et toi, tu as passé un bon week-end?

   – Oui, très bon. J'ai joué au volley sur la plage – très amusant.

6 – Tu as fait quelque chose de beau dimanche?

   – Oui, dimanche, j'ai fait du VTT avec mon frère.

4 C'est quand?

Solution: **1** 21h30, **2** 15h00, **3** 14h30, **4** 18h00, **5** 19h00, **6** 16h20, **7** 20h45, **8** 13h40

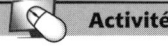

transcript

1 – Le film commence à quelle heure?

   – Il commence à 21 heures 30.

   – À 21 heures 30.

2 – Salut Suzanne, le match commence à quelle heure cet après-midi?

   – À 15 heures.

   – Bon, à 15 heures.

3 – Le musée ouvre à quelle heure aujourd'hui?

   – À 14 heures 30.

   – À 14 heures 30, oui.

4 – Et il ferme à quelle heure?

   – À 18 heures.

   – À 18 heures, bon, merci.

5 – On mange à quelle heure le soir?

   – Normalement, nous mangeons à 19 heures.

   – À 19 heures, d'accord.

6 – Le train pour Paris part à quelle heure?

   – Il part à 16 heures 20.

   – À 16 heures 20, merci.

7 – Le concert commence à quelle heure?

   – Il commence à 20 heures 45.

   – À 20 heures 45, bon merci.

8 – Tes cours commencent à quelle heure l'après-midi?

   – À 13 heures 40.

   – À 13 heures 40, c'est ça.

 sb 137 **cm** 10/9

Sommaire

A summary of the main structures and vocabulary of this unit.

Activité (int08)   **AT3**

Vocabulaire (10)

An online game which tests the vocabulary of the unit.

Plenaries (pages 136–137)

Fiche de travail (ws02)

1 Use the *Sommaire* to review the objectives of the unit and what has been learnt. Discuss how the language could be used in different contexts.

2 **Writing challenge** If appropriate, set this challenge: how many lines could students write entirely in French without any prompts.

   Hand out blank sheets of paper and give students five minutes writing time. They can write anything they want in French.

   Then ask who has written: 1 line/2 lines/3 lines, etc. (Hopefully many hands will be raised.)

   When eventually only 3–4 hands are left up (perhaps at 7–10 lines) ask a volunteer from those remaining to read out what they have written.

Review of Stage 1

Students review what they have learnt in Stage 1: which topics they have found most useful/interesting; which grammar points they have found easy/difficult. They discuss their views in pairs and groups and compare their choice with others.

Unité 10 Consolidation and assessment

Épreuves Unité 10

 10/10 Écouter • **5 tr 17–20** AT1

A Tu aimes ça?

Solution: **1** a, **2** d, **3** e, **4** f, **5** c, **6** b (mark /5)

transcript

A Tu aimes ça?

1 – Est-ce que tu joues du piano?
– Oui, je joue du piano.

2 – Tu aimes le patin à roulettes?
– Le patin à roulettes? Oui, j'aime ça.

3 – Tu fais de la voile de temps en temps?
– Oui je fais de la voile quand je vais à La Rochelle, chez mes cousins. Ils habitent au bord de la mer.

4 – Qu'est-ce que tu fais? Tu dessines?
– Oui, je dessine et je fais de la peinture. J'aime la peinture.

5 – Tu aimes faire de la natation?
– Oui, j'adore la natation. Je vais à la piscine tous les mercredis.

6 – Tu aimes jouer aux échecs?
– Oui, j'aime bien jouer aux échecs, mais je ne joue pas très bien.

B Quelle heure est-il?

Solution: **1** b, **2** a, **3** d, **4** f, **5** e, **6** c (mark /5)

transcript

Quelle heure est-il?

1 – Le film commence à 13 heures 10.
– C'est vrai? À 13 heures 10!

2 – Le musée ferme à 16 heures.
– À 16 heures! C'est extraordinaire!

3 – Le film finit à quelle heure?
– À 22 heures 45.
– À 22 heures 45?
– C'est ça.

4 – Venez ici, tout le monde! Il est 24 heures! Il est minuit!
– Hourra, il est minuit!

5 – Le train arrive à 17 heures 15.
– À 17 heures 15, merci beaucoup.

6 – Il est 18 heures 30. Est-ce que le magasin est ouvert?
– À 18 heures 30? Mais oui, bien sûr!

C Une présentation

Solution: **1** c, **2** a, **3** b, **4** a, **5** b, **6** d

transcript

C Une présentation

Je vais parler de mon passe-temps: la musique. La musique est très importante pour moi. Ma mère est professeur de musique et elle joue du piano et de la flûte. Moi, je joue du violon. C'est un très bel instrument et j'aime beaucoup écouter des airs de violon. Je joue du violon tous les jours et j'ai un cours de musique chaque semaine, le jeudi soir. Ça dure trente minutes. Pendant la fête de la musique j'ai joué avec des amis à l'église près de ma maison. Je joue dans l'orchestre du collège et dimanche dernier j'ai joué dans un concert à l'hôtel de ville. Plus tard, je voudrais apprendre un autre instrument, peut-être la trompette.

D Au club des jeunes

Solution: **1** vrai, **2** vrai, **3** faux, **4** vrai, **5** faux, **6** vrai (mark /5)

transcript

Au club des jeunes

1 Ce soir, au club des jeunes, on fait du sport, on fait de la musique et on fait de l'informatique.

2 Deux filles jouent au ping-pong et d'autres jeunes font de la musique.

3 Trois filles et un garçon jouent aux cartes et les autres jouent au Monopoly.

4 Une jeune fille joue de la batterie – je crois qu'elle adore ça!

5 Un garçon joue de la trompette. Il porte un pantalon noir très chic et une chemise blanche.

6 Il y a aussi un ordinateur et deux garçons surfent sur le Net.

 10/11 Lire AT3

A Un message de Sarah

Solution: **1** d, **2** a, **3** b, **4** e, **5** c, **6** f (mark /5)

B Questions et réponses

Solution: **1** b, **2** d, **3** h, **4** c, **5** f, **6** a, **7** e, **8** g (mark /7)

C Sébastien est en vacances

Solution: **1** V, **2** F, **3** F, **4** V, **5** F, **6** F, **7** V, **8** V, **9** F (mark /8)

10/12 Écrire et grammaire **AT4**

A Un serpent

Solution:

la voile, le volley, la natation

le violon, la flûte

le dessin, la peinture

faire

(mark /4: 1/2 mark for each item, including the example)

B Un questionnaire sur les loisirs

Solution: **1** *au,* **2** *au,* **3** *fais,* **4** *joue,* **5** *de la,* **6** *aux* (mark /5)

C Un message

There are additional distractors listed.

Solution: **1** *fais,* **2** *village,* **3** *joue,* **4** *promenades,* **5** *musique,* **6** *ai* (mark /5)

D À toi!

This is an open-ended task. (mark /6)

 **138–139** **106–107**

Presse-Jeunesse 4

These pages provide reading for pleasure. They can be used alone or with the accompanying worksheets. See the notes on TB 4.

 **138** **106**

Un bon repas pour Mangetout

Solution:

A

français	anglais
1 *dormir*	to sleep
2 *quelque chose*	something
3 *couverte de .....*	covered in
4 *.... provisions*	provisions
5 *un peu*	a little
6 *un gros morceau*	a large piece
7 *soudain*	suddenly
8 *s'échapper*	to escape

B Ça commence par ...

1 *un chat,* **2** *la cuisine,* **3** *une carotte,* **4** *deux,* **5** *le déjeuner,* **6** *le dessert*

Complète la grille

Solution:

Il mange ça: du pain, de la salade, du gâteau, du fromage, des carottes, du poisson, de la viande, des tomates.

Il ne mange pas ça: des pommes, des petits pois

Une recette

Solution: **1** 125g, **2** 2, **3** *oui,* **4** *les jaunes d'œufs,* **5** *oui,* **6** *le chocolat*

Mots croisés

Solution:

Horizontalement:

1 *poisson,* **4** *jambon,* **6** *lait,* **8** *fromage,* **12** *potage,* **13** *pâté,* **14** *chou*

Verticalement:

1 *poulet,* **2** *salade,* **3** *tomate,* **5** *carotte,* **7** *tarte,* **9** *gâteau*

 **139** **107**

La page des sports

Solution:

Un acrostiche

1 *jeux olympiques,* **2** *judo,* **3** *joueur,* **4** *natation,* **5** *volley,* **6** *équipe,* **7** *gymnastique,* **8** *planche à voile*

Chasse à l'intrus

1 *l'équipe – ce n'est pas un sport.*

2 *le judo – ce n'est pas un sport de raquette.*

3 *la gymnastique – ce n'est pas un sport nautique.*

4 *le rugby – ce n'est pas un sport individuel.*

5 *le volley – ce n'est pas un sport individuel.*

6 *le vélo – ce n'est pas un sport collectif.*

Le sais-tu? Les sports

Le volley-ball

1 *6,* **2** *simple* **3** *de toutes les saisons*

La planche à voile

1 *individuel,* **2** *mer, lac,* **3** *voile*

Le judo

1 *le blanc, le jaune, l'orange, le vert, le bleu, le brun, le noir*

2 *5 ans*

3 *le Japon*

La natation synchronisée

1 *faux,* **2** *vrai,* **3** *vrai*

Tricolore Total 1
Contrôles

The three *Contrôles* provide blocks of formal assessment of the vocabulary and structures introduced during the course. They assess all four National Curriculum Attainment Targets. See TB 20 for the Assessment Introduction.

The National Curriculum Level is indicated in brackets after the title. The tasks test elements of performance at that level.

The Listening and Reading sheets are designed to be written on, but the Speaking and Writing sheets are re-usable.

Mark scheme:

Do not include a mark for the example. Each *Contrôle* has a total of 100 marks (25 for each Attainment Target).

Record sheets:

A record sheet for students is provided on CM 126. They will need one for each block of *Contrôles*.

Listening:

All items are repeated. For Level 1 assessment only, the recording can be played twice (so that students hear it four times altogether). At all levels, the pause button can be used at any time to give students time for reflection and for writing.

Speaking:

Decide how you wish to conduct this assessment:

- invite students out individually and ask the questions yourself;
- invite them in pairs, listen to the conversation and mark the answers;
- offer your students the option of recording the assessment with a partner, for you to listen to and mark afterwards. It is important, if students record their conversations at home, to obtain some assurance that they are not reading the questions and answers. Depending on the facilities available, the assessment could be carried out in a computer suite.

Unités 1–4

| | 108–109 | 5 tr 21–24 | 5B |

Premier contrôle: Écouter

A Loto mathématique (NC 1)

Make sure that students understand that they should only put three crosses (not including the example) on each card.

Solution: *Carte numéro un* – 24, 30, 45, 3; *Carte numéro deux* – 12, 11, 17

(mark /6: 4+ shows understanding of short statements, with no interference and with plenty of repetition)

transcript

Loto mathématique

Carte numéro un:

vingt-quatre, trente, quarante-cinq, trois

Carte numéro deux:

douze, onze, dix-sept

B Dans ma chambre (NC 1)

Solution: **1** a, **2** b, **3** b, **4** a, **5** a, **6** b, **7** a

(mark /6: 4+ shows understanding of short statements, with no interference and with plenty of repetition)

transcript

Dans ma chambre

1 Voici mon baladeur.
2 J'ai une table et deux chaises.
3 Il y a des stylos et une règle.
4 Ça, c'est mon ordinateur.
5 Mon chat s'appelle Tom.
6 Voilà trois cahiers.
7 Et voilà mon poisson.

C À la maison (NC 2)

Each item is repeated once, slowly and clearly. It is not necessary to replay the recording for the purposes of assessing at Level 2. It is acceptable, however, to pause the recording at any time to give your students more time for reflection.

Solution: **1** *vrai*, **2** *faux*, **3** *faux*, **4** *faux*, **5** *faux*, **6** *vrai*, **7** *faux*, **8** *vrai*

(mark /7: 5+ shows understanding of a range of familiar statements)

transcript

À la maison

1 Maman est dans la cuisine.
2 Le chien est dans le jardin.
3 Le chat est sous la télé.
4 Ma sœur est dans sa chambre.
5 Mon père est dans la salle de bains.
6 Je suis dans le jardin.
7 Le téléphone est sur la chaise.
8 Mon grand-père est dans le salon.

D Deux familles (NC 2)

Solution:

	brother	sister	cat	dog	rabbit
Sylvie	1	0	2	–	–
Richard	1	2	–	1	1

(mark /6: 5+ shows understanding of a range of familiar statements)

Deux familles

transcript

– Bonjour. Je m'appelle Sylvie. Voilà des photos de ma famille. Voici Paul, mon frère. Je n'ai pas de sœur. Voilà mes deux chats.

– Salut. Je suis Richard. J'ai des photos aussi. Voici Marie et Isabelle, mes sœurs. Voici mon petit frère, Patrick. Marie a un lapin. Moi, j'ai un chien. Le voilà, il s'appelle Bruno.

 110

Premier contrôle: Parler

Students should be given the sheet up to a week before the assessment, to give them time to choose whether they prefer to do 1 and 2 or 2 and 3 or 1 and 3, and to prepare and practise all three conversations (two structured ones and the open-ended one) with their partners.

Mark scheme:

Section A: mark /16: 2 marks per response

- 1 mark for conveying the requested information, but with a minimal response, e.g. one or two words. Repetition of the question and prompting by pointing to the visuals may be necessary.

- 2 marks for a response that is clear and conveys all of the information requested, in the form of a complete phrase or sentence, though not necessarily an accurate one. The question and answers may seem disjointed, like separate items rather than part of a coherent conversation.

Section B: mark /9: 2 marks per response, as above, + 1 bonus mark for one or more extra details, e.g. names of animals, their size or their colour. The extra information must be in the form of a complete phrase or sentence, though not necessarily an accurate one.

Summary:	Marks	7–15	16–25
	Level	1	2

 111–112

Premier contrôle: Lire

A Dans la salle de classe (NC 1)

Solution: 1 g, **2** e, **3** b, **4** a, **5** f, **6** d, **7** c

(mark /6: 4+ shows understanding of single words presented in a clear script – illustrations provide context and visual support)

B Les animaux (NC 1)

Solution: 1 f, **2** e, **3** d, **4** b, **5** a, **6** h, **7** g, **8** c

(mark /7: 5+ shows understanding of single words presented in a clear script – illustrations provide context and visual support)

C La famille (NC 2)

Solution: 1 faux, **2** vrai, **3** vrai, **4** faux, **5** faux, **6** vrai, **7** vrai

(mark /6: 4+ shows understanding of short phrases presented in a familiar context)

D Des questions et des réponses (NC 2)

Solution: 1 c, **2** b, **3** g, **4** f, **5** d, **6** a, **7** e

(mark /6: 4+ shows understanding of short phrases presented in a familiar context)

 113

Premier contrôle: Écrire

A La maison (NC 1)

Solution: 1 la grande salle de bains, **2** la chambre de Lucie, **3** la chambre de Thomas et de Marc, **4** la chambre de Monsieur et Madame Duval, **5** la petite salle de bains, **6** le salon, **7** la salle à manger, **8** la cuisine, **9** le jardin

(mark /8: do not allow spelling mistakes as the vocabulary is given; 6+ shows ability to copy single familiar words or short phrases correctly)

B Quelle image? (NC 2)

Solution:

1 J'ai quatre ans.
2 J'habite en Écosse.
3 J'habite dans une ferme.
4 Voilà un cinéma.
5 J'ai huit ans.
6 Voilà une rue.
7 J'habite dans un appartement.
8 Voilà un café.
9 J'ai six ans.
10 J'habite en France.

(mark /9: do not allow spelling mistakes as the vocabulary is given; 7+ shows ability to copy short familiar sentences correctly)

C Des questions (NC 2)

Solution: 1 âge, **2** habites (accept es), **3** frères, **4** animal, **5** appelles, **6** ordinateur, **7** stylo, **8** couleur, **9** chat

(mark /8: 6+ shows ability to write familiar words from memory – note that, at this level, it does not matter if spelling is approximate, as long as the meaning is clear and unambiguous without reference to the contextual picture)

Unités 5–7

 114–115 5 tr 25–28

Deuxième contrôle: Écouter

A À Granville (NC 1)

If helpful for students, play the recording again so they hear the information four times altogether.

Note, there is an additional distractor, h, so not all symbols are used.

Solution: 1 d, **2** e, **3** b, **4** a, **5** g, **6** f, **7** c

(mark /6: 4+ shows understanding of short statements, with no interference and with plenty of repetition)

transcript

À Granville

Qu'est-ce qu'il y a pour les touristes à Granville?

1 Il y a le marché le samedi.
2 Il y a une grande piscine.
3 La tour Saint-Jacques.
4 Le camping n'est pas loin.
5 Il y a un cinéma avec trois salles.
6 La cathédrale est magnifique.
7 L'Escargot, c'est un bon restaurant.

B Les activités de la famille Giroux (NC 2)

Before the assessment, check that students understand that 20.30 means 8.30pm (item 4).

Solution: **1** *faux,* **2** *faux,* **3** *vrai,* **4** *vrai,* **5** *faux,* **6** *faux,* **7** *vrai,* **8** *vrai*

(mark /7: 5+ shows understanding of a range of familiar statements)

transcript

Les activités de la famille Giroux

1 – Je cherche un bon cadeau, c'est l'anniversaire de Pierre le 23 mai.

2 – Pierre? Il regarde un match de football avec son copain Alexandre.

3 – C'est la fête des Mères aujourd'hui. Alette a offert des chocolats à Maman.

4 – Il y a un concert à l'église ce soir, à huit heures et demie. Je joue dans l'orchestre.

5 – Alette travaille dans sa chambre avec sa copine Jeanne.

6 – Il y a un match de tennis de table au Collège Émile Zola. Il a lieu le 9 octobre.

7 – Le 15 juin, je vais au musée Maritime avec le collège.

8 – Papa ... papa ... PAPA!
   – Je suis là. J'écoute de la musique.

C C'est où exactement? (NC 2)

Solution:

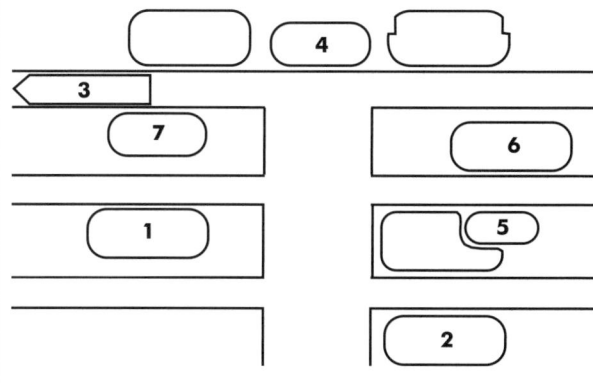

(mark /6: 4+ shows understanding of a range of familiar questions and answers)

transcript

C'est où exactement?

1 – Pour aller à la poste, s'il vous plaît?
   – Prenez la deuxième rue à gauche, et c'est à gauche.
   – Merci, monsieur.

2 – Pardon, il y a un supermarché ici?
   – Oui, voilà, à droite!
   – Oh, pardon.

3 – L'auberge de jeunesse, c'est loin?
   – C'est assez loin, c'est à quinze kilomètres.
   – Quinze kilomètres, ça va.

4 – Le restaurant Renaud, c'est loin?
   – Non, continuez tout droit. C'est entre l'hôtel Pasteur et l'église.
   – Ah, oui, merci.

5 – Maman, il y a des toilettes ici?
   – Oui, derrière l'office du tourisme.

6 – Où est l'hôpital?
   – Ce n'est pas loin. Prenez la deuxième rue à droite, et c'est à gauche.
   – Oh, merci.

7 – Pour aller au marché, s'il vous plaît?
   – Vous prenez la troisième rue à gauche, et le marché est à gauche.
   – Merci beaucoup.

D Quel temps fait-il? (NC 3)

Solution:

	temps	*opinion*	*activité*
Charles	e	c	a
Magalie	a	d	d
Robert	d	b	c

(mark /6: 4+ shows understanding of short dialogues, spoken at near normal speed without any interference, identifying personal responses, including opinions)

transcript

Quel temps fait-il?

– Et voici notre premier joueur. C'est Charles, qui habite à La Rochelle.
– Allô.
– Charles, c'est Annie ici!
– Ah oui, bonjour Annie.
– Il fait beau à La Rochelle?
– Euh, non, il y a du vent. Mais ça va, j'aime le vent.
– C'est vrai?
– Ah oui, je fais de la planche à voile!
– Ah.
– Et maintenant Magalie, à Lyon.

- Allô.
- Salut, Magalie.
- Salut, Annie.
- Quel temps fait-il à Lyon, Magalie?
- Il y a du soleil – j'adore le soleil.
- Moi aussi.
- Je vais à la piscine avec mes amis.
- Super!
- Et le numéro trois habite à Lille. Il s'appelle Robert.
- Allô.
- Salut, Robert.
- Ah, bonjour, Annie.
- Qu'est-ce que tu fais aujourd'hui?
- Oh, il pleut. Je n'aime pas ça. Je reste dans ma chambre et je surfe sur le Net.
- Ah, bon.
- Alors, trois personnes, Robert, Magalie et Charles. On joue!!

 116

Deuxième contrôle: Parler

Students should be given the sheet up to a week before the assessment, to give them time to choose whether they prefer to do 1, 2 or 3, and to prepare and practise both conversations – the structured one (A) and the open-ended one (B) – with their partners.

Mark scheme:

Section A: mark /12: 3 marks per response

- 1 mark for conveying the requested information, but with a minimal response e.g. one or two words. Repetition of the question and prompting by pointing to the visuals may be necessary.

- 2 marks for a response that is clear and conveys all of the information requested, in the form of a complete phrase or sentence, though not necessarily an accurate one. The question and answers may seem disjointed, like separate items rather than part of a coherent conversation.

- 3 marks for a clear and complete response that conveys all of the information requested, in the form of a complete phrase or sentence, though not necessarily an accurate one. The language flows reasonably smoothly, and is recognisable as part of a coherent conversation.

Section B: mark /13: 3 marks per response, as above, + 1 bonus mark for adding one or two items of extra information about personal preferences (i.e. using knowledge of language to adapt and substitute single words and phrases).

Summary:

Marks	7–13	14–18	19–25
Level	1	2	3

 117–118

Deuxième contrôle: Lire

A Cico le clown (NC 1)

Solution: **1** c, **2** g, **3** e, **4** b, **5** a, **6** f, **7** d

(mark /6: 4+ shows understanding of single words presented in a clear script)

B Sophie à Cherbourg (NC 2)

Solution: **1** d, **2** b, **3** e, **4** g, **5** f, **6** a, **7** h, **8** i, **9** c

(mark /7: 5+ shows understanding of short phrases presented in a familiar context)

C Calais (NC 3)

Solution: **1** f, **2** d, **3** a, **4** g, **5** b, **6** c, **7** e

(mark /6: 4+ shows understanding of a short text in a topic studied)

D Les cadeaux de Coralie (NC 3)

Solution: **1** *faux*, **2** *faux*, **3** *vrai*, **4** *faux*, **5** *vrai*, **6** *faux*, **7** *faux*

(mark /6: 4+ shows understanding of a short text, identifying and noting main points, including likes, dislikes and feelings)

 119

Deuxième contrôle: Écrire

A Les activités (NC 1)

Solution: **1** *téléphone*, **2** *dansent*, **3** *surfes*, **4** *jouons*, **5** *dessine*, **6** *écoute*, **7** *allez*, **8** *chantent*, **9** *regarde*

(mark /8: 1/2 mark for correct word; 1/2 mark for correct spelling – round up the odd 1/2 mark; 5+ shows ability to select appropriate words to complete sentences and copy them correctly)

B Quel temps fait-il? (NC 2)

Solution: *À Marseille, il fait beau. À Paris, il y a du vent. À Cherbourg, il y a du brouillard. À Bordeaux, il fait chaud. À Grenoble, il fait froid. À Toulouse, il y a du soleil.*

(mark /9: 1 mark for key weather word, even if the spelling is inaccurate (this includes completing the Paris sentence); 1 mark for each correctly-constructed sentence, apart from Marseille and Paris, accepting only the smallest spelling errors; 5+ shows ability to adapt given patterns correctly and add further vocabulary from memory)

C Le week-end (NC 3)

Solution: This is an open-ended task.

(mark /8: 1/2 mark for comprehensible phrase, even if the spelling is inaccurate; further 1/2 mark for each of the four phrases that is accurate or virtually accurate; 5+ shows ability to write two or three short sentences on familiar topics, adapting a model and adding own vocabulary)

Unités 8–10

 120–121 5 tr 29–32

Troisième contrôle: Écouter

A La soirée d'Anne-Marie (NC 2)

Solution: **1** a, **2** b, **3** a, **4** b, **5** a, **6** a, **7** b

(mark /6: 4+ shows understanding of a range of familiar statements)

La soirée d'Anne-Marie

1 Je quitte le collège à cinq heures.
2 À cinq heures et quart, j'arrive à la maison.
3 Je prends le goûter dans la cuisine.
4 Après le goûter, je regarde la télé.
5 Nous mangeons à sept heures et demie.
6 Je commence mes devoirs après le dîner.
7 Je me couche à dix heures.

B Rendez-vous à quelle heure? (NC 3)

Solution: 1 1h30, b, **2** 6h30/18h30, d, **3** 8h00/
20h00, e, **4** 10h15, c

(mark /6: 4+ shows understanding of short
dialogues, spoken at near normal speed without
any interference)

transcript

Rendez-vous à quelle heure?

1 – Tu veux aller en ville cet après-midi?
   – Oui, je veux bien.
   – Alors, rendez-vous à la gare à une heure et
      demie, ça va?
   – Très bien, une heure et demie à la gare.
2 – Tu veux aller voir un film ce soir?
   – Ce soir, ce n'est pas possible, mais vendredi
      soir oui.
   – Alors, rendez-vous à six heures et demie
      devant le cinéma?
   – Six heures et demie. À vendredi.
3 – Tu veux fêter l'anniversaire de Pierre avec
      nous samedi soir?
   – Oui, super!
   – Alors rendez-vous à la maison de Pierre à
      huit heures?
   – Huit heures. OK. À samedi.
4 – Tu veux jouer au tennis dimanche matin?
   – Oui, nous deux?
   – Et Lucie et Claire. Rendez-vous au parc à dix
      heures et quart, ça va?
   – Ça va. Dix heures et quart. À dimanche.

C Deux interviews (NC 3)

Solution:

Sabine		Paul	
lettres	opinions	lettres	opinions
d	♡♡	c	⚔⚔
h	⚔	e	♡

(mark /7: 5+ shows understanding of short
dialogues, spoken at near normal speed without
any interference, identifying and noting personal
responses, including likes and dislikes)

transcript

Deux interviews

Sabine

– Sabine, qu'est-ce que tu aimes manger ou boire?
– Moi, j'adore le chocolat chaud, surtout quand il
   fait froid.
– Et … est-ce qu'il y a quelque chose que tu
   n'aimes pas?
– Je ne sais pas … Ah oui, le chou-fleur. Je n'aime
   pas le chou-fleur.

Paul

– Et Paul, il y a quelque chose que tu n'aimes pas
   manger ou boire?
– Il y a beaucoup de choses que je n'aime pas,
   mais je déteste surtout le lait.
– Et qu'est-ce que tu aimes? Beaucoup de choses
   aussi, je suppose.
– Bien sûr, mais j'aime surtout les fraises. Mmm.

D Théo parle à Hugo (NC 5/6)

Only use this task if the class has completed *Unité 10*
and has covered the section on the perfect tense (*j'ai
joué, j'ai fait*).

Solution: 1 a, **2** c, **3** b, **4** a, **5** c, **6** a, **7** b

(mark /6: 4+ shows understanding of the main
points of longer passages, and recognition of
people talking about present and past OR future
events. Correct answers to questions 4, 5 and 6
shows ability to recognise people talking about
present and past and future events.)

transcript

Théo parle à Hugo

– Ça va, Théo?
– Oui, ça va. J'adore le ski. Il y a beaucoup de
   neige pour le ski, mais il fait du soleil!
– Tu fais du ski le matin et l'après-midi?
– Oui, il y a une classe de dix heures à douze
   heures, et une classe de quatorze heures à seize
   heures.
– Et qu'est-ce que tu fais à midi?
– Nous allons au restaurant à la montagne et nous
   mangeons un grand repas chaud.
– Il y a des activités le soir aussi?
– Oui, ce soir, par exemple, je vais faire de la
   natation. Mercredi prochain, je vais jouer au
   volley. On va organiser un match à l'auberge de
   jeunesse.
– Et les autres soirs, qu'est-ce que tu as fait?
– Lundi dernier, j'ai joué au tennis de table. Un
   autre soir, j'ai fait du shopping. C'est très bien.
   On organise des activités intéressantes.
– Tu as ton appareil-photo avec toi?
– Oui, j'ai un appareil-photo numérique. Il y a un
   café avec Internet au village. Je vais t'envoyer
   un e-mail avec des photos.
– Ah oui. Ça, c'est une bonne idée!

122

Troisième contrôle: Parler

Students should be given the sheet up to a week before the assessment, to give them time to choose whether they prefer to do 1, 2 or 3. Conversation 1 is entirely about the present. Conversation 2 includes an exchange about the future (using *aller* + infinitive). Conversation 3 enables students to demonstrate that they can talk about present, past and future. The open-ended conversation B includes a question about future activities using *aller* + infinitive.

Students should prepare and practise both conversations – the structured one (A) and the open-ended one (B) – with their partners.

Mark scheme:

Section A: mark /12: 3 marks per response

- 1 mark for a response that is clear and conveys all of the information requested, in the form of a complete phrase or sentence, though not necessarily an accurate one. The questions and answers may seem a little disjointed, like separate items rather than parts of a coherent conversation.

- 2 marks for a response that is clear and conveys all of the information requested, in the form of a complete phrase or sentence, though not necessarily an accurate one. The language must flow reasonably smoothly and be recognisable as part of a coherent conversation.

- 3 for a clear and complete response that flows smoothly as part of a coherent conversation. The language must be in complete sentences or phrases that are reasonably accurate and consistent as far as grammar, pronunciation and intonation are concerned.

Section B: mark /13: 3 marks per response, as above, + 1 bonus mark for adding one or two items of extra information about personal preferences (i.e. using knowledge of language to adapt and substitute single words and phrases).

Summary: Marks 7–13 14–18 19–25
                Level   2   3   4

Students who talk about present and future or past are operating at Level 5.

Students who talk about present, future and past are operating at Level 6.

 123–124

Troisième contrôle: Lire

A L'emploi du temps (NC 2)

Solution: **1** *mardi*, **2** *jeudi*, **3** *jeudi*, **4** *lundi*, **5** *samedi*, **6** *vendredi*, **7** *mardi*

(mark /6: 4+ shows understanding of short phrases presented in a familiar context)

B Le déjeuner au restaurant (NC 3)

Solution:

	hors d'œuvre	plat principal	dessert
Mme. Dubois	Ex. -	e	h
M. Colin	a	g	j
M. Martin	b	f	-

(mark /7: 5+ shows understanding of short texts, identifying and noting main points, including likes, dislikes and feelings)

C Le message de Richard (NC 4)

Solution: **1** *faux*, **2** *vrai*, **3** *vrai*, **4** *faux*, **5** *faux*, **6** *faux*, **7** *vrai*

(mark /6: 4+ shows understanding of a longer text, identifying and noting main points and details, including likes, dislikes and feelings)

D Un week-end à Boulogne (NC 6)

Solution: **1f** *merci*, **2c** *dernier*, **3a** *ai*, **4b** *allée*, **5d** *intéressant*, **6e** *joué*, **7g** *vas*

(mark /6: 4+, if it includes 7g, shows understanding of a longer text, recognising text relating to present, past and future.)

 125

Troisième contrôle: Écrire

A Une boisson ou un fruit? (NC 2)

Solution:

1 *Monsieur Mally prend un café.*
2 *Adèle prend une banane.*
3 *Madame Bijou prend une pomme.*
4 *Robert prend une limonade.*
5 *Julien prend une poire.*

(mark /8: 1 mark for each key word, even if the spelling is inaccurate; 1 mark for each correctly-constructed sentence, accepting only the smallest spelling errors; 5+ shows ability to adapt given patterns correctly)

B La famille Boulot va au cinéma (NC 3)

Decide whether you want your students to write the times out in full and make sure they are aware of this.

Solution:

1 *Maman travaille, elle rentre à la maison à cinq heures et quart.*
2 *Julien, tu manges/prends le dîner à cinq heures et demie/5h30.*
(*manges/prends* = 1 mark, *mange/prend* = 1/2 mark, *manger/prendre* = 0 marks)

3 *Nous prenons le bus à six heures moins dix/ 5h50.*

(*prenons* = 1 mark, *prendrons/prennons* = 1/2 mark, *prendre* = 0 marks)

4 *Le film commence à six heures vingt/6h20.*

(*commence* = 1 mark, *commences* = 1/2 mark, *commencer* = 0 marks)

5 *Après, maman et moi, nous allons/mangeons/ prenons le dîner au restaurant à neuf heures/9h.*

(*allons/mangeons/prenons* = 1 mark, *alons/ mangons/prendons* = 1/2 mark, *aller/manger/ prendre* = 0 marks)

(mark /8: 1 mark for each correctly conjugated verb, or 1/2 mark for an attempt that shows understanding of the conjugation, rounding up an odd 1/2; 1 mark for each reasonably accurate sentence; 5+ shows ability to write short sentences on familiar topics, adapting a model and vocabulary from a word bank)

C Samedi (NC 4/5)

There is potential to use the perfect tense introduced in *Unité 10*, but the task can also be done using just the present tense and *aller* + infinitive.

Solution:

This is an open-ended task.

(mark /9: 6+ shows ability to write simple sentences, relying largely on memorised language)

Mark scheme:

- for each weekend activity comprehensibly mentioned: 1 mark (up to max. of 2)
- for each comprehensible reference to time of activities: 1 mark (up to max. of 2)
- for each comprehensible expression of an opinion of an activity: 1 mark (max. of 2)
- for fairly accurate spelling throughout (comprehensible with a little effort): 1 mark

  or for generally accurate spelling throughout (easily comprehensible): 2 marks